Further praise for HOW TO WRITE **ANYTHING**

"A terrifically useful resource." —*Small Business Resource*

"Brown's ideas of inspired framework and hip-pocket lists of suggestions assured me that I will be rescued from writer's block when it happens. I think you'll find this book just as life-saving for your business communication needs."
—*Small Business Trends*

"Laura Brown's *How to Write Anything: A Complete Guide* is the most comprehensive guide to writing I've seen. I wish the book had been available when I was in college more than 50 years ago." —*Huntington News*

"Laura Brown has written the *ultimate* guide for anyone who needs to create clear, concise, and compelling written communications. Students, businesspeople, and even seasoned professional writers should keep it handy, right between their dictionary and thesaurus." —Michael Snell, literary agent, writing collaborator, and author of *From Book Idea to Bestseller*

"An invaluable guide. If your job or your business depends on delivering clear messages with impact, you need this book."
—Bernd Schmitt, professor, Columbia Business School

"Laura Brown's ability as a writing coach is unparalleled, and *How to Write Anything* offers the best of her guidance on business writing. Laura has a gift for helping business writers focus, refine, and develop their ideas, and express those ideas in a compelling way. Whether you are a CEO or a first-time manager, *How to Write Anything* will help you craft your message for the highest possible impact."
—Robert C. Daugherty, executive dean, Forbes School of Business and Technology

"*How to Write Anything* is the first book I've seen that addresses the very core of writing for today's digital communications channels. The lessons in this book are for everybody." —Mary Olson, digital business design and development pioneer

"To author a book called *How to Write Anything: A Complete Guide*, you have to be foolish, delusional, *or* be Laura Brown, who pulls it off with grace and wisdom. Brown provides readers with an overview of the writing process—the infrastructure on which all writing is built—and specific strategies for hundreds of situations. Of course, eventually writers have to face each task alone, but they will be well-equipped thanks to Laura Brown."

—Alan Ziegler, author of *The Writing Workshop Note Book*

"As a writing instructor of over thirty years, I know full well the demands on young writers. Laura Brown answers the tough questions on how to get started, how to craft tone for a target readership, how to develop succinct content, and how to master argumentation."

—Roger Marheine, assistant professor, Pasadena City College

also by LAURA BROWN

BUILD YOUR OWN GARAGE:

Blueprints and Tools to Unleash Your Company's Hidden Creativity

(with Professor Bernd H. Schmitt)

HOW TO WRITE
ANYTHING

A Complete Guide

LAURA BROWN

W. W. NORTON & COMPANY
Independent Publishers Since 1923
New York | London

For my parents,
the late Lois H. Brown and Justin W. Brown

Copyright © 2014 by Laura Brown

For information about permission to reproduce selections from this book,
write to Permissions, W. W. Norton & Company, Inc.,
500 Fifth Avenue, New York, NY 10110

For information about special discounts for bulk purchases, please contact
W. W. Norton Special Sales at specialsales@wwnorton.com or 800-233-4830

Manufacturing by LSC Harrisonburg
Book design by Fearn Cutler de Vicq
Production manager: Julia Druskin
Page layout: Carole Desnoes

Library of Congress Cataloging-in-Publication Data
Brown, Laura Marie.
How to write anything: a complete guide / Laura Brown.—First Edition.
pages cm.
Includes bibliographical references and index.
ISBN: 978-0-393-24014-6 (hardcover)
1. English language—Rhetoric. 2. Report writing. I. Title.
PE1408.B8573 2014
808'.042—dc23   2013045078
ISBN 978-0-393-35518-5 pbk.

W. W. Norton & Company, Inc., 500 Fifth Avenue, New York, NY 10110
www.wwnorton.com

W. W. Norton & Company Ltd., 15 Carlisle Street, London W1D 3BS

1 2 3 4 5 6 7 8 9 0

HOW TO WRITE
ANYTHING

A Complete Guide

LAURA BROWN

W. W. NORTON & COMPANY
Independent Publishers Since 1923
New York | London

For my parents,
the late Lois H. Brown and Justin W. Brown

Copyright © 2014 by Laura Brown

Printed in the United States of America
First published as a Norton paperback 2017

For information about permission to reproduce selections from this book,
write to Permissions, W. W. Norton & Company, Inc.,
500 Fifth Avenue, New York, NY 10110

For information about special discounts for bulk purchases, please contact
W. W. Norton Special Sales at specialsales@wwnorton.com or 800-233-4830

Manufacturing by LSC Harrisonburg
Book design by Fearn Cutler de Vicq
Production manager: Julia Druskin
Page layout: Carole Desnoes

Library of Congress Cataloging-in-Publication Data
Brown, Laura Marie.
How to write anything: a complete guide / Laura Brown.—First Edition.
pages cm.
Includes bibliographical references and index.
ISBN: 978-0-393-24014-6 (hardcover)
1. English language—Rhetoric. 2. Report writing. I. Title.
PE1408.B8573 2014
808'.042—dc23   2013045078
ISBN 978-0-393-35518-5 pbk.

W. W. Norton & Company, Inc., 500 Fifth Avenue, New York, NY 10110
www.wwnorton.com

W. W. Norton & Company Ltd., 15 Carlisle Street, London W1D 3BS

1 2 3 4 5 6 7 8 9 0

Contents

SECTION III: THE ENTRIES   45

HOW TO WRITE
ANYTHING

Introduction

This book is the product of thirty years' experience helping people with their writing—at work, at school, and in their personal lives. I've learned over my career as a business writing coach, a ghostwriter, and a college and high school instructor that there's no such thing as a person who "can't write." I've met people who hate to write and I've met people who think their writing is no good. But I've never met anyone who "can't write." Anyone can write, and anyone can write anything they need to. All that's needed is an understanding of the writing process, an understanding of the particular task you're working on, and a little dedication. If you'll supply the dedication, this book will supply the rest.

How to Write Anything is divided into three sections. Section I offers guidance about the writing process and techniques you can use with any writing task you'll ever have to do. Here you'll find the "Writing Spinner," a novel approach to the writing process that can make all your writing tasks go more quickly and easily. The spinner frees you to think and write in the way that works best for you. You can read this section from beginning to end, browse around, or use the index to find exactly what you're looking for.

Section II is devoted to what I call "e-writing," that is, writing that's done on a computer, a smartphone, an iPad, or any device connected to the Internet. E-writing has changed some of the rules of writing, providing new opportunities and creating new risks. This section offers you guidance about navigating the world of e-writing, including e-mails, instant messages, and social media platforms.

Section III is an encyclopedia of nearly two hundred different writing tasks you're likely to encounter at work, at school, and in your personal life. Each entry discusses how to manage the writing process for that task, offers a series of dos and don'ts, and provides models for you to use for your own writing tasks.

I've tried to be as comprehensive as possible in developing *How to Write Anything*. If you think I've left anything out, I'd love to know about it. Please send your ideas and suggestions to info@howtowriteany thing.com. I look forward to hearing from you!

THE WRITING PROCESS

CHAPTER 1

You Can Write Anything

A man may write at
any time, if he will set
himself to it.

—*Samuel Johnson,*
writer, poet, editor, and
lexicographer

With a few simple tools, you can write anything you'll ever have to write—at work, at school, or in your personal life. Business e-mails and presentations, term papers and application essays, condolence notes and eulogies. Even notes to reclaim lost property or letters to fight parking tickets. As I said, anything.

I've been teaching writing for nearly thirty years to people of all ages, from high school students to corporate executives and everything in between. In all that time, I've never met a person who "can't write." But I have met a lot of people who are intimidated by the writing process.

Not to worry. In this book, I'll present a proven process and show you how to make it work for you every time, no matter what you have to write. We'll take care of that in the first few chapters. Then, in the rest of the book—which, as you can probably tell, constitutes most of the book—I'll hold your hand through every conceivable type of writing you might ever have to do.

If you've ever played one of those children's board games with a circular spinner, where you spin the pointer to determine your next move, you're actually well prepared for my writing process. Here, ladies and gentlemen, is Dr. Laura Brown's Writing Spinner:

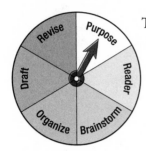

The moves on my spinner will look familiar to you if you've ever taken a writing class or even high school English. You've heard this before: writing involves figuring out your **purpose**, identifying your **reader**, **brainstorming** your ideas, **organizing** your content, **drafting**, and **revising**. But in most writing classes, these steps are presented in a linear fashion, like this:

Purpose → Reader →Brainstorm →Organize →Draft →Revise

In theory, following this sequence should get you to a polished draft in an organized and logical way. This system works for some people, but if you're like most people, it probably *doesn't* work for you. In the real world, most people aren't linear writers.

There's nothing wrong with the six-step process. What's wrong is dictating the order in which you take the steps. When step-by-step becomes lockstep, it prevents you from being the writer you can be.

Successful writers know that it's possible to start *anywhere* in this process and still emerge with an excellent document. (The obvious exception is revising, of course.) You can start by brainstorming. You can start by writing an outline. You can start by drafting. (In fact, most of my clients and students start here; maybe you do, too.) The real key to success is not going through these six steps in any particular order but simply in ensuring that you've touched all these bases at least once as you go through the writing process.

For most of us, the process of writing isn't a line but rather a circle made up of a series of steps. We can start the process with any of the steps on the circle and go around the circle as many times as we like, until we're completely satisfied with what we've written.

In the next chapter, I will show you how to use the spinner approach to discover your own ideal writing process. Once you find your ideal process and practice it a little, writing will be much easier for you, you'll write much faster, and your end product will be much better. In the rest of the book, I'll refer to the spinner process frequently, showing you how it can be applied to a wide variety of different writing tasks.

When we read, we start at the beginning and continue until we reach the end; when we write, we start in the middle and fight our way out.

—*Vickie Karp, poet*

When I am ready to write a book, I write the end first.

—*Marcia Davenport, novelist*

CHAPTER 2

Finding Your Process

I n the last chapter, we looked briefly at six steps of the writing process that sit at different positions on the Writing Spinner. In this chapter, we'll look in detail at each of these steps and see the part each one of them plays in your own writing process. For the sake of simplicity, I'm presenting them in a linear fashion here, but remember . . . you can start your process anywhere you want!

UNDERSTAND YOUR PURPOSE

When you sit down to write something, you need to understand—in a very specific way—what your **purpose** is. What exactly are you hoping to accomplish with this piece of writing?

At first glance, your purpose in writing might seem self-evident, and many times it is. If you're writing a note of congratulations, your purpose is to give the reader some well-deserved recognition for her accomplishment. If you're writing a condolence note, your purpose is to offer comfort to the reader. However, sometimes understanding your purpose is more complicated than it appears. If you don't have a clear idea of what you're trying to achieve, you can easily go astray.

Let's say you're applying for a job, and you need to write a cover letter to accompany your résumé. What is your purpose in that cover letter? You're trying to get a job, right? So isn't that the purpose behind the cover letter? That's your long-range goal, but can the cover letter get you hired? No, it can't. It's only a part of a much larger process that has many different components. Many elements go into the hiring decision: your résumé, your references, and your performance during the interview, among others. So what specifically is your purpose in writing a cover letter to accompany a résumé?

The cover letter actually has two purposes: to encourage the reader to look carefully at your résumé and to motivate the reader to call you for an interview. The horrifying truth is that the average hiring manager reviewing a pile of résumés spends about ten seconds on each. If you can say something in your cover letter to pique your reader's interest, she will be much more likely to give your résumé a serious look. The cover letter also gives you a chance to mention some things that don't appear on the résumé or to point out exactly how your experience makes you a perfect fit for the job—just the kinds of things that will make a hiring manager put your résumé in the follow-up file rather than the circular file.

You can see, then, that there's a world of difference writing a cover letter with the thought "My purpose is to get a job" versus thinking "My purpose is to give my reader information that will encourage her to interview me." The second is more realistic, more focused, and actually much easier to write.

Let's look at another example, the complaint letter or e-mail. We're usually angry when we write a complaint or at least disgruntled enough to devote the time to it. But what's the purpose behind your message? It may be just to blow off steam. But if you want more than that, it's worth thinking carefully about what you're asking for. Do you want a refund? Do you want a replacement? Do you want an apology, an explanation, a recount, a redo? Once you identify your purpose, you can make a specific request of your reader. If you don't ask for what you want, how will the reader know? Remember the old saying "Ask and ye shall receive"? It may not always be true, but you're much less likely to receive if you don't ask!

Thinking specifically about your purpose helps you figure out what to say and how to say it. Interestingly, it also makes things easier on your reader. If you've ever been in a position where you had to review a stack of résumés, you know what a relief it is to read a cover letter that's thoughtful, well written, and targeted for the position you're trying to fill. If you've ever been on the receiving end of a complaint, you know it's much easier to deal with a specific request for a remedy than simply to endure a page worth of angry abuse. Making things easier for your reader increases your chances of getting what you want.

Thinking hard about your purpose is an excellent way to start your writing process. However, if you've started someplace else—for instance, if you've started by writing an outline or writing a draft—you can use this phase as a check-in. Review what you have so far, and check to see if what you're working on really addresses the right purpose. Keep your purpose in mind when doing a final check, too. When you review your final draft, ask yourself if your purpose is clear and sensible to the reader and if you've suggested to your reader a specific way to act on that purpose.

UNDERSTAND YOUR READER

Every time you write, unless you're writing a personal journal, you're writing for an audience. You're directing your writing to specific **readers**. Sometimes your readers' needs and expectations will be clear. It's not hard, for instance, to imagine the needs and expectations of the reader of a condolence letter. The reader of a recipe or driving directions also has pretty straightforward needs.

Some situations are more complicated, however, especially when you're asking your reader for something. Since your readers are the people who can grant or deny your wish, it's worth thinking hard about who they are, what their expectations are, and what they need from you.

When you consider your readers, put yourself in their shoes. Ask yourself how you would respond if you were the person receiving this communication. Think from your reader's point of view.

There are two key issues for you to consider as you think from your reader's point of view:

- Information
- Attitude

What kind of *information* should you give your readers? How much information do they have already, and what information do they need in order to make the decision or take the action you want from them? Imagine, for instance, that you're writing a letter of recommendation for someone who's applying to an MBA program. The reader is going to be looking for information that will convince him the candidate will perform well academically, has a good basic understanding of business, and will work well with other students in the program. If you're creating a sales pitch for a product, your reader will want to know exactly what that product can do and how it can address his needs. In a case like this, the information you include will depend on who you're targeting for the pitch. If you're trying to sell a software product, for instance, you'll likely select different information to present to an audience of IT professionals than to an audience of end users.

The golden rule for selecting information is this: *include* enough *of the* right kind *of information to get readers to do what you want them to do.*

Understanding your readers' potential *attitude* is also key to successful writing. How are your readers likely to respond? Will they be open and receptive? Defensive? Hostile? The importance of this question depends a lot on what you're writing. If you're writing a note of congratulations, for instance, you really don't have to worry about your reader's attitude. However, if you're writing a proposal that asks for funding, and you know your reader is planning budget cuts, you can expect her attitude to be cautious or skeptical. If you're sending an e-mail to an employee requesting a meeting about a performance problem, you can expect that your reader might be defensive, and you can tailor your tone accordingly.

Thinking about information and attitude can help you anticipate any questions your reader might have. When you anticipate questions, you can include the answers to those questions in your document, thus saving yourself extra rounds of follow-up communication and, in the process, time. You might also choose to hold that information aside for now and simply be prepared when the questions actually arise. In either case, being forearmed about your reader's information and attitude—and hence her potential response—will help you do a better job.

Even with writing tasks that seem very cut and dried, it's worth taking the time to think seriously about how your writing can best serve your reader's needs. Instructions are a good example. Writing instructions seems completely straightforward, but we've all been in the situation where those "perfectly simple" instructions were impossible to follow, because an important step had been left out. In cases like this, the writer has taken for granted that the reader knows everything she does. Putting yourself in your reader's shoes can help ensure you do a careful job, even on a "foolproof" piece of writing.

You can see by now that understanding your reader often works hand in hand with understanding your purpose. If you understand your reader, it's easier to write something that will help you achieve your purpose.

Spending a few minutes at the beginning of the writing process thinking about your readers and their needs can help you get off on the right foot, but it's not etched in stone anywhere that you *have* to start this way. It's equally helpful to consider your reader a few times as you work your way through the writing process. In fact, I highly recommend you do so! Often that "lost" feeling you get when you're writing is a sign that you've lost your focus on your reader and you're starting to drift. Going back to consider your reader is a useful touchstone at any point in the process, and an excellent place to check in just before you finalize your draft.

BRAINSTORM YOUR CONTENT

Brainstorming is traditionally the third step of the writing process: once you've considered your purpose and your audience, you're ready to generate the content you need. Some pieces of writing are simple and straightforward. For instance, if you're writing to your child's teacher letting her know that your son will miss school because of a doctor's appointment, you probably won't have to work very hard to be sure your note is complete. However, many writing tasks are more complex, and it's worthwhile spending some time making sure you're including all the necessary content. Brainstorming is the process of compiling all the possible relevant content and putting it all down in one place, for use when you actually start to write.

Get a grasp on your subject and the words will follow.

—*Cato, Roman statesman and writer*

There are a few rules to observe in brainstorming (don't worry, these rules make things easier for you, not harder). You may have come across these rules if you've ever participated in group brainstorming sessions at work or in school.

1. **Try to come up with as many ideas as possible.** If you focus on quantity rather than quality, your chances of generating useful pieces of content increase. The more the merrier.
2. **Don't censor or criticize.** When you're brainstorming, let your ideas flow freely. Now is not the time to judge your ideas, to decide this one isn't good or that one doesn't fit. Turn off that critical voice in your brain, and just write down everything that comes to you. You can sort things out later.
3. **Be open to unusual ideas.** Don't be concerned if some of your thoughts seem off the mark. You may come up with some ideas that are totally unanticipated. One of these unusual ideas might prove to be your most useful point or at least lead you in the direction of your most useful point. Let your imagination do its job.
4. **Combine and improve ideas.** If your ideas are flowing freely, you're likely to come up with some that overlap at least a little bit. Notice similarities and note them.

The more you practice brainstorming, the better you get at it. In many people, the impulse to censor is very strong. There's a little voice in your head saying, "That's not very good" or "That's not interesting" or "That's not relevant." Learning to turn off that voice can be a challenge, but once you do it—or at least get it under control—you can use the whole force of your creativity in generating content for your writing project.

Let's look at an example of how brainstorming can work. Say that you're creating a PowerPoint presentation to pitch a new software product your company has developed. You might brainstorm for a while and end up with a list like this:

If you buy our software, you'll be more efficient
You'll save money

It's better than competing products

We offer great support

We can customize it for you

It's easy to use

It's going to be the leading software package in its category

More economical

Works on all different platforms

Easy to understand

Other companies in your industry are using it

Its main competitor has features that are useless

New version in the pipeline right now

Looking over this list, you can see that not all the information will be relevant to the presentation the writer is planning. Some of it is repetitive. Some of it is vague: for instance, exactly how does the product save the customer money, and how can it make the customer more efficient? However, this list is as complete as the writer could make it during this brainstorming session, and it provides her with an excellent basis for moving forward in the process and developing her slides. With a little editing and a little reorganizing, this list will become a strong first draft.

As you brainstorm, it can be particularly helpful to think about the two phases of the writing process that we've already discussed: understanding your purpose and understanding your reader. If your purpose is to convince your reader to buy the new software, what kind of information could you include that would help in that regard? Remember, think from the point of view of your readers. What are they looking for in a software product, and why? What software are they using now, and how can your product improve their experience? What information will be most persuasive to them? What information won't interest them in the least? These considerations can help feed your brainstorming process.

Is brainstorming a good place to start your writing process? Absolutely! Many people start a writing project by brainstorming ideas. Sometimes getting everything down in a list helps writers organize their ideas and plan their project. But wherever you start your writing process, remember that brainstorming isn't over once you've written an outline, and it isn't even over once you've written a draft. It's a technique you can come back to as many times as you like, as many times as will be helpful to you.

Say you've already written a first draft of the presentation, for instance. When you review what you've written, you might find areas that seem less complete or less convincing than they should be. You might even remember an important piece of information that's missing altogether. That's the time to go back and brainstorm some more and then return to your draft with the new information you've developed. You might find the same thing happens when you write an outline: some parts of the outline are more developed than others. If you think the imbalance is a problem, go back to the drawing board, brainstorm a little more, and fill in the blanks. You can return to this part of the spinner as many times as you need to, until you're comfortable that you have all the content you need.

ORGANIZE

There are many different approaches to **organizing** a written document. In school, many of us learned a fairly rigid outline format, a format that involves roman numerals, Arabic numerals, and letters of different sizes. This kind of outline format can be helpful because it offers a logical way to organize large quantities of information. However, most of what we write isn't long enough or complex enough to justify using such a formal outline, and trying to force our content into this format can be frustrating and unrewarding.

The way we organize a document depends a lot on what kind of document it is and what our objectives are. If you're writing a set of instructions or driving directions, then a *step-by-step* outline makes sense. If you're describing an event that took place, you might organize *chronologically*. If you're trying to persuade someone, you might want to rank your reasons in *order of importance*, either beginning with the most important reason first or placing the most compelling reason last in order to end on the strongest possible note. If you're presenting *pros and cons*, you might group those together. Organizing most documents usually follows a simple logic. Working your way around the spinner, you may find that returning to a consideration of your reader can help you find the best way to organize your document. What do you think your reader expects? What kind of organization will be the most persuasive or the easiest for him to follow?

As long as we're spinning the spinner, can you start your writing process with organizing, before you've considered your purpose and your reader and before you've brainstormed the content you want to include? Absolutely you can. In fact, organizing and outlining isn't a bad place to start. Doing the organizing first can help guide you as you brainstorm your ideas and content.

Let's look at an example to see how this might work. Say you want to e-mail your boss to recommend postponing an event you've been planning. Here's a quick outline you might throw together:

✓ Let's postpone till May.
✓ May would be better because we'd get a better turnout.
✓ The catering isn't set yet.
✓ There are staffing problems.
✓ We haven't done good promotion.
✓ Two department heads asked for it to be postponed.
✓ If we postpone, we can promote it in the e-newsletter.

You see this outline is very sparse—no roman numerals or letters, or even numbers—but it's a jotting down of the major topics to cover in the e-mail, and it took about forty-five seconds to do. The writer can go ahead and create a draft from this outline, or he can revise the outline a bit, taking into consideration his reader's potential response. Say that the boss isn't going to be happy about this suggestion. Let's also say that some of the reasons for the delay aren't going to reflect well on the writer himself; the boss is likely to wonder why he hasn't done good promotion and why he hasn't finalized the catering arrangements. Reordering the outline can improve his chances of getting a good response from his boss.

✓ Let's postpone till May.
✓ Two department heads asked for it to be postponed.
✓ Some logistical problems.
✓ If we postpone, we can promote it in the e-newsletter.
✓ May would be better because we'd get a better turnout.

With this new outline, the writer is less likely to get resistance from his boss. He leads with his most persuasive point—that two department heads have requested the postponement. He buries some of the information that might make him look bad in the single heading about "logistical problems." And he ends on a promising note: that postponing will allow more time for better promotion and yield a better turnout.

All of this organizing took no more than a couple of minutes: a couple of minutes well spent on solving a big problem and staving off a bad response from the reader. The writer is ready now to write a draft, and because of this outline, he knows where he's going.

Reverse Outlining

Do you have to write an outline before you start writing your draft? No, not if it doesn't work well for you. Many writers prefer to start writing a draft and then do what we call "reverse outlining." When you reverse outline, you take a draft you've already written and jot down a brief outline of what you actually have. You can make notes paragraph by paragraph or idea by idea. Reverse outlining can help you see if your draft is really organized in a sensible way or if you need to go back and reorder things a bit. It can also expose any gaps you might have in your information, gaps that you can fill in by brainstorming additional content.

> Few things are more interesting than revising. Having seen what you said, you begin to discover what you meant. It's like psychoanalysis—except it's free.
>
> —*Zibby O'Neal, novelist*

DRAFT

Drafting is the process of sitting down and getting it all written out for the first time. Conventional wisdom suggests that you should start drafting only after you've carefully brainstormed and outlined your content. However, most people ignore conventional wisdom and start their writing projects by jumping right in and writing a draft. There are lots of reasons people do this. Sometimes we're in a big rush and writing an outline seems like a waste of time. Sometimes we think we know exactly what to say, so we start off by just saying it.

In spite of what your English teachers may have told you, there's absolutely nothing wrong with starting by writing a draft. If you want to start writing, start writing. There's also some practical support for this approach, as many writers find that the process of writing helps them generate new ideas. Just be aware that if you start writing a draft before you've given any thought to your purpose or your reader, and before you've really brainstormed your content, you're probably going to have to do some major revising. If that works well for you, then you shouldn't hesitate to proceed!

The great irony about drafting is that although most people start here, it's probably the most anxiety-producing part of the entire writing process. Drafting can create worry because it's so near the end of the process, and we put ourselves under a lot of pressure to get it right the first time. Of course, we've already seen that getting it right the first time is unlikely. So how can we reduce the anxiety associated with drafting and work through the cycle of the writing process efficiently and effectively?

If you've started a draft, my best advice is to keep going until you feel stuck or until you have serious questions about what you're doing. You know you're going to have to go back and take another look at it, so relax and keep going. If you come across an area where there's something missing, flag it and keep going. If you're writing on a computer, mark the section with ALL CAPS or *italics* or put it in a different color. If you're writing by hand, underline it or mark it with stars or question marks. Once you're on a roll, use that momentum and keep going as long as you can.

How do you know when it's time to stop and think? Signs that you're having problems include wondering "Why the heck am I writing this?" or "Is this relevant?" or thinking "This stinks." If you find you've hit the wall, stop and take a break. Go over what you've written and check it by going around the spinner. Is your purpose clear? Will it appeal to your reader? Do you have all the content you need, or do you need to brainstorm more? Is it organized effectively? Work on the areas that seem skimpy or weak to you, and then go back and fill in.

> Convince yourself that you are working in clay not marble, on paper not eternal bronze: let that first sentence be as stupid as it wishes. No one will rush out and print it as it stands. Just put it down; then another.
>
> —*Jacques Barzun, historian and essayist*

> Too often I wait for the sentence to finish taking shape in my mind before setting it down. It is better to seize it by the end that first offers itself, head or foot, though not knowing the rest, then pull; the rest will follow along.
>
> —*Andre Gide, novelist*

REVISE

The perfect first draft is almost as rare as a sunny day in Vancouver or a polar bear in Florida. It happens but not very often. **Revising** is part of the writing process; it's not a sign of failure. Regardless of the writing project you're working on, you should plan time to revise your drafts.

Revising can mean anything from doing a complete rethink and rewrite to simply proofreading and fixing typos. The extent of the revising you do depends on a few things: how long the document is, how complicated it is, and how important it is. Whatever it is, you need to give it at least a quick proofread before you let it out of your sight.

Spending just a few seconds to proofread your documents can help prevent costly misunderstandings. Imagine, for example, that you've written a letter requesting a postponement in your jury duty service, and you've written this sentence:

I will be available to serve until June 21 of this year.

That sounds all right, right? The trouble is that you *won't* be available to serve until June 21. What you meant to write was this:

I will not be available to serve until June 21 of this year.

You dropped out one little word (*not*), didn't proofread, and sent off the wrong information to the clerk of the court. It's going to take far longer to untangle this mess than it would have taken to proofread the letter before you sent it.

Even e-mail should be proofread. You may feel it's an unreasonable hassle to proofread personal e-mails, but failing to do so can have annoying and time-consuming consequences. Once I sent out an e-mail to twenty friends, inviting them to dinner at a restaurant at 3:00 p.m. on Tuesday, April 17. Eleven people wrote me back, asking if I was really proposing to have dinner at three in the afternoon. I had to send out a correction—the invitation should have been for 7:00. I'd wasted my time and my friends' time, and it would all have been very easy to avoid had I taken a moment to proofread my message before I sent it.

The stakes become much higher when we e-mail at work. Sending an e-mail that contains typos will, at best, make you look unprofessional. The consequences of sending out the wrong information can be more serious. We'll look at e-communication in greater detail in the next chapter. For now, it's enough to remember to proofread!

For documents that are longer and more complex, you'll want to go beyond proofreading and really think critically about your draft before you revise it. Here is a useful list of questions to ask yourself as you review and revise:

> You have to allow yourself the liberty of writing poorly. You have to get the bulk of it done, and then you start to refine it. You have to put down less than marvelous material just to keep going to whatever you think the end is going to be—which may be something else altogether by the time you get there.
>
> —*Larry Gelbart, scriptwriter*

✓ Is it clear what I'm trying to accomplish here? If I'm asking for something, have I asked clearly?

✓ Do I address the readers appropriately?

✓ Do I give the readers enough information to act on my request? Is that information interesting or inspiring to them? Does it motivate them to act?

✓ Is my information complete? Have I left out anything important?

✓ Is the information presented in a logical and compelling order?

✓ Is my document free from errors in spelling, punctuation, and grammar?

Revise in passes

For long and very important documents, some people like to revise in passes. That is, they go through the document several times, each time checking for a different question above. It can be difficult to keep all these questions in your head at once, and dividing the task into its component parts can make it less overwhelming. You can develop your own set of questions and your own way of working through them. The key is to find a way to make the task as comfortable and efficient as possible for you.

Enlist help

No matter how conscientious you are, it's very easy to lose perspective on something you've just written. When you comb through a draft immediately after you've written it, you're likely to miss problems. Having another person review your draft, even very quickly, is an excellent way to solve this "I'm too close to it" problem and get a different perspective on your writing.

> One must be ruthless with one's own writing or someone else will be.
>
> —*John Berryman, poet*

Sometimes co-workers develop a buddy system whereby they regularly check one another's writing. People who work together this way build trust and can significantly improve each other's work. If you're asking someone for help for the first time, be sure you let him know exactly what you need. If you're just looking for a quick proofread, for instance, let your reader know that before he spends an hour developing a detailed critique of your content. If you have any specific questions about what you've just written—for instance, if you're worried it might not appeal to the reader or if you think the introduction is too long—be sure tell your "editor" so he can focus on the areas where you need help.

To Reach Your Readers, Get Feedback First!

When Mark Victor Hansen and I started work on the first of our *Chicken Soup for the Soul* books, we knew we wanted to create a book that would touch and inspire our readers with unforgettable stories. We had collected a lot of stories, and we wanted to choose the ones that would mean the most to our readers. How did we choose? Through reader feedback!

We selected a group of forty reviewers and asked them to rate every story on a scale from 7 to 10. A 10 is a great story that gives the reader goose bumps; a 9 is a good story with a great message. An 8 is an OK story that lacks emotional punch, and a 7 is a flat-out rejection. We sent each of our reviewers a letter explaining the feedback process and letting them know that it would be *their* input that would make the final book meaningful to readers. From the results, we created an Excel spreadsheet and averaged all the scores, which showed us exactly how all our reviewers felt about every story we were considering.

We've used the same feedback process for each of the nearly 250 *Chicken Soup* titles. Today there are over 500 million copies of the *Chicken Soup* books in print, and I firmly believe that wouldn't have happened without the feedback our many reviewers provided. That's an important lesson for anyone writing anything for any audience.

So the next time you're writing something that's very important to you—something that has to have a real impact on your readers—make the effort to get feedback on your writing before you finalize it. If you can get feedback from people who are similar to your intended readers, your message will truly reach and touch its audience.

Jack Canfield is the best-selling cocreator of the Chicken Soup for the Soul series of books. He is also coauthor (with Janet Switzer) of *The Success Principles: How to Get from Where You Are to Where You Want to Be.*

Take a break

In an ideal world, you'll have time to write a draft and then take a break before you review it. Letting a day or two pass between drafts is an excellent way to gain some perspective on what you've just written. Unfortunately, the demands of the real world often make this difficult. Even under harried circumstances, though, it's often possible to let that draft "rest" long enough to improve your revision process. Say, for instance, that the document has to be done by close of business today. If your schedule allows, plan to write a draft first thing in the morning, let it rest through lunch, and then return to it later in the afternoon. Even a span of a few hours can help you take a fresh approach to the document. If you've had a colleague proofing your draft in the meantime, you'll be in even better shape when you return to the document to revise it.

SPEED AND THE SPINNER

As we've seen, the spinner approach to the writing process gives you a lot of freedom to work in the way that's most productive for you. Using the spinner, you can start your writing process anywhere you like and work through the process in the way that works best for you. We all learn to do things in the most efficient and comfortable way for us. Folding laundry, preparing a meal, making a purchase decision—we have a preferred process for anything we do regularly, whether or not we've thought consciously about that process. The spinner approach frees you to find and develop your own best process for writing.

However, any kind of systematic approach to writing is bound to seem a little idealized to people who have to write in the real world. Whether you see the process as a line or as a circle, going through all these steps may seem like an impossible luxury to people who are under the gun to do a lot of writing, fast, every day. In both our personal and professional lives, the pace of communication is increasing, and the notion of stopping to think may seem like little more than a charming fantasy.

I think I can offer some comfort here. The more you interact with the spinner, the more the process will become ingrained in your everyday mode of working. The more exposure you have to it, the more you will begin to use it. Even unconsciously, you'll become more aware of your purpose and your reader, you'll be more conscientious about the content you include, you'll begin to think instinctively about outlining, and your drafting and revising skills will improve. By working the spinner approach, even occasionally, you'll figure out *your optimal writing process*, the one that allows you to write quickly and effectively—which is bound to be more efficient than any process handed to you by others.

The spinner approach to writing has yet another advantage over the linear, step-by-step approach. It's ideal to use for a quick check when you really don't have much time to plan and revise. You can dash off a draft and then take yourself once or twice around the spinner to check that you haven't forgotten something important. You can even use it literally as a spinner, to select an area to work on at random, knowing that focusing attention on that area is bound to improve the document you're working on (and also, over the long run, make you a better writer across the board).

The spinner is yours to play with and to use as you like. It includes everything you need to know about writing. It's purposely designed to be flexible, to help you find the best possible writing process for yourself, and to help you get your writing done within your time constraints. You'll see the spinner icon return throughout the book as we discuss different kinds of writing tasks and look at examples, both successful and unsuccessful. I hope it will open the door for you to an approach to writing that's sensible, straightforward, and comfortable.

E-WRITING AND THE TECHNOLOGY REVOLUTION

When the Internet first came into popular use in the mid-1990s, some people predicted writing would soon be extinct, replaced by some kind of nonverbal, digital communication. By now, we're all aware that these dire predictions didn't come true. Not even close. In fact, the multiple options for e-communication have created an explosion in writing. A typical day for many people consists of e-mailing all day at work, using text messaging to keep tabs on our kids and to make after-work plans, and spending the evening catching up with friends on social networking sites or posting on discussion boards. While we certainly write less on paper than we used to, most of us are writing more than ever before, and writing is playing a more important role in both our professional and personal lives.

> Regardless of the changes in technology, the market for well-crafted messages will always have an audience.
>
> —*Steve Burnett, The Burnett Group*

Although the technology revolution didn't kill writing, it definitely changed it. The advent of personal computers, the Internet, and cell phones has given rise to a new, accelerated kind of writing, which I call "e-writing." What's e-writing? Any kind of writing using an electronic device, whether it's a computer connected to the Internet, a cell phone, or a device like an iPad. E-writing is fast, technologically enabled writing, and we're doing more of it every day.

Although life without the Internet and cell phones may seem unimaginable now, the fact is that these technologies are still relatively new, and people still have a lot of questions about digitally based writing. What are the rules? *Are* there rules? How can you know what the rules are when the technology is changing so fast, creating new devices and platforms for writing all the time? Even younger people who have been using the Internet for much of their lives face challenges when they make the transition from school to the workplace, where the rules for e-writing are different and the costs of making mistakes are higher. Although many of us are immersed in e-writing and typing as fast as we can, doing it well isn't as easy as it looks.

The next two chapters are designed to answer all your questions about e-writing. In section III of this book, you'll find detailed guidance about specific kinds of e-writing: personal and work-related e-mails, text messages, instant messaging, blogging, posting on social networking sites, and creating copy for web pages. In this section, you'll find general guidance you can use for *any* kind of e-writing—at work, at home, or at school.

CHAPTER 3

Choose Your Weapon

The advent of computers and cell phones has created a sort of a Wild West of communication options—all fast and convenient—and the future is likely to bring even more. But although these communication options are all quick and easy, they're not all created equal. Some are better suited for personal communication, others for business. Some create a permanent record of communication that's easily accessed; others are more ephemeral. Before you send a text or an e-mail, or post on a social media website, or make a phone call, or even speak to someone face-to-face, you'd be wise to spend a minute thinking about whether you're choosing the right medium to convey your message.

TO WRITE OR NOT TO WRITE

The first decision you need to make when you want to communicate with someone is whether you should write at all. Writing may seem like a convenient option, but sometimes a phone call or a face-to-face conversation is really a better choice. Why might you prefer to talk rather than to write? There are a few reasons.

One important consideration is that e-mails and text messages are far more likely to be misunderstood than spoken communication. Tone of voice and facial expressions are simply not available in writing—and smileys are useful only in the most basic of situations. During a face-to-face conversation, or even over the phone, either party can ask for clarification or stop and rephrase what they're saying, so it's easy to nip any potential misunderstandings in the bud. Written communication doesn't allow the real-time give-and-take of a conversation. The fact that we're usually in a hurry when we're e-mailing or texting doesn't improve the clarity of our writing.

Another important issue to consider is that any written communication creates a record. In most cases, this presents no problem. However, if your topic is at all personal or sensitive, you might want to think twice before you put your thoughts in writing. We'll talk more about the permanent and public nature of e-writing—and the associated risks—below. For now, ask yourself if you're comfortable having a written record of your message floating around for others to see. If the answer is no, you're better off using the phone or having a conversation face-to-face.

Courtesy is another reason you might want to speak to someone rather than write to them. If you have something especially difficult or complicated to convey, it's tempting to take shelter in the written word instead of starting a potentially uncomfortable conversation. But there are some kinds of communication that you really should handle face-to-face or at the very least over the phone. Important conversations about personal relationships should be done in person. Apologies often mean more when you say "I'm sorry" while looking the person in the eye. Has anyone ever broken up with you via a text message? It's not nice, to say the least. It may feel easier for you to put difficult communications in writing, but trying to sort out problems in writing can actually be more difficult than doing it in person. What's more, the person on the other end will know that you're trying to avoid facing her, and that in itself can make a bad situation worse. Stop and think for a moment before you compose that e-mail or text message. Are you hiding behind your writing so you don't have to face the person you're writing to? If so, consider whether an in-person meeting—or at least a phone call—might be the better choice for the message and for the relationship.

Another way we hide behind our writing is through the "e-mail tag" we sometimes engage in at work. Have you ever felt in such a rush that you've fired off an e-mail simply to get a particular issue out of your inbox and into someone else's? When you do this, you may look like you're being productive . . . but are you really moving things closer to resolution? Usually not. If you have an ongoing round of e-mail communication that's getting you no closer to resolving the issue at hand, you might be better off picking up the phone and sorting it all out. If you need a written record of the decisions you made on the phone, you can follow up with an e-mail confirmation. But sometimes it's just more sensible to work things out through a conversation rather than sending a seemingly endless string of written messages.

Ninety-nine times out of one hundred, you can successfully make the decision about talking versus writing if you follow these two simple steps: (1) slow down, and (2) think. As you think, ask yourself if writing would be the best way to resolve what you're trying to resolve. Ask yourself how you would feel if you were the person on the other end of the communication and whether you would rather do it in writing or by speaking personally. Most of the time, the decision is really a matter of common sense and common courtesy. Exercise both, and you'll find the best way.

IF YOU WRITE

Once you've given yourself the green light to communicate in writing, you'll want to make sure the medium you choose is *convenient for your reader* and *appropriate for your message.*

I once had a colleague who responded to all my e-mails by immediately sending me an instant message (IM). It didn't matter how pressing the issue was, or how complicated. He was sitting at his desk, he liked instant messaging, and that's the way he wanted to communicate. In fact, I once overheard him telling another colleague about how efficient he was, using instant messaging to get things done right away rather than leaving issues languishing in his e-mail inbox. What he was overlooking, of course, was that it might not be convenient for others to respond to his IMs right away. Very often people choose to send an e-mail because it gives both parties the time to think and respond at their own convenience. You can conduct an e-mail conversation very efficiently during the little spaces between other activities during your day or even continue the discussion at three o'clock in the morning if you so choose. By moving the discussion to instant messaging, my colleague changed the terms of the communication and, perhaps unconsciously, imposed his own schedule on mine.

Even if we're not as fanatical (and irritating) as my former colleague, most of us have a preferred method of communication and will tend to default to it. Some people e-mail. Some people text. Some people prefer the phone. There's nothing wrong with having a preference, of course, but if you really want to communicate effectively, you need to consider whether your preferred method of communication is *convenient for your reader*. It may be easy for you to send a lot of messages through Facebook, but if your friends aren't checking their messages there, you won't be heard. You might like texting, but if your friend has his phone off while he's at his desk, you're not going to reach him. If it's important for you to get in touch, you may have to be flexible about the medium you use to contact people.

You'll also need to ensure that the medium you choose is *appropriate for your message*. How can you tell? There are a few parameters for you to consider: *length, complexity, formality, number of readers*, and *permanency*. Looking at these parameters in combination—and in terms of what you want to say—can help you decide the most appropriate form of e-communication for your message.

Let's take a quick look at some e-communication options with these parameters in mind.

Instant messaging is ideal for short, simple communications, like informal chats with friends. It can also be a very useful way to ask and answer quick questions at work. Instant messaging works best when your message is brief and uncomplicated and when the message is directed to a small number of readers. A conversation that involves more than three or four people can be confusing: separate cross-conversations spring up, answers get separated from questions, and it can be hard to trace the thread of your own discussion. Because the instant messaging conversation typically disappears when you close the window or shut down your computer, instant messaging is not a good choice if you need a permanent record of the communication. Although IMs can be cached, they're not easy for the average user to recover. If you're conveying information that people will need to refer to later—for instance, giving instructions or finalizing an action plan—you're better off texting or e-mailing.

Texting is great for quick, informal messages, like making or confirming plans. It's easily accessed when you're on the go, and it's especially good for last-minute changes and updates. If your message is brief, uncomplicated, and informal, texting is a good medium for it.

It's worthwhile taking a minute to assemble your thoughts before you send a text. If you forget something and need to send a follow-up text before your reader has replied, there's a chance that they will never see the original message, depending on the kind of phone they're using. Speed isn't always your friend.

Like instant messaging, texting is more effective when there aren't a lot of people involved and when the topic is not complex. A friend of mine tells this story about a frustrating experience in communicating via text message: "I was trying to arrange a meeting with two friends who didn't know one another and were both the non-e-mailing types. Every change in plans that one of them wanted (and they wanted quite a few) had to be filtered through me. I found myself texting these detailed messages back and forth until they finally came to an agreement! By the time we met, they were both fine, but I was feeling both anxious and put upon."

As my friend's situation illustrates, it's not unusual for a text message communication to grow into something too complex for the medium to handle. If you find yourself at this point, you might just want to pick up the phone. If you still prefer to communicate in writing, though, you should consider sending an e-mail instead of a text.

E-mail is a long-established, flexible, and widely accepted form of e-communication. It's a staple of the business world and a part of people's personal lives. E-mail is generally easily accessible to most of us. It's sitting there on our work and home computers, and mobile devices make it easy to check e-mail many times a day. E-mail can accommodate long and complex messages (though, as we'll see in the next chapter, your chances of being read are greater when you keep your e-mails as brief as possible). It's appropriate for informal discussions between friends and also for formal business communications.

E-mail is a good way to get a message across to a large number of readers. It's also a good way to share information that everyone will need to access again: e-mail creates a permanent record that everyone on the thread can find easily.

Although e-mail is usually an excellent default choice for e-communication, remember this caveat: don't make the decision without first considering your readers and their preferences. There are still people who don't get e-mail on their mobile devices, and there are others who have abandoned e-mail in favor of texting. If you really want to be heard, you'll need to select a medium that reaches your reader.

Posting on **social media sites** like Facebook or Twitter is another way to get your message out. Most of these sites have a word or character limit for posts, so they force you to stick with brief messages. If you're sure that your target readers are looking at these sites frequently or following you, this can be an excellent way to reach large numbers of readers. Bear in mind, though, that the attention span of the average reader on social media sites is very short: if you have a complex message to convey, this might not be your best option. Social media sites are ideal for announcements, less ideal for complex messages that require thoughtful consideration.

An even more serious concern about social media sites is the public nature of these postings: anything you post on a website is public and permanent, so be sure you're comfortable with those two conditions before you post. Be warned that even if you reconsider and take down your post, you can't assume that it's "gone." It's been seen by your audience and possibly shared with others. And, as we'll see in the next chapter, most forms of e-writing are cached somewhere. If you wouldn't write your message on a sign and hang it out your bedroom window, don't post it on any website!

WHAT ABOUT THE FUTURE?

The world of e-communication is always in flux. New devices and forums become available, and their popularity changes over time. Websites come and go. Mobile devices become more sophisticated. Although it feels to some of us that the Internet has been around forever, the fact is that we're still in the very early days of electronic communication, and there are doubtless many changes to come.

Whatever changes in the future, though, you can be confident in your e-communication if you follow the guidelines set out in this chapter. No matter how things change, your selection of the best medium for communication will still be guided by considering what's convenient for your reader and what's appropriate for your message.

As in the past, early adopters of new technology will always run the risk that those they wish to communicate with aren't yet using the new technology; in such a case, early adopters need to be flexible in their communication choices. On the other hand, those who cling to outdated forms of communication (and things get outdated faster and faster, it seems) also risk not connecting with their readers. These writers will also need to be flexible and willing to keep up with the times. No matter how things change, showing a mutual concern for the convenience of others will improve our success in communication.

Whatever new devices and forums for e-writing come along, the same parameters for determining appropriateness will still be important to consider—*length, complexity, formality, number of readers,* and *permanency*. Bear these in mind, and you're well equipped to make the appropriate choices for all your e-communications in the future.

Keeping Your Kids Safe in the World of E-Communication

Kids grow up surrounded by all kinds of electronic communication. But even though it's omnipresent, it's not always benign. These two important guidelines can help students stay out of trouble in the world of e-communications.

Assume everyone can see it. There's no such thing as privacy in e-communication. Facebook status updates are seen not just by your friends, but also by your friends' friends, and anyone can grab your words or your pictures and share them with the world. The same goes for anything you post on Twitter, discussion boards, and other websites. Your text messages can be forwarded. You'll be safer if you assume that anyone—including everyone in your school, even college admissions officers—can see everything you write on your computer or your mobile device.

You can't take it back. Everything you post on the web or write on a smartphone is permanent. Deleted Facebook accounts remain accessible for an undetermined time after deletion, and deleted tweets continue to show up in search results long after you take them down. If someone wants to find something you wrote, they will. Never post or text anything that you don't want sticking around forever.

CHAPTER 4

The Process of E-Writing

I n chapter 2, we looked at a six-step writing process designed to help you write anything you need to write. The process involves using a spinner that contains the following points: **purpose**, **reader**, **brainstorm**, **organize**, **draft**, and **revise**.

The process is flexible and adaptable, and it's useful for any writing task you might attempt. In this chapter, I'm going to show you a shortcut that makes the spinner approach especially relevant for e-writing.

You'll recall from chapter 2 that when you write with the spinner you can start anywhere you want and work your way around until you're happy with the result. But because most e-communications are brief and composed quickly, I'm going to assume you'll start with a **draft**. Most of us just sit down at the computer and start writing, right? There's absolutely nothing wrong with that, but most of us don't write perfect first drafts, so we need to do a little more work before we hit Enter or Send.

Exactly how much work? If you have a long or especially important message to write, if you're writing a blog post, and certainly if you're writing copy for a website, I encourage you to implement the full spinner approach we looked at in chapter 2, and to touch on all six points at least once before you finalize your draft.

However, if your message is short and to the point, I recommend an abridged approach to using the spinner, a quick diagnostic you can use with your drafts to make your writing as successful as possible. Although this process takes just seconds, it can save you a lot of time by helping you avoid messages that are unclear, incomplete, and ineffective.

Let's assume you're starting with at least a partial draft. Now I'd like you to touch on just three of the other points on the spinner and check how your draft is working: purpose, reader, and revise. You can use this mini-spinner approach every time you send an e-mail, post on a website, or even send a text message.

IS YOUR PURPOSE CLEAR TO YOU AND YOUR READER?

Let's say you've just dashed off a quick draft of an e-mail, a comment on a website, or a brief announcement on your blog. When you're writing in a hurry, it can be especially easy to lose focus on your **purpose**. We tend to start writing before we're really finished thinking, and e-writing makes it especially easy to send or post something before you've really thought through what you're trying to accomplish. How many e-mails have you received that are full of information but leave you wondering, "What exactly do they want from me?" Or messages that contain the vague request "Let me know what you think"? If you stop for a moment and consider your purpose, you can avoid creating these problems for your readers.

Remember, your readers are in a hurry, too. In this busy e-world, people aren't likely to spend a lot of time trying to figure out what you want. In fact, readers often ignore messages that contain vague or unclear requests. If they do take the time to follow up and find out what you wanted, they're likely to be unhappy about the wasted time. Spending a minute to clarify your purpose can save you and your reader a lot of time and effort in the long run, and it improves your chances of getting what you want.

Ask yourself a few questions about the purpose of your communication. Why am I writing this? What do I want? Do I want someone to take action? Do I want someone's opinion? Do I need a reply at all, or am I just passing along information? When you slow down to consider these questions, you may find that your answer is "I don't know." No worries—it's lucky you've found out now, before you've bothered your readers with a vague or meandering message or a purposeless post. Take a second and figure out exactly why you're writing, and then get to work revising your draft to make your purpose clearer to your reader.

Before you send a message or post on a website, take a moment to ask yourself these questions:

- Do I really understand what my purpose is?
- Have I made my purpose clear to my reader?

If you've answered no to either of these questions, then it's time for a little more work to clarify your purpose. The effort will pay off!

IS YOUR MESSAGE TAILORED TO YOUR READER?

Of course you can achieve your purpose in writing only if your **reader** agrees to it. Have you given any thought to your reader in writing your draft? It's not too late to do so! First ask yourself, "Who is my reader?" Are you writing to your boss? A colleague? A friend? Who's reading that blog? Customers? Potential customers? Consider how you address your reader, and consider whether your tone is appropriate, given your relationship. Now think about how your reader might react to your draft. Different types of readers will likely have different needs and expectations, and if you think from your reader's point of view, you'll have a better chance of writing a draft that will appeal to her. Think in terms of *information* and *attitude*. What information does your reader have, and what information does she need in order to make the decision or take the action you're requesting from her? What is her attitude likely to be? Do you expect her to be open and receptive, or do you expect her to be resistant or skeptical? All these reader-related considerations should help shape your message as you continue to develop your draft.

Before you hit Enter, Send, or Post, ask yourself the following questions:

- What's my relationship to my reader?
- Have I addressed my reader appropriately, given our relationship?
- Have I given my reader the information she needs?
- Have I taken the reader's likely attitude into account?

If you find you're not happy with the answers, take a moment to rework your draft to make it more interesting and compelling to your reader.

REVISE, REVISE, REVISE

Having clarified our purpose and made sure our message is relevant to the reader, let's go around the spinner to **revise**. To help you get through your revision as quickly as possible, here's a quick checklist covering the most common problems that turn up in e-writing:

- ✓ Is Your Message as Brief as It Can Be?
- ✓ Have You Included Everything?
- ✓ Is Your Message Courteous?
- ✓ Is Your Tone Appropriate?
- ✓ Does Your Message Pass the Newspaper Test?

Let's look at each of these in a little more detail.

✓ Is Your Message as Brief as It Can Be?

Hurried readers prefer short messages. Keeping your messages, posts, or blog entries brief is the key to being read. Busy colleagues might not read long e-mails, or they might not read them in full. People browsing the Internet and reading website content expect short paragraphs. Social media sites limit the number of words or characters you can use. Even when we're "doing nothing" on the Internet, we still have the sense that time is at a premium, and we're likely to skip web pages or status updates that look too long.

Once you've finished a draft, look it over and see if you can condense it. Think from your reader's point of view. Have you given her what she needs, or have you given her far more? If it's the latter, take a moment to cut out the excess language and streamline the reader's experience.

If you do need to send a long e-mail or make a long post on a website, you can use formatting to break up long paragraphs and bullet points to call out important information. People tend to *scan* rather than read when they're in a hurry, and these formatting tricks can make your text more scannable and thus more accessible to your reader.

Before you hit Enter or Send, ask yourself these questions:

- Is my message or post as brief as it could be?
- Have I cut out any unnecessary verbiage?
- Have I used formatting to break up long blocks of text, to make them easier to read?

> If it is possible to cut a word out, always cut it out.
>
> —*George Orwell,*
> *novelist and essayist*

If you find your draft is too long or too dense, spend a few minutes trimming, rewriting, and reformatting until it's as efficient as it can possibly be.

✓ **Have You Included Everything?**

Keeping your e-communications as brief as possible is great . . . unless you leave out important information. Speed is often the culprit here: sometimes we're in such a rush, we forget to tell the reader everything he needs to know. Of course this kind of omission defeats the purpose of rapid communication, because we end up taking more time to clarify what we should have said in the first place.

Once you're finished reviewing your message for length, have a look and be sure you haven't forgotten anything essential or cut it out by mistake in a frenzy of editing. Also check to see that you haven't condensed your message so much that you've made it incomprehensible. It's better to send a slightly longer message and get your point across than to send something brief but impossible to understand.

Ask yourself:

- Have I left out anything important?
- Is there anything ambiguous in my message or post that I should clarify?

If your message is incomplete or unclear, revise it!

✓ **Is Your Message Courteous?**

Common courtesy is an all-too-frequent casualty of our quest for speed. Yes, we're all in a hurry. But it doesn't take long to type "please" and "thank you," and it doesn't take long to read them. Another good practice is to use salutations in your e-mails. It takes just a second to begin your message with a greeting, but it raises the courtesy level of the message tremendously.

E-writers use a wide variety of styles, from chatty to blunt. Business writing tends to be more direct than personal communication. Even in business, though, there's a difference between being direct and being rude. It's well worth the small effort to make sure your message is courteous and to make sure you haven't unintentionally said something that might offend someone.

Composing a draft when you're angry or upset can lead to a curt or even rude tone. If you find yourself typing furiously when you're upset about something, *stop*. Cool off and return to the task when you're more levelheaded. You can revise it later or throw it out if you prefer. To be safe, delete the text you've written from your e-mail program and paste it into a Word file so that you don't send it by accident.

Before you fire off an e-mail or post your opinion on the web, ask yourself these questions:

- Is my message or post courteous?
- Have I read over my text to be sure nothing might offend?
- If I'm angry or upset, have I taken some time to cool off before sharing what I've written?

If you've forgotten to show courtesy in your message, take a moment to add "please" and "thank you." If you've written anything potentially offensive, explosive, or abusive, revise it.

✓ **Is Your Tone Appropriate?**

While you're at it, take a moment to consider if you're using the appropriate tone in your message or post. What do I mean by tone? In a nutshell, tone refers to the feelings or attitude that the writing conveys. Tone can be shaped by things like vocabulary, sentence length, and adherence (or not) to the rules of grammar.

How can you tell if your tone is appropriate? Tone is generally governed by two things: the *context* of the communication and your *relationship* with your reader. The context of your message might be professional or personal. Are you at work or at home? Is your message business-related, or is it purely personal? Your relationship with your reader might also be professional or personal. In a professional context, is your reader a person who works for you, a peer at your job, your boss, a business associate outside your organization, or a customer? Is your reader a professor at your school, your child's teacher, a contractor you might hire to work on your house?

All of these factors should influence the tone you use. Let's start with the easiest one. When writing to friends or family, your tone can be relaxed and informal. Of course, you should still take the trouble to be courteous, but you're otherwise pretty safe in writing to these people just as you would speak to them.

Things get a little more complicated when you're writing in a work or professional context. There, your tone should be more formal. If you work in a company, it's wise to follow the lead of your colleagues when it comes to tone. Some organizations tend to use a formal tone; others are more relaxed. If you're in charge of a company blog or Facebook page, remember that your readers are customers, not friends: you can certainly be warm and friendly, but you must also show the appropriate respect.

I'm belaboring this point because many people have trouble understanding and controlling tone when they write. According to Chris Aisenbrey, director of global university relations at Whirlpool Corp., "We still see a tremendous amount of e-mail from students who are writing to the recruiter like they are sending a message to a friend asking what they are doing that evening."[1] Clearly these young people don't know that their tone is inappropriate and that their lack of control is endangering their prospects of finding a job. If you arm yourself with a little information and make the commitment to think before you send your words out into cyberspace, you can avoid making the same kind of mistake.

---

[1] Ronald Alsop, "Poor Writing Skills Top M.B.A. Recruiter Gripes," Vault Career Intelligence, March 31, 2009, http://www.vault.com/wps/portal/usa/vcm/detail/Career-Advice/Career-Advancement/Poor-Writing-Skills-Top-M.B.A.-Recruiter-Gripes?id=316&filter_type=0&filter_id=0.

How exactly does tone manifest itself in writing? Here are a few things to consider as you look at your draft:

Complete sentences. In formal writing situations, it's a good idea to use complete sentences rather than fragments. Fragments are all right in less formal situations as long as you're sure your meaning is clear.

Word choice. Formal writing requires that you use accurate, descriptive vocabulary rather than slang. For instance, your competitor's solution is "not adequate." It doesn't "suck." Your corporate retreat was "exciting," not "kick-ass." You would "very much appreciate" the opportunity to meet with a recruiter; it wouldn't be "awesome."

Profanity. Don't use profanity in work-related or professional communications, ever.

Abbreviations. Texting abbreviations like "u" for "you," "r" for "are," and "2" for "two" are not acceptable in formal writing. Abbreviations like LOL and TTYL are also informal. It's safer not to use them at work unless everyone else in the company is doing so.

Emoticons. Using smiley faces (☺) instead of making your attitude clear through your actual words is not appropriate in formal writing. People use them all the time in informal work-related writing, like instant messaging, but even here you should exercise caution. If you're pinging with your boss, for instance, let her be the first one to send you a smiley rather than taking it on yourself to do so.

When it comes to tone, be thoughtful and use your best judgment when you're writing in a professional or business setting. Please don't send an e-mail asking your boss "WTF????"; don't send your company's general counsel a smiley, don't ask your English professor "r u going to be in ur office 2morrow?" If you don't trust your judgment, your best bet is to err on the side of being too formal, then gradually relax your tone as you become more familiar with the organization and its expectations.

The time you spend understanding and controlling the tone of your writing will be some of the most profitable time you've ever invested. New tone-checking software promises to review your writing and save you from embarrassment, but its results are very spotty.[2] No software can

---

[2] Rachel Z. Arndt, "Tonecheck Test Drive Spots 'Unprofessional' Email, Knows Dick Cheney Sounds 'Sad,' 'Angry,'" Fast Company, http://www.fastcompany.com/1672974/check-the-tone-of-your-emails-before-sending-dummy.

possibly understand the nuances of your relationship with your boss or your customers. You're far better off learning to check and adjust your tone yourself. The effort you put into it will make you a more skillful and powerful writer in the end.

Before you release your writing into the world, ask yourself these questions:

- Is my tone appropriate for the context (personal vs. professional)?
- Is my tone appropriate for my reader?

If the tone of your message isn't appropriate for your reader or the context of the communication, revise it.

✓ **Does It Pass the Newspaper Test?**

E-writing can feel very intimate: after all, it's just you and your device, right? Actually, no. E-writing may feel private and ephemeral, but it's really neither. To be absolutely safe, you should assume that all e-writing is *public* and *permanent*. If you're not comfortable with the idea that anything you write on a computer or mobile device might be seen by anyone, at any time, *don't write it*!

I hope we all understand that the e-mails we write at work belong to our employers; they can be retrieved (even if we delete them) and can get us and our companies into trouble. Almost everything you post on the Internet is cached somewhere. Even if you post on a website as "Anonymous," your IP address is logged, and you can be found. Instant messaging programs contain a logging feature that saves your chats on your computer—which means they're also saved on the computer of the person or persons you were chatting with. Cellular phone carriers maintain "transaction logs" of your text messages and have produced the content of actual text messages when ordered to do so by the courts. To be safe, you should always assume that anything you write using an electronic device is going to be there forever, and if someone really wants to get it, they will.

In the words of Richard M. Smith, an Internet security and privacy consultant at Boston Software Forensics, "Computers are really, really good at saving things. . . . If you don't want something to get out, don't put it in any computer form at all."[3] Or on any cell phone or on any other device that electronically broadcasts what you've written to other people.

This reality is a little scary, but there's a very easy way to check yourself before you do something unwise. Before you turn your words loose on the e-world, imagine how you would feel if they appeared on the front page of a major national newspaper, attributed to you. If the answer is "embarrassed," "horrified," "ashamed," or anything along those lines, don't do it. Rewrite it—or cut it out completely—before you hit Enter, Send, or Post.

Other variations on the newspaper test include the "mom test" and the "boss test." I recommend you choose the image that has the greatest impact for you: a major newspaper printing that snarky e-mail you sent about a co-worker, your mom reading the drunken Facebook status you just posted, or your boss seeing what you just said about him in an IM. Whichever prospect frightens you the most, use it as a yardstick to measure the appropriateness of your e-writing, and revise your drafts accordingly.

Before you hit Send, Post, or Submit, ask yourself:

- How would I feel if what I just wrote was printed on the front page of the *New York Times*?
- How would I feel if my mom read what I just wrote?
- How would I feel if my boss read what I just wrote?
- How would I feel if a prospective employer read what I just wrote?

If your message doesn't pass the newspaper test, protect yourself by deleting or rewriting the offending material.

✓ **Have You Proofread?**

Your final step before sending your words off into the ether is to give them a quick proofread. You should make it a habit to proofread everything you write. It takes only a second, and it can prevent misunderstandings and costly errors.

---

[3] Anick Jesdanun, "Instant Messaging Conversations Can Easily Linger for Years," USA Today, October 5, 2006, http://www.usatoday.com/tech/news/internetprivacy/2006-10-05-im-foley_x.htm.

An occasional typo is no big deal. However, if your writing contains too many of them, you'll call attention to yourself as a sloppy and careless writer. Typos and errors in punctuation and grammar can have a serious impact on professional and business communication. According to Chris Aisenbrey, "It is staggering the frequency of typos, grammatical errors and poorly constructed thoughts we see in e-mails that serve as letters of introduction."[4]

Careless errors can do more than damage your reputation: they can also destroy your meaning and cause confusion. Even text messages should be given a quick once-over before you hit Send. Don't believe me? When the iPhone 4 came out, people began to notice, often too late, that the phone's autocorrect feature would sometimes create nonsensical messages. Some of these are howlingly funny; some are obscene. The website Damn You Autocorrect (www.damnyouautocorrect.com) has some brilliant examples, including these:

There's no harm done in either of these examples, but anyone who texts regularly knows that there's a real risk of miscommunication in this hyperfast, hypercondensed writing form.

---

[4] Alsop, "Poor Writing Skills Top M.B.A. Recruiter Gripes."

The risk doesn't come only from the autocorrect feature, either. Anytime you're typing that fast, on such a tiny keyboard, you're likely to make mistakes. Are you planning to meet someone at 6:00? How easy is it to type "5:00" instead, without realizing it? You can cause yourself and your friends serious headaches. It's worth making a quick check before you hit Send. If you accidentally send an unproofed message, go back and have a look at what you've just sent off. If it's wrong, correct the error immediately.

Quick e-mails, especially at work, also need checking. When we get really busy firing off a lot of e-mails, we tend to go on automatic pilot, and that can be risky. One of my clients told me that she had signed an e-mail to prospective customer "Love, Susan." She'd just finished sending off her daily e-mail to her son at college, and she was in "mom mode." Her customer thought it was funny, but you can see there are situations that might not end so happily.

Before you finalize your draft, ask yourself:

- Have I proofread what I wrote for typos, misspellings, missing words, and grammatical errors?

Fix those typos and errors!

MAKE IT A HABIT

I know all this checking and revising sounds like a lot of work. Practically speaking, there will be occasions when you don't have time to do it all, and there are occasions when it matters less. Some messages are more important than others, and some settings have higher stakes than others.

Bear in mind that as more and more business and social contact occurs in a virtual setting, people are increasingly defined by their style of professional and personal communication. You might find yourself working or doing business with someone over e-mail, and it often happens that you never meet that person face-to-face. You may meet a new romantic interest on the web. If you're a sloppy, unfocused writer, you'll create the impression of being a sloppy, unfocused person, and you might not get the deal . . . or the date. On the other hand, if you pay attention to the clarity and accuracy of your communication, you'll create a better impression and get better results.

Make it a habit to check and revise your e-writing. The more attention you give to your writing, the better you'll get at it, and the less time you'll have to spend on it. If you get in the habit of checking over your e-mails before you hit Send, you'll get faster at reviewing and revising. You'll learn to be alert for the mistakes you make most frequently, and eventually you'll stop making them. Checking and revising regularly will ultimately make you a better writer.

The guidelines presented in this chapter will be useful to you no matter how e-communication evolves in the future. Whatever you write, in whatever form, it will always be critical to be clear about your purpose and sensitive to your readers' needs and concerns. Messages will need to be brief but complete. They will also need to be courteous and to use the appropriate tone for the context and the reader. E-writing is not likely to become less public—rather, more so—and the newspaper test will always stand you in good stead. And as long as human beings remain imperfect, proofreading will be a necessary part of the writing process. Whatever the brave new world of e-communication brings, you're now well equipped to handle it!

THE ENTRIES

WRITING IN YOUR PERSONAL LIFE

Writing in our personal lives has become markedly less formal over the past few decades, but it's even more important than ever. E-mails and text messages have taken the place of phone calls and face-to-face communication in many aspects of our personal lives. Clear written communication is critical for the smooth running of our personal business, relationships, families, and homes. Whether you're writing an e-mail to your child's teacher, a letter to fight a parking ticket, or a list of instructions for a babysitter, the ability to write clearly can mean the difference between peace and chaos. In this section you'll find guidance on everyday writing tasks, personal business communications, notes and letters recognizing life's milestones, and guidance on the world of writing for social media.

The Basics

ANNOUNCEMENT

(See also *Engagement Announcement* on page 117, *Wedding Announcement* on page 135, *Birth Announcement* on page 141, and *Adoption Announcement* on page 143.)

We write announcements for many of life's milestones—most frequently for engagements, weddings, and births. Announcements may be published in newspapers, posted on websites, sent through the postal mail, or sent via e-mail. Although e-mail announcements are becoming more common, formal occasions still call for announcements to be professionally printed on card stock and sent through the postal mail.

Introduction

The **purpose** of an announcement is to inform the reader about a happening or a milestone in your life. Depending on the kind of announcement, your **readers** may be a diverse group, including people who know you well and others who don't. Regardless, ensure that your announcement is complete. It's worthwhile to take some time to **brainstorm** your content to ensure you included all the relevant information. Announcements often follow a standard **organizational** template, partly to ensure that you don't forget anything. Unless your announcement is extremely simple, you should plan to go through more than one **draft**. It's surprisingly easy to omit important information, so it's wise to ask someone you trust to proofread your draft and **revise** it accordingly. Pay special attention to typos and other errors. If the event is important enough to announce, the announcement may be saved as a keepsake, so make sure it's perfect!

DO	DON'T
• Keep your announcement brief and concise. If you're announcing something like a new business launch, provide a website where readers can gather more information.	• Don't include extraneous information. The focus of your announcement should be exclusively on the news you're announcing. Don't include long descriptions or explanations.
• Ensure your announcement is complete. Think "who, what, when, where, and why." If you're announcing an event, don't forget essential information like date, time, and place.	
• Allow yourself to express pleasure if you're announcing good news. If you're announcing bad news, get straight to the point and use a formal and businesslike tone.	
• Proofread to ensure that your details—including names, dates, and locations—are accurate. If you're having printed announcement cards made, ensure that the printer allows you to check a proof for accuracy before all the cards are printed. It can be costly to have announcements reprinted, and it's embarrassing to have typos in a formal announcement.	

DIVORCE ANNOUNCEMENT

As divorce has become more common, an increasing number of divorcing couples have taken to sending out formal announcements to their friends and associates to inform them of the news. Divorce announcements are typically handwritten or printed on cards and mailed out to people. Some couples choose to announce their divorce via e-mail. Some readers feel an e-mail announcement trivializes the event, so consider your medium of communication carefully.

Introduction

The **purpose** behind a divorce announcement is simply to inform others of your decision and provide any new contact and logistical information, not to supply information about "what happened" or to solicit anyone's approval of your decision. The last thing you need to worry about at a time like this is other people's opinions. Keep your **reader** in mind as you compose your announcement. Take care not to make people more uncomfortable than necessary, for instance through the misplaced use of humor. Naturally this is an upsetting time, and it's easy to forget important things. **Brainstorm** what you want to say. If you and your ex don't draft the announcement together, it's smart to share notes back and forth before you finalize a **draft**, to be sure you haven't forgotten any critical information, made any errors, or inadvertently insulted each other.

Your tone should be serious and businesslike. A matter-of-fact announcement is easier for your readers to digest than an emotional one. In addition to collaborating with your ex, you might also want to show your draft to a good friend or close family member—someone you can trust to give you objective feedback. **Revise** according to their feedback.

DO	DON'T
• Keep it brief. A long description of how hard you tried to save your marriage or how bad (or relieved) you feel isn't appropriate for a divorce announcement. Save this information for one-on-one communication with friends.	• Don't try to be funny. Humor is very difficult to achieve successfully in a divorce announcement. Sometimes couples try to soften the blow by writing a funny announcement. These often fall flat and leave the reader feeling uncomfortable.

| **DO** (CONTINUED) | **DON'T** (CONTINUED) |

- Keep your tone civil and serious.
- Provide new contact information as necessary—for instance, if one or both parties will have new mailing addresses or home phone numbers. Let readers know when that new information will be in effect.
- Relay any other changes in the status quo that readers might need to know: for instance, if someone is changing their name as a result of the divorce. Readers who have contact with the children (teachers, scout leaders, etc.) will need to know if the children's primary address will change.
- Maintain your dignity. You may be experiencing a flood of emotions right now, but consider what your divorce announcement might look like to you—and your children—twenty years from now. You can vent all you want to your friends, but don't say anything you'll regret in your written announcement.
- Make sure your ex-spouse knows you're sending the announcement and knows, basically, what's in it; the point of a divorce announcement is to make things easier, not to stir up new conflict.

- Don't delve too deeply into emotions. It's just good manners to express regret about the end of the marriage, but there's no need to explore your feelings beyond that.
- Don't talk about the reasons for the divorce. It's not anyone's business. Protect your dignity and privacy by withholding personal details. These discussions are better left for face-to-face meetings with friends.
- Don't mention any of the terms of the divorce settlement. It's personal information.
- Don't mention any logistical arrangements (for the children, etc.) that have not been agreed to by both parties and finalized.
- Don't explain arrangements for the children in the announcement. Your custody arrangements fall under the category of "no one's business."
- Don't go overboard in praising each other. Some couples try to soften the blow by saying wonderful things about each other. No matter how good your motives, though, this approach can make readers uncomfortable.
- Don't put in an e-mail anything you don't want to reach a wider audience. Remember that e-mails can be forwarded. Protect yourself from embarrassment or worse.
- Don't send the divorce announcement to readers' work e-mail accounts, unless they are strictly work acquaintances. Send a written card or use personal e-mail accounts.

NOT LIKE THIS . . .

Providing this much personal information is unnecessary and might make readers uncomfortable.

It's no one's business what custody arrangements have been made. Paradoxically, the more personal information you supply, the more people will feel entitled to question you. If you want to nip curiosity in the bud, don't say too much.

Dear Friend,

It is with heavy hearts that we announce that after 14 years of marriage, we have made the difficult decision to divorce. We have worked hard and diligently, with the help of our pastor, to avoid having to make this decision. In the end, we felt that we have simply drifted too far apart for our marriage to continue to be viable. Our divorce became final last month.

Lisa will remain in the house, which will also continue to be Devin and Kerry's primary home. Ken will be at 47329 Moorcroft Parkway, #27E, from March 24 and will see the boys on the weekends. Our cell phone numbers will remain the same.

We leave this marriage saddened but full of love and respect for one another. We remain the best of friends, and we look forward to productive and fulfilling years ahead raising the boys as a team.

Lisa and Ken Hoyt

There's no need to explain why you've decided to divorce. Keep this very personal information to yourself.

It's nice to reaffirm your respect for each other, but Lisa and Ken are taking it a bit too far here. Some readers are going to feel very uncomfortable, and others are going to wonder why this couple is divorcing if they think so highly of each other.

. . . LIKE THIS

Lisa and Ken express the appropriate regret about the end of their marriage, but they don't offer their readers any further insights about their feelings. It protects their privacy and doesn't draw their readers into the drama.

Dear Friend,

We regret to announce that after 14 years of marriage, we have made the difficult decision to divorce. Our divorce became final last month.

Lisa will remain in the house, which will also continue to be Devin and Kerry's primary home. Ken will be at 47329 Moorcroft Parkway, #27E, from March 24. Our cell phone numbers will remain the same.

We thank all our friends for many years of support and look forward to seeing you soon.

Lisa and Ken Hoyt

This is all the information most readers need about the boys. Anyone who needs regular access to the kids—like teachers, doctors, scout leaders, and so forth—should receive more detailed information once things are settled.

This is a very nice nod to the couple's friends. It quietly acknowledges that it's been a long road, and it affirms the place of their friends in their lives.

NOT LIKE THIS . . .

Dear Friends,

Free at last! After five "interesting" years, Chris and I have finally gotten a clue and thrown in the towel. I'm a free woman as of this month.

Part of recovering my sanity will be resuming using my maiden name. I'll be known once again as Gina Mazzei. The kids will keep their father's name.

Thank you all for your love and support.

Gina

> Gina is trying to be funny here. Maybe she has a few friends who share her giddy excitement, but the tone isn't really appropriate for an announcement to be sent to a larger circle of acquaintances.

> This is beginning to sound like a celebration rather than an announcement. It's not in great taste.

> Am I the only one who detects a little hostility in the phrase "their father's name"? Tone can be very difficult to control, so you should err on the side of being simply factual in your divorce announcement.

> Gina's flippant comment might make perfect sense to her closest friends, but it's not fair to Chris. Has he seen this announcement? Is it simply another volley in their ongoing dispute? No wonder this couple is getting divorced. Readers don't want to be drawn into the drama.

. . . LIKE THIS

Dear Friends,

After five years of marriage, Chris and I have made the decision to divorce. The divorce becomes final this month.

I will resume using my maiden name and be known as Gina Mazzei. The children will keep the name Carlson.

Thank you all for your love and support.

Gina

> This announcement doesn't give Gina the chance to blow off steam, but it's businesslike and it gets the job done. Gina isn't saying anything here that she might regret later. She can vent with her friends in person if she needs to.

RESPONSE TO A DIVORCE ANNOUNCEMENT

As divorce has become more socially acceptable, it has become more common for divorcing couples to send an announcement letting their friends know about their change in status. Close friends of the couple will likely already know, but a wider circle of acquaintances might not have heard the news. Such an announcement can be helpful for people who interact with the couple as a family, and it can help prevent awkward and embarrassing situations.

You may receive such an announcement from the parents of your children's friends, from business associates, or from old friends you haven't recently been in touch with. Whatever the relationship, if you're important enough in a couple's life to receive such an announcement, you must respond to it.

Your reply to a divorce announcement should take the form of the original announcement. If you got an e-mail, reply by e-mail; if you received a card, reply with a card or brief note.

Introduction

The **purpose** of a response to a divorce announcement is first and foremost to acknowledge the news. Divorce always carries with it a minefield of emotions, so your wisest course is simply to acknowledge the announcement and let the parties know that you care about their welfare. Deeper discussions may happen at a later time. Consider your relationship with the **reader** as you write. How well do you know her? In what context? The answers to these questions can help guide your response. It's a good idea to keep your reply brief, so it's rarely necessary to **brainstorm** a lot of content or spend a lot of time **organizing** your reply. However, do take some time to collect your thoughts before you reply. As you **draft**, pay attention to your tone. The tone of divorce announcements can vary widely: businesslike, regretful, loving, angry, bitter, humorous. Regardless of the tone of the announcement, your reply should be kind, serious, and brief. Take a moment to proofread and **revise** your reply before you send it. Put yourself in your reader's position, and ask yourself how you would feel if you received such a response to your announcement. If there's anything in your draft that you don't like, revise it.

DO	DON'T
• Say that you're sorry to hear the news. Even if you think that the divorce is the best decision for the couple, it's still a profound loss, and you should express regret.	• Don't express approval or disapproval about the divorce. A divorce announcement is not a request for permission. Respect the couple's wishes, and refrain from commenting.
• Acknowledge the difficulty the couple are experiencing.	• Don't say anything to indicate that the couple will be better off divorced, even if you think that's true. It can be tempting to offer a pep talk to encourage the couple to be optimistic about the future, but it's not appropriate to do so here.
• Affirm your friendship for the couple if you expect to remain friends with both of them.	
• Express your good wishes to both parties for the future. It may be that you are much closer to one member of the couple than the other and that you may lose touch with one of them. You might even feel strongly that one or the other party behaved badly or is to blame for the dissolution of the marriage. Regardless, it's only polite to wish them both well.	• Don't offer advice. You may feel you have good advice to give the couple, perhaps based on your own experience. But remember, you don't really know how they feel or where the situation stands. A private conversation is a more appropriate setting for offering counsel.
• Keep your reply brief, kind, and unemotional. Feelings are likely to be raw at this point; your reply should not add to the turmoil.	• Don't make jokes. Even if the announcement is humorous, it's not appropriate for you to follow suit. Even good-natured jokes about a divorce have the potential to hurt feelings.
	• Don't say anything about the children, beyond good wishes for their well-being. Arrangements for the children may not have been finalized, and even finalized arrangements may still be a sore spot for the parents. In addition, the couple may feel guilty about the potential effects of the divorce on their children. It's best not to stray into this territory.
	• Don't ask for details. The couple has shared as much as they want to. It's impolite to ask or even hint around about what happened.

NOT LIKE THIS . . .

Mentioning that the couple used to seem happy might be hurtful. And commenting on how hard they tried might stir up bad feelings; it's possible that the divorce is the product of someone's extramarital affair, and the other party might not share your belief that they tried hard to save the marriage.

When even these innocent expressions of goodwill can cause hurt, you're better off keeping your reply as brief as you can.

Dear David and Aileen,

I was so sorry to receive the announcement of your divorce. You're a wonderful couple and always seemed so happy together. I'm sure you both tried very hard, and I'm sorry to hear this is happening.

You know I've been through this myself. I would encourage you both to regard this event not as an ending but as a new beginning. I know you will remain in touch, at least for the kids, and I know you will always have a strong regard for each other. In fact, Bryan and I became even closer friends after our divorce was finalized. While you mourn the loss, don't forget to celebrate the new beginning.

Take care,

Jenn

Advice, no matter how good or how well intended, is often not welcome at this point. Save it for future personal meetings.

"Celebrate" is probably too cheerful a word for this kind of occasion. Again, the sentiment is well intentioned, but the potential to hurt and offend is enormous here.

. . . LIKE THIS

Dear David and Aileen,

I was very sorry to hear the news about your divorce. Thank you for letting me know.

I'm sure this must be a very difficult experience for you both, and I know it will be a big transition. I hope that you are taking care of yourselves. I wish you all the best in the future.

Take care,

Jenn

This reply, though brief, shows real concern about the couple and regret about the parting, without taking sides or straying into territory that might cause pain.

INVITATION

(See also *Wedding Invitation* on page 120.)

We send invitations for all kinds of events, from children's birthday parties to formal gatherings. It's helpful to think of the invitation as part of the event itself: it sets the tone for the event and lets readers know what to expect. An invitation seems simple, but it's important to take the time to get it right. If you leave out important information, you'll find yourself with a lot of work to do catching up.

Invitations to parties are often sent by e-mail or through websites like Facebook or Evite. Invitations to formal events like weddings should be printed and sent through postal mail.

Introduction

The primary **purpose** of an invitation is self-explanatory, of course: to let the reader know you would like him to attend your event and to give him the information he needs to do so. Beyond the basics, though, an invitation can also be important in giving the invited guests important cues about what to bring, what to wear, and so forth. Whoever your **readers** are, they will all need complete information about the event, so be sure to **brainstorm** from their point of view. Ask yourself the journalist's questions "who, what, when, where, why, and how." Don't assume your readers know what you have in mind. Most invitations follow a traditional organizational structure, partly to help you remember all the critical information. If you are using pre-printed invitation cards, consider if you need to do more than just fill in the blanks. Do your guests need extra information like what to wear and what to bring? Be sure your invitation is complete. It's a good idea to give your **draft** to someone to proof for you, both for completeness and for typos. Sending out incorrect information can lead to a lot of follow-up. In addition, for a formal event, guests may keep your invitation as a souvenir. As you **revise**, make sure your invitation is free of typos and other embarrassing errors.

DO	DON'T
• Decide on the tone for your event. How formal is the event? Is there a theme? The invitation will set the tone for the event.	• Don't send e-mail invitations from an unknown e-mailbox, or they may get caught in your guests' spam filters.
• Choose the appropriate form of invitation. Very formal events still require printed invitations.	• Don't fail to consult other interested parties. Be sure that other people who have a stake in the event have a chance to weigh in on the invitation.
• Send your invitation well in advance. Whether you're sending printed invitations or using a social planning website, give your guests plenty of notice: generally three weeks for a party, at least three months for a wedding.	• Don't omit RSVP information. It's surprisingly easy to forget!
• Make sure all your information—including dates, times, and locations—is accurate.	
• Let recipients know if they may bring a guest.	
• Include directions if there are invitees who might not know where the venue is.	
• Specify attire, if appropriate.	
• Let guests know if there's anything you want them to bring—such as food for a potluck. Also mention anything you'd like them not to bring—gifts for a birthday, for instance.	
• Include RSVP information. Consider including a date by which you want to know, so you have time to plan the event.	
• Proofread! Sending out inaccurate information can be worse than embarrassing. If you inadvertently provide the wrong date or the wrong phone number for RSVPs, for instance, you'll have a lot of work to do to clear up the confusion.	

LIKE THIS

(For sample wedding invitations, see page 121.)

DINNER PARTY

PLEASE JOIN US FOR DINNER!
FRIDAY, FEBRUARY 27
6:30 P.M.

KAREN RICHMOND AND DAVID HERMAN
908 ROUNDTREE ROAD
RSVP 888.765.4321

POTLUCK

Potluck Dinner!
Bring Your Favorite Dish

Let's just get together and enjoy
Saturday, May 18, 6:00 p.m.

Lynn and Neil
2334 Oaks Drive
RSVP 888.111.2222

Please join us for a surprise 30th birthday celebration

for Lindsey Sahagian

Saturday, April 20

6:00 p.m. (please be on time)

Dinner & Cocktails

The Shelton Lounge | Boise

RSVP to Louis

888-555-2222

SURPRISE
BIRTHDAY
PARTY

Please join us to celebrate

Shirley Hansen's 90th Birthday

September 5 at 6 o'clock in the evening

Beckham Place Restaurant

657 Fieldstone Road

Ames, Iowa

RSVP to Linda 888-222-1234

NINETIETH
BIRTHDAY

CHILD'S
BIRTHDAY

Come and help us celebrate

Joshua's 8th Birthday!

Saturday, July 23, 2:00 p.m.

 42 Page Drive, Santa Barbara

Bring swimsuits and towels!

Please pick up your child at 5:00 p.m.

GRADUATION

Christina and Cameron Lassiter
are proud to announce
the graduation of their daughter

Yvonne Simone

Class of 2013 — Tulane University

Please share in their happiness
at Commencement Exercises
on June twelfth
at ten o'clock in the morning

McAlister Auditorium
6823 Saint Charles Avenue
New Orleans

Reception to follow at the
Lassiters' home

RSVP 888.222.1111

You are cordially invited to celebrate

Stephanie Alexander

as she retires after 35 years of service in the
Reno Unified School District

Saturday, June 16, 2012
6:00 p.m. – 11:00 p.m.

The Marston Club
7492 Marston Drive
Reno, Nevada

Regrets only to Bill Alexander, by June 1
888-222-1212

BAR OR BAT
MITZVAH

Samuel Evan*

Please join me when I am called to the Torah

as a Bar Mitzvah

Saturday, June 7, 2012 at 9:00 a.m.

Temple Israel

5633 Gellen Drive

St. Paul, Minnesota

Evening Reception at Green Shade

2121 Grand Street

St. Paul

7:00 p.m. Black Tie

Wendy and Jon Silverman

RSVP by June 1 to 888-222-1111

*Some invitations also include the Hebrew name.

YOU ARE INVITED TO JOIN US
FOR THE BAPTISM OF
EMMA LOUISE
ON SUNDAY, JULY 12, 2011
AT TEN O'CLOCK IN THE MORNING
HADLEY LUTHERAN CHURCH
329 COTTONWOOD AVENUE
HADLEY, NEBRASKA

LAUREL AND ROB BOARDMAN
RSVP 888.222.1111

Marta and Leo Villabon
Invite You and Your Family to Join Us
for the First Communion of Our Son

Tomas Steven

Saturday, May 12, 2011
12 o'clock noon
Church of Notre Dame
3766 Carson Avenue
Grant City, Arizona

Please join us afterward
In the Parish Hall

RSVP By May 1
888-111-2222

CONFIRMATION

CAITLYN ANNE RUSSELL
WILL RECEIVE THE SACRAMENT OF CONFIRMATION
FRIDAY OCTOBER 3, 2012
TEN O'CLOCK MASS

ST. ELIZABETH CHURCH
1773 LAKE STREET
LYNN, NEW YORK

RECEPTION AT 3:00 P.M.
BRIOLI'S RESTAURANT
339 VALE ROAD
LYNN, NEW YORK

PLEASE RESPOND BY SEPTEMBER 20
EILEEN AND TOM
(888) 555-1212

BABY SHOWER

For more sample invitations for different occasions, visit www.howto writeanything .com.

Join us as we honor

Thalia Christensen

with a Baby Shower
on May 18 at 2:00 p.m.

Jennifer's Home
507 Homewood Drive
Forest City, Montana

Given with love by
Jennifer Frantzen and Tracee Norling

CONGRATULATIONS

(See also *Wedding Congratulations* on page 135.)

Sending a note of congratulations is a wonderful way to recognize an accomplishment and to let someone know you care about them. As the pace of life has accelerated, people are sending fewer messages of congratulations, but these messages are an excellent way to stay in touch, develop a relationship, and build goodwill. The sidebar "Occasions for Congratulations" offers some suggestions about when you might send such a message.

In informal circumstances, it's all right to send a message of congratulations in an e-mail. However, your message will mean much more to the recipient if you put it on paper. In a professional context, you might write a letter; in a more personal context, your messages should be handwritten on high-quality notepaper. It's also fine to send a preprinted greeting card, but be sure you personalize the card with something more than just your signature.

Introduction

The **purpose** of a note of congratulations is straightforward: to recognize and congratulate the recipient on some wonderful achievement, event, or milestone in her life. A note like this can make your **reader** feel appreciated and let her know you're thinking of her and supporting her in her endeavors. Rather than writing a generic note, really take some time to **brainstorm** your content to make your message special. What do you know about how hard the reader worked to achieve this milestone? Share personal insights and memories, and your note will mean that much more. The Model Outline (page 66) suggests one way to **organize** your note of congratulations. The tone of your **draft** will depend partly on your relationship with the reader: the better you know him, the warmer and more personal your note can be. It's a good idea to write out a rough draft before you actually write in the card or on the nice stationery. As you look over your draft, put yourself in the reader's shoes and try to imagine how you would feel if you received such a note. Can you make it more personal, more meaningful? **Revise** your draft until you know you are sending a message you yourself would like to receive.

OCCASIONS FOR CONGRATULATIONS

Take advantage of occasions like these to send a note of congratulations and show you care:

- Acceptance to school, college, or graduate school
- Academic award, honor, or achievement
- Scholarship
- Graduation
- New job
- Promotion
- Professional achievement
- New business opening
- Retirement
- Meeting a personal goal
- New home
- Engagement or wedding
- New baby
- Anniversary
- Bar or Bat Mitzvah
- First Communion

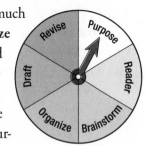

MODEL OUTLINE

Opening: Explicitly congratulate the reader on the specific occasion or accomplishment.

Middle: Let the reader know how much she deserves the honor or how much she paid her dues for it. You can also let her know how proud you are of her, or how happy you are about her good news. Make it personal.

Conclusion: Finish your note by repeating your congratulations and wishing the reader well for the future.

DO	DON'T
• Use the word "congratulations" early in your message.	• Don't wait too long to send it. By sending a note promptly, you create the feeling that you're participating in the celebration of the news.
• Remember that "congrats" is not a word. It's appropriate as an abbreviation for text messaging, but it's sloppy to use in more formal writing. Take the time to write out the whole word in your note.	• Don't attribute the achievement to "good luck." You may mean well, but in doing so you suggest that the reader didn't deserve or earn what she got. If she just got lucky, she doesn't deserve congratulations, does she?
• Mention the occasion for the congratulations early in the message.	
• Be as personal as is appropriate, given your relationship.	• Don't express surprise. Again, when you say something like "I never thought I'd see this," you undermine the reader and undervalue his achievement.
• Appreciate what went into the achievement. People like to be praised for their general wonderfulness, but they especially like to know that you understand what they've been doing and the effort they've made.	• Don't gush. Be careful that your praise of the reader doesn't go over the top. You risk sounding insincere, even if your feelings are genuine.
• Keep the focus on the recipient rather than on yourself. Too much reminiscing about your own college graduation, for instance, takes the focus away from the reader.	• Don't buy a preprinted card and do nothing but sign it. Even if you write just a few lines, make sure the card contains a message that is specific to the reader and appropriate to your relationship.
• Close with wishes for continued success.	

NOT LIKE THIS . . .

Carl's long apology for the lateness of the card takes the focus off its real purpose: to congratulate Jennie. He says the delay is "inexcusable" but then tries to excuse it by saying things have been crazy at his job. You can avoid having to negotiate this kind of situation by getting your congratulations off in a timely fashion.

Dear Jennie,

First, please forgive me for the inexcusable delay in getting you this card. I want you to know I've been thinking a lot about you, but things have been crazy at work.

I'm thrilled for you that you passed your qualifying exams! I know how much work you put into studying, and I know it wasn't easy for you. I'm proud of you for sticking to it and getting through. I'm sure it doesn't seem real yet. I remember when I passed my exams—everyone was congratulating me, but I just felt stunned rather than happy for weeks. I was so exhausted from the studying and the pressure. You deserve to feel happy and very proud of yourself. Well done!

Lots of love,

Carl

Perhaps because he's feeling so guilty, Carl actually forgot to congratulate Jennie. Don't just imply it; say it!

Carl is talking too much about himself, and in the process Jennie is getting a little bit erased. Carl means well in sharing his experience with Jennie, but it doesn't seem to have occurred to him she might not feel the same way he did and she might not need his advice.

. . . LIKE THIS

Carl starts off the note with a warm wish of congratulations.

Carl shares his own experience and uses it to reach out to Jennie.

Dear Jennie,

Congratulations on passing your qualifying exams! I know how rigorous the studying is, and I'm proud of you that you stuck with it and got through.

I hope you're doing something wonderful to celebrate your success. You've earned it!

Passing these exams opens a whole world of professional opportunity for you, and I know you'll be a great success whatever path you choose. Very best of luck with everything.

Lots of love,

Carl

Being "on the inside" himself, Carl understands the implications of passing this exam for Jennie's professional career, and he shares that knowledge with her. He also closes with a vote of confidence in her future performance and good wishes for her future.

NOT LIKE THIS . . .

Dear Steve,

Congratulations on landing the job at Bronson! It's not very often that a position like that becomes available, and there you were with your perfect timing and fabulous good luck. I'm so happy for you! You have always been such a go-getter. You're an inspiration. I wish you all the best in your new position.

Again, congratulations. I'm so happy for you.

Best,

Stephanie

Stephanie's enthusiasm spills over into gushing. Maybe she really does think Steve is the greatest thing in the world, but she sounds a little insincere here. Getting the right tone in a note of congratulations can be a delicate balancing act.

Stephanie's enthusiastic tone might mask some of the undercutting that she's doing here. She implies that Steve got the job because of his "perfect timing" and "fabulous good luck" rather than his actual qualifications for the job.

. . . LIKE THIS

Dear Steve,

Congratulations on landing the job at Bronson! You've managed your career so well, and I really admire the way you've consistently worked to make yourself more valuable to your employer. Bronson is very lucky to be getting the benefit of all your hard work. I hope you'll be really happy there. I wish you all the best in your new position.

Again, congratulations. I'm so happy for you.

Best,

Stephanie

This is more like it. Stephanie recognizes that Steve got the job not because he was lucky but because he was well prepared and he worked hard for it.

CONGRATULATIONS ON RETIREMENT

Retirement is a significant milestone in life, the closing of one chapter and the opening of a new one. It's well worth celebration and congratulations from friends and colleagues. Even if you choose to buy a commercial greeting card, you should take the time to write a personal message in recognition of this very important transition.

DO	DON'T
• Recognize the value of the reader's work. If you are a colleague, you're in a good position to speak with some authority about the reader's contributions at work. Make your message personal and specific.	• Don't say anything to make the reader feel he's over the hill.
• Thank the reader, if thanks are appropriate. If your reader has been helpful to you—a co-worker or employee, your child's teacher, a librarian, your mechanic or gardener or doctor—let him know how much you appreciate what he has done for you during his career.	• Don't get maudlin. Yes, something is coming to an end, and yes, we're all getting older. But keep your tone positive, even if you are sad.
• Stay upbeat. Retirement can be a scary time as well as a happy one, so it's important for your tone to be cheerful.	• Don't use humor inappropriately. People sometimes use humor when they don't know what else to say or when they're uncomfortable with sadness or earnestness, but be sure your tone is really appropriate to your relationship with the retiree.
• Recognize the past, but look toward the future. Say something encouraging about the enjoyable life the reader will have.	• Don't rely on a generic message when you're able to write a specific one. Don't just say "Congratulations on your retirement—it's very well deserved." Take the time to write a more specific message.
• Make a specific suggestion about getting together, if you'd like to do that. Retirement can be isolating.	
• End with good wishes to the retiree.	

Dear Kerry,

Congratulations on your retirement!

This place won't be the same without you. You have always been so generous with your knowledge of the business; you have been an invaluable resource and a wonderful colleague. Thank you for all you've done for all of us. Now it's high time for you to relax and enjoy spending time with your family. I'm very happy for you.

Please make sure to get me your personal e-mail address. I'm looking forward to staying in touch and hearing all about your new beginning in Arizona.

Take care,

Tom

THANK-YOU NOTE

(See also *Wedding Thank-You* on page 136 and *Baby Gift Thank-You* on page 145.)

Thank-you notes are called for on many occasions—for birthday and holiday gifts, for hospitality, for thoughtful gestures, and for many other kindnesses. It's rarely wrong to send a thank-you note, so if you have the impulse, do it!

Thank-yous can certainly be sent by e-mail, but bear in mind that an e-mail thank-you is appropriate only for a smallish gift or gesture. A handwritten card or letter sent through the mail is more meaningful and more appropriate for occasions like wedding or shower gifts, holiday gifts, or a visit to someone's home. Use your best judgment, but when in doubt, err on the side of doing too much—sending a card or letter— rather than doing too little.

Introduction

The primary **purpose** of a thank-you message, of course, is to express your appreciation for something someone gave you or did for you. Another important purpose is to strengthen your relationship with the **reader**. A gracious thank-you can leave a lasting impression. Your relationship with the reader will influence the content and tone of your thank-you message: for instance, a note to a relative will be very different from a note to someone you don't know well. **Brainstorming** your content is an important step—once you've said "thank you," you'll need to flesh out the message with your thoughts about what the gift or gesture meant to you and offer some specific details. **Organize** your message so that the "thank-you" comes right at the beginning and is repeated again at the end. Write your **draft** in your own words and your own natural voice, and express your true feelings. Read over your draft once or twice, putting yourself in the position of your reader. Is your thank-you appropriate to the gift and to your relationship? Do you say enough? Is it sincere? **Revise** and make any necessary adjustments before you send it off.

DO	DON'T
• Send your thank-you message promptly. The late Princess Diana was said to be a fanatical writer of thank-you notes; she wouldn't go to bed till she had written a thank-you for the evening she had just enjoyed. If you get into the habit of sending thank-you notes, you'll never find yourself in the embarrassing position of having to combine the thank-you with an apology for its tardiness.	• Don't send a vague, general thank-you. It only takes a few minutes to make the thank-you specific and personal, and it will mean a great deal more to the reader if you make that effort.
• Remember to say "thank you." Make the message explicit.	• Don't mention the price of the gift or the amount of a cash gift.
• Be specific about what the gift or gesture meant to you. Describe how you'll use the gift, why it was especially needed, or how it made you feel. Personalizing your thank-you this way creates a true connection with your reader.	• Don't simply sign a commercial thank-you card and pop it in the mail. Many readers appreciate the fact that you got a store-bought card for them, but it's not enough just to sign the inside. Make the effort to add a personal note.
• Say something nice about the gift, even if you didn't like it. Maybe that hideous sweater really *is* a nice shade of blue, or you really *do* love kittens, even though they're painted on black velvet.	• Don't write about yourself or other news. Keep the focus exclusively on the gift and the giver. You can write another message to get caught up on the latest developments in your lives.
	• Don't overpraise the gift. While it's nice to offer some specifics about why you like it, don't go overboard. When you praise a gift to extremes, you tip off the reader that your gratitude perhaps isn't sincere.

DO (CONTINUED)	**DON'T** (CONTINUED)
• Mention the context of the gift. Did you enjoy a happy holiday together? Were you touched by their remembering your birthday? • Acknowledge the "cost" to the giver, if appropriate. Obviously, you don't want to talk about the price of a gift explicitly. But if someone has given you an especially generous gift, your thank-you note should reflect that. If someone made you something by hand, or if you know the gift was difficult to find, or if you suspect your visit didn't come at the best time, acknowledge it.	• Don't use phoney, overly formal language. If you're writing to someone you know, don't write "It was a great pleasure to see you and Uncle Ted at the wedding." No one talks that way. Write in your own voice. "Steve and I were really happy to see you and Uncle Ted at the wedding" feels much more personal and will mean a lot more to the recipient. • Don't get on "automatic pilot" when you're writing a stack of thank-you notes. Beware of the impersonal, assembly-line approach, and try to avoid writing essentially the same message to everyone. Make your note as personal as possible.

NOT LIKE THIS . . .

Dear Jenn,

I can't believe it's been nearly a week since we saw you. We all had a fabulous time! The kids are still talking about it and about their wonderful Aunt Jenn. I hope it wasn't too much of an imposition for you. We hope we can return the favor soon and have you and Russ to visit.

We hit the ground running when we got back. Kayla started back to school on Tuesday. Peter is going to a new nursery/day care this year, and he's busy adjusting to a new crowd of kids. Never a dull moment!

Love,

Terri

> Terri's tone is friendly and enthusiastic, but she forgets to say "thank you."

> A thank-you note is the wrong place for Terri to talk so much about her own news. The focus here should really be on Jenn. Although Terri means well, her thank-you feels a little slapdash, especially for a family visit at Jenn's home.

. . . LIKE THIS

Terri recognizes the "cost" of Jenn's hospitality, not in dollars but in the inconvenience to the hostess.

Terri lets Jenn know what her hospitality meant to them: they could not have had the vacation without it.

Dear Jenn,

Thank you so very much for having us all to stay last week. We all had a wonderful time. The kids are still talking about it, and about their wonderful Aunt Jenn.

I know it must have been a hassle for you having us all underfoot, and I know you're not used to having a toddler around. We couldn't have made the trip without your hospitality, and we're so grateful. It was great to spend time with you and Russ, and we hope we can return the favor soon and have you to visit. Shall we make plans for winter break?

Thank you again for a wonderful, memorable end-of-summer visit.

Love,

Terri

Terri makes plans to reciprocate, using the thank-you as a way to deepen the relationship.

The closing repeats the thank-you.

NOT LIKE THIS . . .

You can tell Deb is sitting and writing a lot of thank-you notes for wedding presents, because this is a very impersonal opening. She signs her note with "love," so she and Keesha have a relationship that warrants a warmer tone than this.

Dear Keesha,

It was a pleasure to see you and David at the wedding. Thank you so much for the coffeemaker. We think of you whenever we use it, which makes the experience even nicer.

Let's get together soon, once things have settled down. We'd love to see you!

Love,

Deb

This is a nice sentiment, but it's clichéd.

It's not a *bad* thank-you note, but it's nothing special. With a bit more effort, Deb could write something that Keesha will remember fondly.

...LIKE THIS

Deb's opening is warm and personal.	Dear Keesha, It was wonderful to see you and David at the wedding, even briefly. I've always heard you never get to spend time with your guests at your wedding, and now I know it's true. I wish we'd had the chance to sit and chat a bit.

Thank you so much for the coffeemaker. Byron and I have decided that it's our most important appliance, far more important than the microwave or the fridge. We would never get out of the house without it! I don't know how I survived without one.

> This is kind of silly, but it's sweet and it reflects some real thought about the gift.

Thank you again for everything. Once things have settled down, we would love to get together with you and David. I'll shoot you an e-mail soon.

> Overall it's a warm note that conveys the importance of the friendship.

Love,

Deb

MORE EXAMPLES

FOR A GIFT

Dear Alison,

Thank you very much for the Patrick O'Brian book. I've been hearing great things about his books for years, and I started reading it as soon as it arrived. It's wonderful—really absorbing and interesting. Have you read him? Thank you again for a very thoughtful gift.

Love,

Sophie

Dear Roxanne and Joe,

Thank you for the gift card! It was *exactly* what we needed as we settled into the new house. We used it toward some blinds for the kitchen windows. Having the card meant we could get custom-sized blinds—because the house is so old, the windows are an odd size and the standard sizes don't fit. Your gift is very much appreciated.

We'd love to see you. As soon as we get the rest of the kitchen up and running, please come for dinner!

Love,

Katie and Josh

FOR A GIFT CARD OR GIFT CERTIFICATE

Dear Aunt Linda,

I was overwhelmed when I opened your card and saw the check. Thank you so much for your very generous gift. I think you know this means I'll be able to study next semester without having to get a job. You've given me the chance to pursue my studies full-time, and I'm so grateful for the opportunity. I won't let you down, and I will never forget your kindness.

Love,

Kim

FOR CASH

Dear Steven,

Thanks for taking care of the garden while we were away. I guess I overdid it with the tomato plants this year, and they definitely would have died if you hadn't been there to tend them. I know it was a hassle, and I appreciate it.

Please feel free to help yourself all summer, and make room in the freezer for some of Carol's homemade pasta sauce!

Jim

FOR HELP

Dear Erika,

Thank you so much for driving up and helping me move into the new place. I was completely overwhelmed and feeling so disorganized, and you saved the day. If you hadn't been there, I'd probably still be running in circles and packing boxes. I couldn't have done it without you, and I'm so grateful.

I'm looking forward to seeing you at the holidays!

Love,

Adelle

TEACHING YOUR CHILD TO WRITE THANK-YOU NOTES

Many of us remember being sat down after a birthday or a holiday and told to write thank-you notes to those who had sent gifts. Getting in the habit of writing thank-you notes early in life will serve your children well. Children can be taught how to write thank-you notes as soon as they begin to write.

Gift-givers love receiving thank-you notes from children. On the other hand, sending a gift and never receiving any acknowledgment can be hurtful, especially if it happens over and over again.

Writing thank-yous is not just good manners. The process of learning to write a thank-you note also teaches children larger lessons about gift-giving and thoughtfulness—how much care goes into the process of choosing a gift and how it feels to receive a particularly appropriate gift or a gift that was chosen thoughtlessly. Children also learn to be diplomatic and courteous in saying thank you for a gift they didn't particularly like.

Discuss with your children why it's important to send a thank-you note. Provide them with age-appropriate cards or notepaper, and be available to help them as they write. Some parents have a policy of not allowing the child to play with the toy, wear the clothes, or spend the money until a thank-you has been written. Other kids write thank-yous with less prodding. A thank-you note should always been sent promptly.

You can help your children understand what they should include by sharing with them the list below. Encourage them to add creative details or drawings to make the note more personal and fun to write.

- Say "thank you."
- Mention the gift by name.
- Say that you like the gift.
- Talk about how you're going to use it, how much you'll enjoy it, or how it will help you.

EXAMPLES

Dear Aunt Heather,

Thank you for the dress. Blue is my favorite color. It is very pretty. I'm going to wear it to school.

Thank you!

xoxo,

Carly

Dear Mr. Brown,

Thank you for letting us pick the avocados in your yard. They look really good. Mom is going to teach us how to make guacamole with them.

Thank you again,

David and Jacob

Dear Grandpa and Grandma,

Thank you very much for the check. It was really nice of you. Mom said I can spend some of it, so I'm going to get a new game. I'm going to put the rest of it in the bank and save it for college. I hope you are both doing well.

Love,

Scott

> Dear Uncle Dave,
>
> Thank you for sending the old pictures. It's great to see them! My favorites are the ones with you and Dad in the costumes. Where were those taken? I'd like to call you and talk to you about them sometime. I really appreciate having this piece of family history.
>
> Love,
>
> June

MODEL OUTLINE

A note of apology should get to the point right away and make the message very clear.
Opening: Begin your message with an apology for the transgression.
Middle: If relevant, explain why you behaved as you did. Don't make excuses, but let the reader know you were not motivated by malice or lack of concern for her.
Conclusion: Restate your apology. If relevant, let the reader know what you are doing to fix the problem. Close by letting the reader know that the relationship is important to you.

APOLOGY

Writing a sincere note of apology can go a long way toward repairing the damage done by a careless or thoughtless action. It's important to choose the right medium for your apology. Some apologies are best made face-to-face. Others require a written message.

In an informal situation where the stakes are not high, it can be fine to send an apology by e-mail. A more serious breach requires a handwritten card or note. If you have any doubt at all, you're always wise to err on the side of caution and put your apology on paper. Let your reader know that your relationship is important to you by investing in an apology card or writing your message on good-quality stationery (visit www.crane.com for some ideas about writing paper).

Introduction

The **purpose** of an apology is to let your reader know that you're aware you made a mistake and that you're sorry for the pain or distress you caused. You may also want to let the reader know what you are doing to fix the situation or prevent it happening again. Understanding your **reader** and her likely attitude is key to writing a good apology. What is your history with the reader? How is she likely to react to your message? How much have you hurt her? Be sure you **brainstorm** from her point of view. You may not enjoy revisiting the event, but putting yourself in your reader's shoes will help you craft a better message. What would you want to hear if you were in her position? What might make things better? It's easy simply to write "sorry"; it means more to say something more personal and specific. It's a good idea to **organize** your apology so that the actual apology—the "I'm sorry"—comes first. Use the Model Outline (page 78) to help structure your message. Unless your apology is very simple and straightforward, you should plan to go through a couple of **drafts** before you send it. Getting the tone right can be a little tricky; the tone will depend on your relationship with your reader and the seriousness of the transgression. Once you have a draft, leave it alone for a little while. Then go back and consider your draft from your reader's point of view and **revise** from there.

DO	DON'T
• Write as soon as possible. Delaying your apology can make a bad situation worse.	• Don't make excuses. There's a difference between offering an explanation and making excuses for bad behavior. If you made a mistake, admit it. You don't have to beat yourself up, but be sure you don't say anything to suggest that your behavior was really no big deal.
• Apologize. Be explicit in saying that you are sorry. If the reader feels you're fudging, your apology could backfire.	
• Keep it brief. An apology that goes on too long can make the reader uncomfortable.	• Don't blame the reader. An apology that says "I'm sorry, but you should have . . ." is not going to be received well. Sometimes people are so uncomfortable with admitting they've behaved badly that they unconsciously blame the reader. This attitude can sneak in when you're not aware of it, so be alert to the risk.
• Be sincere.	
• Explain. Let the reader know the cause of the breach. If you hurt him, he's entitled to an explanation.	
• If there is something you can do to rectify the situation, focus on doing it. You can't change the past, but you can demonstrate your commitment to the relationship by changing your behavior in the future.	• Don't shift the blame to others. If others genuinely played a role, you may include that information in your explanation, but don't use it to evade taking responsibility for your own actions.
• Keep the focus on the reader's feelings, not on your feelings of regret.	• Don't make a halfhearted apology. If you've decided to apologize, go for it.
• If appropriate, assure the reader that it won't happen again.	• Don't grovel. You may feel really terrible about what happened, but you and your reader will both be more comfortable if you maintain your dignity.

NOT LIKE THIS . . .

Sara hasn't actually apologized. It would be better for her to come out and say "I'm sorry" explicitly.

Sara's writing a bit too much about her feelings, taking the focus off Denise's.

The focus here is still really on Sara, and she's beginning to grovel.

Ouch. By mentioning the content of the remark, Sara inadvertently hurts Denise again. It's better to allude to an insult rather than repeat it.

Sara is laying on the compliments a little thick, and she risks sounding insincere.

By pointing to the group's behavior, Sara subtly avoids taking full responsibility for what she's said.

Dear Denise,

The remark I made about your weight at Karen's on Saturday was careless and hurtful, and it was terrible of me. I appreciate your friendship so much. You are always so unfailingly sweet and kind, and you didn't deserve that. I want you to know that I don't feel that way about you at all.

I've been thinking a lot about why I said what I said. I feel so awful about it, and I hate to think of myself as the kind of person who would say something like that to a friend. Frankly, I think we all get too involved in being witty with this group, and I really need to rein it in.

Again, I'm really sorry. I feel terrible to think I've hurt you, and I hope you will forgive me.

Love,

Sara

. . . LIKE THIS

Sara has taken the incident seriously, and she lets Denise know that her behavior will be better in the future.

This is a nice way of paying a compliment to Denise and reaffirming the friendship.

Sara apologizes right up front, and she's diplomatic about the offensive remark.

Sara mentions the group dynamic but takes full responsibility for her own actions.

Dear Denise,

I want to apologize for that remark I made to you at Karen's on Saturday. It was careless and unkind, and I'm very sorry I hurt you. You didn't deserve that, and I want you to know that I value our friendship very much.

I've been thinking a lot about why I said what I said. Frankly, I think I get too involved in being witty with this group, at all costs. The fact that I hurt someone I care about is a wake-up call for me to change my behavior. I have a lot to learn from you about being kind.

Again, I'm really sorry. I'd love to take you to tea, just the two of us, and reconnect. I'll give you a call over the weekend. ·······················

> Sara offers an olive branch and indicates that the relationship is important to her.

Love,

Sara

NOT LIKE THIS . . .

> Even if his mom put him up to it, Kyle should just go ahead and apologize directly without mentioning his mother's intervention.

Dear Aunt Jill,

Mom let me know how upset you were about my missing your party, and I want you to know how sorry I am. I will never forgive myself for blowing it so badly and making you unhappy.

> You can tell Kyle is sincerely sorry, but he's getting a bit hyperbolic here.

It's no excuse, but I've been putting in really long days at school. I'm taking five classes, including two labs, and I'm totally sleep-deprived all the time. Probably trying to work during the vacation wasn't a good idea. I had turned off my phone, and I was basically just out of it. I think students today are under more pressure than ever before, and the demands on us have grown so much. But obviously I just need to learn to cope. ·······················

> Kyle actually seems undecided about whether he's making an excuse or not. He claims not to be, but the balance of the paragraph goes beyond an explanation into a kind of justification, hinting that older people don't really understand the stress college students are under. He needs to dial this back and take responsibility in a more straightforward way.

I hope I can make this up to you at Christmastime.

> A nice idea. It would be even nicer for Kyle to suggest how.

Love,

Kyle

...LIKE THIS

Kyle recognizes the reason Aunt Jill might have been upset.

Dear Aunt Jill,

I apologize for missing your party. I know how much work you put into it, and it was awful of me to miss it.

Kyle doesn't mention his mom and makes the apology under his own initiative.

I need to learn to manage my time better. I have a heavy course load at school, plus work, and I've been kind of overwhelmed. I was really looking forward to seeing you and Uncle Kevin, and I just blew it. It won't happen again.

Kyle offers a reasonable explanation for his behavior—not an excuse—and promises it won't happen again.

Kyle proposes a nice get-together to make up for his absence at the party.

I'll be home again at Christmastime. Could I take you to Blum's like we used to do? I would love to see you.

Love,

Kyle

APOLOGIZING FOR SOMEONE ELSE

Typically you should not apologize for someone else if that person is able to do it himself. However, in situations where you bear responsibility for someone else's actions—such as for a child or for a group—you should take the initiative to apologize if that person's actions have caused harm or trouble.

- Make it clear who you are—for instance, the parent or the person who rented the space.
- Let the reader know that you have communicated with the responsible party and they do indeed regret their actions.
- Don't make excuses or try to minimize what they did. If you're apologizing, apologize.

Dear Mario,

    I want to apologize for the damage my scout troop did to your restaurant last Wednesday. They were out of line, and I didn't do my job in getting them under control. As you and I have discussed, we will pay for the repairs to the planters that were damaged. I have talked to the girls about their behavior. They understand it was inappropriate and they feel very sorry for the damage they caused. We all extend our sincere apologies to you and your staff.

    Sincerely,

Jennifer Parks

HOLIDAY FAMILY NEWSLETTER

With families increasingly busy and the population more mobile than it's ever been, staying in touch with friends and family is getting harder. Many families take advantage of the holiday card tradition to include a newsletter reporting all the latest developments in the lives of the family members, usually with a group photo. Sometimes this annual newsletter is the only way we know what's going on in the lives of our old friends who may now live far away from us.

Traditionally, people have included paper newsletters folded into their holiday cards. As communication becomes more electronically based, more and more families are opting to send an e-newsletter with their e-greeting at the holidays. The form you choose depends entirely on your own preferences.

Introduction

The **purpose** of a holiday family newsletter is to send greetings and bring people up-to-date on the activities of your family. Your **readers** are friends and family who are eager to hear what's going on with you and your family. Bear them in mind as you write.

As you **brainstorm** your newsletter, try to focus on the most important events of the year for each family member. You may want to ask your children what they want included. Help them to

TIP

Be selective about who you send your family newsletter to. Relatives and friends are likely to be interested in your news. People like business associates, your children's teachers, and the mail carrier are probably not all that interested in the family news and will be happier and more comfortable with a simple holiday greeting card.

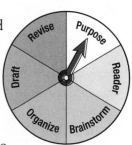

understand that there's not space for them to say absolutely everything. The Model Outline can help you organize all this material.

MODEL OUTLINE

Your family newsletter should be kept to one page in length. Your first paragraph should be devoted to greetings and good wishes to your readers.
It's typical to devote one short paragraph to each family member.
A paragraph about a shared family activity, like a vacation, can follow.
Your closing paragraph should repeat your warm holiday wishes to the reader.

In keeping with the holiday spirit, the tone of your **draft** should be friendly and warm. Reading your newsletter should be like a little visit with your family, and it should bring a smile to the face of the reader.

Writing an engaging newsletter that your friends will enjoy reading requires a little art and attention. There are two main pitfalls in creating a holiday family newsletter: being boring and being boastful. Our lives are pretty routine most of the time, and a faithful recounting of the previous year might be a little tiresome for friends to read. On the other hand, focusing on your family's achievements can create the impression that you're bragging about them. There are some people who feel there's a fine line between sharing news and bragging. No matter how fine that line, I encourage you to locate it and respect it.

If you start working on your newsletter early, and allow time to write and **revise** a few drafts, you'll have more fun with it and prevent it from becoming another chore at a busy time of year. Revising and rewriting will also help you craft a family story that your friends and family will really enjoy reading.

DO	DON'T
• Open with a warm greeting that focuses on the reader rather than jumping right into reporting about your family.	• Don't send more than one page. Of course you could probably write endlessly about your kids, but readers are not likely to read any more than a single page. If you send a very long newsletter, people are likely to put it aside to read "later."
• Be careful about your tone. Your newsletter is not an occasion to brag about your family's achievements. It's really about staying in touch and keeping friends up-to-date. By all means you should let your readers know about your family's accomplishments, but it's even more fun to focus on what family members have enjoyed over the previous year: your kids' new interests, activities that the family enjoyed together, or settling into a new home.	• Don't present a list of achievements. Your family newsletter is not a competition or a job application. Including information like AP test scores or rattling off a long list of colleges where Junior was accepted can be obnoxious.
• Give equal billing to each family member. The newsletter can be a family writing activity. You might let each child draft his or her own section.	• Don't use a lot of superlatives. Focus less on how great, talented, and brilliant your kids are and more on how much they enjoyed their various activities.

THE BASICS | 85

Some families even rotate authorship from year to year and allow different family members to be the "author of record." (Just make sure you edit it before it goes out!)

- Get approval from all family members before you send out your newsletter, to ensure that no one will be embarrassed or surprised by the content that you're sharing.
- Keep it brief. Everyone is busy during the holidays, so be considerate about your readers' time.
- Use short paragraphs. A newsletter with several short paragraphs is far more inviting that large blocks of text.

TIP

Most holiday family newsletters focus on good news. However, if something bad has happened in your family, it can be appropriate to include that information in your newsletter, too. Perhaps a child is struggling with a chronic illness; your letter can report the news factually and quickly touch on her courage and the hope you feel for her recovery. Perhaps a grandparent has passed away. Note the passing and the family's sadness, and emphasize the many happy memories you all share.

People who truly care about you want to hear about what's important to your family, not just the good news.

NOT LIKE THIS . . .

It's hard to believe that another year has passed! But it's been a blessed and wonderful one for the Taylor family! In June, we moved from Santa Ana to our new home in Houston, and we're enjoying it so much. The house is big enough that at last everyone has their own bedroom, and we even have a few rooms to spare! It's been a challenge keeping up with such a big place, and we're still working out a chore schedule so that not everything falls on Mom!

> The entire first paragraph is devoted to the Taylor family. How about a greeting to the reader?
>
> The focus on the size of the house sounds a bit boastful.

Tom is enjoying his new job as director of IT Development for SciEx. Ann is (as usual) busy keeping up with the kids.

> Mom and Dad get short shrift in this newsletter. This often happens, but remember that your old friends are at least as interested in you as they are in your kids.

Mike will be graduating high school next May, if you can believe it! He's decided to attend University of the Northwest in the fall, with a major in communications and a minor in industrial relations. The whole family is planning to take a road trip to Oregon to get him settled in, then back in time to get the rest of the kids in school.

> This is too much information about Mike's plan of study. It won't interest readers.

Jeannie is enjoying her junior year in high school, where she's head of the debating team, an officer on student council, homecoming coordinator . . . and somehow maintaining her 4.0 average on top of all that!

> Jeannie is an impressive kid, but this paragraph brags too much about her accomplishments.

Pat will start high school next year. He's continuing in his father's footsteps with his interest in technology and has developed an interest in astronomy and physics.

| Poor little Pat doesn't get much copy, and it's pretty vague. |

Danny is eleven and enjoying fifth grade. His passion for model cars seems to have faded, and now it's the guitar. He's been taking lessons weekly. His teacher says he has real talent . . . if only he would practice! Danny's the baby, of course, but now he's nearly as tall as Pat. It looks like he got his father's height, after all.

| This paragraph creates the impression that Danny is the favorite, and manages to be both boastful and boring. |

The highlight of our year, in addition to the move, was a trip to Disney World in August. We spent nine days exploring every corner of the place and buying nearly every DVD, T-shirt, and souvenir on offer. We have so much Disney stuff in the house now, we figure we never have to go back!

| The message here seems to be that the Taylors have plenty of disposable income. |

We miss you all, and we wish you and yours a very Merry Christmas and the happiest of New Years!

Love,

Tom, Ann, Mike, Jeannie, Pat, and Danny

. . . LIKE THIS

It's hard to believe that another year has passed! We hope it's been as wonderful for you as it has been for us. The Taylor family wishes you and yours the very happiest holiday season!

| The revised opening, which first extends holiday greetings, focuses more on the reader. |

Our big news this year was our move from California to Houston, Texas (please note our new return address if you don't already have it). It's been a big adjustment for everyone, but we're crazy about the new house (more space!) and we love our new lives here.

| This is a friendly and nonboastful way to let readers know what the family loves about the house. |

Tom is enjoying his new job as director of IT Development for SciEx. Ann is (as usual) keeping busy with the kids and has also begun a new volunteer role with Church of the Nazarene here in Houston. We've taken up horseback riding, which gets us some exercise and some quality time together.

| Tom and Ann's friends will appreciate this additional information about them. |

Mike will be graduating high school next May. He's decided to attend University of the Northwest in the fall, and the whole family is looking forward to a road trip to Oregon to get him settled in.

:

Jeannie is enjoying her junior year in high school, where she is unbelievably busy and especially enjoying her activities with the debate team.

Pat will start high school next year. He remains very interested in science and technology and will be volunteering at a local observatory this year.

Danny, eleven and now in fifth grade, has taken up the guitar, which he's enjoying very much. He's also hard at work on becoming the tallest kid in the family.

The highlight of our year, in addition to the move, was a trip to Disney World in August. We exhausted ourselves over the course of nine days, but everyone had a wonderful time and returned ready to face their new schools in good humor.

We miss you all, and we wish you and yours a very Merry Christmas and the happiest of New Years!

Love,

Tom, Ann, Mike, Jeannie, Pat, and Danny

> The paragraphs about the kids are shorter, less laden with detail, and lighter in tone. Everyone gets more or less equal attention, and we feel we know a little more about the kids as people rather than as feathers in the Taylor family cap.

> This account of the trip is more modest and more interesting, and we understand why a family vacation was good for them all.

> The overall tone of this version is less frantically competitive, and more low key and friendly. Removing some of the unnecessary detail has also shortened the letter, which makes it more pleasant to read.

LOVE LETTER

A love letter is one of the most personal messages you'll ever write, and you are the undisputed authority on what you want to say in this message. No matter how strong your feelings, it can be hard to get started. You might feel embarrassed, and it can be hard to find a "voice" that seems real to you. With a little guidance, though, you can write a love letter that comes from your heart.

You can send a love letter via e-mail, but how romantic is that really? Love letters should be written by hand. It's nice to imagine that your loved one will keep your letter tucked away in a safe place. Invest in some nice stationery (try Crane fine papers, at www.crane.com), and make your love letter worth treasuring.

> To write a good love letter, you ought to begin without knowing what you mean to say, and to finish without knowing what you have written.
>
> —*Jean-Jacques Rousseau, philosopher*

Introduction

The **purpose** of a love letter is simply to share your feelings. Don't spoil the spontaneity, but do think about your **reader**'s likely response as you write. How well do you know him? Are you declaring your love for the first time, or are you both so in love you're walking on air? Part of the fun of writing a love letter is **brainstorming** the content. The box "What to Say in a Love Letter" offers some suggestions. Write your **draft** freely, and don't censor yourself as you write. Leave the draft alone for a day or so, and then read over it. Don't obsess—and don't chicken out—but do allow yourself to **revise** a bit. Proofread to catch errors like misspellings and missing words, which might distract your beloved from your message.

What to Say in a Love Letter

It's kind of funny. You have all these feelings, but you don't know what to say. Writing a love letter can feel embarrassing. It can be hard to get started, but that's no reason not to do it! Here are some ideas about what you might write about:

A memory you share that's special to you

Something she said that was thoughtful or revealed her character

The moment you first realized you loved him

How your life has changed since you first met or first got together as a couple

How you have changed as a result of loving her

Some gesture he makes that endears him to you

What you've learned as a result of loving her

Some physical characteristic you particularly love about him

Something he does that lets you know he cares about you

What about her makes you grateful

How much you miss him when he's away

So you see, it doesn't have to be of an epic proportion to mean the world to the two of you. Nothing is too trivial to write about in a love letter, as long as you mean it sincerely.

DO	DON'T
• Take your time. Don't rush through this. Give yourself time to think and write.	• Don't feel that you need to use poetic or elevated language. Not everyone is good at writing poetry. Your loved one will value a message written from the heart, in your true voice, more than an imitation of a greeting card.
• Share your real feelings.	
• Use your own words. Don't feel you need to use poetic or flowery language. Your love would much rather hear your own voice in the letter than hear you trying to be someone you're not.	
	• Don't feel that you have to write about flowers, the moon, or any other clichéd image.
• Use quotations sparingly. If you want to quote a favorite writer, that's fine. But remember your own words will mean more to your beloved than any famous quotation borrowed from another.	• Don't worry that you're "not a good writer." You're as good as you need to be!
	• Don't say things you don't mean. It's easy to go over the top in pursuit of the proper "romantic" tone and sentiments.
• Offer some specific details: times you think of her, an incident that reminded you of him, something she did that you will always remember, something about him that you particularly admire.	• Don't be afraid to say silly things. If you love the way she opens the car door or the way he chops vegetables, say so.
	• Don't be creepy. If you're writing to someone who doesn't have any idea how you feel, don't go overboard describing your feelings and your desires.
	• Don't forget to say "I love you." It may be implied, but it's nice to hear!

LIKE THIS

Dear Alison,

I was walking into the office the other day, and I saw a young woman. I was sure it was you. Of course I knew it wasn't, but my heart just leaped up when I saw her. She had long dark hair and she was about your height. She turned around, and she wasn't you, of course. I was incredibly disappointed. And that's when I knew that I loved you.

Love,

Steve

Bunny,

It took me so long to find you. Sometimes I thought it would never happen. I thought I had missed the boat. They say it always happens when you're not looking. Honestly I had really given up. I can't believe how much you have changed my life. You've changed everything about how I see the world and everything in it. I love you so much. Saying you were worth the wait is putting it mildly. You're my miracle.

Love,

David

Dear Jon,

I was watching you leave for work yesterday while Kyle was getting ready for school. I watched you walk out to the car, open the door, and toss your briefcase in the back, and suddenly it came to me how much I love you. I've known that for years, of course, but yesterday morning I knew it more profoundly than I've ever known it before. You are my love and my soul mate, and I was put on Earth to love you.

Love,

June

FAN LETTER

Sending a fan letter can be a nice way to share your admiration with your favorite actor, athlete, author, or other celebrity. Use this advice to get the best results from your letter . . . and to avoid embarrassment.

Introduction

Before you write your fan letter, think a bit about your **purpose**. Do you just want to express your admiration, or would you like an autograph? If it's the latter, be sure you ask for it explicitly; otherwise you may be disappointed. Of course you're envisioning that your **reader** will be that person you admire so much. However, you should be aware that most famous people have someone at their management company screening their letters. Remember, then, your correspondence is not entirely private. **Brainstorming** a fan letter can be great fun, and a creative letter can stand out from the pack. If you can tell a special story and catch your reader's attention, you stand a better chance of being noticed. Pay attention to readability as you **organize** your letter. Make any requests early in the letter; don't bury a request for an autograph or a photo in the middle of your message. Be careful with your tone as you write your **draft**: it's fine to be enthusiastic, but do try to sound rational. If you sound like a crazy person, you might not get the outcome you want. Take a break from your draft before you send it. Reread it and **revise** as necessary.

DO	DON'T
• Decide what you want. Are you writing just to express your appreciation or to ask for something? If you want an autograph or a photo, say so.	• Don't be creepy. Don't say anything to suggest you've been stalking the reader or that you intend to do so. Don't say that you "know" you have a special spiritual connection with the celebrity. Don't try to draw your reader into your fantasies. There are lots of weirdos out there—don't you be one of them.
• Make your letter interesting and worthwhile for the reader. Celebrities read lots of letters from people who love them and want to marry them. If you can tell a personal story or share something of real value, your letter is more likely to stand out. You might offer specifics about how they inspired you or affected your life in some way. Really think about how your reader might feel about the	• Don't be sexually inappropriate, even if you feel you love them. No disturbing sex or love talk. No matter how you feel about this person, remember you've never met him, so be respectful.

DO (CONTINUED)	DON'T (CONTINUED)
comments you make in your letter, and tailor them accordingly.	• Don't ask invasive personal questions. Believe it or not, celebrities have feelings too, and inappropriate questions can be hurtful.
• Keep it brief. Remember, their time is at a premium. Long letters are less likely to be read than short ones that make a compelling point.	• Don't send weird gifts: no sexy pictures of yourself, no food, nothing valuable, nothing irreplaceable or of great value to you.
• Provide a self-addressed, stamped envelope if you want an autograph sent back to you. Make it easy for your reader to reply.	• Don't lie. Don't say you've met before (unless you have), that you're distant cousins, that you were his sister's best friend in high school, or that you're dying of a terminal disease and must meet him before you depart this earth. Celebrities have heard it all before, and ultimately it degrades you.
• Close your letter by wishing your reader well.	
• Respect the celebrity's preferences when it comes to fan mail. If you have an agency or management address for him, don't use the Internet to find his home address and slip your letter under his garden gate. Most celebrities just shred mail that finds its way to their personal address.	

NOT LIKE THIS . . .

Even if that's true, don't put it in your letter. It's a little scary. Fandom can border on obsession and still be quite harmless, but don't try to draw the celebrity into your fantasy life.

Think about how the reader might react to what you write. If you think he might squirm or want to stick his head in the oven, keep it to yourself. You can find another way to express appreciation that won't make him uncomfortable.

And Tim Curry wishes he had a nickel for every time he's heard that remark. Actually, he really wishes he'd never heard that remark at all. Really *think* about who you're writing to and how he might respond to your comments.

It's beginning to look like Ashley is a fan of Frank-N-Furter rather than Tim Curry. Ashley can feel however she likes, of course, but this kind of comment might not make an actor very happy.

Dear Tim,

I just wanted to let you know I think you're the best actor in the world! I've seen *The Rocky Horror Picture Show* thirty-seven times, and I still think you're incredibly hot! You are soooo sexy in that movie! I wish my legs looked that good in fishnet stockings!

I haven't even seen anything else you've done, although I know you've done a lot. If you never did anything besides *Rocky Horror*, I'd still think you were the best actor in the world.

Don't dream it, be it!!!!

Lots of love,

Ashley Marquette

... LIKE THIS

Dear Mr. Curry,

I went to see *The Rocky Horror Picture Show* last night. It wasn't my first time, but I just enjoy your performance so much, and every time I see it, I notice new things about it. It really is amazing.

This may sound strange, but I think *Rocky Horror* has actually made me a better person. The first time I saw it I thought it was weird and the characters were freaks. Since I've seen it a few more times with my friends, I think I understand it better, and it's made me a lot more tolerant of different kinds of people. I don't know if that was the intention, but I think that's what it's done.

I can't wait to find some of the other movies and TV you've done and to learn more about your career.

I hope to see you in a new project again soon. I'm really looking forward to that.

Best wishes for the future,

Ashley Marquette

> Ashley has seen *Rocky Horror* thirty-seven times, but she spares Tim that detail and instead offers meaningful praise of his performance.

> This is a really nice compliment. It involved some serious thought, and it's the kind of thing most celebrities like to hear: that their work has made a difference.

> Ashley expresses interest in learning more about Tim's career. She's taking him seriously as an actor and not mistaking him for a character he played.

> Ashley wishes Tim well for the future.

PERSONAL JOURNAL

I know what I know
and I write it.

—*Octavio Paz, writer,
poet, and diplomat*

There's no right or wrong way to keep a personal journal. Your journal should serve a purpose for you, and you're the only one who can decide what that purpose is. If you'd like to keep a personal journal, these hints and tips can help you get started and keep going once you have.

DO	DON'T

DO

- Decide why you want to keep a journal. There are no rules, but it can be easier to develop and maintain a journaling habit if you have a clear idea about why you're doing it. Will your journal be a place for personal reflection? Are you keeping track of an activity or a march toward a goal? Planning weekly or daily goals? Do you think you'll want to refer to the journal later, or is it just for the experience of writing it now?

- Choose a medium. On the computer or on paper? Online, by e-mail, or in a Word file? If you want to write on paper, buy a journal or notebook. It helps to have a single place where you write your journal rather than doing it on separate pieces of paper. Consider what will be most convenient and what will be most satisfying to you.

- Make a schedule. It's easier to stay consistent if you plan to write at the same time every day. Some people wake up a little early to write; others write just before bedtime. The baby's nap time can be a good quiet time. Look at your day and see where your likeliest times are.

- Find a good place to write. It's best to find a place where you can be alone. You don't have to write in the same place every day, but doing so helps reinforce the habit.

DON'T

- Don't censor yourself. Your journal is only for you, so feel free to write what you please. Don't feel you have to write the same thing every day. If you suddenly feel like writing a song or a poem, go for it!

- Don't criticize yourself. Going back and correcting your grammar after the fact can make journaling a drag. Let the journal do its thing without beating yourself up.

- Don't give up. It's natural to miss a day or two or even a week, but don't let that discourage you. It's better to miss a few days and pick it up again than to abandon it altogether.

- Don't show it to others unless you're really prepared to do so. Sharing your journal can violate your privacy and might hurt others. It's yours to do with as you please, but be sure you think carefully before showing it around.

- Write as consistently as you can. There may be days when you simply cannot find the time, but be as consistent as possible, given the demands of your life.
- Develop templates if you are using your journal to track daily activities.

HABIT JOURNAL

Some people keep a journal to track a habit—what they eat and how much, how often they exercise, how much money they spend, and so on. You can also keep a journal to track your progress in developing new—and presumably healthier—habits. To be most useful, habit journals should be written as regularly as possible. Journaling itself might become a new and rewarding habit!

DREAM JOURNAL

Keep a notebook and a pen by your bed and record your dreams as soon as you wake up or even in the middle of the night. Write while the dream is still fresh in your mind.

BABY JOURNAL

Make your own baby book and record milestones, funny stories, and happy memories. You can also use the journal to record medical history, growth, and other important information.

EXPERIENCE JOURNAL

Some people find it helpful to keep a journal about their feelings when they are going through a particularly significant experience: the death of a loved one, going back to school, a divorce, a move to a different part of the country. Recording your feelings can help you understand them, and it can be interesting to go back and reflect later.

BIRTHDAY JOURNAL

Write a journal entry every year on your birthday, and include photos. You can write about your birthday celebration and who you spent it with. You can also use the journal to reflect on the previous year and make plans for the upcoming one.

For more journaling ideas and advice, visit www.howtowriteanything .com.

GET-WELL NOTE

When someone is ill or recovering from surgery, a get-well note can help cheer them. The personal touch of a real note or card rather than an e-mail is called for in this case. The gesture will mean more if the message is handwritten and delivered by mail. Buy a commercial get-well card and personalize it with your own message, or write your note on nice stationery.

MODEL OUTLINE

A get-well message can be brief.
Opening: Tell the reader you are sorry to hear they're not feeling well.
Middle: Explicitly state your hope they will feel better soon. Offer to help if you're willing to do so.
Conclusion: Finish your message on a warm note of hope for a speedy recovery.

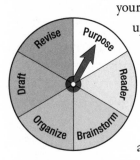

Introduction

The **purpose** of a get-well note is to wish the reader well and to let him know that he is in your thoughts. When you compose your note, be yourself: think about what you might say to your **reader** if you were talking on the phone, and take it from there. A get-well note should be brief, so it won't require a lot of **brainstorming**. Take a moment to put yourself in your reader's shoes. What might she be feeling? What might cheer him up? The Model Outline can help you **organize** your get-well message. It's a good idea to write out a **draft**, or at least a quick outline, before you write in the card or on the fancy notepaper. As you write your **draft**, use an upbeat and encouraging tone. Review your draft from the reader's point of view. How would you feel if you received this note? **Revise**, write your message in the card or on the notepaper, and send it off. It will be appreciated.

DO	DON'T
• Send your note promptly. A get-well note means more if it arrives in a timely fashion.	• Don't allude to the diagnosis unless you've been officially notified of it. Some people prefer to keep medical issues private. If you've just heard through the grapevine, it's enough to mention "your surgery," "your hospitalization," or "that you've been ill."
• Take the time to personalize a commercial get-well card with your own message. You don't need to write a lot, but be sure you do more than just sign it.	• Don't go overboard with your cheerleading to the extent that the reader feels you're downplaying her condition. Someone who has just had major surgery probably won't be back to normal in "no time." Be encouraging, but don't gloss over the challenges the reader is facing.
• Be yourself. Write in your own voice and express your own feelings. A message in your own words will mean the most to your reader.	
• Mention the illness, accident, or procedure, but don't delve too deeply into it.	• Don't write at length about a similar experience you've had. If you have had a similar illness or procedure, you're in a good position to offer encouragement to the reader, but remember—this isn't about you, and your reader's experience is not likely to be exactly the same as yours.
• Express your concern and good wishes explicitly.	
• Offer to visit or help in some way, if it's appropriate and if you're truly willing to do so.	
	• Don't offer a miracle cure. You might have just read a convincing article about ginkgo biloba or vitamin D or kelp extract, but avoid giving your reader off-the-cuff medical advice.
	• Don't make a vague offer of help or offer to help if you really don't want to or can't. "Please let me know if there's anything I can do" sounds nice, but your reader is not likely to take you up on such a vague offer. It's better to spend a moment thinking about what your reader might truly need—for instance, help with grocery shopping, gardening, or errands. Making a specific offer shows your thoughtfulness.
	• Don't offer to visit if you don't intend to.
	• Don't talk about God or religion unless you're sure about the reader's views on the subject.

NOT LIKE THIS . . .

Jackie's talking a little too much about herself here. She means well, but she should really keep the focus more on Karen.

Jackie is cheerleading, but she doesn't really know the details of Karen's condition. She should tone it down a bit.

It's a nice offer, but does she mean it? Karen would feel more comfortable calling on her for help if Jackie made a specific offer.

Dear Karen,

Ronnie let me know about your ovarian cyst, and I wanted to let you know I'm thinking of you. I had my appendix removed years ago, and I know how you're feeling now. The appendix had burst, and I was laid up for about six weeks. I've never been so bored! I know just what you're going through, and you have all my sympathy.

I hope you're taking good care of yourself and feeling better and better with each passing day. Just take it easy, and you'll be up and around before you know it! Please let me know if there's anything at all I can do to help.

xoxo,

Jackie

It's better not to mention the specific diagnosis unless you're sure it's public information or the reader has told you directly.

Jackie probably doesn't know exactly what Karen is going through. She's trying to be encouraging, but she's actually a little dismissive.

. . . LIKE THIS

Jackie shares her experience just to commiserate with Karen, not to tell her she knows exactly how she feels. This is the way to do it.

Jackie's focus is on Karen throughout the note.

Dear Karen,

Ronnie let me know about your surgery, and I wanted to let you know I'm thinking of you. I had a similar procedure years ago, and I still remember how painful it was. I hope you're taking good care of yourself and feeling better and better with each passing day. Please get plenty of rest so you can heal.

Do you need any help around the house? I remember from my own surgery that lifting was a problem for a while. I'd be happy to come over and help with chores or shopping—just say the word!

xoxo,

Jackie

This is a sincere and practical offer of help. Jackie refers to her own experience to imagine the kind of help Karen might need. If you make a specific offer, the reader will feel more convinced that you mean it, and she'll be more likely to ask for the help she needs.

SERIOUS ILLNESS

In the event of a serious illness with an uncertain outcome, take some extra care in crafting your message.

DO	DON'T
• Let the reader know you're sorry he is ill and that you are thinking of him. If you pray, and if you know the reader is a believer, you can mention you are praying for him.	• Don't send a jokey or silly card. Some commercial get-well cards—those with busty nurses or dogs wearing cones on their heads—are not appropriate for a serious illness. A card that makes someone smile is fine, but don't send anything that trivializes the illness.
• Keep your focus on the reader, not on your feelings. Although you are writing to express your concern, the focus of your letter should be on the reader rather than on your feeling upset.	• Don't offer medical advice or suggest a miracle cure. Sometimes people do this because they are too overwhelmed by the news to accept it. By all means keep hoping for a miraculous recovery, but it's ultimately selfish to draw your reader into this kind of wild hope.
• Learn about the reader's illness. Having some information about the reader's situation will help you craft your message. (Don't discuss the condition explicitly—this research is just for your own understanding.)	• Don't write about God or religion unless you know the person is a believer. Respect your reader's beliefs.
• Let the reader know you would like to see him, if you would and if it's practical and possible to do so.	
• Follow up and stay in touch.	

Dear Alan,

I was so sorry to hear about your diagnosis. I hope you are taking good care of yourself and keeping your spirits up. I would love to drop in and see you one day after work if you are feeling up to it. Does that sound good? I'll give you a call and check in.

In the meantime, please know I am thinking of you and sending all my very best wishes. Please do take good care.

xoxo,

Stephanie

TERMINAL ILLNESS

If someone is diagnosed with a terminal illness, your message requires special sensitivity and care. Your message will depend on how close you are to the reader and how public the diagnosis is. If you're writing to someone with whom you have a close relationship and whose diagnosis is out in the open, you can speak more freely. Be very sensitive to your relationship with the reader and his attitude toward the diagnosis.

If you don't expect to see the person before he passes away, your note will essentially be a kind of good-bye message. Choosing what to write will be a very personal decision. Rather than saying good-bye explicitly, try to express what that person has meant to you, and how you value the relationship. Recall a happy memory or an incident where you learned something from the person. It's a blessing to have the opportunity to say what you want to say.

DON'T

- Don't procrastinate. If you know someone is terminally ill, send your message right away.
- Don't send a get-well card. If you don't expect the reader to recover, write your note on a blank card or stationery, or choose a commercial card that says simply "thinking of you" rather than "get well."
- Don't mention death unless the reader has done so first or unless you are very sure she is comfortable talking about it openly.
- Don't ruminate about mortality or the nature of life unless the reader has initiated that discussion.

Dear Helen,

I was very sorry to hear about your illness. I hope you are taking good care of yourself and that you have all the help you need.

I have been thinking so much about you, particularly your friendship with Mother over the years. I remember so many afternoons coming home from school to find you and Mother having tea and talking. (I also remember the time Shadow stole the cookies right off the plate!) I want you to know that Mother considered you one of her very best friends and was especially grateful for your loyalty and support after Daddy got sick. I don't know if she ever expressed that to you, but I want you to know how much this family appreciates you.

I'll phone you this weekend and see if you feel like talking. Please know I am thinking of you and your family.

Much love,

Diane

OBITUARY

There are many things to do when a loved one passes away, and writing an obituary can be one of the more daunting tasks on the list. Writing an obituary for the local newspaper is a way of getting the news out to that person's wider circle of acquaintances and inviting them to the funeral or memorial service. Although writing an obituary can be difficult, people will appreciate hearing the news and having the opportunity to say good-bye.

Introduction

The **purpose** of an obituary is to provide a public notice of someone's death and to offer information about any funeral or memorial service that is planned. Writing an obituary can also be a way of paying tribute to the deceased. Your **readers** may be old friends and acquaintances of the deceased. An obituary can contain a vast array of different information: use the Model Outline (page 102) to help **brainstorm** content and **organize** yours. Plan to go through more than one **draft** of the obituary, unless it is going to be a simple death notice with little or no additional information. Consider sharing your draft with one or more trusted parties. It can be helpful to get other people's perspectives, and they might remind you of something you've forgotten. **Revise** and edit accordingly.

Model Outline

———•———

An obituary can contain a great deal of information or very little. Choose from these categories:

NAME / ANNOUNCEMENT

Full name of the deceased, including nickname, if any

Maiden name, if any

Age at death

Place of residence

Date of death

Place of death

Cause of death

LIFE

Date of birth

Place of birth

Names of parents

Childhood: siblings, schools, friends

Marriage(s)/partnership(s): date, place, name of spouse/partner

Education

Awards and honors

Employment

Places of residence

Hobbies, interests, activities

Charitable, religious, fraternal, political, and other affiliations; positions held

Accomplishments

FAMILY

Survived by (and place of residence):

Spouse/partner

Children (in birth order, and their spouses)

Grandchildren

Great-grandchildren

Great-great-grandchildren

Parents

Grandparents

Siblings (in birth order)

Other relatives, such as nephews, nieces, cousins, and in-laws

Friends

Pets

Predeceased by (and date of death):
  Spouse
  Children (in birth order)
  Grandchildren
  Siblings (in birth order)

  Others, such as nephews, nieces,
    cousins, and in-laws
  Pets

SERVICE
Day, date, time, place
Visitation information (if
  applicable)
Reception information (if
  applicable)

Other memorial, vigil, or graveside
  services (if applicable)
Clergy and pallbearers
Place of interment
Funeral home

CLOSING
Memorial funds established
Other suggestions for memorial
  donations

Thanks to hospital, care workers,
  and others

DO	DON'T
• Try to do what the deceased would have wanted. The wishes of the deceased are more important than yours right now. Focusing on his wishes can relieve the burden on you and can help smooth over any disagreements.	• Don't rush or cut corners. There's a lot going on when someone dies, but the obituary is important. A sloppy obituary that doesn't include accurate information, or one that appears too late for people to plan to attend the service, can be hurtful.
• Be sure the obituary is accurate and complete. Have you omitted any family members or other important information? Ask someone to read your draft to catch anything you might have inadvertently left out.	• Don't manifest old grudges or hard feelings in the obituary. You may be angry at a family member for some reason, but don't take it out on them by leaving them out of the obituary or slighting them.
• Try to convey something about the deceased's values and passions. In addition to listing family members and other facts, think a bit about her volunteer and free-time activities.	• Don't include anything in the obituary the deceased would not have wanted there. For instance, some people are uncomfortable with sharing the cause of death.

DO (CONTINUED)	**DON'T** (CONTINUED)
• Consider writing several versions of the obituary. You may wish to write a short notice for the newspaper and develop a longer one for other publications, a family scrapbook, or a website. • Consider drafting your own obituary. You can save your loved ones time, struggle, and indecision if you write your own obituary in advance. Make sure they have a copy or know where they can find it when they need it.	• Don't share your draft with too many other people. It's very wise to get input from others, particularly when you're upset and possibly not thinking very clearly. However, remember that everyone who reads it will have an opinion, so be careful about how many different opinions you solicit. • Don't print a home address in a public obituary. Doing so can alert thieves to an empty house or a widowed spouse, as well as risking identity theft.

Writing Your Own Obituary

Increasingly, when death is anticipated, people are writing their own obituaries. In this way, they save their loved ones the difficulty when the time comes, just as paying for your funeral in advance can take pressure off those who survive you. Although some people feel uncomfortable writing their own obituary, this practice does have advantages. Surviving family members might not remember specific dates (for instance birth, employment, retirement, deaths of other family members). Survivors might not recall relevant people, places, employers, or organizations and might not have the correct spelling for these. In addition, surviving family members might be unaware of your memberships in volunteer or community organizations. Finally, writing your own obituary allows you to specify charities for donations that your survivors wouldn't have thought of. If you do draft your own obituary, make sure your loved ones have a copy of it or know exactly where to find it when the time comes.

Some people have found that starting to write their own obituary has launched a personal memoir-writing project. A memoir can be a very nice legacy for those you leave behind, as well as an enjoyable project for you.

LIKE THIS

HARRISON—Matthew Robert. Professor of Climatology at the University of Arizona, father to three and grandfather to four, died from complications of Alzheimer's disease April 3 at his home in Scottsdale, AZ. He was 89.

Samantha B. Vasquez

Samantha B. Vazquez, 66, of Brooks Farm, passed away Wednesday, May 30, 2012, at St. Mary's Hospital. She was born May 20, 1946, in Walker City. Sam graduated in 1969 with a degree in pharmacology from the University of Illinois. She met her husband, Leo, at Pfizer, where they both worked. More recently, Sam spent much of her time enjoying her recently acquired Thoroughbred horse, Zoot. She also was working at Second Chance Thoroughbred Rescue, where she nurtured her love of animals.

Sam is survived by her husband, Leo Vasquez, whom she married June 4, 1973; her children, Jennifer McCormick and John Vasquez; her mother, Phyllis (Morton) Ledbedder; and her in-laws, Luis and Elizabeth Vasquez.

The visitation will be from 10 a.m. to 1 p.m. Tuesday, June 5, with a service at 1 p.m. at Thomasson Funeral Home, 659 Beechwood Road, Brooks Farm.

In lieu of flowers, memorials would be appreciated to Second Chance Thoroughbred Rescue, 209 Lennox Road, Moscow, IL 60010.

For information, call the funeral home at 800-800-1111. Online condolences may be made at thomasson.org.

For more sample obituaries, visit www.howtowriteanything.com.

CONDOLENCE LETTER

Writing a condolence letter can be a difficult challenge. It's hard to know what to say when someone has died, and we sometimes feel that nothing we say can possibly help relieve the pain the bereaved is suffering.

No matter how inadequate it may seem, a kind letter from a well-wisher can be a tremendous comfort to someone who has just lost a loved one. A sensitive and thoughtful sympathy letter will tell the bereaved that her loved one is fondly remembered and show her how much you care. Although it may be a struggle, a good condolence letter can be one of the most important things you'll ever write.

An expression of condolences must be done through a card or letter. E-mail, no matter how well intended, is simply too informal for this occasion.

Introduction

A condolence letter serves three **purposes**: to express sympathy to the bereaved about the death of a loved one, to share your affection or regard for the deceased, and to let the bereaved know you are thinking about him and willing to help. Anything that goes beyond addressing these three purposes can get you into trouble, so make sure everything in your letter works toward achieving them.

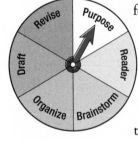

Keep your relationship with your **reader** in mind, and tailor the content of the letter accordingly. To make your letter as effective as possible, it's good to **brainstorm** content, thinking back over your relationship with the deceased, looking for some special memories or insights to include in the letter. Following the Model Outline can help you **organize** your thoughts.

MODEL OUTLINE

Three paragraphs is a good length for a condolence letter. This simple outline can help guide you:
Paragraph 1: Express your sympathy for the bereaved.
Paragraph 2: Demonstrate your regard for the deceased, perhaps by relating an anecdote or describing how special he was.
Paragraph 3: Express your concern for the well-being of the bereaved, and offer any help you are genuinely willing to provide.

As you **draft**, try to keep the letter brief and to the point. Sincerity in these letters is prized above all things, so don't worry too much about whether your writing is at its finest—write from the heart, and your message will be heard and appreciated.

To be safe, you should keep the tone of your condolence letters rather formal. Even if you choose to relate an amusing anecdote about the deceased, your overall tone should be one of respect; this is not the time to push the envelope when it comes to style.

Because these letters can be difficult to write, it's a good idea to allow yourself extra time to **revise** the letter once you've drafted it. Ideally, let the first draft sit overnight and read it with a fresh eye the next day to make sure you're saying exactly what you want to say and that you haven't inadvertently included anything that could offend.

DO

- Express your sorrow at the death and your heart-felt sympathy for the reader.
- Make the effort to relate a little anecdote about the person who has passed—perhaps something amusing, an incident that you think expresses the character or personality of the deceased, a good time you had together, or a time when the person was especially helpful to you. What you say depends on your relationship with the reader and the person who has died, but selecting some personal details lets the reader know that people appreciated her beloved and that there is a community of remembrance and continuation. This is likely the part of your letter that your reader will remember and appreciate most.
- Let the reader know that he is not alone. Tell him that he is in your thoughts. And if you are willing and able to help out in a more direct way, say so. For example, let the person know that he should feel free to call anytime, or say you'll call him in a week or so just to check up on him. Grieving is a long process, and it's good to know that people will be there for you beyond the first round of condolence cards.
- Handwrite the card or letter to make your message more personal.

TIP

The late Jacqueline Kennedy Onassis was a great letter writer, and she often included well-known quotations in her letters of condolence.

If you're struggling for the right words, try consulting a book of quotations or an online source. Don't limit yourself to quotations about death; search for topics like "loyalty," "kindness," or other characteristics that you feel describe the deceased.

DON'T

- Don't put it off. The difficulty of writing a condolence letter makes it hard to get started, but a timely expression of sympathy does the most good. A belated condolence letter is better than none, so if you have put off writing the letter, do it as soon as you can.
- Don't send an e-mail. A condolence letter is one of those cases in which an e-mail simply won't do: you must send a paper letter or card. There are a few extraordinary exceptions: if the bereaved is traveling and away from her mailbox, an e-mail message is better than none. But make sure a card or letter from you is waiting for her when she arrives home.
- Don't rely on a commercial sympathy card to express your feelings. It's fine to buy and send such a card, but to show you really care you must personalize it with a handwritten note.
- Don't dwell on how bad you feel about the loss. You may feel that you are sharing the reader's pain, but remember that the purpose of the letter is to offer sympathy and support to the reader, not to make a display of your own grief.
- Don't allude to religious or other spiritual or philosophical views of death unless you're quite sure the reader shares those views. Mentioning God's purpose, for instance, may offend a reader who does not believe in God. Remember, your focus should be on the reader and her needs at all times.
- Don't offer advice. Now is not the time to help the reader "move on" or achieve "closure." The grieving process takes time and is different for everyone who experiences it. The purpose of your letter is to acknowledge the loss and to express

DON'T (CONTINUED)

condolence and support in the here-and-now, not to push the reader along into the future. The only exception to this rule is that you may wish to gently urge the reader to take good care of herself at this time; in doing so, you're expressing your concern for her.

- Don't say anything to suggest that the death was a blessing or a relief. Even if the deceased suffered for a long time before death, this is not the time to say "He's better off now" or "At least he is no longer in pain." Your letter should treat the death as a loss to be mourned. In situations in which the death was long anticipated, survivors often experience difficult conflicting emotions; rather than stir up such emotions, your letter should be an unqualified expression of sympathy and condolence.

- Don't offer to help if you're really not prepared to. Most people take these offers as pro forma, but be aware that if you offer help you may actually be called upon to do so.

NOT LIKE THIS . . .

However terrible you feel, it's a sure thing that Carol feels worse. Don't write about yourself or how difficult it is to write this letter. Focus on Carol and her feelings.

Dear Carol,

I can't tell you how terrible I feel about Justin's passing. It's been on my mind day and night since I got the news, and I find it very difficult to express my feelings about this loss. He was a wonderful man, and we will all miss him terribly.

Instead of simply listing the deceased's good qualities, why not illustrate them with a special memory that the reader can enjoy and cherish?

Justin was unfailingly cheerful, friendly, helpful, and kind. He was a wonderful neighbor—always good-natured and willing to help.

I know you must be going through a very difficult time. I hope it is of some comfort to know that God has a purpose in all things, though it may not be clear to us. In time, I'm sure we will all come to accept what has happened.

Marc and I send our love and deepest sympathies to you at this difficult time.

Love,

Louise

> Unless you're very, very sure about Carol's religious beliefs, you should keep your religious ruminations to yourself. Carol may not believe in God, or she may be very angry with God right now. Remember, the objective of your letter is to express sympathy and support, so focus on crafting a sensitive letter that will help Carol without risking offense.

. . . LIKE THIS

Dear Carol,

Marc and I were deeply saddened by the news of Justin's death, and we send our heartfelt sympathy to you.

My most vivid memory of Justin is from a cold, rainy Christmas Eve. Marc and I were new in the house and had brought home an enormous Christmas tree, far too big to fit in the stand. When we came over to borrow a saw to trim the trunk, Justin came back with us to help. After about an hour of effort, Justin managed to cut through a stubborn knot in the trunk and get our tree into the stand. I'm sure he wasn't anticipating spending his Christmas Eve struggling with the neighbors' tree in the cold and damp, but he kept his sense of humor long after we had lost ours, and it was thanks to him that we had a Christmas tree our first year in the house. Justin was a wonderful, kind, and generous neighbor, and we will miss him very much.

I want you to know that you are in our thoughts and prayers. We hope you are taking good care of yourself at this difficult time. I will give you a call during the next week or so to see how you are doing. In the meantime, if there is anything at all we can do for you, please let us know and we will be there for you.

Love,

Louise

> A simple and direct opening can often be more eloquent and effective than something flowery and elaborate. Write from your heart.

> Sharing this memory of Justin's kindness will comfort Carol and let her know that others cared about and appreciated her husband.

> This closing paragraph expresses concern for Carol's well-being and the commitment to follow up with her, without being intrusive, as she moves through the grieving process.

TIP

A personal condolence letter should always be handwritten. A letter for a business associate, especially one written on behalf of the company or all the deceased's co-workers, should be typed.

SUICIDE

When a person takes his or her own life, writing a condolence letter can be particularly delicate. Often families and loved ones are taken completely off guard by a suicide and are suffering a terrible shock. In cases in which the deceased was known to have been troubled, a tactful acknowledgment of the difficult situation is usually best. Simply ignoring the circumstances of the death may make the bereaved feel shut out and stigmatized.

Dear Steve,

I was deeply sorry to learn about the passing of your son Victor. Victor was an unfailingly kind and charming young man, and he will be missed terribly. I wish you and your family the strength to find the answers you seek. Please know that you are not alone; Paul and I are thinking of you.

With best wishes always,

Lisa

VIOLENT DEATH

The same principles apply in a case in which a person was murdered or died in unpleasant or shocking circumstances.

Dear Janice,

All of us at Weston share your grief and shock at John's death. He was an exemplary colleague, always willing to share insights and support team members. What's more, everyone here knew what a devoted husband and father John was. He spoke with great pride about Peter's soccer games and Tania's enthusiasm for ballet. Such a sudden loss is difficult to understand, but we hope you can take some comfort in knowing that John's colleagues held him in the highest regard and will never forget this wonderful man. We offer our sincere condolences to you at this difficult time.

Sincerely,

Simon and the Technical Support Group

LOSS OF A PREGNANCY

A condolence note for the loss of a pregnancy requires some special care. The impulse to say something to "make it right" can be very strong, but be aware you can't do that. Your message should simply be one of sympathy and support.

DO	DON'T
• Say how very sorry you are.	• Don't say "At least you can have another one."
• Focus on being supportive.	• Don't say "At least the pregnancy wasn't that far along."
• Be aware there's very little you can say to make the reader feel "better" about what happened. This should not be your goal.	• Don't mention God or religion unless you are sure the reader is a believer.
• Keep it brief. There is so little to say besides "I'm sorry." Don't force yourself to write a long note.	• Don't say "There's a reason for everything."
• Offer to help, visit, or spend time with her if you so desire and are able.	• Don't say anything that might make the reader feel the loss of the pregnancy was her fault. Many women blame themselves groundlessly for the loss of a pregnancy. Be sensitive about her feelings and simply offer your support.
	• Don't speculate on the reasons for the loss of the pregnancy.

Dear Shelly,

I am so very sorry to hear about your loss. Please know that you are in my thoughts daily and that I am here for you if you need anything at all. I hope you are taking good care of yourself. I would love to see you, if you're feeling up to it. I'll give you a call over the weekend to check in.

Much love,

Rhonda

DEATH OF AN ANIMAL

As domestic animals have evolved from "house pets" to "companion animals," so has sensitivity to the feelings that people have about the animals they live with. The loss of such an animal can be very sad, and sending a sympathy note is entirely appropriate in such a case.

> Dear Erika,
>
> I was very sorry to hear about Mimi's death. She was a beautiful, sweet cat, and even a casual visitor could see what a happy and vital presence she was in your home. I hope you can take comfort in knowing that you gave her the best possible care. She was very fortunate to have such a loving home with you.
>
> Take care,
>
> Jill

EULOGY

The word "eulogy" comes from the Greek *eu*, which means "good" and "logos," which means "word." A eulogy is a set of good words about the dead. A eulogy can be one of the most difficult things you'll ever write, but it can also be one of the most important and rewarding. A eulogy is a gift to the deceased and to the survivors.

Introduction

The **purpose** of a eulogy is to honor the dead and to comfort the living. Rather than a **reader**, you will have listeners, among them the loved ones of the deceased. You should keep them in mind as you write. Your eulogy will be the product of **brainstorming** through many memories and insights and selecting those you feel best about presenting. Try making a list of your most vivid memories of the deceased or a list of his strongest traits or most important accomplishments. Take your time to reflect and cull through what you want to say. It's a good idea to make a formal outline, as it's very easy to ramble. As you **organize** the eulogy, remember that people will be listening to it, not reading it. Make it easy to follow. You should plan to go through a couple of **drafts**. Consider showing your draft to someone you trust to get feedback. Have you forgotten anything? Is there anything that rings false? Since this is a speech, it's also an excellent idea to read your draft out loud to see how it sounds. **Revise** any places that don't flow smoothly. Ideas will probably continue coming to you as you draft and rehearse. Be open to memories and insights that arise. Read your final draft out loud and time yourself, to make sure you're not going on too long. Rehearsing can also help you manage your emotions when the time comes to deliver the eulogy.

DO	DON'T
• Allow yourself enough time to reflect and write. You'll do a better job and feel better about your effort if you take your time. You'll only have one chance to do this.	• Don't dwell on your own feelings in your eulogy. Everyone at the service is sad, and your focus should be on the deceased rather than yourself.
• Focus on the deceased rather than yourself. Everyone understands you're upset.	• Don't violate the tone of the event. Some events are more relaxed than others. Try to get a sense of what it's going to be like. You might enjoy telling a funny story, but if it's going to offend your mother's friends, it's not worth it. Be considerate.
• Explain a bit about how you knew the deceased, if it's not clear. Some memorial services welcome brief eulogies from volunteers. Unless everyone at the service knows who you are and what your relationship was with the deceased, take a moment to make that clear to your listeners.	• Don't go on too long. Especially at a service where several people are speaking, keep your remarks brief and pithy. If you're not sure how long is too long, check with the other people speaking or the religious officiant, if there is one.
• Make sure your eulogy is appropriate to the relationship you had with the deceased.	
• Choose material that lets the character of the deceased shine through, perhaps an anecdote that shows how she related to other people, an act of kindness, or a decision that she made that demonstrated her values.	

TIP

If you are one of several people speaking at a funeral or memorial service, try to touch base with the other speakers and briefly discuss what everyone plans to say. This way you can avoid being caught by surprise if someone else tells the very story you were planning to tell. You can also plan a more balanced program and retrospective of the person's life.

DO (CONTINUED)

- Talk about what you know. If you knew the deceased from work, offer insights from that part of his life. Your own relationship with the deceased can help illuminate the whole person for the audience.
- Use humor judiciously. If it's appropriate to your relationship and the circumstances, you may want to tell a funny story involving the deceased. Be sure the humor isn't mean-spirited and that it is something the deceased would have laughed about, too. A well-placed laugh can be a very healing emotional release, as people remember the deceased in joy.
- Consider finding an appropriate quotation, perhaps a poem or a passage from scripture. Read from a poet or writer whom the deceased particularly liked, or find a passage that you feel conveys who she was.
- Be extremely careful of your listeners' feelings. They're vulnerable, so think about the potential impact of your words.

NOT LIKE THIS . . .

The speaker is focusing on himself a bit too much.

This is a very sad day for me, and I know it's hard for all of us to be here. Alan Wilson was a central part of my professional life for thirty-five years. I am shaken and saddened by his passing. He was an exemplary physician and a fine husband and father, and the world is poorer for his loss.

All nice sentiments but rather vague. It would be nice to hear more specific details.

Alan was a senior colleague of mine at St. Luke's. He was always fair and caring to staff and patients alike. I looked up to him as a mentor, and he had a profound influence on the way I practiced medicine. Alan took special care with his younger colleagues. In addition to his students, he watched over those of us who were just beginning our careers. I was always extremely grateful to him for smoothing my transition to St. Luke's and for providing a model of a caring, conscientious physician.

As important as his professional responsibilities were, Alan's personal life was even more important to him. He was a devoted husband and father. His family meant the world to him. He adored you, Elaine, and he was deeply proud of you, Garth and Terry. He always had stories of your latest accomplishments and never failed to brag about each of your triumphs.

> Again, this is nice, but it's so general it might apply to almost anyone. This is an opportunity to provide a real insight into the deceased and his life and values. It sounds as though the speaker didn't really know the family.

Alan's loss will be deeply felt by everyone whom his life touched, his family, friends, and colleagues. It was my privilege to know him and to serve with him. He will be sorely missed.

. . . LIKE THIS

For those of you who don't know me, I'm Steven Kelley, and I was privileged to be Alan's colleague at St. Luke's Hospital for thirty-five years. Alan was a mentor to me, as he was to many physicians, and his loss will be deeply felt by all of us.

> Steven introduces himself. There will certainly be people at the service who don't know Alan's professional colleagues.

I remember my first year like it was yesterday, and the help Alan offered me. I was a young physician, just out of residency. Of course I thought I knew everything, and of course my attitude was just a cover for the fact that I was terrified. It was a big-city hospital, with big-city demands. I was proud to get the job, but secretly I felt out of my depth. Alan saw right through my cocky attitude. He didn't try to change it. He didn't try to get me to confess my uncertainty. He simply offered his friendship. He was a quiet, steady presence. And when I had my first crisis—losing a patient I didn't expect to lose—it was Alan I turned to. Asking for help wasn't easy for me in those days, but Alan made it very easy to talk. He offered his views on life and death, which by the way I thought I had all squared away by then. His words helped me see that wherever we are and whatever we think we know, we're all still at the beginning of understanding life and death, a lesson I am drawing on again today in trying to understand this loss.

> Steven offers a very personal anecdote that reveals a lot about Alan's character and his personality and how he interacted with people. Steven describes exactly what Alan meant to him.

Our personal lives didn't intersect much. My family and I live in Evanston, and we spent most of our weekends at the lake. But Elaine, Garth, Terry—I feel as though I've known you all for years. Alan was so, so proud of you all. Every year there were new pictures of you in his office. He kept us posted on your most important activities. Garth, I still remember your dad telling us all about your balsa wood model airplanes and your feats of engineering. Terry, Alan shared with us your joy at getting your first horse and kept us abreast of your adventures. And Elaine, when he talked about you—which he did frequently—his whole face lit up. When my first child was born, Alan smiled, congratulated me, and quietly said, "This is the best thing that can ever happen to anyone." He knew, and he was right.

Alan was not a religious man, but I know he believed in love. I'm sure he wouldn't mind me quoting Paul's letter to the Corinthians: "If I have the gift of prophecy and can fathom all mysteries and all knowledge, and if I have a faith that can move mountains, but have not love, I am nothing." Alan had love, and we are all the richer for it.

Alan was a fine physician who fathomed the mysteries and knowledge of his profession, but it was his understanding of love that marked him as an extraordinary person.

> Steven admits he didn't know the family well, but he offers what he does know as a tribute to Alan's commitment to his family. The incidents he recalls are personal and specific and will be remembered by the family.

> A really nice little incident that shows Alan's values.

> Steven handles this very nicely. He acknowledges that Alan was not religious, but he justifies the use of scripture by showing its relevance to Alan's life and beliefs.

Weddings and Births

ENGAGEMENT ANNOUNCEMENT

(See also main entry *Announcement*, page 47.)

Engagements have traditionally been announced by the parents of the bride. As society has changed, so has etiquette, and today many different styles of engagement announcements are acceptable. Engagement announcements are often made before the wedding date is set and therefore include only the month or season of the planned wedding, not the date. Your engagement may be announced in a local newspaper, through cards or notes sent through the mail, or both.

LIKE THIS

PARENTS
ANNOUNCE

> Mr. and Mrs. Thomas Peters of Weldon, South Dakota, announce the engagement of their daughter, Marina Ann, to David Evan Morrison, son of Phyllis and James Morrison of Red Wing, Minnesota.
>
> The future bride graduated from the University of Minnesota with a bachelor of arts. She is employed as a marketing analyst at Jones Creative.
>
> The future groom received a bachelor of arts degree and a master of science degree from the University of Minnesota. He is employed as a teacher at the Greenwood School in St. Paul.
>
> A November wedding is planned, and the couple will live in St. Paul.

DIVORCED
PARENTS,
BRIDE'S
MOTHER
ANNOUNCES

> Mrs. June Stevens of Norman, Oklahoma, wishes to announce the engagement of her daughter, Carin Lee Murphy, to Simon Harrison, son of Mr. and Mrs. Bradley Harrison of Austin, Texas. Miss Stevens is also the daughter of Dr. William Murphy of Austin, Texas. The wedding will take place in December.

Alternatively, without titles . . .

> June Stevens of Norman, Oklahoma, wishes to announce the engagement of her daughter, Carin Lee Murphy, to Simon Harrison, son of Gail and Bradley Harrison of Austin, Texas. Ms. Stevens is also the daughter of William Murphy of Austin, Texas. The wedding will take place in December.

June and Derek Stevens and Dr. William and Colette Murphy announce the engagement of their daughter, Carin Lee Murphy, to Simon Harrison, son of Gail and Bradley Harrison of Texas.

The couple met at their alma mater, the University of Texas at Austin.

The future bride recently received a master of arts degree in biometrics from the University of Texas. Her fiancé is pursuing a master of arts degree in chemistry at Riverside University. Both are educators.

A November wedding is planned at the Church of Our Lady.

DIVORCED AND REMARRIED PARENTS, PARENTS AND STEPPARENTS ANNOUNCE

The engagement of Marina Ann Peters, daughter of Mrs. Thomas Peters and the late Mr. Peters, to David Evan Morrison, son of Mr. and Mrs. James Morrison of Red Wing, Minnesota, is announced by the bride's mother. A July wedding is planned.

WIDOWED PARENT ANNOUNCES

Mr. and Mrs. Robert Peters would like to announce the engagement of their niece, Marina Ann Peters, to Mr. David Evan Morrison, son of Mr. and Mrs. James Morrison, of Red Wing, Minnesota. Miss Peters is the daughter of the late Mr. and Mrs. Thomas Peters. A July wedding is planned.

BOTH PARENTS DECEASED (A CLOSE RELATIVE ANNOUNCES)

Marina Peters, a marketing analyst at Jones Creative, and David Morrison, a teacher at the Greenwood School, are planning an autumn wedding in the coming year. Ms. Peters is the daughter of Lori and Tom Peters of Weldon, South Dakota. Mr. Morrison is the son of Phyllis and James Morrison of Red Wing, Minnesota.

COUPLE ANNOUNCES

ANNOUNCING THAT AN ENGAGEMENT HAS BEEN BROKEN

If you are faced with the unhappy task of announcing that an engagement has been broken, be brief and to the point. Do not discuss the reason or reasons that the engagement was broken. You owe no one an explanation.

NEWSPAPER ANNOUNCEMENT

> The engagement of Victoria Simon and Michael Tasso has been broken by mutual consent.

ANNOUNCEMENT CARD

> Mr. and Mrs. Christopher Simon announce that the marriage of their daughter, Victoria, to Mr. Michael Tasso will not take place.

WEDDING INVITATION

(See also main entry *Invitation* on page 56.)

Traditionally the bride's parents have paid for the wedding and sent the invitations. As society has changed, so have wedding invitations, and many different styles of invitations are regularly used.

In addition to the invitation itself, your invitation package should include a response card and a self-addressed, stamped envelope, to make it easy for guests to RSVP. Some couples also include an at-home card to update guests on their contact information. For an example, see the box "At-Home Cards: A Tradition Revived" (page 128).

LIKE THIS

There are many acceptable formats for wedding invitations. Here are just a few. For examples of other family configurations, see Engagement Announcement (page 117).

FORMAL

MR. AND MRS. THOMAS PETERS
REQUEST THE HONOUR OF YOUR PRESENCE
AT THE MARRIAGE OF THEIR DAUGHTER
MARINA ANN
TO
MR. DAVID EVAN MORRISON
SATURDAY, THE NINTH OF JUNE
TWO THOUSAND AND TWELVE
AT FOUR O'CLOCK IN THE AFTERNOON
THE BIGELOW HOUSE
57 SMIT ROAD
WELDON, SOUTH DAKOTA
RECEPTION TO FOLLOW AT
THE VALLEY STREAM COUNTRY CLUB

LESS FORMAL

Jan and Thomas Peters
request the pleasure of your company
at the marriage of their daughter
Marina Peters
to David Morrison
Saturday, June 9, 2012
at 4 p.m.
The Bigelow House
57 Smit Road
Weldon, South Dakota
Reception to follow at the Valley Stream Country Club

**HOSTED BY
BOTH SETS OF
PARENTS**

MR. AND MRS. STEVEN WATANABE
AND
MR. AND MRS. KEVIN HOLDER
REQUEST THE HONOR OF YOUR PRESENCE
AT THE MARRIAGE OF THEIR CHILDREN
DANA ELISE AND PETER SEAN
SATURDAY, NOVEMBER 17, 2012
3:00 P.M.
THE BALLICOE MUSEUM
2856 ENDICOTT ROAD
RIVERTON, VERMONT
RECEPTION TO FOLLOW

Together with their families,
Marina Peters and David Morrison
invite you to join them
at the celebration of their marriage
Saturday, June 9, 2012
at 4 p.m.
The Bigelow House
57 Smit Road
Weldon, South Dakota
Reception to follow at the Valley Stream Country Club

Please join us
For a celebration of love
as
Madison Christina Lewis
and
Brian Carlos Thompson
Join their hands in holy matrimony
Friday, June 28, 2013
8 o'clock in the evening
Knox Presbyterian Church
Savannah, Georgia
Champagne and dessert reception to follow

RESPONSE CARD

> THE FAVOR OF A REPLY IS REQUESTED
> BEFORE THE FIRST OF JUNE

or

> PLEASE REPLY BEFORE THE FIRST OF JUNE
> M _____
> _____WILL ATTEND
> _____WILL NOT ATTEND

CIVIL UNION

> *Maria and Jon Kusnir*
> *and*
> *Victoria and James Anderson*
> *request the pleasure of your company*
> *at the Civil Union Ceremony of their sons*
> *Alexander Louis Kusnir*
> *and*
> *Matthew Peter Anderson*
> *on Saturday, the eighth of September*
> *two thousand and twelve*
> *at seven o'clock in the evening*
> *The George Club*
> *Greenville, South Carolina*

Jan Marie Parker and Linna M. Harrison invite
you to share in a
Commitment Ceremony
joining them as a couple
Saturday, the ninth of April
at one o'clock in the afternoon
The Crystal Lake Hotel
957 Crystal Lake Road
Charles, Wisconsin
Reception to immediately follow

RECALL OF INVITATION

If you have already sent out your invitations and find you have to post-pone the wedding, you can recall the invitation with a short message like the one below. There is no need for you to explain why you're recalling the invitation.

MR. AND MRS. THOMAS PETERS REGRET
THAT THEY ARE OBLIGED TO RECALL
THE INVITATIONS TO THE MARRIAGE OF
MS. MARINA PETERS AND MR. DAVID MORRISON
JUNE 9, 2012

Styling the Perfect Wedding Invitation

The wedding invitation is the first impression your guests will receive for your big day. Make it really count. This seemingly simple piece of card stock will introduce your friends and family to the style, the formality, and the personality behind your wedding. It will give them a sense of what to wear, what to gift, and what to expect from your celebration. So when it comes to choosing the perfect words, it's important to approach your invitation with the same sense of style you would treat your wedding as a whole.

For a classic, timeless affair your invitation should be issued by whomever is hosting the affair. There are slight variations in the way that you word your invitations, depending on where you will be tying the knot: in a house of worship (use "the honour of your presence") versus in a nonsecular venue (use "the pleasure of your company"). Dates and times are all spelled out in their entirety, as are city and state locations. Gifts and attire are generally not mentioned on traditional invitations, though exceptions can be made for black tie affairs. Here is the wording used for my own, formal wedding invitations:

> Mr. and Mrs. William McLucas request
> the honour of your presence
> as they celebrate the marriage of their daughter
> Abigail Dee
> to
> Mr. Tait Elliott Larson
> Saturday, the twenty-seventh of August
> two thousand five
> at five o'clock in the evening
> Old South Church
> Boston, Massachusetts

A response card is generally included in the wedding invitation, as are other pieces like a reception card noting the address of the reception.

For a more casual affair, many brides choose to break all of the rules and have a bit of fun with their invitation. Some choose to approach their wedding with a fun, humorous, or often sweet approach:

Boy met girl. Girl loved boy. The rest is history.
Please join us as we celebrate even more history in the making
with the marriage of
Abby McLucas to Tait Larson
Saturday, the 31st of August
at 5 o'clock
Old South Church
Boston, Massachusetts
dinner, dancing, and a midnight snack to follow
The Parker House

And some simply stick to a more relaxed variation of a traditional invitation:

Abby McLucas and Tait Larson
invite you to share in their celebration of marriage
Saturday, the 31st of August
at 5 o'clock
Old South Church
Boston, Massachusetts
a reception to follow at The Parker House

If you're going for that casual, fun, or silly approach, just make sure that all of the necessary details that the guest needs are included in your language! Think "who, what, where, and when" to frame the basics of your invitation—then sprinkle the rest on top.

Abby Larson is the founder of the popular wedding blog *Style Me Pretty* (www.stylemepretty.com).

At-Home Cards: A Tradition Revived

By Crane & Co.

The original purpose of the at-home card was to let guests know when the newlyweds would be back from their honeymoon (often a grand tour of Europe) and at which address they would be residing.

Couples still use them for such a purpose, but they are also used today to communicate new contact information. It is also a lovely way to present a bride's new name.

Included with the wedding invitation or marriage announcements, at-home cards are small enclosure cards that match the card stock, lettering style, and ink color of your invitations. In addition to the return-home date and the new address, many couples now include their phone numbers and e-mail addresses on their at-home cards.

The wording for at-home cards sent with announcements is different from the wording for at-home cards sent with the invitations. At-home cards sent with announcements show your names together as "Mr. and Mrs." since you are already married when they are sent. When sent with invitations, your names are not used since you are not yet married and cannot use "Mr. and Mrs."

While the principal purpose of at-home cards is to let people know your new address, when sent with announcements they can also let people know that you have chosen to continue to use your maiden name. Your name appears on the first line, followed by your husband's name on line two. The remainder of the card reads as it normally would. Since you could have presented yourself as "Mrs." but did not, it will be assumed that you are still using your maiden name.

At-home cards are not gift-request cards and should never be interpreted as such.

Instead, think of at-home cards like the change-of-address cards you might send when you move. They simply announce your new address and are a great convenience for anyone who wants to keep in touch with you—which will certainly give you a chance to use that new personalized stationery.

Mr. and Mrs. André Lucas Hildebrand

at home

after the first of September

———

Apartment No. 10

105 East Fifty-fifth Street

New York, New York 10021

212 555 1212

Premier stationery purveyor Crane & Co., Inc. has been dedicated to the art of classic correspondence for more than two centuries. The website is www.crane.com.

WEDDING TOAST

Toasts are often made at rehearsal dinners and wedding receptions. It is traditional for the best man and the maid of honor to make toasts, but at many events the floor is open and anyone is welcome to speak. The prospect of making a toast strikes fear into the hearts of many. With a little preparation, though, making a toast can be a very rewarding—and fun—way to honor someone special.

DO	DON'T
• Take the time to write the toast well in advance. This occasion means a lot to people, particularly the honorees. Don't wing it.	• Don't put off your preparations. Give yourself plenty of time to write a draft, rehearse it, and revise it if necessary. Your friends are worth it.
• Bring notes, if necessary. Don't read your notes word for word, but a few prompts on an index card can help you stay focused.	• Don't say anything that will make anyone uncomfortable. Gentle teasing is fine, but anything much beyond that is not.
• Introduce yourself, if necessary. If there are a lot of people at the event who don't know you, offer a quick introduction.	• Don't give the toast if you're very drunk. You'll embarrass yourself, the honorees, and the other guests, and it will all be recorded on video for everyone to see over and over again, forever.
• Keep it simple, and use your own words. It's fine to quote from a poem or something, but your toast will mean more to your friends if you speak in your own natural and sincere voice.	• Don't read your speech. It's fine to use an index card for a prompt, but you should practice enough, and be sober enough, that you don't have to read the toast word for word.
• Keep it brief. If you choose to tell a story, cut to the chase. It will be more enjoyable and more memorable if you keep it short and punchy.	
• Make sure the tone of your toast is consistent with the occasion and with the honorees' personalities.	
• Use humor judiciously. It's fine to share a laugh or smile around a memory, but don't go over the top and don't humiliate anyone.	
• Keep the focus on the honorees, not on yourself.	
• Rehearse. Allow yourself some time to practice. Rehearsing lets you hear if your toast sounds natural and good-natured, and it will prepare you to perform better at the event.	
• Remember to end your comments by actually proposing a toast to the honorees.	

WEDDING VOWS

Some couples feel that traditional wedding vows don't express exactly what they want to say at their wedding. They want something more personal that conveys their personalities and their feelings, so they write their own vows. Some adapt traditional wedding vows, whereas others write their own completely from scratch. The tips below will help you get started on yours.

DO	DON'T
• Be sure your officiant will allow you to use your own vows at the ceremony. Some houses of worship require you to use traditional vows. As a courtesy, send the officiant a copy of your vows before the wedding.	• Don't wing it. Leave yourself plenty of time to decide what you want to say, revise until you have the vows just right, and practice so that you're comfortable on the day.
• Work together, and be sure you both agree about what you want from your vows.	• Don't go on too long. Very long wedding vows can be tiresome to your guests. The vows should be a maximum of one minute long.
• Read through traditional vows from various traditions to get inspiration. It's a good starting place, and you may find that you like some of the traditional wording.	• Don't be too personal. Remember your vows are made in public, so don't mention private jokes, and don't reveal anything intimate.
• Read poetry books, books of quotations, websites, and song lyrics to find inspiration. Don't be afraid to borrow and patch together different sources.	
• Be yourself. Your vows don't have to be deadly serious or sound traditional—write something that truly expresses how you feel and that you will be comfortable saying.	
• Rehearse. You don't want to be stumbling over your vows or, even worse, forgetting them. Take time to memorize and practice them before the big day.	
• Time yourself. Be considerate of your audience, and be sure your vows aren't so long that people will find them tedious.	

LIKE THIS

Reading traditional and popular wedding vows is a good way to get started writing yours. Below are some you can sample from.

TRADITIONAL VOWS

I, _____, take you, _____, for my lawful wife/husband, to have and to hold from this day forward, for better, for worse, for richer, for poorer, in sickness and health, until death do us part.

. . .

I, _____, take you, _____, to be my husband/wife. I promise to be true to you in good times and in bad, in sickness and in health. I will love and honor you all the days of my life.

. . .

In the name of God, I, _____, take you, _____, to be my husband/wife, to have and to hold from this day forward, for better or worse, for richer or poorer, in sickness and health, to love and to cherish, until we are parted by death—this is my solemn vow.

. . .

In the presence of God and these our friends, I take thee to be my husband/wife, promising with Divine assistance to be unto thee a loving and faithful husband/wife so long as we both shall live.

POPULAR NON-TRADITIONAL VOWS

_____, I declare my love for you, I invite you to share my life as my husband/wife. I promise always to respect your needs, and to accept you as you are. I will be kind, unselfish, and trusting. I will work for a happy life for both of us.

. . .

_____, I want to be with you always just as you are. I choose you above all others, to share my life with me in marriage. I love you for yourself, and I want you to become all that you can be. I vow to honor this pledge as long as I live.

· · ·

_____, today I take you to be my husband/wife. Together we will create a home, becoming a part of one another. I vow to help create a life that we can cherish, inspiring your love for me and mine for you. I vow to be honest, loving, and truthful, and to love you as you are and not as I wish you to be, and to grow old by your side as your love and best friend.

· · ·

I _____, take you, _____, as my spouse, my lifelong partner. I will do everything I can to maintain our love. I will talk to you and listen to you. I will give to you and I will take from you. Your success and happiness will be mine.

· · ·

I pledge to remain your companion and friend. I promise to be with you always, to care for you, and to love you no matter how far apart we may be. I will be with you in your heart and keep you safely in mine. When you are happy, I will be happy with you. When you are sad, I will make you smile. I will encourage you and stand with you as your friend and husband/wife. I promise to give you love, honesty, trust, and commitment and, in general, keep your life interesting as we grow old together.

Wedding Poems

Many couples choose to have a poem read or recited at their wedding. Whether the tone is romantic, serious, playful, or a combination of these, a poem can express the couple's love for one another and uplift the guests at the wedding. Here are some popular poems for weddings.

"Touched by an Angel," Maya Angelou
"How Do I Love Thee?," Elizabeth Barrett Browning
"The Good-Morrow," John Donne
"Invitation to Love," Paul Lawrence Dunbar

"Resignation," Nikki Giovanni

"When two people are at one in their inmost hearts," I Ching

"Your love is from life's great mystery," I Ching

"You are my husband, you are my wife," Inuit love song, traditional

"May the road rise to meet you," Irish blessing traditional

"Beauty That Is Never Old," James Weldon Johnson

"Fidelity," D. H. Lawrence

"The Passionate Shepherd to His Love," Christopher Marlowe

"More Than," Ogden Nash

"May the sun bring you new energy by day," Native American wedding ceremony, traditional

"Love's Coming," John Shaw Neilson

Sonnet XVII ("I don't love you as if you were the salt-rose"), Pablo Neruda

"The Married Lover," Coventry Patmore

"As Once the Winged Energy of Delight," Rainer Maria Rilke

"A Birthday," Christina Georgina Rossetti

"The Minute I Heard My First Love Story," Rumi

Sonnet 116 ("Let me not to the marriage of true minds admit impediments"), William Shakespeare

"Love's Philosophy," Percy Bysshe Shelley

"Wedding Prayer," Robert Louis Stevenson

"These I Can Promise," Mark Twain

For the full text of these poems and for more suggestions, visit www. howtowriteanything.com.

WEDDING ANNOUNCEMENT

Wedding announcements are typically published in the newspaper and may also be printed and mailed to people who did not attend the wedding.

Some newspapers prefer to write the announcement from content you provide them; others will publish the copy you write.

Traditionally, the bride's parents have made the announcement, but changes in society have made other formats acceptable. For more contemporary styles that you can adapt for your wedding announcements, see Engagement Announcement (page 117).

> Mr. and Mrs. Barton M. Carver have the honor of announcing the marriage of their daughter Andrea Louise to Mr. Daniel Jacob Lewis, Saturday, the tenth of July, Two Thousand Ten. St. Andrew Church, Pleasantville, Montana.

BRIDE'S PARENTS ANNOUNCE

> Ms. Andrea Louise Carver and Mr. Daniel Jacob Lewis are pleased to announce their marriage Saturday, the tenth of July, Two Thousand Ten. St. Andrew Church, Pleasantville, Montana.

COUPLE ANNOUNCES

> Andrea Louise Carver and Mr. Daniel Jacob Lewis announce we were married Saturday, the tenth of July, Two Thousand Ten in Pleasantville, Montana.

WEDDING CONGRATULATIONS

When you attend a wedding or receive a wedding announcement, it's time to write a note of congratulations to the happy couple. Even if you choose to use a commercial greeting card, it's important to write at least a few lines to personalize your message.

A wedding is a major milestone in a person's life and deserves a much more substantial recognition than an e-mail. Buy a greeting card or use good-quality notepaper to write your message.

DO	DON'T
• Speak from the heart. Your sincere sentiments are more important than poetic language. • Express your happiness for the couple. • Express your fondness and regard for the couple. • Say something optimistic about the future. • Consider choosing an appropriate quotation. Including a quotation isn't a substitute for expressing your own feelings, but if you find something appropriate, by all means use it. • Keep your comments appropriate to your relationship with the readers. If you don't know them well, your note should not be excessively personal.	• Don't offer advice. This is a very personal thing to do, and it's best left to close family members or for face-to-face conversations.

> Dear Michele and Alex,
>
> Congratulations on your wedding! I am just thrilled for you. I've never seen anyone as happy as you two are when you're together, and I've never known anyone who deserved that happiness as much as you do.
>
> I wish you many more years of happiness, fulfillment, and love.
>
> My best always,
>
> Frank

WEDDING THANK-YOU

(See also main entry *Thank-You Note* on page 70.)

You've received a gift at a wedding shower, at the wedding itself, or after the event. Now it's time to say thank you. A thank-you note for a wedding gift can be brief, but it should be warm, sincere, and personalized.

Your wedding thank-yous should always be handwritten and sent through the postal mail. E-mail is simply too impersonal for this important communication.

DO	DON'T
• Keep careful track of who gave you what. At a shower, ask a friend to keep a list for you. Collect the gift tags and cards immediately after the wedding and make notes on them. The time around the wedding will be very busy, and wedding gifts may continue to come in for up to a year after the date. It's a good idea to create a file or special notebook to keep track of gifts and givers and to make a note of which thank-yous you have sent.	• Don't send your thank-yous via e-mail. Your note can be brief, but you must make the effort of handwriting it.
• Send your thank-you notes promptly. Build time into your schedule for writing thank-yous.	• Don't write your notes in advance. Your thank-you should be a personal response to the gift and the kindness of the giver. It's fine for your note to be brief, but when someone goes to the trouble and expense of buying you a gift, he deserves a thoughtful and personal thank-you.
• Make sure you get the names right. You may have received gifts from people you don't know well, such as friends of your parents. Ensure you have the correct spelling of their names when you write your thank-you.	• Don't use the impersonal, assembly-line approach to thank-you notes, even if you have a lot to get through. Try to avoid writing essentially the same message to everyone; people will hear it in your writing. Approach each note as a message to a person you know and care about.
• Write several at a time. If you have a lot of thank-you notes to send, tackle the project in stages. If you write five to seven thank-you messages every evening, you'll finish them much faster than if you plan to do them all at once and keep putting it off.	• Don't mention the amount of the check—it's tacky. Instead, thank the reader for her generosity. You might also let her know how you intend to spend the money if you're going to use it to buy something special.
• Remember to say "thank you" in your note. Make the message explicit.	
• Be specific about what the gift means to you. Describe how you'll use it, why it was especially needed, or how it made you feel. Personalizing your thank-you this way creates a true connection with your reader.	
• Write in your own voice. Your thank-yous don't have to be formal. It's much nicer if they're friendly and personal.	

LIKE THIS

Traditionally, the bride wrote the thank-you note for a wedding gift, mentioned the groom's thoughts in the note, and signed the note herself. More relaxed social norms mean that either partner—or both—can write and sign the note.

TO PARENTS

Dear Mom and Dad,

Avi and I want to thank you for everything you've done for us. We were floored by the generosity of your gift, and we are so grateful.

The last few months have been so hectic, but you were always there for us. We really appreciate being able to turn to you for advice and common sense when everything seemed to be in chaos. I don't know what we would have done without your support and love.

Thank you for everything.

Love,

Marina

TO RELATIVES

Dear Aunt Patty and Uncle Dave,

Thank you very much for the beautiful pewter mugs. We are so touched that you would entrust us with this family heirloom, and we promise to take good care of them for the next generation. It was wonderful to see you at the wedding. I'm just sorry we didn't have more time together, though I suppose that's to be expected. We're moving into the new place next week, and I'll give you a call then.

Thank you again for everything.

Much love,

Connor

Dear Carl and Ingrid,

Allen and I thank you so much for the check you sent as a wedding gift. We are saving for a down payment on a new car, and with your gift we are nearly there. We'll swing by one day soon and take you for a drive!

Thank you again.

Love,

Marina

FOR A CHECK
OR CASH

Dear Mr. and Mrs. Ziegler,

Thank you so much for the antique clock you sent us as a wedding gift. It's beautiful, we both love it, and it looks lovely on the piano. I'm very sorry that you couldn't attend the wedding—we missed seeing you there. We'll be home next week and will be in touch.

Again, thank you for your kindness.

Love,

Marina

TO SOMEONE
WHO DID NOT
ATTEND THE
WEDDING

Dear Mr. and Mrs. Grose,

Thank you very much for the beautiful coffee set. It was very thoughtful of you, and Marina and I will enjoy using it. It was very nice to see you at the wedding. Thank you for coming and helping us celebrate.

Best wishes,

David Morrison

TO SOMEONE
YOU DON'T
KNOW WELL

OTHER WEDDING THANK-YOUS

TO MAID OR MATRON OF HONOR

Dear Andrea,

What would I ever do without you? Thank you to the most wonderful maid of honor anyone ever had!

You were a lifesaver more than once during this whole process. You kept me sane during the fittings, you calmed me down through many little crises, and you made sure everything was just right on the day. I can't thank you enough.

I'm very lucky to have a friend like you, Andrea. Thank you for being there for me.

Much love,

Marina

TO BEST MAN

Dear Rob,

Thank you for everything you did for our wedding. The bachelor party was great, and Marina wants me to thank you for making sure I was coherent on the day. You handled all the details perfectly during the wedding, and it was great to know I could rely on you absolutely. Your support was incredible.

It was an honor to have you by my side on my wedding day. You are a great friend and I can't thank you enough.

Love,

David

Dear Kimberly,

Thank you so much for being my bridesmaid. I appreciate your patience and care throughout the long process—the dress selection, the fittings, the rehearsals, and the very nervous bride. Your support made everything much easier. You looked just beautiful in the dress, and I was proud and touched to have you with me.

Thank you for being such a wonderful friend.

Love,

Marina

TO BRIDESMAIDS

Dear Ron,

Thank you for being there for me on my wedding day. You did a great job keeping everything under control and helping the guests. My mom thought you were very charming, by the way.

Marina and I are grateful for your help, and I am proud to call you my friend. Thank you again.

See you soon,

David

TO GROOMSMAN OR USHER

BIRTH ANNOUNCEMENT

(See also main entry *Announcement* on page 47.)

Birth announcements are typically sent by parents as soon as possible after their baby's birth, although it is acceptable to wait as long as six months. It's a good idea to get a head start on birth announcements and begin to prepare them even before the baby arrives.

Traditional birth announcements include the birth date, weight, and length of the baby. Some parents also include the time of the birth. Most parents also include a photo of the baby.

Gretchen and David Hardman announce the birth of their son
Max Henry
August 12, 2013
8 pounds, 7 ounces
20 inches

Callista Montgomery and John Sheehan
are pleased to announce the birth of
Emily Joy Montgomery Sheehan
June 6, 2013
6:09 p.m.
7 pounds, 11 ounces
18 inches

A very simple birth announcement without the vital statistics is also perfectly acceptable.

We welcome with love Elizabeth Catherine Hunter
—Mary and Leo

Some parents choose to include elder siblings in the announcement.

Raina, Jacob, Lauren, and Sam Parker
Joyfully welcome
Oliver Charles
February 27, 2013
1:22 a.m.
7 pounds, 3 ounces
18 inches

Claudia and Jordan Cohn are proud to welcome
David's baby sister
Ruth Elaine Cohn
who was born on December 7, 2012
weight: 8 pounds, 6 ounces
length: 18 inches

ADOPTION ANNOUNCEMENT

Adoption announcements are handled very much like birth announcements, although it is acceptable to wait longer than six months to send the announcement, if you wish. Don't send an adoption announcement before the adoption has been legally finalized.

Adoption announcements generally include the "gotcha date"—the date the child is brought into the new family—as well as the child's birth date. They may also include the country of the child's birth if the child was born abroad.

Nora and Matt Rose
are thrilled to announce the arrival of
María Luisa
born in Guatemala on July 12, 2011
welcomed home on November 1, 2012

Tim Posner and Stephen Holt
are proud and happy to announce the arrival of
Laura June
born on January 29, 2013
welcomed home on May 1, 2013

BABY SHOWER INVITATION

(See also main entry *Invitation* on page 56.)

Traditional baby shower invitations provide the name(s) of the hostess(es); the name of the mother-to-be; and the date, time, and place of the party.

Join us as we honor
Thalia Christensen
with a Baby Shower
on May 18 at 2:00 p.m.
Jennifer's Home
507 Homewood Drive
Forest City, Montana

Given with love by
Jennifer Frantzen and Tracee Norling
RSVP to Tracee by May 15
888.222.1111

Please come to a Baby Shower
Date: Sunday, June 27, 2013
Time: 2 o'clock in the afternoon
Place: Janet Lee's House, 266 Hawser Street
Guest of Honor: Joanna Wong

Regrets only to Miriam Green
(888) 222-1111

Showers given after the baby is born may include the baby's name and may even list the baby as the guest of honor.

A shower for Sophie!

You're invited to a shower
in honor of her mother
Esme Martin
on April 23 at 1 p.m.
1887 Glencoe Road
Laramie, Wyoming

Sarah and Jenn
RSVP to Sarah by April 19
800.111.2222

Sometimes there are special gift requests for a baby shower. The mother may want to start a library for her baby and would like the guests to bring their favorite children's book. Some mothers may prefer a gift card to an actual gift. It is not appropriate to put these requests on the invitation itself. Either enclose a brief and polite note with the invitation or phone your guests and let them know.

BABY GIFT THANK-YOU

(See also main entry *Thank-You Note* on page 70.)

You've received a gift at a baby shower or after the arrival of your darling. Now it's time to say thank you. A thank-you note for a baby gift can be brief, but it should be warm, sincere, and personalized.

A thank-you for a baby gift should always be handwritten and sent through the postal mail. E-mail is simply too impersonal for this kind of communication.

DO	DON'T
• Keep careful track of who gave you what. At a shower, ask a friend to keep a list for you. At home, find a place to keep a running list of gifts as they arrive. This is a busy time—don't rely on memory alone to keep track of gifts and givers.	• Don't send your thank-yous via e-mail. Your note can be brief, but you must make the effort of handwriting it.
• Send your thank-you notes promptly. It's both polite and practical—once the baby arrives, you're not going to have a lot of extra time on your hands.	• Don't use the impersonal, assembly-line approach to thank-you notes, even if you have a lot to get through. Try to avoid writing essentially the same message to everyone; people will hear it in your writing. Approach each note as a message to a person you know and care about.
• Write several at a time. If you have a lot of thank-you notes to send, tackle the project in stages. If you set aside an hour to write thank-you notes every evening, you'll finish them much faster than if you plan to do them all at once and keep putting it off.	• Don't mention the amount of the gift card or gift certificate. Simply thank the reader for her generosity. If you know what you intend to buy with the card, it's nice to share that information with the reader.
• Remember to say "thank you." Make the message explicit.	
• Be specific about what the gift means to you. Describe how you'll use it, why it was especially needed, or how it made you feel. Personalizing your thank-you this way creates a true connection with your reader.	
• Write in your own voice. Your thank-yous don't have to be formal. It's much nicer if they're friendly and personal.	

LIKE THIS

Dear Sarah,

Thank you so much for the beautiful baby quilt—I just love it. The colors are so pretty and soft. I put it on the crib right away, and I can't wait to wrap the baby in it.

It was lovely to see you, as always. Thank you for helping make my shower so special.

Love,

Caitlyn

Dear Judith-Anne,

Thank you very much for the books. It was a very thoughtful gift, and I appreciate all the care you put into it. I've enjoyed reading through all of them. I know Patrick will love them, and we will always think of you when we read them.

I loved seeing you at the shower. Thank you so much for coming! You always make everyone smile.

Love,

Renate

Dear Wendy,

Thank you for the natural baby products. I've been so careful with what I've put on me and in me during the pregnancy, it's wonderful to have pure and safe things for when the baby comes. I want to learn more about this from you. Thank you again for the thoughtful and useful gift.

And thank you for coming to the shower. It's always fun to spend time with you!

Love,

Alana

Dear Shaoyan,

A deluxe pedicure—what an incredibly thoughtful gift! I haven't even seen my feet in months, it seems, and will be so lovely to have the poor things massaged and pampered. Thank you so much. You can't imagine how much I'm looking forward to this.

Thank you also for coming to the shower. I'm so glad you got to meet my sisters. It meant a lot to me to have you there.

Love,

Catie

Dear Eileen,

What darling dresses! Thank you very much. What a brilliant idea, to buy something for when she's a little older. She'll grow fast, and I'll need them before I know it. That was very thoughtful. I am so looking forward to dressing her up in these pretty things.

And thank you for coming to the shower. It was such fun seeing you again. I hope we'll be able to stay in closer touch.

Love,

Fiona

Dear Stephanie, Renee, Marilyn, and Janet,

Thank you very much for the gift card. We are really bowled over and so excited. There are so many things we need, and your generous gift means we can really stock the nursery. We're so touched. Thank you.

It's wonderful to have such kind friends.

Love,

Elizabeth

Personal Business

COMPLAINT

I t seems as though there are always plenty of things to complain about: products that fall apart, airline delays, rude cashiers. The list goes on and on. Writing a complaint message allows you to bring the problem to light and request the appropriate remedy.

It's important to understand the difference between venting and complaining. In the context of a complaint message, they are not the same thing. Venting is expressing the emotion caused by the problem. Complaining is the tactical, dispassionate process of letting people know what happened and requesting a fix. Vent, by all means, but don't do it in your complaint message!

A complaint may be a letter or an e-mail. A letter is more formal and may get more attention than an e-mail, but that depends on the organization. Some companies have feedback forms on their websites where customers can offer comments.

Introduction

The **purpose** of a complaint is to inform the reader about something unsatisfactory. You may also ask for a remedy, such as a refund, a replacement, or even an apology. The **reader** of a complaint may be the person

MODEL OUTLINE

A message of complaint should be concise, brief, and focused.
Opening: Let the reader know up front you are writing about a problem about a specific product or service. State that you are hoping for a remedy.
Middle: Calmly relate the facts about what happened and what its consequences were for you.
Conclusion: Restate your request for a remedy, and suggest that a mutually satisfactory solution is best for both parties. Thank your reader. Let her know the best way to get in touch with you, and give her a deadline.

who caused the problem in the first place or—more likely—someone in a large company who might be on a different continent from the culprit. Show some consideration for your reader, and be clear and rational in your complaint. State the issue clearly and without rage. It's not just a matter of courtesy, although that should be enough. If you blow your stack and abuse your reader, you're less likely to get the remedy you're asking for. It's very important to **brainstorm** all the content for this kind of message. If you're upset about something that's happened, you're very likely to overlook important information. Even if you start your process by writing a draft, take the time to think out everything you need to say.

Organize your complaint so that it's easy for the reader to follow. The Model Outline can help you structure your message. You should plan on writing more than one **draft** of your message and going through at least one round of **revision**. You're very unlikely to do it perfectly the first time around. Your first draft will likely be too long, and it may include extraneous details that the reader really doesn't need. Ask a friend or colleague to proofread your draft to make sure your tone is appropriate, the description is concise, the remedy is clear, and the complaint is free of typos and misspellings.

DO	DON'T
• Direct your complaint to the right person, if you can find her. If you write to a specific person, you'll have a better chance of getting a reply and getting the appropriate action taken.	• Don't write the message when you're still very angry. Take notes when the information is still fresh in your mind, but cool down before you write.
• Be very clear about your objective. Focus on what you want to accomplish.	• Don't display excessive anger. When you lose your cool in a complaint letter, it's much easier for the reader to dismiss you as a crank. Stay calm and professional, and keep your objective firmly in mind. Vent to your family or friends, not in this letter.
• Provide specific details about your complaint. What happened? When?	
• State the consequences to you. Did you miss a half day of work waiting around for the service person who never showed up? Did your daughter cut herself on the badly designed oven door? Did you miss taking your medication because your bag was lost? Say so.	• Don't use abusive language, ever, even if you really feel like it. No matter how angry or frustrated you are, there's never any excuse to be rude.
• Keep calm and be polite. If you're writing a complaint, chances are you're not in the best frame of mind. But you must be polite. If you're irrational and abusive, your reader will be less likely to take your complaint seriously.	• Don't use an accusatory tone. The person reading your letter is likely not the person who made the mistake, so continually harping on what "you" did wrong is not productive.
• Be brief and concise. Cool down to the point where you can state what happened and focus on the important things. It may be emotionally satisfying to you to tell the whole story, but pare your message down to just what your reader needs to know.	• Don't be sarcastic or insulting. Your tone should be firm and serious. You'll be taken more seriously if you can keep the snark under control.
• Say something nice if you can. If you've been a loyal customer for years, say so. If you're happy with another of the company's products, say so. Doing so improves your credibility and will make your reader less defensive.	• Don't hurl general insults at the company or the industry. Your message should focus on your specific situation only and on the remedy you're requesting. Ranting about the generally awful state of affairs won't do you any good and could actually hurt your case.
• If you want something as a compensation or remedy, say so. Do you want a refund, credit to your account, coupon, miles, an apology, a replacement? Think about what would be reasonable, and ask for it.	

DO (CONTINUED)

- Be flexible. Ask for the remedy you prefer, but express your willingness to find a mutually agreeable solution to the problem.
- Include copies of any documentation you have related to the complaint: photos of the defective item and the damage it caused, copies of relevant correspondence, medical bills, and so on.
- Set a deadline for response. Make sure it's reasonable. Providing a deadline suggests there will be follow-up action if you don't hear from your reader.
- Remember, the person who reads your complaint is almost never the party who created the problem. Put yourself in her position, and don't give her a hard time. Think back about your objective and how to accomplish it.

NOT LIKE THIS . . .

To Whom It May Concern:

In July of this year, I applied for a Jackson's credit card in the store. My application was approved, and I was given a temporary pass to use until my credit card arrived by mail. I used this pass several times. However, my credit card never arrived, nor did a statement.

Last Tuesday I received an automated voice mail message from Jackson's requesting I call back about my account. When I did so, the representative I talked to could not find my account. After much back-and-forth, he told me that he was in the **bankruptcy department** (!!!!) and might not have access to my records. He gave me another number to call.

I called this number and was immediately put into an automated menu. It kept asking me for my account number, which of course I did not have because **I never received my card or my statement**. There was NO WAY to get to a representative directly off this menu. Eventually I was connected with a representative. When he picked up the line, he said, "Account number, please?" I gave him my name and explained to him what had happened. He then ASKED ME FOR MY NAME, although I had just given it to him. I gave it to him again, and eventually he was able to find a record of my account. He asked me to confirm the billing address. I gave him my address: 1437 Wilson Street, Sheldon, MI. He told me that was not the address you had on file and asked if there could be another address. I said no, that I had lived here for twenty years. He then repeated that was not the address you had on file. I asked him what address he had. He replied that he could not give it to me. I asked to talk to a supervisor. We went back and forth for a while, and he finally told me the address you had on file for me was simply "Wilson Street, Sheldon, MI." How absurd! I'm the only person who lives on Wilson Street? Who even thinks that's a real address? What idiots are doing your data entry? I gave him my correct address, and he entered it in the system. He told me you had been sending my statement to that address, which of course DOESN'T EXIST.

I then asked if I could pay the account in full with him. He said no, there was another department for that, and gave me THE EXACT SAME PHONE NUMBER I HAD JUST DIALED. I told him that. He repeated that I had to call the number again. I told him about the infuriating menu. He said just press "pound" and I would be connected directly with a representative.

Well, I did that, and guess what—I was NOT connected to a representative. I had to sit through the whole stupid menu again. I paid my bill and I am keeping my fingers crossed the payment was processed correctly so I don't have to spend another hour on the phone with your store.

I sincerely hope this matter is resolved. It TERRIFIES me that incompetent people like this can **affect my credit rating**. I would appreciate it if you would confirm with me that this matter has been resolved correctly.

Sincerely,

Erin Lellyveld

Easy there. It was a dumb mistake, but being insulting won't do any good and could undermine your position.

Poor Erin. We've all had customer service nightmares, so her anger is very understandable. But she's going on too long and providing too much detail. It's not clear yet what she wants from her reader. She's just venting.

The saga continues. Erin needs to calm down and focus on what she really wants. She begins to hint at it here, but she should make it more explicit, earlier in the letter.

At last Erin makes her request, but it is not very explicit, and she does not give a deadline. She hasn't made it very clear to the reader why she's writing.

. . . LIKE THIS

To Whom It May Concern:

In July of this year, I applied for a Jackson's credit card in the store and was issued a temporary pass, which I used several times. There have since been several serious record-keeping errors on my new account. I am writing to request written confirmation of the following:

1. My latest payment (October 3) has been received and credited to my account.
2. My account is in good standing.
3. You have my correct address on the account.

On October 3, I received an automated voice mail message from Jackson's. I called back and spoke to a representative who told me you have an incomplete address on file for my account and had been sending bills to this nonexistent address. Therefore, my account had gone past due.

The bad address was the result of a careless data entry error, and I find it extremely disturbing that my credit rating might have been threatened by such sloppy work.

In addition, it took me a full hour to resolve this problem, because Jackson's phone menus are so difficult and cumbersome. Moreover, the customer service representative I talked to, although courteous, was poorly trained and inefficient.

I have been a credit card member of Jackson's for only four months, and I am extremely disappointed in the quality of your customer service.

Please provide written confirmation of items 1–3 above by Friday, October 30. Thank you.

Sincerely,

Erin Lellyveld

Erin has reined in her anger enough to make a very clear and explicit request of her reader.

Erin has had to leave out a lot of details. Doing so can be a hard decision, but Erin has her eye on achieving her objective rather than venting about her bad experience.

Instead of describing the scene blow by blow, Erin condenses it here.

Erin finds a way to express her displeasure without being abusive.

Erin provides a deadline and thanks the reader for his help.

MORE EXAMPLES

Premier Airlines
Customer Service:

I am writing to complain about very poor baggage service and to request an award of 1,000 frequent flyer miles to compensate me for my experience.

On July 8, I was booked on flight 678 from LGA to MCI. Because of weather delays, my bag and I ended up on different flights. I understood my bag might arrive at MCI later in the day.

On arrival at MCI, I was given a phone number to check on my bag's arrival. I called this number eight times between 4:00 and 11:30 p.m., and there was never any answer. I called again at 8:00 the next morning and was told my bag had already been picked up for delivery. When the bag finally arrived—at 3:00 that afternoon—the driver told me he had picked it up at 2:00. Apparently my bag had been sitting there since 4:30 the previous day.

It would have been easy for me to return to the airport and pick up the bag, had I known it was there. Instead, the desk was evidently not staffed and then gave me inaccurate information. As a result, I was without fresh clothes and needed medication for over 24 hours.

I believe that 1,000 frequent flyer miles is a modest request given the degree of distress this incident has caused. Please respond by close of business Friday, August 9. Thank you.

Sincerely,

Molly Lake

Agriplex, Inc.
Customer Service:

I am writing to complain about quality control on one of your products, to request a full refund, and to request further compensation.

On March 3, I opened a bag of your Frozen Vegetable Medley and found a potato bug—not a potato, a POTATO BUG—embedded in the vegetables. I am attaching a photograph. I understand it's only a bug, but

I think you'll agree it's a truly disgusting one, and finding it was shocking and upsetting.

I would like a full refund of the purchase price (receipt attached) and some coupons to compensate me for this experience. (Please do NOT send coupons for Vegetable Medley—I don't think my heart could take it.)

Thank you,

Malika Johnson

Three Keys to a Successful Complaint Letter

Companies want happy customers, and most will respond favorably to a well-written complaint letter. These three tips will help you cut through the emotion and write a letter that gets results.

- Be brief. Tell just enough of the story that your reader will understand what happened. Don't vent.

- Be courteous. Use a businesslike tone, and never be rude or abusive.

- Ask for exactly what you want. Don't assume your reader knows what you would like as compensation. Spell it out for her.

LETTER TO A NEIGHBOR

The pen is mightier than the sword.

—*Edward George Earle Bulwer-Lytton, English writer and politician*

Good fences make good neighbors, but good communication helps, too. You may want to write to a neighbor with a complaint about a problem—like noise, overhanging limbs, or misbehaving pets—or to let them know about a potential disruption. Whatever the reason, writing a careful and diplomatic message can go a long way toward keeping peace in the neighborhood.

Introduction

The **purpose** of a letter to a neighbor might be to discuss a problem like noise or to notify him of an upcoming event. A secondary purpose is to preserve your relationship with the neighbor, and that goal should be in your mind as you write your letter. No matter how inconsiderate your neighbor might have been, you gain nothing by making him your enemy, and you stand to lose a lot. It's very important to keep your **reader** in mind as you work on this letter. Try hard to put yourself in his position. How will he react to your message? How can you craft your message to make the best possible impression? Even if you are complaining, remember your goal is to solve the problem, not to tell your neighbor that he's a jerk. As you **brainstorm**, consider what information might persuade your neighbor to cooperate with you. The Model Outline suggests a strategy for **organizing** your letter. Plan to go through more than one **draft** of this message, especially if you're angry or frustrated. As you draft, focus on keeping your tone civil. It's a good idea to show others your draft before you send it. **Revise** to ensure the letter is clear and courteous.

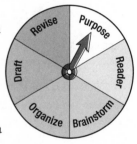

MODEL OUTLINE

A letter to a neighbor should be brief and courteous.
Opening: If there's a chance your neighbor doesn't know you, identify yourself and let her know where you live. Briefly state the reason you're writing.
Middle: Briefly and courteously explain the issue you're writing about. If your letter is a complaint, let your reader know the impact her behavior is having on you. Propose a reasonable remedy to the problem.
Conclusion: Finish your message on a note of goodwill, by thanking your neighbor and looking forward to a resolution of the problem.

DO	DON'T
• Assume the best. You may feel your neighbors are the rudest people on earth, but they may be completely astonished that their behavior is bothering you. You'll likely get a better result if you give them the benefit of the doubt.	• Don't accuse or attack your neighbors. Your letter should be calm, factual, and cooperative. If you take an aggressive approach, you will likely put your neighbors on the defensive, causing them to become entrenched.
• Check any applicable laws and rules before you write. Whose responsibility is it to trim those branches? Are you really sure where the property line is? The point here is not to rub your neighbor's nose in it, but simply to be sure you're on solid ground before you write.	• Don't exaggerate. State the extent of the problem and no more.
	• Don't be histrionic. Don't say your neighbors are ruining your life when they're really just annoying you. It's easy to dismiss a complaint that's overdramatic.

DO (CONTINUED)	**DON'T** (CONTINUED)
• Explain your perspective, and state facts. If you're writing about something that annoys you, let your neighbors know exactly how their actions are affecting you. Does their noise wake up your children late at night? Do the dropping pine needles kill your tomato plants? Calmly let them know how things are affecting you. • Be cooperative. Suggest ways to solve the problem. Make yourself available to discuss it in person.	• Don't start by threatening. Don't threaten to call the police or file a lawsuit in your first communication with your neighbors. Give them a chance to respond to an initial cordial request. Needless to say, you should never threaten any illegal action. • Don't make threats you don't intend to follow up on. Making empty threats tells your neighbors you're not serious and gives them license to ignore you.

Brainstorming Notes

———————•———————

Brainstorm your content before you write your draft. Get it all down on paper first, and then select what you want to use.

Alex's drumming is driving us CRAZY!

He WAITS until they leave the house to start up—sneaky.

He leaves the window open.

I work at home. Can't use earplugs, because I need to be on the phone. Why the hell should I use earplugs in my own house?

He keeps Talia awake at night—her bedtime is 8:30.

It's illegal to make noise after 8:00 p.m.—I looked up the noise code.

You need to say NO to that kid once in a while. He's going to be a monster of a teenager if you don't.

NOT LIKE THIS . . .

This is a very accusatory and emotional opening, which Joann and Martin will likely find offensive. Holly needs to get her emotions under control before she sends this message.

"Deafening" is probably a little hyperbolic and dramatic.

Threatening to call the police about someone's kid is not the way to begin this discussion. Holly is very upset, and she's allowing her feelings to shape the note in a way that's not constructive.

Dear Joann and Martin,

Alex's drumming is out of control. I'm not sure if you're aware how much he plays, or how loud, because a lot of it happens when you're at work. He cranks the music, opens the windows, and just lets rip.

As you know, I work at home, and the noise is deafening. It's impossible to concentrate. I've tried working with earplugs in, but obviously I can't take phone calls while wearing earplugs. Talia's bedroom is on the west side of the house, and when he plays after 8:30 he keeps her awake. This has to stop immediately.

If we can't resolve this amicably, I will be forced to call the sheriff and have Alex cited the next time he starts up. I really can't stand this anymore.

Thanks,

Holly

Holly hints that Joann and Martin are bad parents, or that Alex is a bad kid, or both. It may all be true, but she's not going to enlist any support this way.

It sounds as though Holly thinks Alex is being obnoxious on purpose.

This message is quite confrontational. The neighbors will have a lot of fence-mending to do just to get past this note, even before they begin working on the noise problem.

. . . LIKE THIS

Holly avoids blaming Alex for being inconsiderate.

Holly makes the point that Alex is drumming when his parents aren't home, without being accusatory.

Dear Joann and Martin,

Alex's drumming has become a bit of a noise problem for us, and I'm hoping we can discuss ways to solve it.

I'm sure Alex has no idea how the sound carries. It's quite loud in the afternoons after school, and it makes it hard for me to concentrate on my work. Talia's bedroom is on the west side of the house, and when Alex plays after 8:30 the noise keeps her awake.

Could we brainstorm about how to solve this? I think it would help a lot if he could keep his win-

Holly soft-pedals the problem in the beginning, as a way to ease into the topic. She opens her message with a suggestion that they all collaborate on a solution.

Instead of saying that Alex keeps Talia awake, Holly says *the noise* keeps her awake. This is a subtle difference but one that might make the neighbors feel less defensive.

dow shut while he's playing. Please give me a call at 626.888.1111 so we can work this out.

Thanks,

Holly

> Holly makes a concrete suggestion about how to solve the problem, without blaming anyone. She makes herself available to discuss the solution.

MORE EXAMPLES

Bob—

Would it be possible for you to wait to put out your garbage till Tuesday night for collection Wednesday morning? When it sits out from Sunday onward, the raccoons get into it and throw stuff around. Yesterday I saw a coyote in broad daylight rummaging through it.

I know your schedule is crazy, but I'm concerned about attracting wild animals.

Thanks,

Alan

Hi Caren and Joshua—

I hope all's well with you.

You may not be aware of this, but Lucy starts barking in the morning when you leave for work and keeps it up all day long with only a few breaks. Because she's shut in the sunroom and I'm home all day with the twins, I can't get away from it, and it's driving me crazy.

There must be a solution for this. Maybe Lucy needs a friend to keep her company or more space to patrol. Please give me a call so we can figure out what to do.

Thanks so much,

Heather

NOTIFYING A NEIGHBOR ABOUT A FUTURE DISRUPTION

If you're planning a party or other event that might cause disruption in the neighborhood, it's courteous to notify the neighbors in advance. Many people invite the neighbors to a planned party to forestall any complaints. Whatever you choose to do, be courteous, provide complete information, and thank your neighbors for their understanding.

Dear Neighbors,

We're writing to let you know that we will be having our daughter Andrea's wedding reception in our backyard on Saturday, June 23, starting at 2:00 p.m. We expect about fifty guests.

We will have a dance band that will play for no more than two hours. The party will be finished by 7:00. We hope we don't disturb you. Please let us know.

Many thanks,

Joan and Steve Chu

LETTER ABOUT JURY DUTY

Most of us accept that performing jury duty is a civic responsibility. The rest of us are constrained by law to turn up anyway. If you're summoned at a time that's not convenient for you, you may request to be excused altogether or to defer your service to a more convenient time.

Different areas have different regulations about jury duty, and the smartest thing for you to do is read the instructions on your summons about how to make an appeal. Some areas have websites or automated phone systems that allow you to reschedule your jury service. In other areas, you must write a letter or an e-mail.

Introduction

The **purpose** for writing a letter about jury duty is to ask to be excused from serving or to request that your service be deferred to a later date. In your letter, you should be explicit about which remedy

MODEL OUTLINE

A letter about jury duty should be brief and concise.

Opening: State the date for which you have been called, and state up front what you would like from the reader: an excuse or a deferment of service.

Middle: Briefly and courteously explain why you cannot serve during the dates you've been summoned. Make it clear to the reader that you cannot serve, not just that you prefer not to.

Conclusion: Finish your letter by restating your request for an excuse or deferment and by thanking your reader.

you're asking for. Your **reader** will be a civil servant who is used to all kinds of rudeness and arrogance. You can make her day a little better—and improve your chances of getting what you want—by being courteous. **Brainstorm** to ensure your letter is complete. What is your reason for asking for an excuse or deferment? What negative impact would you suffer if you had to serve at the time called? When will you be available to serve? Use the Model Outline to **organize** your letter. As you **draft**, make sure your tone is polite and professional. On no account should you show irritation or be snarky. **Revise** your draft to make sure it's complete and that your request is clear.

DO	DON'T
• Look at the summons for any instructions offered for rescheduling your appearance. Follow those instructions to the letter.	• Don't wait until the last minute to send your request. Get your letter out as soon as you can after you receive the summons.
• State what you are asking for: an excuse from jury duty or a deferral to a later time.	• Don't complain about the judicial system or the system used to select jurors.
• State clearly and without emotion the reason that you cannot serve at the time assigned to you.	• Don't be rude or dismissive.
• If you are requesting a deferral, state the dates you are available to serve.	• Don't talk too much about your feelings. The basis for claiming an excuse or deferral must be that you are unable to serve, not that it upsets or annoys you to serve.
• Provide documentation of any circumstance that prevents you from serving at the time you are summoned: a note from a doctor stating disability, a statement from your employer, and so on.	
• Ask explicitly for a response.	
• Be sure you're sending it to the right place. If your summons does not specify where the letter is to be sent, call the phone number supplied and get the address where you should direct the letter.	
• Send the letter return receipt requested.	

NOT LIKE THIS . . .

Mike's cutting it a little close if he's supposed to turn up for service in ten days.

May 13, 2013

Clerk of the Court:

I have been summoned to serve as a juror beginning May 23, 2013.

This may be true, but the person reading Mike's letter doesn't make the rules and would probably change them if she could, if only to avoid listening to people complain like this.

The reader is probably less interested in Mike's feelings than in his purpose for writing this letter—which he hasn't revealed yet.

The current system of juror selection does not take into account the fact that many people work as independent contractors or on a consulting basis. Such is the case with my small company, and it creates a significant burden on the company as a whole when a team member has to be missing from a project. It is extremely frustrating.

I will be unable to serve starting May 23 owing to work commitments. Hence I must defer my service as a juror.

Thank you for your consideration.

Sincerely,

Mike Ennis
Mike Ennis

Finally, in the last paragraph, Mike makes his request for a deferment. Except he hasn't phrased it as a request; it's more of a demand. He sounds a little high-handed here. He'd likely get more cooperation if he were more polite. He's also failed to mention when he *will* be available for service.

. . . LIKE THIS

Mike has written promptly, allowing plenty of time for the court to make arrangements.

March 13, 2013

Clerk of the Court:

I have been summoned to serve as a juror beginning May 23, 2013. I am writing to request a deferment in my service till July of 2013.

Mike helps the reader by stating right up front his reason for writing—to request a deferment—and the date he will be available to serve.

Mike makes a compelling case for the deferment.

My reason for requesting the deferment pertains to my job. I work as a management consultant, and my company has just won a contract that will go through June of this year. No one else in my small company can do the work I do. Leaving the project to serve on jury duty would jeopardize this contract and have a serious financial impact on the company and its employees.

I am willing and able to serve as a juror starting July 1, 2013. I appreciate your understanding of my situation. Please let me know if you will grant me this deferment.

Thank you for your consideration.

Sincerely,

Mike Ennis
Mike Ennis

> Mike is courteous and shows goodwill. He's also smart to ask for a reply to his request.

LETTER TO FIGHT A PARKING TICKET

MODEL OUTLINE

A letter to fight a parking ticket should be concise and easy to follow.
Opening: State the purpose of your message: to contest a parking ticket and request it be expunged from your record. Provide the details, including the citation number and the time, date, and location of the incident.
Middle: Clearly and politely explain why you believe the citation was made in error. Cite the facts, and refer to photographs.
Conclusion: Repeat your request that the ticket be reversed. Offer additional information. Close your message by thanking the reader.

You return to your car to find a dreaded—and expensive— parking ticket waiting for you. It's bad enough when you know you deserve it, but it really stinks when you don't. When you know you've parked legally, or when there is no signage to let you know you were parking illegally, sending an appeal letter can sometimes get the ticket thrown out. With the rising cost of parking tickets in many areas, it's worth taking the time to write a convincing letter.

Some communities have web forms you can use to dispute a parking ticket. Others supply an e-mail address for that purpose. In other areas, you still need to send your letter via postal mail.

Introduction

A letter to fight a parking ticket is a persuasive letter. Your **purpose** is to convince your reader that the citation should be reversed. Your **reader** is a civil servant who very likely spends much of his day reading this kind of appeal. You can make his job easier and more pleasant—and increase your chances of success—by providing clear evidence and expressing yourself rationally. As you **brainstorm** your content, be sure you have the complete facts for your message, including all the details of the citation and your reasons for disputing it. It can be easy to overlook important information when you're upset. **Organize** your letter logically and for maximum efficiency. The

Model Outline provides a structure you can adapt for your letter. It's wise to go through more than one **draft**. Show your draft to a friend or family member and ask her to read it from as objective a point of view as possible. Is your content complete? Is your tone appropriate? **Revise** according to her feedback.

DO	DON'T
• Send it promptly. Find out what the deadline is to contest the ticket, and make sure your appeal arrives well before then.	• Don't vent your emotions to the reader. No matter how frustrated you are, losing your temper in the letter won't help you, could hurt you, and might just ruin someone else's day.
• Be courteous. The person reading your letter didn't write you the ticket and probably receives a lot of rude and angry messages. You'll get a better result if your letter is respectful and polite and if you remember to say "please" and "thank you."	• Don't make any snarky remarks about the citing officer's intelligence or eyesight, or mention anything about monthly ticket-writing quotas.
• Make your letter easy to understand. Use simple language and short sentences. You'll gain more sympathy if you make your reader's job easier.	• Don't be condescending. Your tone should be businesslike, not arrogant.
• Keep it as brief as possible.	• Don't cite laws and ordinances gratuitously. If you've been cited for something obscure, it's all right to mention the ordinance. But throwing legal language around can make you sound officious and silly.
• Provide complete information, including the number of the ticket and the date, place, and time of the citation.	
• Make your request clear.	
• Explain the reasons you feel the ticket was erroneous. Don't rely on your reader to understand how absurd the citation was. Spell it out.	
• Provide proof. One of the best weapons you have is photographs of the scene, especially if you can demonstrate that there was no sign there or that the sign indicates that you were in fact parked legally. Include the photographs with your letter.	
• Explain what your photos prove. Don't leave it to your reader to figure it out.	

NOT LIKE THIS . . .

Teresa Moy
5666 Live Oak Street
San Gabriel, California 91101
Tsmoy434@mmail.com

December 21, 2012

To Whom It May Concern:

On December 15, my vehicle was given an erroneous citation for parking in a red zone, when it in fact was NOT parked in a red zone. I am enclosing two photos. I don't know why the officer could not see what is obvious in these photos, that I am NOT PARKED IN A RED ZONE, especially since it was not the end of the month. I would appreciate your help in this matter. Thank you.

Sincerely,

Teresa Moy
Teresa Moy

It would be helpful for Teresa to spell out exactly what the photos show and what they prove.

Insulting the officer may be tempting, but it won't help your case.

Remarks about ticket quotas are typically not helpful. Imagine how tired the reader gets reading remarks like these over and over again; you can make her day a little better by refraining.

It may seem self-evident, but Teresa should request explicitly that she wants the citation reversed.

Teresa should supply more information in her letter, including the citation number and her vehicle license number. The easier you make it for the reader, the more likely she is to help you.

. . . LIKE THIS

Teresa Moy
5666 Live Oak Street
San Gabriel, California 91101
Tsmoy434@mmail.com

December 21, 2012

Citation number: ZY00987U27PT
Date of citation: December 15, 2012
Vehicle license: NNU 838

> This is a good way to provide the key information in an easily scanned format.

Re: Parking Ticket Dispute

To Whom It May Concern:

My vehicle was issued the above-numbered ticket for parking in a red zone. However, my car was *not* in fact parked in a red zone, and the citation was issued in error. I would appreciate it if you would cancel this citation.

> Teresa does a good job of explaining the problem and making her request explicit in the opening paragraph of her letter.

I am attaching two photographs taken when I discovered the ticket.

- Photo #1 shows my car parked on Green Street with the citation on the windshield.
- Photo #2 is a close-up of the rear wheel. *You can see that the wheel is not in the red zone.* Please note that the time stamp and date stamp on the photos correspond to the date and time the ticket was issued.

> Teresa explains what each photo illustrates. Presenting them in a bulleted list, with the key finding in bold, makes it easy for the reader to scan.

The photos demonstrate that my vehicle was not parked illegally and that the citation was erroneous. I would appreciate it if you would reverse the citation. I would like to request notification within 30 days that the ticket has been canceled.

> It's smart to request verification that the citation has been reversed.

Thank you very much for your assistance.
Please contact me if you have any questions.
Sincerely,

> Teresa's letter is courteous and makes it easy for the reader to understand what she wants and why she wants it.

Teresa Moy
Teresa Moy
Enclosures (2)

NOTE TO YOUR CHILD'S TEACHER

You may write a note to your child's teacher for a number of reasons: in response to a note you received from her, to explain your child's absence from class, to request clarification about a homework assignment, or to ask for the teacher's help in resolving a problem—either academic or social—that your child is having at school. Most teachers appreciate hearing from parents, if the communication is constructive. Being in touch shows that you're interested and involved in your child's education, and it can make the teacher's job easier.

Most communication between parents and teachers takes place through e-mail, because it's fast and convenient.

Introduction

The **purpose** behind a note to your child's teacher is generally to convey information or to discuss a problem. Unless the note is very simple, it's a good idea to spend a moment and clarify your own purpose for writing. If you're writing because you or your child is upset about something, it's even more important to be clear about what you're trying to accomplish with the note. If you're not sure, you might end up just venting or saying something ill considered.

Building a good relationship with your **reader** is key to getting results. Regardless of your reason for writing, you should always work toward collaboration and cooperation with your child's teacher, as well as showing respect for the teacher's professional expertise. You and the teacher are on the same team: you both want the best for your child. Your communications should reflect that understanding.

The amount of **brainstorming** you do will depend on the complexity of the issue you're writing about. If an incident has occurred, it's a good idea to list everything out, confirm with your child that your list is complete, and then take some time to **organize** the information. Refer to the Model Outline for guidance.

If you're writing to the teacher because something upsetting has happened, it's a good idea to plan to write a first **draft** and then **revise** it rather than firing it off immediately. Ideally, you should show your draft to someone else before you send it, to check it for tone and to be sure you haven't inadvertently said anything to

MODEL OUTLINE

The structure of your note will depend on the issue you're writing about.
Paragraph 1: If you haven't corresponded with the teacher before, introduce yourself. Briefly say why you're writing.
Paragraph 2: Explain your understanding of the problem and the impact it's having on your child. You may want to provide additional information about your child or the issue at hand.
Paragraph 3: End on a cooperative note, and let the teacher know how to reach you.

insult the teacher or lay blame inappropriately. Fostering a sense of cooperation is often the key to solving problems, all the more so when emotions are running high.

DO	DON'T
• Introduce yourself unless you're already having regular contact with the teacher. Don't expect the teacher to know who you are, especially if you and your child don't share the same last name.	• Don't lose your temper. It's natural to be very protective of our children, but showing anger is rarely the best way to solve a problem, and it's never the best way to engage the cooperation of others. If you feel very angry, wait until you cool down a bit before you write your note.
• Be polite and cordial. Even if you're upset about something, you'll get better results if you treat the teacher with respect and politeness.	• Don't assign blame. The focus of your note should be to engage the teacher in a cooperative effort to solve whatever problem has occurred. If you blame the teacher, it is natural for the teacher to become defensive, and it becomes much harder to solve the problem.
• Explain your concern directly, simply, and without judgment.	
• Let the teacher know you're interested in his perspective rather than just presenting your views about the situation.	
• Take a cooperative approach. You want the best for your child, and you have to assume the teacher does, too. Your note should make it clear that you're looking forward to working together to solve whatever the problem is.	If there's a problem in the classroom or with your child, it's only natural to believe your child's version of events. But try to keep your mind open to the possibility that a misunderstanding has occurred, at least until you've had the chance to communicate with the teacher.
• Focus on what can be done to remedy the problem rather than on assigning blame.	• Don't say anything to suggest that the teacher is insensitive to your child's feelings, or that the problem arises from the teacher's lack of understanding of your child.
• Provide information that the teacher might not have. For instance, the loss of a family member or a pet, the arrival of a new baby, or problems at home can all cause stress that can affect how your child behaves and performs in school. Has your child been diagnosed with a learning disability? Does your child require medication? Let the teacher know.	• Don't be disrespectful or condescending. Teachers are professionals and deserve to be treated as such.
• Provide insights into your child's personality. Especially early in the school year, the teacher might not know your child very well. Help the teacher understand who your kid is.	• Don't be high-handed. Teachers do not "work for you," even if you are a taxpayer or a payer of tuition. This kind of attitude is guaranteed to yield bad results.

DO (CONTINUED)

- Let the teacher know how your child feels about the situation.
- Try to keep your note as concise as possible. Teachers have a tremendous amount of work to do outside classroom time, so be respectful of their time.
- If you can, include a positive comment about the teacher's work or your child's experience in the teacher's class. Doing so will foster goodwill and cooperation.

NOT LIKE THIS . . .

Before you criticize the teacher like this, consider the possibility that your child has misunderstood what's expected of him. Your first step should be to clarify the assignment rather than to blame the teacher for having unreasonable expectations.

Many teachers are happy to be addressed by their first names, but you should err on the side of caution if you're not sure.

This comment implies rather bluntly that it's the teacher's fault Jason is having a problem now. This is not the best way to clarify or solve the problem.

Dear Andrea,

Jason came home from school extremely upset yesterday. He doesn't understand the math assignment, and it's an overwhelming amount of work for a child his age. I must say I don't understand why you would assign the class so much work.

Jason has always worked hard in school and done very well. We have never encountered a problem like this before.

Cynthia Carter

This message ends abruptly, on a note of accusation rather than cooperation. Better to ask the teacher to get in touch with you so you can talk over the problem together.

. . . LIKE THIS

If you haven't corresponded with the teacher before, it's a nice courtesy to address her formally rather than by her first name.

Dear Ms. Taylor,

I'm Jason Carter-Brinkman's mom. I'm hoping you can help clear up some confusion we're having. Jason came home extremely upset yesterday. He doesn't understand the math assignment, how much of it is required, or when it's due. He showed me what looked like a lot of work, and I'm not sure either. Can you please explain it to me so I can help him?

The opening paragraph includes a friendly introduction, a nonjudgmental statement of the problem, and a request for cooperation from the teacher.

Jason expects a lot of himself, and he feels that he should "get" everything right away. When he doesn't, he feels like a failure. We're working with him on this. I suspect that if he had asked for clarification about this assignment, we wouldn't be in this situation. He really is a very conscientious kid, and he enjoys your class very much.

This is a valuable piece of information about Jason, and something that will help his teacher help him. Providing this information also helps explain why the misunderstanding occurred, without laying blame on anyone.

The message concludes on a positive note, invites collaboration with the teacher, and lets her know how she can best reach the parent.

Please call me so we can sort this out. You can reach me anytime on my cell at 212-555-1234. I'm looking forward to talking with you.

Many thanks,

Cynthia Carter

MORE EXAMPLES

Hi Miriam,

Lilly was not in school today because she cut her hand on a bread knife and I had to rush her to the hospital. I'm sorry I didn't let you know sooner, and I hope you weren't worried—things were a bit crazy this morning.

Lilly has three stitches, but she's absolutely fine and will be in school tomorrow.

Thanks!

June Newman

Dear Stuart,

We hope all is well with you.

We would like to take Ming-Hua out of school for four days next month, April 25–28. His grandparents will be visiting from Taiwan, and we are planning a family trip to Washington, DC.

We would like to work with you to ensure he does not fall behind in his studies. Could you please call us at (609) 555.1111 when you have time?

Many thanks,

Mei-Feng and Steven Li

NOTE ON THE WINDSHIELD

Someone has parked so close to your car that you can't get out of your parking space or so close to the driver's side that you had to climb in through the passenger's side of the car. Rude parking behavior is nearly as provoking as rude driving behavior, and almost as widespread. The difference is that you can leave a note for a rude parker and try to correct her behavior.

Introduction

Having your car blocked or your rightful parking place usurped can be infuriating. You may want to leave a nasty note just to blow off steam. A higher **purpose**, though, would be to leave a constructive note to let the person know the consequences of his actions and, with luck, to keep him from doing it again.

Spend a moment thinking about who your **reader** might be. Consider how you would like to be addressed if you were the one parking rogue.

Not much time needs to be spent in **brainstorming** or **organizing** a quick note like this. However, if you can let your reader know exactly how she's inconvenienced you and why she should stop, she will likely be more receptive to your message.

As you **draft**, bear in mind that your tone should be civil no matter how frustrated or angry you may be. Selfish parking behavior is far more likely to be the result of thoughtlessness than of pure evil. The person who blocked your car may have been late for a meeting or perhaps upset by the behavior of some other rude driver. If you really lose it when you're writing the note, take a moment to **revise** and rewrite it.

DO	DON'T
• Let the driver know exactly what he has done that's caused a problem for you. • Tell the driver exactly what the consequences are of his behavior. Don't assume that he must know how badly he's inconvenienced you. Explain it to him, calmly and rationally. • Ask him to stop. • Focus on solving the problem rather than venting your anger.	• Don't use profanity. It's not constructive. Although it might feel good in the moment, using profanity will ultimately undermine your position. No matter how angry or frustrated you are, take the high road. • Don't use sarcasm. The person may have done something really stupid, and it might feel good to blow off steam by insulting her, but you're guaranteed not to get a good result if you do so. • Don't engage in personal abuse or name-calling. • Don't make any threats, with the exception of appropriate and legal actions that you are actually prepared to take. For instance, if someone persistently parks in a spot that's officially designated for you, you're within your rights to tell him that the next time it happens you'll have his car towed.

NOT LIKE THIS . . .

Nice alliteration but not likely to encourage cooperation.

This kind of personal insult may be gratifying in the moment, but it's bound to make the other driver mad and uncooperative.

To the Moron in the Mazda,

It doesn't take much intelligence to see that when you park here, I can't get out, does it? Next time maybe I'll just go ahead and back into your door. Maybe you'll get the point then. Would it be too terribly difficult for you to pull up about ten feet and park there so I can get my car out?

Snide, sarcastic comments like this aren't going to win you any cooperation.

This is a clear and very unconstructive threat. Do you really mean you're going to hit her car on purpose? Really? This kind of threat will make the offending parker angry and defensive. And what if someone does hit her car and do some damage? You've just provided written evidence making you the first suspect.

. . . LIKE THIS

> This is a calm and courteous way of letting the parker know that his behavior is having a negative impact on you.

Hi,

I live directly across the street, and as you can see my driveway is parallel to where you're parked. I'm sure you didn't think of this, but when you park here it's extremely difficult for me to get out of my driveway without backing into you. In the future, could you please pull up about ten feet when you park? I really don't want to back into your car.

Thanks.

Steve Tanner

> Signing your note puts a face (or at least a name) behind the complaint and keeps things aboveboard. It also might make the reader take your complaint more seriously.

NOTE TO RECOVER LOST PROPERTY

You think you left your watch at the gym. You come back from the laundromat and discover there's a pillowcase missing. Your favorite pen has disappeared at work. It can be really painful to lose something you care about. Your best bet is to write a note that will motivate people to have a look around and return the missing item to you.

Introduction

The **purpose** behind a note to recover lost property is self-explanatory. You want to let people know you've lost something and motivate them to give it back to you. No matter how frustrated or upset you may be, keep your focus on recovering your property, not venting about the party who may or may not have carried it off.

As you write, consider your **readers**—how they might feel reading your note and what might motivate them to help you. As you write your **draft**, pay attention to your tone. Don't show anger, and don't make people defensive. Make an earnest appeal for their help. Ask someone else to check your draft and provide feedback. **Revise** to ensure your note is complete and your tone is friendly and cooperative.

DO	DON'T
<ul><li>Be specific about what it is you lost and where and when you think you lost it.</li><li>Mention whatever special value or importance the item has for you.</li><li>Focus on recovering the object, not on scolding or punishing the person who may have taken it.</li><li>Use formatting to help you. Give your note or flyer a headline, and put important words in bold.</li><li>Offer a reward, if you can.</li><li>Remember to sign your note, if it's appropriate to do so, and to provide your contact information if necessary.</li><li>Thank people for their help.</li></ul>	<ul><li>Don't assume that the missing item was stolen. Instead, write your note in the spirit of cooperation and assume someone has taken it by mistake. If it was really stolen, you're unlikely to get it back anyway.</li><li>Don't express anger or blame in your note. You may be upset that you've lost the item, but writing a nasty note is the quickest way to ensure that people won't cooperate with you to recover it.</li><li>Don't go on too long. Think from the point of view of your readers, though: what do they need to know in order to help you? Keep your message brief, accurate, and concise.</li></ul>

NOT LIKE THIS . . .

To Whoever Walked Off with My Red Folders:

Last night when I left the office, there was a stack of red folders sitting on top of my file cabinet. I ordered those on purpose, because I NEED THEM FOR PACKETS FOR THE BOARD MEETING TONIGHT! These were a special order from Pendaflex, and I can't just go out and buy more. This morning when I walked in, they were gone, and Jill has no idea what happened to them.

Calm down. Stop shouting.

The writer, whoever he is, is going on too long. He needs to take a breath and organize this note rather than just venting.

If you're the person who walked off with my folders, kindly RETURN THEM TO MY OFFICE immediately. And in the future you might learn to order your own supplies instead of stealing other people's.

Whoa. Using the word "steal" isn't going to motivate people to help out.

This note is nasty and angry. No one is going to want to help this person. And who is this person anyway? He's forgotten to sign his note.

... LIKE THIS

Missing Red Folders

> Jim's used a good headline. You don't even have to read the note to know what the problem is.

> The boldface type here draws the reader's attention to some important information, without shouting about it.

A stack of red folders disappeared from my office last night or this morning. I need those folders for the packets for **tonight's board meeting!** Has anyone seen them? Put them away for safekeeping? Please let me know.

> Jim assumes the best about his readers rather than assuming they are thieves.

> Jim thanks his readers, capping off a very pleasant note. People will be motivated to help him.

Thanks for your help!

> Since Jim signed the flyer, readers will know where to return the folders.

Jim

FINDING A LOST ANIMAL

If you're in the sad position of finding your pet missing, a smart thing to do is make flyers and post them around your neighborhood, or go door-to-door to hand them out. Describe the pet as accurately as possible, and put a picture of him on the flyer. Note where and when the pet was last seen. Be sure to note if your pet answers to his name, and list any other distinguishing characteristics. If you can offer a reward, say so. And don't forget your phone number or e-mail address.

For sample lost-pet notices, visit www.howtowriteanything.com.

CLASSIFIED AD AND ONLINE AUCTION LISTING

(See also *Job Advertisement*, page 446.)

> Never write an advertisement which you wouldn't want your family to read. You wouldn't tell lies to your own wife. Don't tell them to mine.
> —*David Ogilvy, British advertising executive*

There are all kinds of ads, from traditional newspaper ads to online classifieds to auction listings on eBay. Print ads generally limit the amount of text you get for your money. Online ads are also limited—by the attention span of the reader. In either case, you'll want to write punchy, efficient copy that will draw the attention of potential buyers.

Introduction

The **purpose** of a classified ad or auction listing is to capture the interest of people scanning a newspaper or website and to motivate them to contact you. An ad is a sales tool, so remember that your purpose is to motivate rather than to provide an exhaustive description of the item you're trying to sell or rent. Your **readers** may be in desperate need of just the thing you're offering, but it's smarter to assume that they have a number of attractive choices and focus on attracting them to your offering. Think from the point of view of your readers as you **brainstorm**. Make a list of all the attributes of the item you're offering, and then narrow the list down to what would make potential buyers want to pursue it. There are a number of ways to **organize** a classified ad or auction listing; the Model Outline provides one you can adapt. Your initial **draft** will likely be too long. Take a break and come back to the draft with a fresh eye: you'll find it much easier to tighten the copy when you go to **revise** it. Be sure your ad is as concise and punchy as possible and that it's free from typos and other errors.

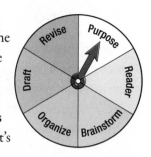

MODEL OUTLINE

A classified ad or auction listing has to say a lot in a short space.
Headline: Write a strong headline to catch the reader's attention.
Basic information: Provide identifying information—what kind, how big, what color, how old, and so on.
Special features: Describe special features that set this item or this deal apart from others. Mint condition? Collector's edition? Ocean view?
Contact information: Let readers know how they can reach you.

DO	DON'T
• Lead with a catchy headline. Your headline could make the difference between a potential buyer reading your ad and passing it by.	• Don't overuse abbreviations. Some abbreviations are standard, but if your ad is packed with them, readers may be put off or simply confused.
• Catch the readers' eyes with compelling key words. Readers will scan your ad before they read it. Notice what words catch your attention when you're browsing, and identify the key words that describe the product, service, or deal you're offering.	• Don't be bland. As long as you're running an ad, make the effort to make it attractive to readers. Don't just list the basic attributes and expect buyers to come flocking to you.
• Keep your ad brief. Remember your readers have limited attention and may be browsing through many similar ads. You can provide more details during a phone call or e-mail. A brief ad can also create a sense of urgency that can help motivate the reader to act.	• Don't go on too long. Print ads and some Internet ads have word limits. Be aware that your readership will diminish the longer your ad is, so be judicious.
	• Don't let an ad go to print or be posted online without checking it for errors. If you find a newspaper has made an error in a printed ad, ask for it to be corrected immediately.

DO (CONTINUED)

- Provide the appropriate contact information. Make sure you supply a phone number where you can be reached easily. If you're not always available, note the best time to reach you.
- Mention your location. Potential buyers are more attracted to places closer to them.
- Classify your item in the right place. No one's ever going to find it if it's listed under the wrong category.
- Proofread your ad, even after it's in print or posted on the web. The ad can be useless to you if there's a typo in the phone number or other key information, so you'll want to correct errors ASAP.

LIKE THIS

MULTIFAMILY YARD SALE FROM KITCHENWARE TO COMPUTERS

Kitchenware / adult and baby clothing / toys and games / DVDs / books / glassware / laptops / auto parts / pet supplies . . . more! Saturday, June 9, 9 a.m. to 5 p.m. 1870 Wilbur Rd.

BEAUTIFUL FULLY RENOVATED SPANISH STYLE $799,000

Beautiful 4 BR 3 BA on half-acre lot. Formal DR. Mountain and city views. Hardwood floors, Spanish styling throughout. Fully renovated kitchen and baths, new electric, plumbing, tile roof—move right in! Call David at 310-800-1111.

1967 VW Beetle—$10,000

Totally restored, rebuilt from the bottom up. 2,000 miles on new engine. New paint, tires, everything. Pristine. MUST SEE. Will consider trades. Call Jeff at 434-800-1111.

COLUMBIA SAILBOAT—$1500

1998 Columbia 22-foot fixed-keel sailboat in mint condition. Includes Johnson outboard motor, plus 3 NEW sails: 1 main sail, 1 roller furling Genoa, 1 storm jib VHF Ship to Shore Radio. Bottom was painted in October 2012. Boat is located in Galveston Bay in water, rigged and ready to sail. Call Robert at 409-999-0000 (evenings only).

Quiet, spacious rental

3br/2ba town house, $2100/mo, enclosed garage. Great area. Landscape maintenance, water, electric included. Landlord references. Pets OK. Call Kari, 777-800-1111.

CRAIGSLIST

Craigslist is the most popular of the classified ad sites. The competition on Craigslist can be intense, so write a listing that stands out from the others.

- Write an enticing headline. A compelling headline is the single most important part of your listing. Getting buyers to click through can be a challenge, so make sure your headline contains information that will motivate people to take a closer look.
- Describe the item completely and accurately. Have someone else check your listing before you post it, to be sure you haven't left anything out.
- Use bullet points to make your listing easy to scan. People won't read block paragraphs.
- Include good pictures. Pictures are actually more important than text on Craigslist. A listing with a great description and no pictures—or bad pictures—simply won't generate results.
- Remember to mention your location. This seems like an obvious point, but many people overlook it.
- Don't use all caps. It's hard to read a posting written this way.

ONLINE AUCTION LISTING

There are several venues for online auctions, eBay being the most popular. Buyers using eBay have become discriminating and read auction listings carefully, so take care in crafting yours.

DO	DON'T
• Write a catchy title. Use all the available characters to write a title that responds to search terms, such as brand name, size, color, and any other information that might make your item attractive ("vintage," "antique," "mint condition," etc.). • Be thorough in your description of the item. If you leave out important information, shoppers will simply move on to another listing. • Be honest about flaws and defects.	• Don't create a messy listing. Listings with too many colors, too many fonts, and too many sizes of fonts are annoying and may drive people away. • Don't copy the text from other listings word for word. By all means refer to similar listings as a way of checking yours, but other sellers will not be happy if you just swipe their copy. • Don't make inaccurate statements. For instance, don't say an item is "rare" if there are several

DO (CONTINUED)	DON'T (CONTINUED)
• Browse through similar auctions on the site to see what works—and what doesn't.	others of the same item currently for sale. It makes you look silly and, worse, untrustworthy.
• Use formatting to make your text more readable. No one likes to read a big block of text, and online shoppers don't have to; they just click on to the next offering. Use paragraph breaks or bullet points to break up the text and make your auction more easily scannable.	• Don't rant about bad experiences you may have had with previous buyers. State your payment and shipping policies clearly and concisely, and leave it at that. Nothing scares away buyers like a seller who is already angry, aggrieved, and resentful.

For model Craigslist and eBay listings, visit www.howtowriteanything .com.

RECEIPT

You'll need to write a receipt whenever you've accepted money for goods or services you've sold, rented, or leased. A receipt serves as a statement that the transaction is finished, and that neither party owes the other anything. You can use a receipt to acknowledge the payment of a deposit and to specify the balance due. If you sell your car or large items at a yard sale, or if you rent out a room or an apartment, you'll need to be able to provide a receipt for those transactions.

Introduction

A receipt is a simple business communication that proves that a sale or transaction has been completed. Its **purpose** is to confirm what has been paid for an item or service and to state if there is a balance due or if the price has been paid in full. A receipt can prevent misunderstandings and can protect both parties should a dispute arise in the future. There is little **brainstorming** to do apart from providing complete information about the transaction. The sample below provides an organizational format you can adapt. Especially if you are handwriting a receipt for a one-off transaction, it's a good idea to ask your **reader**—the buyer—to look at the receipt and confirm its accuracy. **Revise** if there are any errors.

DO	DON'T
• Date the receipt.	• Don't note the payer's full credit card number on a receipt.
• Include your name and contact information on the receipt.	• Don't take anything for granted. The point of writing a receipt is to provide an accurate and complete record of the transaction to protect both parties. Don't assume anyone will "just remember" the details—write them out.
• Include the name of the payer on the receipt.	
• Specify exactly what has been paid. Break down the amounts into any relevant categories: cost of goods, labor charges, taxes, any discounts applied.	
• If there is a balance due, note it. If the amount is paid in full, note that fact on the receipt.	
• If there is a deadline for paying the balance due, state the deadline on the receipt.	
• State what has been paid for. Include a detailed description, including serial numbers if applicable. If there are any relevant exclusions, state them.	
• State the billing period, if relevant, for instance for rent.	
• Note the method of payment: cash, check, money order, credit card. Note the number of the check or money order or the last four digits of the credit card used. If the payment is in cash, the receipt will be the only evidence of the transaction, so make sure that both parties agree it's accurate.	

LIKE THIS

Bill of Sale for Vehicle: Without Warrantee

I, Dwayne LaFayette, of 5978 Parkside Dr., certify I am the legal owner of the vehicle 2009 VW New Beetle 2.5L PZEV, red, VIN I38oK9LL572 and have the authority to sell it. I hereby acknowledge the receipt of $9,995.00 in the form of check #776 from Tom Gutierrez as full payment for the purchase of said vehicle AS IS. I hereby state that the mileage of the vehicle at the time of sale is 81,443.

I do hereby grant, sell, and transfer ownership of this vehicle to the buyer. I certify that this vehicle, at the time of sale, is free from all encumbrances, taxes, fees, and liens except as those specified on the Title or listed below and that I will be held fully responsible for such lawful claims and demands with respect to the vehicle, if any.

Buyer accepts full liability for the vehicle, damages, and any third-party liability incurred from the vehicle use from the date of sale.

Dwayne LaFayette   *Tom Gutierrez*
4/3/13   4/3/13

Rental Receipt

August 25, 2012

I, Steve Ohanessian, do acknowledge receipt of $1,250 from tenant Julianne Chiang, by cash, as payment in full for rental 255 Ambrose Avenue, Unit 315, for the rental period of September 1–October 1, 2013.

Community Life

EDITORIAL

There are two kinds of editorials. One presents the publication's official opinion about an issue and reflects the majority vote of the editorial board. The other, the guest editorial, is written by a contributor who is not on the publication's staff. Many publications invite guest writers—sometimes people with a particular expertise in the topic—to contribute editorials. Others accept submissions from the general public.

Introduction

An editorial may have several **purposes**: to highlight a problem, to criticize the way that problem is currently being handled, or to argue in favor of a potential solution. In addition, some editorials praise government or other organizations for a job well done. As you write your editorial, it's helpful to imagine an intelligent, engaged **reader** who is undecided about the topic you're writing about. Treat your reader with respect, and try to imagine what information and arguments would be the most compelling from her point of view. A good approach is to **brainstorm** as much content as you can, then cull your strongest arguments from there. Editorials typically follow a

MODEL OUTLINE

Space is typically extremely limited for an editorial, so you should keep yours as concise as possible.

Opening: State the topic, and provide timely context—some recent political decision or a recent event that brings the issue to the fore, for example. State your position on the question.

Middle: Fairly state the opposing point of view and present your arguments against it.

Conclusion: Finish your editorial with a punchy ending that restates your position and contains a call to action.

standard organizational pattern that readers expect, consciously or otherwise. The Model Outline can help you **organize** your content. Plan to go through several **drafts** as you write your editorial. Show your drafts to others, and ask them if your editorial makes sense and is persuasive. Especially when you're writing about something you have strong feelings about, it's important to get some distance and perspective. Use your readers' comments to help you **revise** your draft before you send it in.

DO	DON'T
• Be sure you understand the publication you're submitting to. Look at its editorial pages to get a sense of what it publishes, and request guidelines for guest editorials.	• Don't engage in name-calling or character assassination. It's poor argumentation, and it insults your readers' intelligence. Using personal abuse or other dirty tactics will make it easy for readers to dismiss your opinion.
• Get your facts straight. Open your editorial with a fair statement of the current situation. Make sure your assessment is accurate and dispassionate. Don't distort the facts to your own advantage.	• Don't rely on readers to know what abbreviations and acronyms mean. Define them.
• State the opposition position fairly and unemotionally.	• Don't drift off topic. You don't have much space to make your point, so it's especially important that you pick a thesis and stick to it.
• Select a strong argument to oppose. Present the opposition's strongest case, and refute it. Although it may be tempting to offer up their weakest argument and then smash it like a bug, that tactic ultimately undermines your position.	• Don't use "I." It's understood that the opinion is yours. Editorials written by the newspaper staff sometimes use "we." Your argument will be stronger if you don't dilute it by saying "I believe."
• Concede a valid point from the opposition. Acknowledging that the opposition may be partly right enhances your credibility. Just be sure you don't undermine your main argument.	
• Make sure you can state the point of your editorial in a single sentence. Having a clear and simple thesis is very important for an editorial, which is by definition brief and condensed.	
• State your position firmly and clearly, not abusively.	

- Provide facts and evidence that support your position.
- End with a punch. Take some time to craft an ending that restates your position clearly and urges others to agree with you.
- Keep it brief. You may have a word limit, but even if you don't, you'll get more readers if you keep your editorial brief and easy to read.
- Choose a catchy title for your editorial. The publication may choose to retitle it, but try to come up with a title that will grab readers' attention.
- Include some information about yourself, if you have special expertise on the topic, to enhance your credibility.

NOT LIKE THIS . . .

Huntersville's retrograde, dim-witted city council has once again proven that it's on the wrong side of history and the wrong side of common sense by abolishing our very popular curbside recycling program.

> This is a little abusive. It's fine to take a strong position, but insulting the opposition won't win over anyone who is undecided, and it can make you look bad.

> "Abolishing" seems like an overstatement.

The recycling program was so popular, in fact, it had real potential to become an income source for the city. After four years of strong promotion, the program enjoyed the support of an overwhelming majority of households in Huntersville. Our rate of participation was far above that of comparable communities nationwide. Experts predicted that the recycling program was on the cusp of turning the tide and generating income for Huntersville. The city council claims to be interested in saving money, but it seems apparent that there must be some other agenda at work. Canceling a profitable program is no way to save money.

> Some statistics would lend support to this contention.

> How soon would this have happened?

> What is Jean suggesting here? That the city council is taking bribes? If she wants to make that accusation, she should make it directly and offer evidence rather than hinting around about it.

> This doesn't seem quite fair. Is the program really profitable now? Jean has just said the program was "on the cusp" of generating income. It's hard to follow her argument, and the lack of clarity might make some readers doubtful of her honesty.

Jean H. Holder

...LIKE THIS

> The title is catchy and counterintuitive, making it intriguing for readers.

Abandoning Recycling: A Costly Decision for the City

> Jean states her position clearly and firmly right at the beginning

The city council made a shortsighted and fiscally irresponsible decision when it voted last week to suspend Huntersville's very popular curbside recycling program.

> Jean acknowledges that spending cuts are necessary in the city.

> Jean concedes an opposing position without compromising her own argument. In doing so, she enhances her credibility.

We're all aware that budget shortfalls require the city council to make some painful cuts in spending. Councilman Hernandez was correct when he stated that the recycling program was not profitable. What he neglected to mention, unfortunately, is that the recycling program was so popular it was on the cusp of actually becoming an income source for the city. After four years of promotion, the program had gained the participation of 67 percent of households in Huntersville, well above the national average of 38 percent participation in comparable communities nationwide. Experts predicted that the recycling program was only a year or two away from turning the tide and generating income for Huntersville. The little money the city council is saving this year would have been offset, and the city would have continued to enjoy the benefits of recycling. As it stands now, if the program is dismantled it will likely take years to put it together again. In the meantime, untold quantities of recyclable paper, plastics, and metals will have been dumped into landfills, forever unavailable for use by future generations . . . and the city will actually have lost money.

> The statistics and estimates included here bolster Jean's case.

> The editorial concludes with a strong call to action.

It's not too late to reverse this unfortunate decision. If citizens of Huntersville will call and e-mail the city council members, we can save our recycling program. Let's contact the city council and urge them to reinstate the curbside recycling program, for the sake of our current fiscal welfare and for the sake of our children's future.

Jean H. Holder

LETTER TO THE EDITOR

You might write a letter to the editor of a publication in response to an editorial or other article or to offer your opinion about current events. The letters-to-the-editor section is one of the mostly widely read sections of the newspaper, so it provides a good forum for sharing your views. Letters to the editor are often submitted via e-mail. Check with the publication in question for the best way to send yours.

We will not be driven by fear into an age of unreason if we . . . remember that we are not descended from fearful men, not from men who feared to write, to speak, to associate and to defend causes which were, for the moment, unpopular.

—Edward R. Murrow, journalist

DO	DON'T
• Write promptly if you're responding to an editorial or article in the publication. Editors often have very tight deadlines for letters such as these, and the window of opportunity closes quickly.	• Don't argue from emotion. Even if the topic is something you feel passionate about, your argument will get more respect if it comes from reason rather than feelings.
• Check the publication's guidelines for letters to the editor. Your chances of getting published increase if you comply with the guidelines, and some publications won't even consider your letter if you don't.	• Don't be snarky or sarcastic. You may think that article was the dumbest thing you've ever read, but being snarky about it isn't going to convince anyone.
• Check other examples of letters to the editor in the publication to get an idea of appropriate style and content.	• Don't attack the author of the article or editorial you're responding to.
• Keep it brief. The publication will very likely trim your draft anyway because of space restrictions. Your letter should be a maximum of three paragraphs, with two or three sentences per paragraph.	• Don't write too often. Serial letter writers are often regarded as cranks. Your chances of publication go up if you don't submit too often: once every three months is a good outer limit.
• If you are responding to a recent news article or editorial, refer to it by date and headline.	
• State your point early and clearly, in the first sentence of your letter.	
• Stick to a single point. Remember that your letter may be cut dramatically. Focus on the single most important thing you really want to say.	
• Use facts and statistics to support your argument, if possible.	

DO (CONTINUED)

- Mention any qualifications you have that give you special expertise about the topic.
- Sign your letter and include your contact information. Publications rarely print anonymous letters.

LIKE THIS

The *Tribune*'s editorial "Time to Reconsider the Death Penalty" (January 17) completely misses the point made by opponents of the death penalty: that it does *not* act as a deterrent to crime. There has never been a shred of credible evidence that the death penalty deters criminals, yet death-penalty proponents continue to repeat this argument as though it were fact. It is not.

The editorial also harps on the severity of the crimes committed by Mr. Gaynor and Mr. Olson. Presumably none of us endorses crime, and no one thinks criminals are doing right. Wallowing in the horror of the crime does not constitute an argument for killing the criminal.

The wisdom and the morality of the death penalty in our society remains a topic of legitimate disagreement among concerned people. But death penalty proponents need to put forward factual and legitimate arguments if they wish to be taken seriously.

Steven J. Hintz

For more sample letters to the editor, visit www.how towriteany thing.com.

I disagree with Victor Tilden's position on the city's attempt to limit sugar ("The Nanny State Rides Again," June 24). The term "nanny state" is nothing more than name-calling, and it begs an important question: should the government concern itself with public health issues? If your answer is yes—and for most reasonable people it would be—then you need to address yourself to the real issues: the harm that sugary drinks are doing to the health of the population and how we can act to prevent that harm. Simply stomping your feet and calling names suggests that maybe you do need a nanny to look after you.

Denise Chen

How to Write an Op-Ed

If you've got an opinion that you want to send in to your local newspaper, blog, or other online site, first the good news—we editorial page editors need good copy just the same as you need to get something off your chest. We may sound crusty on the phone or in an e-mail, but it's the plain truth. We've got pages to fill, and our charge is to do so with interesting material, regardless of whether we agree with it or not.

First, if you can write what you want to say in 200 words or so, just make it in the form of a letter to the editor. No shame in that. Especially if you are not one of the usual suspects—smaller papers tend to get letters for publication from the same crowd of 20 or 30 people—your opinion will be especially valued. If the subject is an upcoming election, just make sure you don't send it in two or three days before the vote and expect to see it published. Most of us have cut-off dates of the Saturday before the Tuesday election, as there would be no time for opposing views to respond otherwise. Write about an unusual topic of interest to you and you will be almost certain to see it published.

If you really need more space, drop a note to the opinion editor—e-mails are better than phone calls—and say so: "Gee, I've tried, but this really needs 400 words or so, and I was wondering if you could find the space. It's such an important issue to the community." Again, we always need well-written copy, particularly if it's local, rather than the generic national or international ranting about something we all have heard before.

Write tight. Don't use clichés ("kicking the can down the road again," "that socialist/fascist president of ours"). Impress the editor by knowing that "op-ed" means "opposite editorial," not "opinion editorial"—which is the same thing said twice. Check your grammar and spelling thrice so that it can be copied and pasted into the system without too much trouble on the editor's part. Suggest—don't demand—a headline, and don't call it a title. Write in the body of an e-mail, not in an attachment we may not be able to open—and not by snail mail, which must be re-keystroked. Be strong but fair in your opinion. Keep it light, even humorous—not bombastic. Be sure to sign your real name, address, phone number.

You'll be a favorite around the editorial pages. And you'll see your thoughts in print very soon indeed.

Lawrence Wilson writes a thrice-weekly column for the *Pasadena Star-News* and is a member of the editorial board for the Los Angeles News Group.

FUND-RAISING LETTER

A good fund-raising letter can play a key role in any campaign for community-based organizations, schools, religious organizations, and other causes. Think of a fund-raising letter as a kind of sales letter—the more convincingly you can "sell" your reader on your cause, the better results you'll get.

Introduction

The **purpose** of a fund-raising letter is to motivate readers to contribute money to a cause. Your **reader** may be someone who has donated in the past, someone who has never been solicited before, or somewhere in between those extremes. Whoever your reader is, people are rarely eager to part with their money, so you need to make a compelling case to motivate your reader to help. **Brainstorm** your content from your readers' point of view. What will make them feel good about giving? What benefits will they accrue? **Organize** your letter to hook your readers' attention early and sustain their interest. The Model Outline provides a structure you can adapt for your own letter. As you **draft**, try to maintain an enthusiastic tone, without tipping over into hype. Don't worry if your first draft seems long. Unlike many forms of writing, fund-raising letters can actually benefit from additional length; the longer you sustain your readers' attention, the more likely they are to make a donation. Take a break after you've written your first draft, review it with a fresh eye, and then **revise** accordingly. Does it hold your interest? If there are sections of the letter where your interest flags, tighten them up. Fill in missing information. Ask others to read it and give you their feedback.

MODEL OUTLINE

A fund-raising letter must grab the reader's attention and hold it.

Opening: Hook your readers with a compelling story. Describe an acute need or a compelling fund-raising activity or goal. State the need, and ask your readers to make a donation.

Middle: Describe the cause, the event you are organizing, and the benefits of supporting the cause. Suggest an amount or list amounts.

Conclusion: Finish your message with a call to action, urging your reader to make a donation and thanking them for their support.

PS: Consider using a postscript to reinforce your message and repeat the call to action. Many readers will read the postscript first.

DO	DON'T
• Know your readers. Have they donated in the past? Many organizations segment their mailings according to giving history and further segment according to how much people have given.	• Don't be shy. Your cause is a good one; otherwise you wouldn't be asking for support for it. Let your confidence in the cause shine out.
• Thank people for prior donations. In letters to existing donors, show your appreciation. In letters to those who haven't previously contributed, show the difference that others' contributions are making.	• Don't assume readers understand the benefits of a potential contribution. Let them know what their donations can buy and how they can make a difference.
• Open your letter with a hook. Tell a compelling story of need or an inspiring success story.	• Don't hesitate to write a long letter. Readers are unlikely to read every word, so you don't need to worry about being concise. Use effective format- ting so that readers can browse through and pick up your message more than once.
• Address the reader as "you." Direct address involves the reader in your appeal.	
• Use short sentences and everyday, conversational language. Your reader should feel as if you're talk- ing to him.	• Don't hype. A fund-raising letter is a motivational message, but you shouldn't sound like a used-car salesman. Let your sincere enthusiasm for the cause shine through, but don't go overboard.
• Ask specifically for money. Many people are uncomfortable asking for money and will default to using a euphemism like "support." Ask for money. Your cause is good, it needs money to suc- ceed, and no one will be offended if you ask for what you need.	• Don't use a lot of acronyms or abbreviations. Your letter should be as accessible as possible.
• Ask for a specific amount, and don't be shy. Ask for a significant donation. You'd be surprised how often people say yes. And even if they contribute less than the suggested amount, they have still contributed.	
• Let your readers know what benefits their donations will provide. Be explicit about what the money will buy. People are more inclined to donate when they can connect a tangible benefit to their donation.	
• Create a sense of urgency. People will put off giv- ing, so set a deadline. Natural deadlines include	

the end of a fiscal year, the deadline for a tax deduction, or the looming expiration of a matching grant. Also consider fund-raising for a holiday or special event.

- Use formatting to make your letter easy to scan. Readers aren't obliged to read this letter, so make it attractive. Bulleted lists and short paragraphs can make the letter easier to scan and help keep readers' attention longer. Use subheadings to break up a long letter.

- Use a PS under your signature. Most readers are unlikely to read your entire letter, but a postscript will catch their attention. Include a call to action in your PS.

- Give readers specific instructions about how to make their donation. Depending on your method of delivery, provide them with a reply envelope and/or a link to a website where they can donate.

LIKE THIS

Dear Mr. Smith,

I'd like to introduce you to Tamra Sullivan, a senior graduating from Portland Independent School this June. **Tamra's studies at Portland Independent would not have been possible without financial aid, funded in large part by the generous support of gifts to the Portland Independent Annual Fund.**

Tamra attended public school through 6th grade. She was a bright student with an aptitude for science and a love of animals. A trip to the Bayside Aquarium introduced her to the world of marine biology, and her ambition was born. "I love the ocean," Tamra says, "and I'm fascinated with everything living in it." Tamra's father died when she was 8, and Tamra's mother,

Heidi Sullivan, worked hard to support Tamra and her two younger sisters. "I wanted Tamra to have the best possible preparation for college. I knew she would work hard wherever she went. We applied to Portland on a wing and a prayer. When the financial aid came through, it was like a miracle."

Tamra has thrived at Portland. She has participated in Mr. Rose's field trip to the Coastal Islands every year, and this year she developed a mini-course for the Lower School called Oceans and the Life in Them. Next year, Tamra starts at the University of Southern California as a marine biology major. "I was able to get into my first choice of college and pursue my dream, because of a scholarship at Portland Independent."

Tamra's story is much like mine—and perhaps like yours, too.

I would not have been able to study at Portland Independent without financial aid and scholarships. The funding I received opened the doors to learning for me, as it did for Tamra and many other students.

Today I am thrilled to be able to open those same doors for a new generation of Portland Independent students through my gifts every year to the Annual Fund. My support—and yours—goes directly to financial aid. **Gifts to the Annual Fund help to ensure that the school continues to attract and support students like Tamra. Please show your support with a gift of $100 today.**

Thank you in advance for your gift to the Portland Independent Annual Fund. We're deeply grateful for your support.
Sincerely,

Lisa Monroe Wilson
Lisa Monroe Wilson '74
President, Portland Independent Alumni Association

PS. You can make your gift to the Portland Independent Annual Fund by using the enclosed envelope or by visiting our secure giving site at www.giving .portlandindependent.org.

APPEAL FOR VOLUNTEERS

Community organizations of all kinds organize volunteers, and many people are more than willing to donate their time for a good cause. An effective letter or an e-mail can inspire volunteers to come out and lend a hand.

Introduction

An appeal for volunteers is really a kind of sales pitch. Its **purpose** is to motivate readers to share their time and energy in a situation in which they don't have to. Accordingly, you'll want to make your recruitment appeal inspiring and attractive. Depending on the cause you're writing for, your **readers** may or may not be interested already. If you're writing to people for the first time for a cause they don't know about, you'll have to work that much harder to motivate them. On the other hand, if you're writing to an established group, they might think you already have enough volunteers. Think hard from your readers' point of view, and develop a pitch you think will motivate them. **Brainstorm** about the benefits, not just for the cause but also for the prospective volunteers. Will you raise needed funds for the school? Great! Can your volunteers have fun and meet new friends in the process? Even better! The Model Outline provides an **organizational** structure you can use. Use a friendly tone as you **draft**. Your initial draft will likely be too long. Remember that people are not obliged to read your letter, so make it as concise as you can. Take a break after you write your first draft, and show it to someone for feedback. **Revise** your letter to make sure it's as engaging and compelling as possible.

MODEL OUTLINE

An appeal for volunteers should be brief.
Opening: Identify yourself, let your readers know why you're writing, and ask explicitly for their help.
Middle: Your middle paragraphs outline the volunteer opportunities, what's expected of volunteers, and how these activities can benefit the cause (and the volunteers themselves).
Conclusion: Finish your appeal by thanking your readers and asking again for their participation. Be sure you provide your contact information at the end of your appeal.

DO	DON'T
• Introduce yourself. You're initiating a cooperative relationship with readers who may not know you, so make a personal introduction.	• Don't assume that people will agree to help just because it's the right thing to do. Your letter must motivate them to want to help.
• If you're writing to a group of people who have volunteered in the past, thank them for their service and let them know their efforts have benefited the cause.	• Don't take your volunteers for granted. Be sure to show your gratitude for their attention and efforts.
• Use a friendly, upbeat tone. You're trying to motivate people to do something they don't have to do, so your letter should be as encouraging and welcoming as possible.	• Don't use guilt to motivate readers. There may be a fine line between inflicting guilt and urging people to take responsibility, but if you cross that line you'll alienate readers.
• Be clear about who or what will benefit from volunteers' efforts. Will students enjoy a better-organized library? Does the sports team need new equipment? Will the neighborhood enjoy a spruced-up park? Let volunteers know exactly why their efforts are needed.	• Don't write your letter before you're sure what you're asking for. A vague appeal for help won't likely get any responses. If you're still trying to figure out the best thing to do, ask for volunteers for an exploratory committee.
• Be explicit about what you're asking for. Baked goods for the sale? People to work in the booth or make phone calls? Gardening, cleaning, other heavy lifting? Or are you asking people to contribute ideas and work together on a committee?	• Don't go on too long. Your potential volunteers are busy, so don't expect them to read a long, too-specific letter. Even if the letter comes from their child's school, readers are likely to regard your letter as a form of junk mail and will be inclined to recycle it rather than reading it. An initial letter should pique readers' interest and motivate them to learn more.
• Be clear about how much time you're asking for. If you're organizing an event, give the exact times of the event and the times you'll need the volunteers to be present. If you're organizing a committee, let potential volunteers know how often you plan to meet, for how long, and if any additional participation will be expected.	• Don't use long block paragraphs. Readers won't read them.
• Mention that the activity will be enjoyable and rewarding for volunteers. A community garden cleanup can mean fun in the fresh air. Working on a committee can be an opportunity to meet and network with people who have similar interests. There's nothing wrong with appealing to volunteers' self-interest in soliciting their help.	• Don't overformat your letter with too many different fonts or too much bold and italics. By all means use formatting to make your text more accessible, but don't let it get messy.

DO (CONTINUED)

- Let readers know if you're going to provide refreshments. There's nothing like a little free food to bring people out in droves. On a more serious note, it also helps readers plan their time if they know they can count on lunch or a bite to eat during the time they're spending with you.
- List a variety of different opportunities for volunteers to help.
- Highlight past successes of similar volunteer efforts. For instance, "Last year, we were able to raise enough money to fund second-grade field trips to the children's museum and the aquarium." If your goals are similar—or higher—this year, say so.
- Consider including some testimonials from previous volunteers about how enjoyable, rewarding, and productive the volunteer opportunity was.
- Be sure to thank potential volunteers for their support, even before they say yes.
- Use formatting to make the letter easy to scan and absorb. Break up long paragraphs into shorter ones, and create numbered or bulleted lists where appropriate.
- Be sure you make next steps clear. If you'd like potential volunteers to contact you, make your phone number or e-mail address easy to find.

LIKE THIS

Dear Neighbors,

My name is Fiona Gorman, and my husband Mike and I live at 1564 Falstaff Road (the Spanish house with the rose garden in front). I'm writing today because I'm hoping to organize a group of neighbors this coming Saturday to help clean up Madison Park.

As you know, the park had a lot of damage in the recent windstorm. The city has removed the downed power line and the big branches, but there's still a lot of cleanup to do, and the city won't get to it for several months. I figure if enough of us turn up, we can make the park usable again in a couple of hours.

Let's meet at the park on Saturday at 12:30 p.m. Mike and I will bring some lawn bags. Please bring whatever tools you might have. A few things we might do:

- Rake up small branches, twigs, and leaves.
- Repair the broken fencing along Madison Drive.
- Repair the slide, if possible.
- Clean up the wading pool and get it ready for the season.

If we all lend a hand, we can get the park ready to use for spring and summer!

Mike and I would like to invite you back to our place at 5:30 for margaritas and snacks.

If you'd like to join us, please give me a call at 555-123-4567 (so we know how much tequila to buy). Hope to see you Saturday!

All the best,

Fiona Gorman

Fiona introduces herself and provides a context in which readers might know her.

Fiona lets people know why she's writing early in the letter.

Fiona explains the need for the volunteer effort.

The task seems reasonable and palatable.

It's helpful to outline exactly what the volunteers will be doing, so people know what they're getting into.

That's a nice little incentive.

Free snacks! Free drinks! I'm there!

Fiona's letter is friendly and engaging. She makes the task sound enjoyable and lets readers know the benefits of participating.

Instructions

You're about to go off and leave something or someone you love—your home, your child, or your pet—in the care of another person. Whether you're just going out for the evening or packing up and spending a month away from home, you'll feel better about going if you leave a good set of instructions for your house sitter, babysitter, or pet sitter.

Introduction

The **purpose** of a note to the sitter is to make sure the sitter has all the information he needs to do a good job taking care of your home, your kids, or your pets. It can also take a load off your mind and help you have more fun if you're sure everything will be taken care of in your absence. To write a successful note, **brainstorm** the content for the note from the point of view of your **reader**. Don't take for granted that he knows what you know, such as where you keep the extra batteries, what's an appropriate bedtime snack for your kids, or what to do with the empty pet-food cans. **Organize** your note in a way that will make the most sense for the sitter. For instance, a note to a babysitter might be organized chronologically—from the start of the evening to the finish. A note to a pet sitter might be organized around categories:

feeding, litter, toys, emergency information, and so on. If the instructions are long or complicated, you should plan to go through a couple of **drafts** to ensure your note is clear, complete, and accurate. Put yourself in your reader's shoes as you **revise** to clarify your message.

DO	DON'T
• Give yourself plenty of time to write the note. Leaving it until the very last minute before you depart increases the likelihood that you'll omit something important. For long instructions, you're wise to start working on your note several days in advance so that you have plenty of time to think about the content.	• Don't take anything for granted. Really think from the point of view of a stranger as you write out your instructions, so that you don't miss anything important.
• Be thorough. Really think from the point of view of your reader, and don't take for granted that she knows as much about your home, your child, or your pet as you do. It's better to supply too much information than not enough.	• Don't leave too much to the sitter's judgment, unless you're really willing to live with the consequences. It's better to write a note that is rather long and detailed than to leave open questions.
• Provide your contact information. It's a good idea to provide two phone numbers, if possible, to make it easier for the sitter to reach you.	
• Provide explicit instructions for the sitter in case of emergency. If an emergency occurs, the last thing you want is for your sitter to be wondering what to do. If you want him to call you to get your guidance before he does anything, let him know. Everyone will rest easier knowing it's all spelled out.	
• Remember to say "thank you."	
• Use a template. If you go out or travel frequently, create a master template for your note to the sitter. Keep the basic information in the template, and update the information as appropriate for each occasion.	
• Provide multiple copies. It's a good idea to e-mail one in advance and leave a hard copy where the sitter can find it easily.	

NOT LIKE THIS . . .

> What's a good bedtime snack for these girls? Don't leave it up to them, or there may be chocolate ice cream and Twizzlers in the bed when you get home.

> Anything in particular? And for how long? Again, don't leave it up to the kids. Giving the sitter a clue about reading material can help the kids feel more continuity when their parents are away.

> Ever? Right before bed?

> Where's the night-light?

Hi Deborah,

Thanks for staying with Jessie and Chloe!

They've had their dinner, and they can have one snack before they go to bed. Bedtime is at 8:00 p.m. sharp. They'll probably ask you to read to them for a little while.

They can watch a movie before bed but no Internet, please.

Chloe is having some issues with the dark, so please leave on the night-light for her.

We'll be back by 10:00. Please call me on my cell if you have any questions.

Thanks again!

> It's wise to leave your phone number in the note, even if you think the sitter already has it. She can reach you faster if your number is right there.

Holly

. . . LIKE THIS

> The note is organized chronologically, so that Deborah knows what to expect at every stage of the evening (as much as you do, anyway, with twin seven-year-olds). Holly's given her some helpful guidance about the choice of a movie, so she's not on her own and won't get tricked into showing the girls a scary movie.

> This section helps guide Deborah through the bedtime transition, including setting limits on appropriate snacks.

Hi Deborah,

Thanks for staying with Jessie and Chloe!

They've had their dinner, and they can watch a movie before bedtime. They've been into *The Little Ballerina* lately, or we also have *Black Beauty*. They MAY NOT watch that insect movie! And definitely no Internet, for the whole evening, no matter what they say.

Start circling the wagons at 7:15 for their 8:00 (sharp) bedtime. They can have a snack before bed—either vanilla yogurt or wheat crackers (on the counter). Please make sure they brush their teeth after the snack.

They'll probably ask you to read to them for a little while. I'm reading them *By the Banks of Plum Creek*. It's on Chloe's nightstand. Just one chapter per night.

> Deborah now knows what to read to the girls, who can enjoy another chapter in their regular book. She also knows how much of the book to read.

Chloe is having some issues with the dark, so please leave on the pink night-light under the window.

> There's the night-light!

We'll be back by 10:00. Please call me on my cell if you have any questions: 212-555-1212.

> Holly's phone number is right there, in case Deborah needs it.

Thanks again!

Holly

NOT LIKE THIS ...

Hi Joe—
Thank you so much for staying and taking care of the place!

Please help yourself to anything while we're gone. Make yourself at home.

> Anything specific?

The back sprinklers will need to be turned on, usually twice a week unless it rains.

> Will Joe know where the faucet is?

There are a couple of lamps on timers. Please don't disturb them.

> How many? Where are they?

Alarm system. The code is 3329. Please make sure it's on when you go out.

> What should Joe do if something goes wrong?

If anything comes up, please don't hesitate to give us a call.

We'll be back on the 20th. Have fun, and thanks again!

> It might be useful to know what time.

—Michele and Bob

. . . LIKE THIS

The note is organized by topic, so Joe knows where to look for information.

Ideally you will have demonstrated the alarm system, but it's a good idea to put a refresher here.

This is exactly the kind of thing that you take for granted but your sitter won't. Good move to remind him.

Giving Joe the number could avoid a visit from armed guards and the police. Always a good thing.

These are helpful details.

It's nice for Joe to know those lamps are on timers and there is not an intruder or a ghost in the house.

Raccoons turning over the trash cans in the middle of the night could be a nasty surprise. Just as well to warn Joe and let him know how to prevent it.

Hi Joe—

Thank you so much for staying and taking care of the place.

House

Alarm system. The code is 3329. Please make sure it's on when you go out. When you go out, please remember to close and lock the patio door, or the system will go nuts. If it goes off by mistake, please call the security company at 626-777-1111.

Please help yourself to anything in the fridge. There's a packet of ground beef in the door. If you don't want to use it, please freeze it right away. There's beer in the pantry.

There are two lamps on timers: one in the living room and one in our bedroom. Please don't disturb them.

Yard

The sprinklers for the front lawn are on automatic. The back ones need to be turned on, usually twice a week unless it rains. The faucet is under the deck, by the hibiscus. Run them for about 20 minutes.

Please make sure you put the lid very tightly on the garbage cans, so the raccoons can't overturn them. If you hear weird tweeting sounds from the backyard in the middle of the night, don't freak. It's the raccoons. ☺ The garbage guys come on Tuesday mornings.

Help yourself to fruit off the trees!

Travel Plans

We'll be in Monterey from the 9th through the 20th. We'll be back home on the 20th by 10 p.m.

Bob's cell is 626-555-4444. Michele's is 626-555-9000.

Thanks again!

—Michele and Bob

RECIPE

You've created the perfect chocolate cake or vegetarian stew or mango salsa, and now you're ready to share your creation with the world. Writing a recipe is not as easy as it seems, but if you follow the guidelines carefully you can ensure that your readers will faithfully reproduce your success in the kitchen.

Introduction

The **purpose** of writing a recipe is to make it possible for you and others to re-create a fabulous dish, and to make it as easy as possible. Assume that your **reader** has only a basic understanding of kitchen skills. If there's anything exotic in your instructions, spell it out for your reader. Your **brainstorming** will involve making sure all parts of the recipe are complete: the ingredients, the necessary implements, and the instructions. This process can be harder than it looks if you're very familiar with the recipe yourself: think from the point of view of your reader, and be sure you include everything. Recipes follow a standard **organizational** format; see the "Recipe Format" for guidance. If you're creating a recipe for the first time, it's important to test it. Even better, have someone else follow the recipe and see what kind of results they get. Use their feedback to **revise** the recipe so that everyone can enjoy your success.

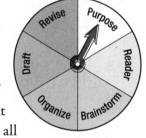

RECIPE FORMAT

Recipes generally follow a conventional format, broken down into two main sections.

List of Ingredients
Provide a list of all ingredients to be used, plus the amount of each. Specify how those ingredients should be prepared, i.e., sliced, grated, chopped, etc. Note any special cookware required by the recipe.

Method of Preparation
Provide step-by-step instructions for preparing the dish:
- preparation of ingredients
- assembling of ingredients
- cooking instructions, including cookware, temperature, and cooking time

Cooking Terms

Here's a list of common cooking terms frequently used in recipes.
Bake—Cook using dry heat inside an oven.
Baste—Moisten food with fat or other liquid during cooking.
Beat—Stir or whip vigorously.

Bind—Thicken liquids by adding a thickening agent like flour.

Blanch—Plunge into boiling water for a few seconds, then into cold water; then drain.

Blend—Mix ingredients thoroughly.

Boil—Cook in a generous amount of bubbling hot liquid.

Braise—Sauté in a small amount of fat, then cook slowly with a small amount of liquid in a covered pan, either in the oven or on the stovetop.

Broil—Cook under direct heat.

Caramelize—Heat gently until sugars turn brown.

Carve—Cut into slices or pieces.

Chop—Cut up into small pieces.

Clarify—Remove impurities from a liquid or fat by heating, skimming, and straining.

Cream—Mix and beat with a spoon or fork until soft and fluffy.

Decant—Separate a liquid from sediment by pouring carefully.

Deep-fry—Immerse in hot fat or oil sufficient to cover food.

Dredge—Sprinkle over food (usually of flour or sugar).

Dress—Shape meat, poultry, or fish before cooking.

Drizzle—Pour liquid slowly and gently over food.

Dry-fry—Fry quickly in pan without oil or fat.

Emulsify—Combine two liquids that do not mix (for instance, oil and vinegar).

Extract—Separate solid from liquid components of fruit or vegetables by pressing or squeezing.

Fillet—Remove skin and bones from raw flesh.

Flambé—Pour small amounts of hot alcoholic liquid over food and then set alight just before serving.

Fold—Combine a light mixture with a heavier one by gently cutting and turning.

Fry—Cook in fat or oil in an open pan.

Garnish—Decorate.

Glacé—Coat with a thin sugar or syrup.

Glaze—Coat food for a glossy finish—usually with a mixture of beaten egg, egg white, milk, syrup, sugar glaze, or reduced juices.

Grate—Cut into small strips by rubbing on a serrated surface.

Grill—Cook under a heat source.

Knead—Work dough by folding, stretching, and pressing with heel of hand.

Marinade—Soak in seasoned liquid to introduce flavor and tenderize prior to cooking.

Pan broil—Cook without fat in a hot frying pan or on a hot griddle.

Parboil—Boil or simmer until partly cooked.

Pare—Thinly peel vegetables or fruit.

Pickle—Preserve in brine, vinegar, oil, and spices.

Plunge—Cool rapidly by immersing in cold water or crushed ice.

Poach—Cook in liquid kept just below boiling point.

Purée—Pulp of fruit or vegetables mashed, sifted, or ground to a smooth, thick paste.

Reduce—Boil liquid rapidly to reduce volume, thus thickening and concentrating.

Render—Heat chopped food to extract fat.

Roast—Cook in the oven.

Roux—Melted butter or fat combined with an equal amount of flour, used to thicken gravies.

Sauté—Cook gently in a small amount of hot fat.

Scald—Heat liquid to just below boiling point.

Score—Make shallow cuts or slashes in the surface of a food.

Sear—Brown raw food in a small amount of fat in an open pan to seal in juices.

Sift—Pass dry ingredient(s) through a fine mesh.

Simmer—Cook in liquid at just below the boiling point.

Skim—Remove scum from the surface after boiling.

Steam—Cook in steam from boiling liquid.

Stew—Cook slowly for a long time in a tightly lidded container, with enough liquid to cover.

Toss—Cover with food coating (for instance fat, flour, or salad dressing) by shaking.

Trim—Remove skin, sinews, or other unwanted parts.

Zest—Thinly peel or grate skin of citrus fruit, without white inner pith.

DO	DON'T
• Note the number of servings the recipe provides.	• Don't abbreviate. Spelling out measurements avoids confusion. If you do use abbreviations, make sure to use conventional and easily under-stood ones.
• List the ingredients in the order they will be used.	
• List the most important ingredients first, if doing so is consistent with order of use.	
• List every ingredient you need to use.	• Don't assume that your readers understand less-common cooking terms. When in doubt, spell it out.
• Make sure to specify the use of every ingredient. Go back and double-check to be sure everything is accounted for.	
• Use subheadings to break out separate elements of the recipe, if relevant, such as "Pie Crust" and "Filling."	• Don't use unconventional measurements, such as ounces when the ingredient is usually measured in cups.
• Mention the appropriate preparation of each ingredient in the ingredient list. For instance, "8 ounces mozzarella, grated" or "1 cup walnuts, chopped."	• Don't use two numerals together without punc-tuation. Set the second numeral in parentheses, for example, "2 (12-ounce) packages grated mozzarella."
• Place your adjectives carefully when you describe ingredients. For instance, when you call for "1 cup of walnuts, chopped," you mean that the walnuts should be measured out prior to being chopped. However, when you call for "1 cup of chopped walnuts," you are suggesting that the reader should measure out walnuts that have already been chopped.	
• Provide the preparation steps in chronological order.	
• Begin every step with an imperative verb, for example, "chop," "slice," "baste." Direct your reader at every step.	
• Specify the appropriate sizes of bowls and cook-ware to be used.	
• Suggest various cooking times, if the dish can be served at different degrees of doneness. If the cooking time is exact, say so.	
• Provide serving instructions, including garnishes.	

- Provide instructions for storage, including how long the item will keep.
- Make it bomb-proof. Especially if you intend to share the recipe on the web, make very sure that it includes all the information anyone would need to prepare it successfully.

NOT LIKE THIS . . .

CHEESECAKE

Crust: Roll out 20 single graham crackers on wax paper. Add 1 cube melted butter. Mix well. Press into 9-inch pie plate and refrigerate.

Filling: Blend 12 ounces soft cream cheese, 2 beaten eggs, ½ cup sugar, 1 t lemon flavoring, 3 t half-and-half. Beat until creamy. Pour into pie shell, bake 20 minutes @ 350.

Topping: 2 cups sour cream, 1 t lemon flavoring, 2 ts. sugar. Stir and spread over cheesecake. Bake at 475 5 mins till set.

It would be helpful to have the list of ingredients at the top, so the reader doesn't have to comb through the recipe to figure out what to buy.

Refrigerate for how long? An experienced cook will understand when the crust is ready, but your recipe should be easy for anyone to use, regardless of their level of experience.

It's helpful to have the parts of the recipe broken out into sections like this. It would be even more helpful to have the separate steps formatted as a list, so they're easy to follow.

More detail would be helpful here, including instructions for pre-heating the oven.

What does "t" mean? Teaspoon? Tablespoon? If you're going to abbreviate, make sure your abbreviations are very clear.

A "cube" of butter is a nonstandard unit of measurement. Better provide the measurement in tablespoons to avoid potential disaster.

Another confusing abbreviation.

"475 5 mins" is confusing. There's a clearer way to express this instruction.

... LIKE THIS

CHEESECAKE

20 single graham crackers

2 tablespoons butter, melted

12 ounces soft cream cheese

2 eggs, beaten

½ cup plus 2 tablespoons white sugar

2 teaspoons lemon flavoring

3 tablespoons half-and-half

2 cups sour cream

> It's clear now how much butter is needed.

> The abbreviations are spelled out, avoiding any possibility of confusion.

> The writer has provided a list of ingredients. The reader can take this list to the market.

> The formatting is even clearer. Each step appears on its own line, and each line begins with an imperative verb.

Crust

Roll out 20 single graham crackers on wax paper.

Add the melted butter and mix well.

Press into a 9-inch pie plate and refrigerate for 20 minutes.

Preheat the oven to 350 degrees F.

> It's helpful to specify how long the crust should be refrigerated,

> We no longer have to wait for the oven to heat after the preparations are done.

Filling

In a large bowl, blend the cream cheese, eggs, ½ cup of the sugar, 1 teaspoon of the lemon flavoring, and the half-and-half.

Beat until creamy.

Remove the crust from refrigerator, pour the filling into the pie shell, and bake for 20 minutes.

Remove from the oven and increase the oven temperature to 475 degrees F.

Topping

Stir together the sour cream, the remaining teaspoon of lemon flavoring, and the remaining 2 tablespoons of sugar.

Spread over the cheesecake.

Return to the oven, and bake for 5 minutes until set.

> Cooking time is easier to understand expressed this way.

On Recipe Writing

The best cooks I know are people who cook without recipes. They may turn to recipes for inspiration and guidance, but when it comes down to actually putting a knife to ingredients and heat to the pan, they are off and running using their own experience and intuition to guide them. More novice cooks, however, will adhere to a recipe closely, referring back to it each step of the way, using it as a careful guide to turning out a good-tasting dish. In this way, recipes act as the threshold between being *able* to cook and *being* a cook, and I approach recipe writing as an opportunity to help people make this leap.

When I set out to write a recipe, I attempt to embed helpful tips and coaching advice into the text so that someone making a dish for the first time will come away with more than just a good tasting dish; they will also have gleaned some basic cooking knowledge. As I write a recipe, I envision myself talking someone through each step, and I do my best to include any information that may lead to success. I encourage people to use all their senses by indicating sights and sounds as well as tastes and touch. I also try to include variables and common pitfalls, and whenever possible I try to explain the reason behind any given step. For instance, in explaining how long to cook a dish topped with feta, I write "Cook until the feta has softened (cooked feta holds its shape, so don't wait for it to melt)."

The true sign of a well-written recipe is when someone can follow it a few times successfully and then advance to making it without having to read each step. In other words, the recipe will have taught them how to cook the dish rather than simply showed them how to do it.

Molly Stevens is the author of *All About Roasting* and *All About Braising*.

Social Media

The advent of blogging has created opportunities for millions of people all over the world to share their opinions, experiences, advice, and artistic creations with an audience of interested readers. Whether you're blogging for fun to or to build a business, you're competing for readers on the web. Putting some time and energy into your blog can make the experience more enjoyable for you and your readers and help build your audience.

Introduction

Find a **purpose** for your blog. You'll attract a more consistent readership if you find a topic or theme and stick to it. Know who your **readers** are, and write with them in mind. Many blogs sound as though they're written entirely off-the-cuff, but that casual tone is often the product of hard work. Take your posts seriously, and **brainstorm** content that is of value to your readers. **Organizing** your posts to grab and keep your readers' attention is key to maintaining an audience over time. There's a lot happening on the web, and it's very easy for readers to leave your page. Experiment with starting your posts with an engaging hook. Plan to go through more than one **draft**, especially in the beginning. As you continue blogging, you'll have a clearer idea of what you're trying to do and what your readers expect, so your first drafts will be closer to the mark. Reread your draft, check for typos, **revise**, and post.

The mere habit of writing, of constantly keeping at it, of never giving up, ultimately teaches you how to write.

—*Gabriel Fielding, novelist*

DO	DON'T
• Read other blogs. One of the best ways to get ideas for your blog and narrow your focus is to read widely on the web. Understand what types of blogs are popular, and see what others are doing.	• Don't be intimidated. Millions of people have personal blogs, and you can, too!
• Decide on a focus for your blog. Of course, you're free to blog about anything at all, but you're likely to find more consistent readers if you find a theme for your blog and stick to it. Is it a personal journal, a collection of reviews, or commentary on current events? Is it devoted to a particular topic that interests you or on which you have special expertise? Whatever focus you've chosen, try to follow it consistently.	• Don't ramble. Of course it's your blog and you can do anything you want, but if you lose focus and ramble, you'll likely lose readers. Keep your posts as concise as they can be.
• Provide value for your reader. Once you know what you want to write about, focus on providing your readers what they want: useful information, clever insights, laughs, whatever.	• Don't bore your readers. Make sure all your posts offer something valuable and interesting to other people, not just yourself.
• Decide about your tone, and stick to it. Your content and your readership will help you decide if your tone should be serious, casual, quirky, or somewhere in between.	• Don't put anything in your blog you don't want the whole world to know. Avoid anything very personal, anything that might offend anyone you know, and anything written in anger. If you're uncertain, write a draft and think about it before you publish it to the web. Blog posts can be found through search engines, so any content you put on your blog is public.
• Give your blog a title.	• Don't plagiarize. If you borrow someone else's words for your blog post, you must say where you got them.
• Use formatting to make your blog posts easy to read. Long block paragraphs can be alienating. Use short paragraphs surrounded by plenty of white space or bullet points to make your text easy to scan. If your post is very long, consider splitting it into two or more shorter entries.	• Don't blog inconsistently if you want to develop a following of readers.

DO (CONTINUED)

- Post frequently. You will have a more loyal readership if readers know they can expect regular updates to your blog. Shoot for a minimum of once a week. You may want to have a few posts "on deck" before you start your blog, and keep a few in reserve for those weeks you don't have time to write original material.
- Title your posts. A blog post with a good title will be more interesting to readers.
- Add pictures. Photos and other graphic images can make your blog more pleasant and interesting to visit.
- Decide whether or not to enable comments on your blog. There are advantages either way. If you allow comments, you have the potential to spark a real discussion among readers. However, enabling comments also means you need to moderate the section, which can become time consuming.

So You Want to Blog . . .

As easy as it is to start a personal blog these days—pretty much all you need is a computer, access to the Internet, and an ego—there are a few important things to consider before you ever publish a single word online. One, anything you say can and will be used against you by your employer, your family, the girl who slighted you in high school, and your child's science teacher. Once you publish something online it becomes permanent property of the Internet and will live far longer than you even if you don't smoke or drink. You can apologize and send flowers, but a copy of your original words will remain in existence forever. Always think twice before hitting publish.

Two, even if you decide to make your blog private or share it with only a few of your friends, you should always ask yourself this: is there a particular person I would not want to read this? Because that particular person will read this. The Internet is sort of magical and evil in that the information on it can maneuver with ease around the most secure roadblocks. Always be mindful that it wouldn't be hard for anyone to see what you're writing.

And three, the anonymity of the Internet can make the most cowardly person a brazen jerk. You will inevitably write something that will elicit a strongly worded and judgmental response. It happens to anyone who has ever written a single word online. Be prepared for the sting. And then be prepared for it to happen again. And again. Keep in mind that you shouldn't take it personally and that many of the people who leave hateful comments could quite possibly be thirteen years old, living in their mother's basement, and eating potato chips for dinner.

Heather B. Armstrong is the creator and writer of the popular blog *Dooce* (www.dooce.com).

ONLINE REVIEW

Everyone's a critic on the web. Writing an online review on sites like Yelp, TripAdvisor, Citysearch, and Amazon gives you a chance to share your experiences with others and help them make decisions about where to stay, what to eat, what to read, and what movies or plays to see. You can also offer helpful reviews about local businesses and service providers. Following a few simple guidelines can make your reviews as useful as possible to the online community.

Introduction

The **purpose** of an online review is to help others by sharing your experiences and insights. Keep in mind that your **readers** are looking to you for guidance in making a decision. Be sure your review is truly helpful rather than just venting. **Brainstorm** from the point of view of your readers. What information would help them? What are they expecting? How does your experience speak to their expectations? **Organize** your review around two or three key insights—don't try to recount your entire experience. Expect to rewrite your **draft** before you finalize your review. As you **revise**, keep your readers' needs in mind. Check your review to confirm that it's really useful, as concise as possible, and free from errors that can damage your credibility.

DO	DON'T
• Keep your review brief and focused. You don't need to record everything that happened at the restaurant or all your impressions of the movie. You can save that for your blog. Focus on providing details that will be useful for your reader.	• Don't write anything untrue. You can seriously damage someone's online reputation through reviews, so stick to the facts, even if you're very unhappy about your experience.
• Offer details. What exactly did you like or dislike? What was wrong with the service? What was good about the food? Was the price fair? Was the experience better than you expected? Why? Specifics are more helpful than generalities.	• Don't write when you're angry. It's fine to start a rough draft when you're upset, but take a break from it and revise it later to ensure you're being fair.
• Try to be balanced. A review that's wholly positive or negative tends to make readers suspicious. Particularly if you have to write a negative review, finding something nice to say (if possible) will make the review more credible.	• Don't exaggerate. Is it really the worst restaurant you've ever been to? Really? Readers won't take you seriously if they think you're exaggerating.
• Write about the product or service and your experience with it, not about yourself. Of course you're writing from your point of view and will mention yourself, but people will abandon long reviews that talk about your evening, your friends, where else you went, how many other Korean restaurants you've been to, why you like Korean better than Chinese, and on and on.	• Don't focus on individuals. Whether your review is positive or negative, it's more helpful to focus on the business rather than on a particular person you encountered, unless that person is the business owner. By the time readers try the place, that waiter or bartender might be gone.
• Give your review a useful and descriptive title.	• Don't be rude. Make your point without insults or abuse.
	• Don't be crude. Foul language undermines your credibility, even if other people are doing it.
	• Don't ruin it for others. If you're reviewing a book or movie, don't reveal key plot points. If you feel you must do so, alert readers at the beginning that your review contains spoilers.
	• Don't leave typos or other errors in your review.

NOT LIKE THIS . . .

Awesome Chinese!

Shun Lee is absolutely the best Chinese restaurant I've ever been too, and I've been to a lot. I would estimate that I've probably eaten in well over 100 Chinese restaurants. In fact, I have a hobby of trying out the local Chinese place wherever I visit travel, and that includes foreign cities like London, Florence, and Paris. Each one has its own distinctive style, and it's fun to observe the local variations. Shun Lee is hands down the best. In fact, it's probably spoiled the other restaurants for me. The food was outstanding, and the service was professional.

> This error—"too" instead of "to"—undermines the reviewer's credibility right from the start.

> Another typo. This reviewer is writing in a hurry and not paying attention. How much weight would you give a review like this?

> Most of this review is really about the reviewer's interest in Chinese restaurants, not about the place he's reviewing.

> Good to know, but it's a little vague. A person trying to decide where to eat would appreciate more specifics.

. . . LIKE THIS

Excellent High-End Chinese Dining

If you're ready for a special experience with Chinese dining, Shun Lee is the place to go. It's hands down the best Chinese restaurant I've ever been to, and Chinese is my absolute favorite.

> This is a good way to show your experience with Chinese cuisine without saying too much about yourself.

I went with a group of four people, and everyone loved it. The food was outstanding. Even ordinary dishes like pork dumplings were delicate and tasty. The garlic eggplant was flavorful and not at all greasy. Peking Duck was crisp and perfect.

> Good to know. They probably sampled a big part of the menu among them.

> A nice detail that shows this restaurant really is a cut above.

> It's good to hear reports about specific dishes.

Shun Lee is a fancy restaurant. Plan to dress nicely, because you'll be surrounded by the pre–theater crowd. The waitstaff are professionals. Waiters wear black suits and are very attentive. Prices are also more in line with high-end restaurants than with the Chinese place around the corner. Expect to pay $20 per entrée. The quality of the food and the overall experience is well worth the additional cost.

> This is very helpful. The reader now knows the atmosphere of the place, the dress code, and the cost.

NOT LIKE THIS . . .

This already sounds like an exaggeration.

No one? Really?

This reviewer has officially lost my sympathy.

"Sucks" is crude and rude and won't win readers to your side.

This personal abuse is ill mannered and won't help your credibility.

Never Again!!!!!!

What a mess. We stayed at the Shelton Arms for two nights in August and it was a total disaster. It's nearly impossible to find your room from the reception desk, and no one in the hotel speaks English. There's NO valet parking. The parking structure is totally dark. There is no restaurant in the hotel. You can drive to a couple places, but the parking sucks and you have to pay to park in a parking structure. When we went to check out, the idiots at the desk didn't have our bill ready and we had to wait around. The nightly rate is incredibly cheap, but I guess you get what you pay for. Totally not worth it. We will not be going back.

. . . LIKE THIS

The reviewer uses this idea—the place is disorganized—to present a lot of the problems she encountered. She's showing some understanding of the place rather than just complaining.

Although the reviewer clearly didn't have a good experience, she is trying to be fair.

An unattended parking garage is a real problem; lack of valet parking is not.

The reviewer thinks from the point of view of her readers, warning them about the parking situation overall.

The writer provides helpful guidance for people who are trying to make a decision. She acknowledges that the hotel might be appropriate for some people, while letting us know that she had a disappointing experience there.

Disappointing

We stayed at the Shelton Arms for two nights in August and did not enjoy it. The whole place seems disorganized. The rooms are not clearly marked and are hard to find. Our bill was not ready when we went to check out, although we had been told it would be. That caused a delay. We had trouble requesting a trundle bed, because we couldn't find staff who spoke English. People were nice, but they were disorganized and simply couldn't understand us.

Parking is a problem in West LA, and this place didn't help. The parking garage was dark and not attended. There is no restaurant in the hotel, and you should be aware that all the local restaurants are attached to expensive parking garages.

The nightly rates are very cheap. The place was clean and functional. If you just need a place to crash, it might be worth it, but it was not my idea of somewhere I want to stay on vacation. We won't be going back.

Popular Online Review Sites

———•———

Looking for the right home for your online review? Visit one of these popular websites to share your experiences and insights. Most of these sites offer guidelines to help you plan and write your review.

Yelp (www.yelp.com) Yelp is a site dedicated to online reviews of all sorts of local businesses, from food and entertainment to health and medical to automotive care to financial services.

TripAdvisor (www.tripadvisor.com) TripAdvisor provides a forum for travelers to share experiences and recommendations. People looking for tips on hotels, restaurants, flights, vacation rentals, and tourist activities will likely find what they're looking for on TripAdvisor.

Urbanspoon (www.urbanspoon.com) Urbanspoon collects restaurant reviews from professional critics as well as food bloggers and average diners. At the moment, this website's coverage is limited to major urban and tourist areas, but its territory is expanding all the time.

Citysearch (www.citysearch.com) Citysearch is a popular online review site that covers restaurants, bars and clubs, spa and beauty establishments, hotels, and shopping destinations.

Insider Pages (www.insiderpages.com) Insider Pages is owned by the same company that owns Citysearch and Urbanspoon, and was developed to cover territory that Citysearch omits, namely businesses in the health and medical, home and garden, auto services, and pet care industries.

Angie's List (www.angieslist.com) Angie's List is a membership site with over 1.5 million members that provides reviews on businesses and service providers in over 550 categories.

Yahoo! Local (www.local.yahoo.com) Yahoo! Local is an add-on to the search engine that offers reviews of all kinds of businesses.

Google Places (www.google.com) Google offers visitors the chance to write reviews of any business that has a page in Google Places.

Many retailers like **Amazon** (www.amazon.com), **Barnes and Noble** (www.barnesandnoble.com), **Costco** (www.costco.com), **Home Depot** (www.homedepot.com), and **Macy's** (www.macys.com) offer users the opportunity to review books and other products purchased on the site.

FACEBOOK STATUS UPDATE

(See also *Facebook Status Update* in the *Writing at Work* section of this book, page 524.)

Facebook is a popular social media site used by people of all ages. On Facebook, the emphasis is on friendship, and it can be a wonderful way to reconnect with old friends and make new ones.

Entries on Facebook are called "status updates," and the original idea was for you to share your latest status with your friends. As Facebook has evolved, people have begun using status updates for all kinds of things— posting pictures, posting links to websites, making political statements, passing along jokes, and so on. With a few important exceptions, you can do anything you like with your Facebook page.

Using Facebook as easy, and most people learn by doing. These tips will help you get started and help you have a good experience on Facebook.

DO	DON'T
• Keep your status updates brief. Everyone is busy; few people will take the time for long updates.	• Don't post anything confidential or private on Facebook. Remember that your friends' friends may see your posts and they may share them. Your posts will therefore likely be seen by a very wide audience. Essentially, anything you post on Facebook is in public view. Protect your privacy.
• Be aware that your status updates can be seen by all your friends and also by your friends' friends. This could be a very wide audience. Make sure that you're comfortable with your status updates being seen publicly.	
• Post every day if you want to be sure that your friends see your updates. Facebook operates on an algorithm such that the more frequently you post, the more "likes" your posts receive, and the more comments your posts receive, the more likely they are to appear in your friends' news feeds. Be active on Facebook if you want to be popular and stay in touch.	• Don't share anything about friends or family on Facebook that they would not want known publicly. You are responsible for protecting their privacy as well as your own.
	• Don't post anything obscene or offensive on Facebook. In addition to the personal offense you may cause, your account may be suspended if other users complain. To cut down on their own work and to keep the greatest number of users happy, Facebook administrators embrace a fairly conservative view of what material is considered obscene. You may regard that nude photograph as art, but Facebook may disagree and require you to take it down.
• "Like" and comment on your friends' updates to improve their visibility.	
• Use the "message" feature to conduct personal communication with just one person or small groups. Your entire group of friends on Facebook	

won't be interested in your personal conversations. However, remember not to put anything confidential *anywhere* on Facebook. You're creating a digital record when you post online anywhere, and you should err on the side of caution.

- Post questions for your friends to answer. Start a conversation and get people interacting.

- Keep up-to-date on Facebook policy changes. Make sure you understand how Facebook works so you can ensure that your friends see your updates.

- Check your privacy settings frequently and ensure you are comfortable with the level of privacy on your account. Facebook is still evolving, and settings may change without your knowing it. Take responsibility for protecting your own privacy by actively managing your account.

- Don't be mean. Unkind remarks about other people and nasty comments on other people's updates can make Facebook an unpleasant place to be. Be civil.

- Don't post too frequently. Although it's important to post regularly to ensure that your friends see your updates, updating your status multiple times per day can annoy people and may cause them to drop you. Exercise some restraint and post selectively.

TWITTER

Twitter is a fast-paced social media platform through which people communicate via "tweets," which are messages of no more than 140 characters. When you join Twitter, you can collect a community of followers and you can also follow other peoples' Twitter feeds. Their tweets will appear on your screen, and yours will appear on theirs. Most people start out following personal friends and favorite celebrities on Twitter and gradually begin to interact with new people they encounter there.

People use Twitter for all kinds of things—as a quick online diary or travelogue, to share links to interesting articles, to pass along jokes, to make political statements, and for many other purposes. During televised events like the Olympics, Twitter is flooded with commentary from people all over the world—it's a real-time conversation happening as events unfold. Tweets may be a condensed form of communication, but there's a lot of potential for connection on Twitter.

DO	DON'T
• Read a lot of tweets. If you're just beginning to tweet, read other people's tweets to get a sense of content and style, and to watch how others interact on Twitter.	• Don't write in all caps. People will think you are shouting.
• Consider your audience on Twitter, whoever they may be, as you tweet. There's a lot of competition for attention on Twitter. Even if you're tweeting just for personal entertainment, try to make sure your tweets are worth your followers' time.	• Don't write anything on Twitter that you don't want the entire world to see. Twitter is a public platform, and there is no such thing as privacy or confidentiality there. Even if you delete a tweet, it can still be found through a search engine. Think before you tweet. If you have any doubt about it, don't tweet it.
• Let your personality shine through. Even in a personal Twitter account, you are representing yourself as a kind of brand. Develop your own style—funny, quirky, serious, whatever you like—and be consistent. Your followers should be able to recognize you through the style of your tweets.	• Don't tweet boring stuff (changed the cat litter; watching the game; had pizza for lunch). The occasional boring update is fine, but don't make a habit of it or your followers may leave.
• Tweet regularly. Your followers want to be able to rely on regular tweets. If you tweet only sporadically, followers will question your commitment and lose interest.	• Don't tweet too frequently. Frequent, regular tweets are a good thing, but don't flood your followers with dozens of tweets a day.
• Shorten the links you post to other websites. Twitter provides a sidebar that makes it easy to create a shortened link that takes up fewer characters.	
• Learn to use hashtags. A hashtag (the # symbol) is used to highlight key words in a tweet in order to make your tweets easier to find for other people who are looking for similar content (for example, #Olympics, #georgeclooney, #dalmations). Check Twitter's support center (http://support.twitter.com) for more information about using hashtags effectively.	
• Learn to use the @ symbol. The @ symbol on Twitter has several uses when affixed to the beginning of someone's name. You can use it to direct a tweet to a particular person (@stephaniesks Where did you find that?), to	

recognize or welcome a new follower (@alocis Thanks for following me!), to mention a person or a brand, even if the tweet is not directed at them (Sitting in Rubio's w Leo enjoying some @Corona), and to give credit for an article you're retweeting (Great article on surfing from @TheTimes).

- Retweet others' content. One way to show reciprocity and build relationships on Twitter is to share —or "retweet"—other people's posts and links. Make a habit of it, and they'll do the same for you.
- Give credit when you retweet someone else's post.

WRITING AT SCHOOL

This section is designed to serve both high school and college students. Writing is an inescapable part of school and college for students in most majors and concentrations. Whether you're studying humanities, social sciences, or even hard sciences, the ability to write well will be an invaluable asset to you in your academic career. In this section of the book, you'll find guidance on writing assignments you may encounter in just about any class, as well as some discipline-specific tasks like lab reports, history essays, and interpretive essays.

As a student, you'll also likely be confronted with a number of non-academic writing challenges: applications of all kinds, e-mails, letters, and even résumés. Here you'll find practical guidance on effective communication outside the classroom.

Writing skills are even more important as you make the transition from school into the "real world." The National Council of Teachers of English describes good writing as "the quintessential 21st century skill,"[1] and recruiters consistently cite writing skills as among the most difficult to find among job applicants. Developing strong writing skills in school will serve you well in your future work life.

---

[1] National Council of Teachers of English, "Writing in the 21st Century," last modified June 16, 2010, http://www.ncte.org/press/21stcentwriting.

The Basics

The ability to take good lecture notes will serve you well in any class you take. Your class notes are an invaluable study tool that reveals what the instructor thinks is important about the subject. Good note-taking skills are also very useful in the work world, so develop good habits now!

Introduction

Taking in-class lecture notes serves several **purposes**. It keeps you awake and attentive in class. In addition, the process of taking notes keeps you learning actively. Finally, your notes will serve you as a study guide in the future. Unless someone borrows your notes, you are the only **reader** you need to consider when taking notes. But that's no reason to slack off: you will need clear and complete notes to prepare for tests. Do yourself a favor and do the best possible job. As you take notes, pay close attention to see if you can discern an outline for the material. Some instructors make this outline easy to see by providing slides or writing on the board. Even if your instructor doesn't do this, you should be able to see some kind of **organization** in the notes, which can help you understand how the instructor thinks about the material. Some students like to copy over their notes after class, using the first version as a kind of rough **draft**, then **revising** and filling in gaps later. Reviewing your notes soon after class is a good idea, even if you don't choose to rewrite them, because it helps you retain the material and can help you identify areas you don't understand well.

DO	DON'T
• Come to class prepared. You'll take better notes and learn more if you've done the assigned reading or other work before the lecture.	• Don't feel you have to write down everything the instructor says. It's virtually impossible to do so, and it's not necessary. Instead, focus on jotting down the main ideas of the lecture. If you wish, you can go back and fill in additional details later.
• Choose the best medium for taking notes. Whether you take notes by hand or on a laptop will depend on your own preference and the content of the course. In math and chemistry classes, you may find it easier to take notes by hand. In humanities classes, taking notes on a laptop or notebook computer may work better. Choose the option that's most comfortable for you and that's acceptable to your instructor.	• Don't think you can cut corners by using a recording device. If you feel more comfortable having a backup recording (and if you have the instructor's permission to record), by all means do so. Remember, though, that to review the recording will take time. You might be better off paying closer attention in class than depending on a recording.
• Listen actively. Active listening means that you're paying attention to key concepts, considering the relationships between ideas, noting transitions, and thinking about how the material fits into the course as a whole. If you just sit and write down what the instructor says without engaging with the material intellectually, you waste a valuable learning opportunity. You're going to have to do this work sooner or later anyway, if you want to pass your exam, so you might as well do it now.	• Don't worry about punctuation and spelling. No one is going to give you a grade on your notes. As long as you can understand them, they're serving their purpose.
• Write down the most important concepts, not every single word the instructor says. Skip unimportant words like "a," "an," and "the."	• Don't sit back and think you know the material already. The instructor may be going over material you've already seen in your reading, but you shouldn't assume there's nothing new you can learn. Pay attention to the way the instructor conveys the information. The instructor's approach to the material will likely be more relevant to the exam than the textbook's approach.
• Mark any content that you don't understand. Put a big question mark next to information that doesn't make sense to you, and ask your instructor to clarify it after class. Depending on your instruc-	

tor's style and preferences, you may want to ask the question during the lecture itself.

- Use abbreviations. Developing a system of abbreviations can make your note taking go much faster. Some will be specific to the class. For instance, you can abbreviate "Shakespeare" as "S," "Reformation" as "Ref," "catalysis" as "cat," "evolution" as "ev," and so on. Make sure you use your chosen abbreviations consistently and that you're not likely to confuse them with other words. Some abbreviations are useful for any subject. See the box "Note-Taking Abbreviations and Symbols" (page 228) for some suggestions.

- Mark assignments. It's easy for assignments to get lost in the body of your notes. Devise a consistent way to mark assignments so that you don't miss them: put a box around them, underline them— whatever works best for you.

- Review your notes promptly after class. Learning is accelerated if you go back over your notes the same day you took them. Some students like to copy their notes and add material from the textbook or from the lecture itself. Others use different-colored pens and markers, or various types of formatting in a Word file, to highlight important information. Whatever you do, keep working actively with your notes.

- Mark it in your notes if you miss a class. If you're writing in a notebook, leave several blank pages so you can copy a classmate's notes.

Note-Taking Abbreviations and Symbols

Listed here are some of the most common abbreviations and symbols useful for many different classes. You can add to these by creating your own to save time on note taking.

>	more than	¶	paragraph
<	less than	re	about
&	and	yr	year
w/	with	c	about (used with dates)
w/o	without	vs	versus, as opposed to
@	at	e.g.	for example
b/c	because	i.e.	that is
b4	before	NB	note (to emphasize
esp	especially		importance)
etc	et cetera, and so on	/	per (6–8 small snacks/day)
sth	something	➡	leads to
nth	nothing	~	about, approximately
v	very	Ψ	psychology, psychologically
∴	therefore	♀	female, woman, women
p/pp	page/pages	♂	male, man, men

Reading Notes

In classes that use textbooks, it can be helpful to take notes on the assigned reading. Here are some tips to help you take reading notes efficiently.

Read or skim the entire piece first. It can be difficult to discern the major from the minor points on a first reading. Skimming the piece first will help you understand how to organize your notes.

Record just the main points of the piece. If you take extremely detailed notes, you'll end up simply rewriting the entire piece rather than noting the highlights.

Summarize the piece. Try writing a summary of just the main points of the reading in five sentences or less. This exercise will force you to digest and distill the material. For help, see Summary (page 237).

Consider taking notes on index cards if you're preparing a research paper. Having your notes on cards can make it easier to move information around as your outline develops. See also Research Paper (page 243).

OUTLINE

An outline is a plan of the content to be used in a written document. An outline lists topics and ideas as well as the order in which those ideas will be presented. It's often a good idea to create an outline prior to writing something to provide guidance for your writing process.

Introduction

The **purpose** of an outline is to help you generate and organize content. Writing an outline can help order material and clarify relationships among the parts. It can also help develop and refine your argument, reveal areas lacking in sufficient content, and identify content that does not belong in your document. **Brainstorming** is a critical part of creating an outline. Pull together all your ideas and all your research and begin **organizing** it. Examples are provided for several outline formats you might use; select the one that seems most appropriate for your task. Unless your outline is very short, you will probably go through several rounds of brainstorming, reorganizing, and **revising** as you develop the outline.

DO	DON'T
• Choose the most appropriate format for outlining the material you have. A very short document does not require a complex outline format.	• Don't rush it. Writing an outline appears to add another step—and more work—to the writing process. However, the point of outlining is to save you time and trouble over the long run. If you rush the outlining process, you may find yourself having to go back and make significant changes later in the writing process.
• Keep your headings parallel. Most outline formats include several levels of headings indicating the relative importance of that content. Make sure that all the content that appears at the same level is of comparable importance.	• Don't allow your word processing software to hijack your outline. The autoformat feature will sometimes, well, automatically format your outline for you as you work. Keep an eye on it to ensure it's really doing what you want.
• Subordinate. Use lower-level headings for information that is a component part of a larger topic or idea. Keep subordinate headings parallel with one another.	
• Be flexible. You may find that your ideas change as you work with your content and develop your outline. Be willing to adjust your overall argument or thesis to incorporate your new ideas.	

LIKE THIS

There are many different types of outlines you can use. Select the one that makes the most sense given the length of your writing project, the complexity of your content, and your own style of thinking and writing.

TOPIC OUTLINE

Very short writing tasks like short papers and exam essay questions may require no more than a simple topical outline. (See also Exam Essay Question, on page 257.)

> Thesis: Shakespeare often uses female characters to question conventional wisdom and practices
> —Comedies. Beatrice and Benedick. Girls dressed as boys.
> —Histories. Women as victims of war, speaking out against war.
> —Tragedies. Women subversive of patriarchy.

ALPHANUMERIC OUTLINE

The alphanumeric outline is the format many people think of when they hear the word "outline." It uses a combination of roman numerals, Arabic numerals, and capital and lowercase letters to lay out the relationships between topics and ideas. Stripped of its content, it looks like this:

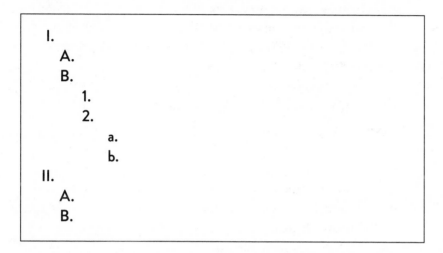

Note that each heading that has subheadings has at least two. If you have only one subheading, you should collapse it into the main heading or consider developing more material.

Alphanumeric outlines can use either full sentences or topics (brief phrases or single words). Whichever you choose, be consistent. Use either whole sentences or topics in your outline, but not both.

ALPHANUMERIC TOPIC OUTLINE

I. Vietnam War
   A. Domestic resistance to war
      1. On college campuses
      2. Broad antiwar movement
   B. Obstacles to military victory
      1. Conscripted army
      2. Difficulties of fighting a guerrilla war
         a. Unprepared for jungle warfare
         b. Unanticipated involvement of civilians
II. Gulf War
   A. Widespread support for war
      1. Very limited press coverage of war
      2. Identification with Kuwaiti sovereignty
      3. Notion of "automated" war
   B. Military victory
      1. Questions about objectives
      2. US/Allied forces overwhelming

ALPHANUMERIC SENTENCE OUTLINE

I. The Vietnam War was the most difficult war the United States had ever waged, both domestically and in terms of achieving military objectives.

    A. Domestic resistance to the war grew steadily among the US population and undermined the war effort.

    B. Obstacles to military victory were unprecedented and unanticipated.

        1. The largely conscripted army felt little support for the war, especially as the years dragged on.

        2. The difficulties of fighting a guerrilla war made military victory very difficult.

            a. The US was fundamentally unprepared for jungle warfare.

            b. The unanticipated involvement of Vietnamese civilians created problems both for strategists and for troops on the ground.

II. The first Gulf War reflected different social conditions and military circumstances.

    A. The US military enjoyed widespread popular support for the war.

        1. Very limited press coverage of war meant that few Americans saw the "ugly" side of the war.

        2. Many US citizens identified with the Kuwaiti struggle for sovereignty.

        3. Many US citizens believed this would be an "automated" war with few US casualties.

    B. Military victory appeared to come about relatively easily.

        1. Many questioned the ultimate objectives of the war, making any declaration of victory somewhat arbitrary.

        2. US and Allied forces quickly overwhelmed the Iraqi military.

DECIMAL OUTLINE

Decimal outlines use sequences of numbers and indentation to show relationships among topics.

1.0 Henry VIII
    1.1 Katherine of Aragon
        1.1.1 Mary
    1.2 Anne Boleyn
        1.2.1 Elizabeth
    1.3 Jane Seymour
        1.3.1 Edward
    1.4 Anne of Cleves
    1.5 Catherine Howard
    1.6 Catherine Parr
2.0 Edward VI
3.0 Mary I
4.0 Elizabeth I
5.0 James I
    5.1 Anne
        5.1.1 Charles
6.0 Charles I
    6.1 Henrietta Maria
        6.1.1 James
7.0 James I
    7.1 Anne Hyde
        7.1.1 Mary (Mary II)
    7.2 Mary of Modena
8.0 William III and Mary II

FIVE-PARAGRAPH ESSAY OUTLINE

The five-paragraph essay is a popular assignment in high school and college. This type of outline can help you organize your material.

I. Introductory paragraph
   A. Topic sentence or thesis statement
      1. Introduce subtopic 1 (to be explained fully in paragraph 2)
      2. Introduce subtopic 2 (to be explained fully in paragraph 3)
      3. Introduce subtopic 3 (to be explained fully in paragraph 4)
   B. Transition to the next paragraph
II. Paragraph 2
   A. Restate subtopic 1
      1. Supporting information
      2. Supporting information
   B. Transition to the next paragraph
III. Paragraph 3
   A. Restate subtopic 2
      1. Supporting information
      2. Supporting information
   B. Transition to the next paragraph
IV. Paragraph 4
   A. Restate subtopic 3
      1. Supporting information
      2. Supporting information
   B. Transition to the next paragraph
V. Concluding paragraph
   A. Synthesis of thesis
   B. Restatement of main topic and subtopics

The Outline in Action

Here is a simple alphanumeric outline for the argumentative essay presented on page 298:

The Great Gatsby and the Dark Side of the Jazz Age

I. Depicts a part of American society between the wars—Jazz Age
   A. Ostentatious display of wealth
   B. Social decay—corruption and decadence
   C. Undermining of the American dream of the past; future uncertain
II. Gatsby charismatic but not what he seems
   A. Casual and frivolous excess of Gatsby's spending
   B. Gatsby not from the wealthy background he claims
   C. Gatsby not an honest "self-made man"—his wealth from crime
   D. Gatsby's abandoned mansion a symbol of emptiness
III. Fitzgerald also critical of "old money"
   A. Tom unfaithful to Daisy
   B. Tom and Daisy letting Gatsby take blame for Myrtle's death
   C. Tom's justification to Nick later in New York City
   D. Tom and Daisy "careless people" who let others clean up the mess
IV. Use of imagery to portray social decay
   A. The "Valley of Ashes" on Nick's train ride
   B. Connection between Myrtle and Valley of Ashes
V. Extremes of wealth and decay—dark side of the Jazz Age
   A. Nick's memory of young people coming and going at Christmastime
   B. Innocence lost
   C. America (and Americans) doomed to seek the past, which is forever lost

SUMMARY

A summary is a condensed version of another written document. A summary should be considerably shorter than the original while still delivering its main points. A good rule of thumb is that a summary should be no longer than 25 percent of the length of the source.

Introduction

Your **purpose** in writing a summary is to create a condensed version of an article or other piece of writing. Imagine that your **reader** is someone who needs the key information from the article but does not have the time to read the whole thing. Your task is to provide that information for her. Your **brainstorming** consists of reading the source very carefully, more than once, and noting the most important parts of it. Take notes, and then make an outline from your notes. Your outline should follow the outline of the original source. **Organize** your summary the same way the source is organized. Follow your outline as you write your **draft**. You may find that your first draft is too long. It can be difficult, especially with a long article, to condense the source material enough. Take a break from your draft, and then go back and reread it. Is there any information you can cut? Are there any areas that are unclear and should be expanded? Refer back to the original source as you reread and **revise** your draft to make sure your summary is complete and accurate. Check carefully for typos and other errors.

DO	DON'T
• Read the source carefully and take notes. You should plan to read the source more than once to become thoroughly familiar with it.	• Don't insert any of your own ideas or opinions into the summary. Writing a summary is rather mechanical and not very creative. Focus on reproducing the author's content in your own words.
• Try to understand the structure of the source material. If you can see how the author organized it, you'll have an easier time summarizing it.	• Don't interpret. Your job is simply to restate the content of the original source in a condensed form, not to explain it or offer your views about
• Look for a thesis statement or a statement of the main idea in the original source.	what it means. If your instructor wants you to write a response to the original, make sure you
• Note the name and author of the original at the beginning of your summary. Some instructors ask	mark your response clearly.

DO (CONTINUED)	DON'T (CONTINUED)
you to provide a complete bibliographical citation of the source. If you're not sure what your instructor wants, ask.	• Don't copy any phrases or sentences from the original. Use your own words. If you must copy phrases in the summary, be sure you enclose them in quotation marks.
• Occasionally remind readers that this is a summary by using phrases like "The author argues . . ." or "According to the article . . ." (Note: if you are writing an **abstract**, which is a special kind of summary, do not mention the article or the author.)	• Don't include examples in your summary. Summaries typically cover just the main points of the original and do not include examples that the author gives for illustration.
• Use the the appropriate verb tense to summarize the source material. Depending on your field, your summary may be written in past or present tense. Consult the appropriate style guide if you are unsure which verb tense to use (see "Common Citation Style Guides for Papers").	
• Use your own words in writing the summary. You should paraphrase the source material.	
• Keep it brief. A good guideline is to make your summary no longer than 25 percent of the length of the original, unless your instructor has asked you to do otherwise.	

Common Citation Style Guides for Papers

The purpose of citing sources in your papers is to make clear to the reader what ideas you have borrowed from others and what words you have quoted directly. (If you're not sure what material you need to cite, refer to the box "Plagiarism and How to Avoid It" on page 287. If you're still unsure, ask your instructor or tutor for guidance. Failure to cite your sources can be a costly mistake, so make sure you understand how to do it.)

Different disciplines and fields of study use different citation style guides. These style guides specify how to format bibliographies, footnotes, and endnotes, and provide other guidance about documenting your sources. They also offer general guidance about grammar, punctuation, word choice, spelling, and other topics.

Here are the major documentation formats currently in use:

Modern Language Association (MLA). Used in most English and literature classes. Consult *MLA Handbook for Writers of Research Papers*, 7th ed. (New York: Modern Language Association, 2009), or visit www .mlahandbook.org/fragment/public_index.

Chicago Manual of Style **(often just called** *Chicago*). Typically used in history and some other social sciences. Consult *The Chicago Manual of Style*, 16th ed. (Chicago: University of Chicago Press, 2010), or visit www.chicagomanualofstyle.org/16/contents.html.

American Psychological Association (APA). Typically used in sciences and social sciences. Consult *Publication Manual of the American Psychological Association*, 6th ed. (Washington , DC: American Psychological Association, 2009), or visit www.apastyle.org/.

Turabian. Often used in high school classes and also used by some historians. Consult Kate L. Turabian, *A Manual for Writers of Research Papers, Theses, and Dissertations: Chicago Style for Students and Researchers*, 7th ed., rev. Wayne C. Booth, Gregory C. Colomb, and Joseph M. Williams (Chicago: University of Chicago Press, 2007), or visit www.press .uchicago.edu/books/turabian/turabian_citationguide.html.

In addition to these widely used guides, your school or department may have a style sheet that explains the preferred style for citation and documentation and may also include guidelines about submitting written work to your instructors. If you're not sure if your school or department has a style sheet, ask.

ANNOTATED BIBLIOGRAPHY

A bibliography is a list of sources—books, articles, reports, video and audio sources, and web pages—that includes author and publication information; it is found at the end of a report or an essay. An annotated bibliography also includes a brief summary and perhaps an analytical evaluation of the source. An annotated bibliography may be part of a report or paper, or it may be a stand-alone assignment.

Introduction

The **purpose** of an annotated bibliography in a research document is to assist and direct further researchers by reporting on sources. Often in a school assignment, it's to demonstrate that you've read your sources and understand them, and it serves as practice for "real" research. Assume that your **reader** is another researcher in the same field. An important part of **brainstorming** this assignment is deciding on the scope and focus of the annotation. Do you intend to provide a simple description of the source, or do you want to provide an analytical evaluation of it? The box "Types of Annotated Bibliographies" offers some suggestions. Your annotated bibliography should be **organized** alphabetically by author's last name. Annotated bibliographies may look simple, but they contain a lot of detail. Allow yourself plenty of time between **drafts** to reread and **revise**. Carefully check the formatting of entries, and be sure your annotations are consistent.

Types of Annotated Bibliographies

Annotations may be descriptive or analytical. A descriptive annotation provides an objective summary of the content of the work. An analytical annotation offers critical commentary on the content, from a particular point of view:

Intended audience: For whom is this work intended? Why is it useful for that audience?

Use: What is the information for?

Significance: Why is this work important in its field?

Methodology: What methodology does this source use?

Value: How is this work especially valuable in the field?

Author's background: What is the author's background and approach?

Theoretical orientation: Does this text use a particular theory? Is it influenced by a particular theoretical orientation?

Usefulness for your research: If you are compiling an annotated bibliography for a project you intend to do, how useful will this source be to you?

As you plan your annotated bibliography, select which focus you want to use.

DO	DON'T
• Start early on this assignment. Make sure you have the time to read all your sources thoroughly.	• Don't attempt to write an annotation of something you haven't read. It defeats the purpose of the exercise, and it's extremely easy to get caught.
• Use the correct citation format. Different fields have slightly different formats for bibliographies. Among the most popular are APA, MLA, Chicago, and Turabian. If you're not sure how to format your entries, ask your teacher or professor. Asking is better than guessing or assuming that "it doesn't matter that much." Format is important. (For resources, see the box "Common Citation Style Guides for Papers" on page 238.)	• Don't go on too long. Whatever the focus of your annotated bibliography, your entries should be brief and concise. Generally six lines per entry is the limit.
• Make sure all your annotations are about the same length. Don't write one sentence for one source and six for another. Give every entry roughly the same amount of attention.	

DO (CONTINUED)

- Make sure your annotation style is uniform throughout. Annotations may be written in full sentences or in phrases. Once you choose a style, use it consistently.
- Make sure your annotations are consistent in terms of information presented. Once you select a focus for your bibliography, stick with it.

LIKE THIS

VALUE

> Shapiro, James L. *Contested Will: Who Wrote Shakespeare?* New York: Simon & Schuster, 2010.
>> Rather than take a partisan approach to the authorship controversy, Shapiro traces the genesis of the controversy and explores why authorship became a question in the first place.

AUDIENCE

> Shakespeare, William. *Hamlet.* Edited by Cyrus Hoy. A Norton Critical Edition. New York: W. W. Norton, 1963.
>> This edition's generous annotations make it especially useful for high school students.

SIGNIFICANCE

> Greenblatt, Stephen Jay. *Shakespearean Negotiations: The Circulation of Social Energy in Renaissance England.* Berkeley: University of California Press, 1988.
>> Greenblatt was the first to coin the term "new historicism." Contains the groundbreaking essay "Invisible Bullets," which explored class and culture in the history plays.

Eagleton, Terry. *Shakespeare and Society: Critical Studies in Shakespearean Drama.* London: Chatto & Windus, 1967. Older work but critical for the development of Marxist criticism of Shakespeare and Renaissance drama.

RESEARCH PAPER

The research paper is a common assignment in high school and in some college composition classes as well. By the time you get to upper-division courses in college, it is assumed that you understand how to write one. Writing your first research paper is kind of a rite of passage, but once you're familiar with the process, the skills you've learned will serve you well in many different classes.

Start early. It can't be emphasized enough that you should start on this assignment as soon as you receive it. A research paper can't be done at the last minute. Many students feel anxious about writing a research paper and procrastinate about starting. The longer you procrastinate, the more anxious you'll get. The best cure for anxiety is working on the paper.

Refer to these other entries and boxes to help you with different parts of your research paper:

Outline (page 229)

Annotated Bibliography (page 240)

"Reading Notes" (page 228)

"Common Citation Style Guides for Papers" (page 238)

"How to Write a Thesis Statement" (page 264)

"Writing Strong Paragraphs" (page 271)

"They Say/I Say": Some Strategies for Quoting and Responding to Sources (page 286)

"Plagiarism and How to Avoid It" (page 287)

Introduction

Step One: Understand the Assignment

The **purpose** of a research paper is to conduct an in-depth investigation of a topic.

The purpose behind the research paper *as an assignment* is often to give you practice in conducting research, developing a thesis, responding to the ideas of other researchers, and maintaining an argument over an extended essay. These are useful skills that will serve you well throughout your career as a student.

The primary **reader** of your research paper will be your instructor, of course. As with any piece of writing, it's important to understand your reader's needs and expectations. Be sure you understand what your instructor wants.

There are two different kinds of research papers:

- An *argumentative research paper* takes a stand on an issue and provides evidence to support a claim. This kind of paper needs a strong thesis and precise thesis statement to let the reader know your point of view. (See also Argumentative Essay on page 282 and the box "How to Write a Thesis Statement" on page 264.)
- An *analytical research paper* proposes a research question—rather than a point to be proven—and explores that question. The writer provides a critical analysis of various sources about the topic. (See also Annotated Bibliography on page 240.)

In addition to understanding what kind of paper you should write, you should also be sure you understand what your instructor expects in terms of length, number of references, and citation style. If you have any questions, *ask*.

Step Two: Identify a Topic

Your instructor may have given you a list of topics from which to choose, or you may be free to find your own topic.

Give yourself plenty of time to explore your topic before you make a firm decision about it. Choose something that interests you. You'll be spending a lot of time on this assignment, and you'll be happier if you're writing about a topic that engages you. Read widely, and be sure there are enough published sources about the topic to support the development of your paper.

If you are allowed to choose your own topic, be sure to discuss your choice with your instructor and get approval before you begin work on your paper. The research paper is far too big a project for you to start down the wrong road and have to begin again.

Step Three: Conduct Research

Your **brainstorming** should be combined with the process of doing research. The content for your research paper doesn't come only from your own head. It's a product of a "conversation" you have with others who have written about the same topic. Don't think of reading and thinking as two separate steps—do them both together.

Look widely for information on your topic—in books, journals, newspapers, magazines, and websites, as appropriate. Don't limit your research only to the web: there is a lot of information in printed sources that is not available on the web.

As you conduct research, create bibliography, citation, and outline note cards (see page 247). Be fair and honest as you write your note cards. Characterize your sources fairly, and be willing to include sources that oppose your position.

As you collect information, you can begin to **organize** your material. The longer and more complex your paper, the more helpful it is to work from a formal outline. A research paper is typically long, and it may be longer than anything you've written before. Start developing your outline early, and be flexible and willing to change it if your ideas change or your research leads you in a new direction. See Outline on page 229 for guidance.

At this stage, you should also begin work on distilling a thesis statement from your broader topic. Narrow your thesis to an idea that's specific enough that you can support it successfully in your paper. For help, see the box "How to Write a Thesis Statement" on page 264.

Step Four: Write Your Draft

Once you have your research done, it's time to start the writing process. Revise and finalize your thesis statement and your outline. Use your outline to write your draft. Leave yourself time to go through several **drafts** of your paper. There are many steps in developing a research paper prior to writing your draft, but don't leave the writing till the last minute. The process of writing may reveal that you have some content missing and need to do additional research or that you need to rethink some of your ideas. Starting too late on the drafting may mean you don't have time to submit a polished draft.

As you write, compile your bibliography (sometimes called References or Works Cited). Be sure you use the appropriate formatting conventions for your citations and bibliography. Most research papers use either MLA or APA formats (see the box "Common Citation Style Guides for Papers" on page 238). If you're unsure what format to use, ask your instructor.

Step Five: Revise

Allow yourself time to do substantial revisions on your paper. Do your revisions in stages, asking these questions at each pass:

- Does the paper meet the requirements of the assignment?
- Is your thesis or research question clear?
- Does your paper flow smoothly? Is anything out of place?
- Are there any places where you need to do more research or explain your position more fully? Do you show support for every claim you make?
- Are your paragraphs well organized with clear topic sentences?
- Do you provide citation information for every source you've used?
- Is your paper free of typos, grammatical errors, and other mechanical flaws?

Proofread carefully. You've put a lot of work into this assignment, and you don't want to lose points for errors you could have prevented.

LIKE THIS

SAMPLE NOTE CARDS

Note cards are an invaluable tool in researching, planning, and writing your research paper. You can use different-colored note cards for these three main purposes:

- Bibliography cards
- Citation cards
- Outline cards

Although there are some digital note card applications available (for instance, NoodleTools), many instructors suggest you use paper cards, and many students prefer them because they're easy to manipulate.

BIBLIOGRAPHY CARDS

Create a bibliography card for every source you use in your paper. It's a good idea to create a card for a source even if you're not yet sure you're going to use that source in the final paper. It's better to have it and not use it than to need it later and have to go back and find the bibliographical information. (Check to be sure you understand which citation format is required in your class. For more information, see the box "Common Citation Style Guides for Papers," page 238.)

Record the information on your bibliography cards using the correct citation format, so you can easily transfer the information to the bibliography in your paper. If you get in the habit of using the correct format as you go, formatting the final document will be easier.

Wiesner, Merry E. *Women and Gender in Early Modern Europe.* Cambridge: Cambridge University Press, 1993.

Bayne, Diane Valeri. "*The Instruction of a Christian Woman*: Richard Hyrde and the Thomas More Circle." *Moreana: Bulletin Thomas More* 45 (1975): 5–15.

CITATION CARDS

Use note cards to record ideas, facts, and quotations taken from your sources. Record quotations *exactly* as they appear in the source, so you don't have to go back and check later. Be sure to note which source the material comes from. There are three ways to take notes from your sources:

- Quote: Copy the text word for word, including all punctuation, and enclose everything in quotation marks.
- Paraphrase: Rewrite what the author says in your own words.
- Summarize: Note the main idea of the passage.

Use these cards when you create the citations or footnotes in your paper. If you have questions about what information you need to cite in your paper, see the box "Plagiarism and How to Avoid It" (page 287).

> The author has two references by this researcher in her bibliography, so she identifies this source using a shortened version of its title.

Wiesner, *Women*, p. 104

English widows often stressed poverty in successful appeals to city and guild representatives

Collinson, p. 74

"unlike their Catholic counterparts, Protestant women had no religious justification for a lifestyle that excluded men and, therefore, they experienced widespread economic and social discrimination."

OUTLINE CARDS

Use outline cards to record your own ideas about the subject you're researching. Put these cards together to outline your essay. Many students spread them out on the floor or pin them up on a wall to get a complete view of their entire paper. Once you have them arranged in the order you want, start inserting your citation cards in the appropriate places. The content on these citation cards provides support for the ideas on your outline cards. For help with outlining, see Outline (page 229).

Widows in Catholic Europe and Protestant England had different options in their lives.

Spanish Catholic widows could go to live at convents.

English Protestant widows did not have the option of retiring to a convent. They had to remain in society.

**SAMPLE TITLE
PAGE**

> Check with your instructor and consult your style guide to see if a title page is required.

Widows in Early Modern England and Spain

Ella Gillespie

History 201

Professor Simpson

December 7, 2013

Gillespie 1

Widows in Early Modern England and Spain

During the early modern period, England and Spain were the two most powerful nations in Europe. How were women treated in these countries? One interesting way to explore this question is to delve into the treatment of widows in these cultures. Widows are an important case, because they represent contemporary women at their most free: no longer under the control of either father or husband. Although some historians have pointed to the Reformation as a key point in the development of women's rights in Europe, other evidence suggests that Spanish widows may have had greater legal protections and social acceptance than their English counterparts.

In Spain, a highly unified, state-sponsored orthodoxy—the Catholic church—laid down strict guidelines for the behavior of widows. They were to spend their lives in quiet contemplation, and they were not to remarry. In Catholic countries, widows might enter convents, either as nuns or, more commonly, as residents.[1]

The teachings of the Christian church were frequently disseminated through popular "behavior manuals." According to P. Renée Baerstein, "The special role of the widow as a model of piety has been developed in Christian thought from early Christian times: Ambrose, Jerome, and Augustine all wrote on the subject. The genre exploded, however, in the late Middle Ages with behavior manuals on the three 'states of life' of laywomen."[2]

---

[1] For a discussion of the convent as a place of refuge for widows in late medieval Milan, see P. Renée Baerstein, "In Widow's Habit: Women between Convent and Family in Sixteenth-Century Milan," *Sixteenth Century Journal* 25, no. 4 (1994): 787–807.

[2] Ibid., 789.

SAMPLE BIBLIOGRAPHY

This section may also be called "References" or "Works Cited" depending on the citation format you're using. Check with your instructor to be sure you know which citation format to use for your paper. For more information, see "Common Citation Style Guides for Papers, (page 238).

Abbott, Mary. *Family Ties: English Families 1540–1920*. New York: Routledge, 1993.

Anderson, Bonnie S., and Judith P. Zinsser. *A History of Their Own: Women in Europe from Prehistory to the Present*. Vol. 1. New York: Harper & Row, 1988.

Bayne, Diane Valeri. "*The Instruction of a Christian Woman*: Richard Hyrde and the Thomas More Circle." *Moreana: Bulletin Thomas More* 45 (1975): 5–15.

Bossy, John. *The English Catholic Community, 1570–1850*. New York: Oxford University Press, 1976.

Camden, Carroll. *The Elizabethan Woman*. Mamaroneck, NY: Paul P. Appel, 1975.

Carlson, Eric Josef. *Marriage and the English Reformation*. Cambridge, MA: Basil Blackwell, 1994.

Collinson, Patrick. *Birthpangs of Protestant England*. Basingstoke, UK: Macmillan, 1988.

Duffy, Eamon. *The Stripping of the Altars: Traditional Religion in England 1400–1580*. New Haven, CT: Yale University Press, 1992.

Durston, Christopher. *The Family in the English Revolution*. Oxford: Basil Blackwell, 1989.

Erickson, Amy Louise. *Women and Property in Early Modern England*. London: Routledge, 1993.

Goody, Jack. *The Development of the Family and Marriage in Europe*. Cambridge: Cambridge University Press, 1983.

Haigh, Christopher. *English Reformations: Religion, Politics, and Society under the Tudors*. Oxford: Clarendon Press, 1993.

Klein, Joan Larsen, ed. *Daughters, Wives, and Widows: Writings by Men about Women and Marriage in England, 1500–1640*. Urbana: University of Illinois Press, 1992.

Leites, Edmund. "The Duty to Desire: Love Friendship and Sexuality in Some Puritan Theories of Marriage." *Journal of Social History* 15 (1982): 383–408.

Macfarlane, Alan. *Marriage and Love in England: Modes of Reproduction 1300–1840*. Oxford: Basil Blackwell, 1986.

———. Review of Lawrence Stone, *The Family, Sex and Marriage. History and Theory* 18 (1979): 103–26.

Orlen, Lena Cowen. *Private Matters and Public Culture in Post-Reformation England.* Ithaca, NY: Cornell University Press, 1994.

Outhwaite, R. B. *Marriage and Society: Studies in the Social History of Marriage.* New York: St. Martin's Press, 1981.

Powell, Chilton. *English Domestic Relations 1487–1653.* New York: Columbia University Press, 1917.

Reay, Barry, ed. *Popular Culture in Seventeeth-Century England.* London: Croom Helm, 1985.

———. *Radical Religion in the English Revolution.* Oxford: Oxford University Press, 1984.

Stenton, Doris Mary. *The English Woman in History.* New York: Schocken Books, 1977.

Stone, Lawrence. *The Family, Sex and Marriage in England 1500–1800.* London: Weidenfeld & Nicolson, 1977.

———. *Uncertain Unions: Marriage in England 1660–1753.* Oxford: Oxford University Press, 1992.

Todd, Margo. *Christian Humanism and the Puritan Social Order.* Cambridge: Cambridge University Press, 1987.

Travitsky, Betty S., and Adele F. Seeff, eds. *Attending to Women in Early Modern England.* Newark, NJ: University of Delaware Press, 1994.

Wiesner, Merry E. "Spinning Out Capital: Women's Work in the Early Modern Economy." In *Becoming Visible: Women in European History*, edited by Renate Bridenthal, Claudia Koonz, and Susan Stuard, 221–50. Boston: Houghton Mifflin, 1987.

———. *Women and Gender in Early Modern Europe.* Cambridge: Cambridge University Press, 1993.

PRESENTATION

PowerPoint presentations are a staple of school and college life. While the basics of PowerPoint are relatively easy to learn, it takes a little more care to learn to create presentation slides that will engage your audience rather than overwhelm or bore them.

Introduction

Typically the **purpose** of a PowerPoint presentation is to provide a visual aid for a live presentation you're making to your class or other audience. The slides are not there to convey all your content; they're there to support your performance. Be aware that your **readers** are primarily listeners who will just scan your content rather than reading it carefully. They should be able to glance at your slides to get your point quickly. Try to do the majority of the research and planning for your presentation before you **brainstorm** your slides. Your slides should contain only the high points of the talk, the important points to help your audience follow and understand your presentation. The **outline** for your slide deck should essentially be the high-level outline for your talk. Allow yourself time to go through a couple of **drafts** of your slides. If you do them at the last minute, your deck will likely be too long and not as focused as it should be. If possible, take a break after you create your first draft, then come back to it later with a fresh eye. Try to see your presentation through the eyes of your audience. **Revise** to streamline and to ensure your slides are free from typos and other errors.

DO	DON'T
• Keep your design simple. Your goal should be to create slides that are easy to scan.	• Don't crowd your slides with a lot of text and graphics. Slides with plenty of blank space are more inviting and easier to read.
• Choose readable fonts, and limit the number of fonts you use. Select fonts that look clean and clear on your slides. As a general rule, limit yourself to no more than two different fonts per slide. If you add more, your slide may look messy and distracting.	• Don't write out your entire presentation on your slides. Remember, the slides should contain just your main points. If the whole content is on the slides, why does the audience need you?
• Keep text to a minimum. You should present just your main points on your slides. When presented with a very text-heavy slide, people will do one of two things: zone out or read it. A zoned-out audience is obviously a disaster, but an audience that's too busy reading to listen can be equally bad.	• Don't present graphics or text that are too small or too detailed for the audience to see easily. If you have a key chart or table that is complex, present a simplified version of it on your slide and give the audience the full version, printed on hard copy, to examine more closely.
• Use light backgrounds and dark text. White or other light-colored lettering is difficult to read.	• Don't distract your audience with busy backgrounds. PowerPoint offers a lot of built-in graphics and backgrounds, but that doesn't mean you should use them.
• Use animation sparingly and strategically to support the message of your presentation. The golden rule is if it enhances the meaning and clarity of your presentation, use it. If it competes with your content and distracts people, don't.	• Don't use meaningless animation. Again, the fact that fancy animation tools are available doesn't mean they're a good idea for your presentation. Use animation when it can help get your point across more successfully, not animation for its own sake. If the audience is sitting there thinking "cool animation," then they're not paying attention to your content.
• In bullet points, use parallel grammatical constructions to help people follow your ideas easily.	
• Use formatting effects like boldface and italics sparingly and consistently. Unless they clearly support your message, avoid using these potentially distracting formatting tools.	
• Proofread your slides carefully. Ideally, have someone else who is not familiar with the presentation proof it for you. A presentation that contains typos, misspellings, and punctuation errors can be very embarrassing.	

NOT LIKE THIS . . .

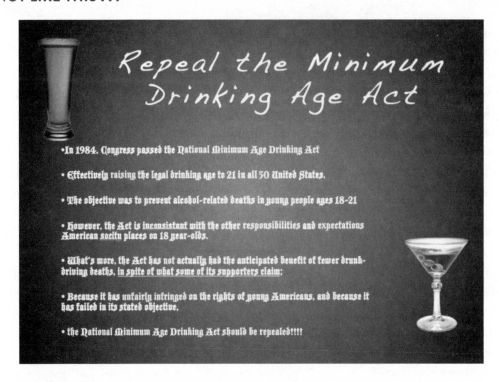

. . . LIKE THIS

EXAM ESSAY QUESTION

An essay exam is enough to strike fear in the heart of many diligent and hardworking students. Unlike with quantitative tests, it's very difficult to know if you're getting the answer "right" when the answer is in essay form.

Fortunately, there are methods to prepare for such tests and techniques you can use during the test to ensure that you perform at your very best. The advice here isn't a substitute for studying the material, of course, but it will help you put your best foot forward when it comes to writing an in-class essay exam.

Introduction

Essay questions have several **purposes**: to demonstrate your knowledge of the subject, to demonstrate that you can synthesize the knowledge you have, to show your ability to think on your feet, and to demonstrate your writing skills. Your **reader**—that is, your teacher or professor—should have made it clear what he expects from you on an exam. Ignore his guidance at your peril. Use your knowledge of your instructor to help you. What kinds of things does he think are important? What has he emphasized in his teaching? **Brainstorm** and **organize** your response *before you start writing*: you don't have the time to do it otherwise. When you receive the question, take time to think about it. Don't start writing until you know what you want to say. Make a brief outline, and follow it as you **draft**; you won't have time to throw everything out and start over again. New ideas will probably come to you as you write. Fit them carefully into your existing outline, and don't let them throw you off track. Once you've finished writing your essay, proofread and **revise**. It may be the last thing in the world you feel like doing, but a thorough proofreading can help you catch a lot of mistakes and omissions. If you have time, you may want to do a little rewriting to clarify your answer, but make sure that any revisions you make are legible and clear.

DO	DON'T
• Answer the easy questions first. If the exam has multiple short-essay questions, warm up by starting with the ones you feel most confident about.	• Don't freak out if the answer doesn't come to you right away. Read over the different questions on the test, answer the ones you feel comfortable with, and try to relax and think calmly about the ones that seem less clear to you.
• Think. Do not panic. Allow yourself to get some ideas rolling before you put pen to paper.	• Don't start writing before you've had time to think about your answer. You don't have to be writing every moment of the exam. You're far better off spending time thinking about and organizing your answer before you start writing than jumping in and starting to write before you're sure what you want to say.
• Make sure you understand each question. If a question seems unclear to you, ask the instructor for clarification.	
• Check to be sure how many questions are really being asked under the guise of a single question—how many parts will your answer have?	
• Read the question carefully, and *answer the question asked*. A good essay on a related topic is not as good as a fair essay that actually answers the question. Be sure you understand the question before you start outlining and writing. To keep yourself on track, try beginning your essay by restating part of the question in your opening sentence.	• Don't feel that you need to write a long answer. A short, accurate essay is better than a long, rambling one. You're not being graded by the word, and teachers appreciate a concise, well-thought-out essay.
• Make sure your essay has a clear beginning, middle, and end—in other words, an introduction, a body, and a conclusion.	

NOT LIKE THIS . . .

> This is a point that many people might dispute, and it's actually not relevant to the question asked. Don't feel you need to open your essay with a big, sweeping, general statement. Focus on responding to the question. This student has got herself in trouble in the first sentence by making a questionable claim that doesn't even address the question.

What were the primary causes of the American Revolution?

The American Revolution, which began in 1775, gave rise to the greatest democracy the world has ever seen. The thirteen colonies were originally established by the British, who considered them their property to do with as they pleased. Over time, the colonists developed a sense of nationalism and began to desire self-determination rather than being governed by a king in a distant country. It was inevitable that the colonists would eventually organize to overthrow British tyranny.

> This is very general background. The student would be better off being more specific earlier in the essay. At this point, it still feels as though she doesn't know exactly what she wants to say.

There were many causes for the American Revolution. The British colonial government imposed many taxes on the American colonists, including the Stamp Act, which required tax stamps to be placed on many things—even marriage licenses—the Townshend Acts, and the Sugar Act, which taxed sugar coming from the West Indies. The Crown also refused to allow the colonists to print their own currency. The Tea Act of 1773 gave the British East India Company a monopoly on importing tea to America. This led to the Boston Tea Party, where colonists disguised themselves as Indians and threw tea overboard into the harbor off British ships. The British responded with the Intolerable Acts, closing Boston Harbor and forbidding public gatherings. In addition, the British forced colonists to house, or "quarter," British soldiers in their homes (Quartering Act, 1765). Finally, in 1775, the first open warfare of the Revolution occurred with the "shot heard round the world" at Lexington and Concord, when the British tried to seize the colonists' store of gunpowder. The Revolution was under way, and the colonists would not stop until they had won their freedom from the British.

> Good. Simple and to the point. This student can throw out her entire first paragraph and begin here.

> This paragraph contains a lot of data. Clearly the student has been studying for the exam. However, it all comes out like a flood in a single paragraph with little or no internal organization. The writer feels rushed, as if she's under time pressure to get everything out of her brain and onto the page. The content is all fine, but it's not held together by an overarching structure, and in the end it doesn't respond to the question about the "primary" causes of the Revolution.

The American Revolution brought about the greatest democracy in the world, and we should all be grateful to the brave colonists who fought for our rights.

> The student is making an effort to tie the essay together by referring back to her introduction, which is a good instinct. Unfortunately, the introduction wasn't really responsive to the question and was factually dubious. In addition, this conclusion is drifting into wider territory, beginning to discuss the indebtedness of contemporary Americans to the early revolutionaries. Resist the temptation to go off in a new direction when you write your conclusion, even if the rhetorical effect appeals to you.

. . . LIKE THIS

What were the primary causes of the American Revolution?

The American Revolution had many causes, and the colonists had many grievances against British rule. These grievances fall into three categories. First, the British caused the colonists financial hardship through taxes and

> This student gets right to the point in the first sentence of her essay.

It's clear that the student has taken some time to organize her thoughts before she started writing the essay. She's organized her information into three categories to make her essay more coherent.

Each of the paragraphs begins with a topic sentence that makes it easy to see the development of the argument.

Each paragraph has a closing sentence that sums up the effect of the events described in the paragraph.

The student uses clear transitional devices to mark the progress of her argument.

This brief closing paragraph connects back to the introduction and wraps up the essay. Overall, the writing in this essay isn't fancy, but it's clear, accurate, and easy to follow. It's better to write a clear essay with little rhetorical flourish than to write a flowery essay that's hard to follow.

duties. Second, the British restricted the personal freedom of the colonists. And finally, several incidents of physical conflict made the colonists resolve to overthrow British rule and form their own government.

The British imposed a series of taxes and duties that the colonists found severe and unfair. The Sugar Act imposed duties on sugar imported from the West Indies. The Stamp Act of 1765 forced colonists to buy tax stamps for many different kinds of goods and services, including newspapers, playing cards, and even marriage licenses. Another tax came about through the Townshend Act, which taxed glass, paper, and tea. In 1773, the British gave a monopoly on the tea trade to the British East India Company, inciting the Boston Tea Party incident. After this series of taxes and duties, the colonists were frustrated and angry.

The British also imposed restrictions on the freedom of the American colonists. They were forbidden to settle west of the Appalachian Mountains. They were forced to quarter and feed British soldiers in their own homes. And after the Boston Tea Party, the British passed the Intolerable Acts, which closed Boston Harbor and outlawed public gatherings. Americans felt their freedom was being abused.

Finally, the American revolutionaries rallied around several incidents in which British soldiers shot colonists. The Boston Massacre of 1770 turned many colonists against the British. The incident at Lexington and Concord, known as the "shot heard round the world," was an armed conflict in which the British were believed to have shot first. Eight colonists were killed. This event was the first open conflict of the Revolutionary War.

The American Revolution took many years to build to a head, and many different incidents shaped the way it happened. In the end, it was a combination of forces and happenings that drove America to gain independence.

Core Writing Assignments

better result if you allow yourself plenty of time to complete your writing assignment. Read the assignment carefully as soon as you get it, and then budget your time sensibly. Allow yourself time to do any necessary research and to think carefully about what you want to say. It takes time to develop an interesting idea, and leaving your paper till the night before will compromise the quality of the finished product. Save yourself the last-minute panic by getting started early on your writing assignments.

3. Use Drafts

If you've started early on your writing assignment, you'll have time to write multiple drafts, which is hands down the best way to ensure you'll be able to hand in a polished final paper. Working with drafts will show you if you have "thin" places in your paper that require more research or deeper thought. Some instructors are willing to read a first draft of an essay and give you feedback before you hand in the final assignment, and it's a good idea to take advantage of this offer. To make the most of writing multiple drafts, you must be willing to make substantive revisions, not just cosmetic ones. Let your ideas grow and develop over time, and your final product will be something you can be proud of.

4. Be Sure You Know What You Mean

Because ideas can change and evolve over the course of writing an essay, your later drafts may seem somewhat disjointed. What you thought when you first started writing the essay might not be exactly what you think by the time you finish it. Rather than just giving up and handing in your paper, go back and reread it carefully. Try reverse outlining to analyze what you currently have in your draft (see page 16 for guidance on reverse outlining). Check to see if your thesis is clear and if the body of your paper supports that thesis throughout. Check to see if your conclusion fits the entire essay. If necessary, spend some time bringing all the elements of your paper into alignment. As a paper goes through successive drafts, it may get messier before it gets cleaner. But the process of revision will help you clarify your thoughts, and you'll end up with a stronger paper in the end.

5. Proofread

Proofreading your final draft carefully is a critical last step. It can be hard to make yourself proofread at this stage, but don't shortchange yourself.

You've worked hard on your paper, and it would be a shame to lose grade points because of sloppy errors. Ask a friend to proofread your writing for you; they'll be more likely to catch errors that your eyes might just pass over. Beware of spell-checkers—they can let errors slide by. Give your paper one more careful review before you submit it for a grade.

Expository Writing

Expository writing is writing that is used to explain, describe, or otherwise convey information. It is based in facts and may be used to support an argument or a claim. Forms of nonexpository writing include creative writing and journalistic writing.

Most school and college writing assignments require some form of expository writing. The techniques of expository writing are used in assignments like interpretive essays, argumentative essays, comparative essays, presentations, research papers, scientific papers, and history essays, among others. These techniques may include one or more of the following:

Description: Present characteristics, features, and examples in order to describe. Useful in many different kinds of writing assignments.

Sequencing: Present items or events in numerical or chronological order. Useful in process descriptions, historical essays, and scientific papers.

Comparison: Explain how two or more things are alike and how they are different. Used in comparison and contrast essays. Also useful in some argumentative and interpretive essays, as well as some history essays.

Cause and effect: Present one or more causes and the resulting effect or effects. Useful in process essays, history essays, and science papers.

Problem and solution: State a problem and propose one or more solutions for the problem. A variation is the question-and-answer format. Useful in argumentative essays, social science and history essays, and science papers.

How to Write a Thesis Statement

A thesis statement is a short statement—usually just one sentence—declaring what your essay is going to be about; it proposes the idea or position you are going to argue for in the paper. Your thesis statement lays down a kind of road map for you as you plan and write your paper, and it also helps your reader follow your argument as it develops: if readers have a clear idea of your argument as a whole, they'll have an easier time understanding its parts.

A thesis statement is a necessity in any kind of argumentative essay in any field. If you're setting out to prove a point, you'll need a thesis statement. Be aware that instructors do not always ask explicitly that you include a thesis statement in your paper; they may assume that you will create one. If you're unsure about your instructor's expectations about the paper, ask for clarification.

A thesis is not the same as a topic. A topic is a broad, general subject. A thesis presents a specific and focused point of view about part of that topic. See the table below to understand how a thesis statement can be developed from a topic.

A good thesis statement has several characteristics:

Asserts your point of view. A thesis statement expresses a position and sets up the rest of the essay to convince the reader that point of view is correct. A thesis is necessary to making a persuasive case in writing.

Justifies discussion. A thesis statement makes a claim that others may disagree with and is therefore worth talking about. A thesis that simply states the obvious—one that everyone would agree with—doesn't make for interesting reading and doesn't allow you to develop an argument.

Expresses a single main idea. Limiting your thesis statement to a single idea makes your paper easier to follow and understand. You'll also find it's easier to develop a paper around a single main idea than around a complex and multifaceted idea.

How to Develop a Thesis Statement

Developing a strong thesis statement is a process that may take some time. It doesn't often happen that your thesis statement pops into your head fully formed. To develop a thesis statement, start with a topic that interests you, and work toward narrowing it down. Consider if you have enough evidence to support your argument. It may take several iterations before you find a specific thesis statement that you can support.

TOPIC	POSSIBLE THESIS	THESIS
Women in Shakespeare	Women characters sometimes disagree with male characters.	Female characters in Shakespeare's history plays challenge the honor-based view of war that the male characters espouse.
Watergate	Watergate changed Americans' expectations of presidential politics.	The Watergate scandal led to a greater tolerance of dishonesty in presidents and presidential candidates among US voters.
Exercise	Exercise helps control weight.	Weight loss programs that include exercise are more successful than those that don't.

Do your best to come up with a specific and defensible thesis before you start writing your paper. Having a clear idea of your thesis at the start of the writing process can save you a great deal of time. However, it's important to remain flexible as you write. You may find that your thesis changes as you develop your paper. Once you have a draft, go back and check to see if your thesis really does summarize the paper you've actually written. If not, be open to the idea of adjusting the thesis to bring it in line with the content of the paper. You may need to go through this process more than once; it's all part of developing and refining an argument.

PERSONAL ESSAY

(See also *College or Scholarship Application Essay* on page 337.)

A personal essay is a reflection about something that's important to you—perhaps an event, a person, or a lesson learned. Personal essays are often required as part of the application for college admissions or scholarships. In that case, the committee is hoping to get a glimpse of who you are as a person and what's important to you—in addition to seeing how well you write. There are many ways to approach a personal essay. This section offers guidance to get you off to a good start.

Introduction

The **purpose** of a personal essay is to share something about yourself—an experience, a relationship, a belief—and to reflect on it. In a personal essay, you invite the reader to know you better and perhaps to share your feelings. As you plan and write your essay, think about the experience of your **readers**. What do you want them to feel or think as they read your essay? What do you want them to understand by the end? Consider that you are taking the reader on a kind of journey, so pay attention to the experience you're designing for them. The box "Topics for Personal Essays" (page 267) offers ideas to help you get started. Allow yourself plenty of time to **brainstorm** about what you want to write about and which details will reveal your story most effectively. The process of brainstorming may actually make you realize how important an event really was to you. Be sure you narrow your focus to something you can treat adequately within the page limits of the assignment. You may find it helpful to begin with just a loose **organization** for your essay, and tighten it up as you rewrite. You should start with a minimum commitment to shaping a clear beginning, middle, and end to your essay, and you should be sure that the ending somehow harks back to the beginning. Write your **draft** freely and try to resist the impulse to edit or revise as you write. It's important to let your creativity flow. Your initial draft will almost certainly be too long. That's not a problem; you can trim it later. The important thing is to develop your idea fully. Once you have a draft, take a break from it. It's a good idea to ask a friend to read it and request feedback. Is anything unclear or confusing? Is it repetitive? Are there parts of the essay that drag and should be trimmed? **Revise** to tighten the essay.

Topics for Personal Essays

If your instructor has asked you to come up with your own topic for your personal essay, you might find some inspiration among these sample topics. Use these suggestions to prompt your memory and start reflecting on what you want to write.

A turning point in your life

A relationship that changed you

A loss

A difficult choice

An event that turned out very different from what you expected

Something that makes you angry

Something that makes you happy

Something you will never do again

An event that taught you something about yourself

An experience with food

An experience with an animal

A time when you did something wrong

A person who has influenced you

A childhood memory

A travel memory

A favorite pastime

A favorite place

A "first" in your life

Something that happened when you weren't paying attention

How you overcame a fear or prejudice

DO	DON'T
• Be sure you understand the assignment. There are many different ways to write a personal essay; be sure you know what your instructor expects from yours.	• Don't feel you need to begin the essay at the beginning of the experience. Consider beginning when the situation was the most absurd or dangerous or frightening. There's no need to relate the incident in strict chronological order. Starting with the most compelling part of the story will grab the reader's attention.
• Focus on a single topic. It's better to focus on one event or idea and develop that fully than to skim the surface of several.	• Don't try to stuff too many themes or ideas into your essay. When we reflect on experiences, it's natural for our thoughts to wander. You may have learned several different lessons from an experience, but your essay will be more engaging if you concentrate on just one. Whatever your topic, make sure your essay has a single tight focus.
• Write a strong beginning. Your opening should draw the reader into your essay and make them want to read more. Instead of "This summer I determined to overcome my fear of heights," try "Dangling 350 feet above the ground was the last place in the world I wanted to be."	
• Feel free to use the word "I." You may have been told in other writing classes that you were not to use the word "I." In a personal essay, it's perfectly acceptable to write in the first person—in fact, it's expected.	• Don't feel you need to use flowery, "literary" language in your personal essay. This essay is about you, so you should feel free to write in your own natural voice.
• Be honest. Your essay will be stronger if you don't try to sugarcoat an incident where you didn't behave very well, or when you write the real ending rather than the happy ending you would have wished for.	• Don't be afraid to use humor. Sometimes the most compelling experiences are funny in some way, even if they didn't seem funny at the time. Your essay doesn't have to be deathly serious to be meaningful.
• Show; don't tell. You'll hear this advice in many writing classes, and its objective is to help the reader experience what you experienced as vividly as possible. If you had intense emotions, don't just say so: help the reader to feel them with you. For instance, say you're writing about the death of your beloved dog. Instead of saying "I felt terrible," provide a scene that shows how you felt and brings the reader along: "I looked at Max's empty bed and realized I would never see him there again."	

- Consider using dialogue, if appropriate. If you do use dialogue, make sure it's interesting.
- Give your essay a specific and engaging title that will pique the reader's interest. Instead of "A Boating Adventure," try "I Know What Swamp Water Tastes Like." Instead of "My Grandmother," try "A Real-Life Rosie the Riveter."

LIKE THIS

Better Late Than Never

I know . . . all little girls are in love with horses. Not me. When I was in grade school, I had friends who were horse-crazy, with posters of horses all over their bedroom walls. I wasn't interested. In fact, I've actually been afraid of horses all my life. When my best friend Alex had pony rides at her eighth birthday party, I wouldn't get on. When my Girl Scout troop went horseback riding, I stayed home. I don't remember having any particularly bad experience with horses that caused me to fear them. They always just seemed very big and very stupid, and that seemed like a dangerous combination.

When my family and I visited our cousins in England this summer, something changed. Our cousins live out in the countryside. They don't have a farm, but there are farms surrounding their house. One of their neighbors in particular caught my attention: a woman who rode by on horseback every morning, followed by a little girl riding a pony. The little girl couldn't have been much more than six years old. She wore a helmet that made her look like some kind of an insect, but under that big helmet she was always smiling. We waved and exchanged greetings as they rode by each day.

Then one morning the woman, who turned out to be named Rachel, asked me if I wanted to go out riding with them. My cousins had told her I was visiting from America, she said, and if I wanted to come out, she would be delighted. Of course I said no. Rachel looked a little surprised. Her daughter, Caitlyn, looked downright shocked. Caitlyn stared at me as if she'd never heard anything so crazy. "Well, my love," Rachel said, "if you change your mind, you know where to find us."

That night I thought about what had happened, and I felt bad. Had I offended them? Was I really that scared of horses? I thought and thought about Rachel, and especially about Caitlyn, who had given me that look. Suddenly I didn't understand why I had said no. There was something about being in a different country—in a place so different from my own neighborhood—that made me see things differently. I decided to go riding with them.

I turned up early the next morning, and Rachel welcomed me warmly. Caitlyn stared. They gave me a big grey horse to ride whose name was Gulliver. I considered telling Rachel that I was afraid, but I didn't want to look stupid, especially in front of Caitlyn.

As we set out, I freaked out a little bit about how high off the ground I was. Horses are big. After a few minutes, though, it began to seem fine. We rode through some beautiful country, with green rolling hills and dark, mossy rocks. When we got to a flat area, Rachel asked, "Fancy a trot?" I nodded yes. This wasn't so bad.

For people who don't know much about horses, a trot is a very rough gait. I bounced up and down on the saddle—hard. I tried hanging on to the saddle, but that wasn't much help. I could feel myself falling off, sliding off the side of Gulliver. And in that moment I knew I had been right in the first place. Horses were big and stupid and dangerous. I was about to fall off one and be trampled to death in a foreign country. And then the horse stopped. He just stopped. Rachel turned and came back to me. Caitlyn stared. I sat there clinging to the saddle. I was suddenly talkative, babbling like a little child: "I thought I was going to fall off. I was really sure I was going to fall off. I was sliding off the side, and then he just stopped." "Of course he did," said Rachel calmly. "They're trained to stop if you're falling, didn't you know?" "Really?" I squeaked. Rachel laughed. "Of course. They feel you falling and they stop. It's in their training."

Suddenly horses didn't seem so stupid anymore. This one had definitely saved my life. We finished the ride quietly, at a sedate walk. Back at the barn, I thanked Rachel and learned how to remove the tack and put the horses away. Once the horses were snug in their stalls, munching on their hay, Caitlyn looked up at me with a smile. "Are you all right then?" she asked. I smiled back. Yes, I was all right.

Did I ride every day for the rest of the visit and come back to the United States an avid horsewoman? No. But I did go out riding with Rachel and Caitlyn twice more, and we even trotted on one of those rides, and that time I didn't slide off. I was definitely all right, and maybe a little bit wiser than I had been.

Writing Strong Paragraphs

The paragraph is an essential building block of every paper you'll write. Paragraphs break longer pieces of writing into small, easily digestible sections, and by doing so they help the reader understand the flow of your argument or narrative. Learning to write a strong paragraph will help you organize your writing and express your ideas in a more logical and convincing way. Strong paragraphs usually have these four elements:

Topic sentence

The topic sentence states generally what the paragraph is about. It is usually, but not always, the first sentence of the paragraph. Using a topic sentence helps readers understand the overall message of the paragraph and follow your argument from one paragraph to another.

Unity

Strong paragraphs have unity; that is, a paragraph generally contains no more than one central idea. If you find yourself starting to write about a different idea, it's time to begin a new paragraph.

Coherence

A paragraph should be internally coherent. All the sentences in the paragraph should support the topic sentence and should be connected logically to one another.

Development

Paragraphs should be fully developed. The main idea of each paragraph should be adequately explained and supported through details and evidence.

It is important to note that each paragraph in the body of the essay must have some logical connection to the thesis statement in the opening paragraph.

Keep this information about paragraphs in mind as you plan your paper. As you write your draft, be aware that it's very easy to let your paragraphs "drift." Once you have a complete draft, go back and read through each of your paragraphs to ensure they are as strong as possible. Is your topic sentence clear and specific? Does the paragraph deal with just one idea? Is the idea well developed and supported with appropriate details? Do the sentences in the paragraph flow logically, lending it internal coherence?

Sample Paragraphs

All the planets always appear close to an imaginary line across the sky, so objects located far from that line cannot be planets. The line is called the *ecliptic*, and it is followed (more or less) not only by the planets but also by the moon. (The ecliptic is actually the path followed by the sun across the background of stars in the course of the year.) Since the earth is but one of the planets, and since all the planets orbit the sun in approximately the same plane, from our point of view the planets and sun must follow roughly the same line across the sky. The moon orbits the earth at only a slight angle to the plane of the planets, so it too always appears close to the ecliptic.

Donald H. Menzel and Jay M. Pasachoff, *A Field Guide to the Stars and Planets* (Boston: Houghton Mifflin, 1983), 6.

In the 1780s the Frindsbury Peninsula was an almost empty expanse of fields and low-lying marshland. There were a few houses in the vicinity of the church, and there was a windmill in the field above the shipyard but little else except for a few grazing cattle. Across the river from the shipyard the ancient city of Rochester huddled beneath the Norman castle and cathedral, the grey stone towers and spires providing distinctive landmarks for ships heading upstream from the Thames Estuary. A mile downstream, around a bend in the river, the redbrick buildings of Chatham dockyard hugged the waterfront, surrounded by windswept pastures and isolated farms. And to the east, beyond the royal dockyard, the river meandered through the desolate marshes, frequented only by seagulls, wading birds and the occasional fisherman.

David Cordingly, *The Billy Ruffian: The Bellerophon and the Downfall of Napoleon* (New York: Bloomsbury, 2003), 7–8.

Ballet may not have a continuous record, but this does not mean it does not have a history. To the contrary: people have been practicing and performing it for at least four hundred years. Classical ballet grew up in Europe's courts; at its origins it was an aristocratic etiquette and political event as much as it was an art. Indeed, perhaps more than any other performing art, the history of ballet is bound up with the fate of kings, courts, and states. What happened to the European aristocracy since the Renaissance also happened, in complicated ways, to ballet. The steps were never just the steps; they were a set of beliefs, echoing as they did the self-image of a noble caste. These larger connections, it seemed to me, were the key to an understanding of the art: how ballet began and what it became is best appreciated in light of the political and intellectual upheavals of the past three hundred years. Ballet was shaped by the Renaissance and French Classicism, by revolutions and Romanticism, by Expressionism and Bolshevism, modernism and the Cold War. It really *is* a larger story.

Jennifer Homans, *Apollo's Angels: A History of Ballet* (New York: Random House, 2010), xxiv.

PROCESS DESCRIPTION ESSAY

The process description essay is a popular assignment in both high school and college English classes, and the skills involved can be useful in many different applications, including assignments in the sciences and social sciences and in writing instructions of all kinds.

Introduction

The **purpose** of a process description essay is to give the reader a step-by-step account of how a process occurs. A process description may also be used in writing instructions for carrying out a process. When you write a process description, it's important to understand your **reader**'s level of knowledge about the content you're describing. Writing for an audience of experts may be different from writing for an audience that is unfamiliar with the process.

Brainstorm your content by writing out the steps of the process in the order they occur. **Organize** your essay chronologically, from the beginning of the process through the end. Include a brief introductory paragraph and a brief conclusion. As you write your **draft**, you may find that you've missed some steps or that you've conflated two steps into one. You can make adjustments when you **revise**. It's wise to show your draft to someone who is not familiar with the process you're describing: he can let you know if your description makes sense or if there is anything that needs to be clarified. Revise accordingly.

DO	DON'T
• Be sure you understand the process thoroughly before you start writing your essay. Brainstorming your content by listing all the steps of the process is a good way to discover if you're missing any information. • Make sure your steps are of comparable size and scope. Don't merge two processes into a single step. • Use transitional words to show the order of steps and to indicate the time elapsed during and between steps. (See the box "Useful Transitional Expressions" on page 275.) • Choose a title for your essay that will help readers understand exactly what it is.	• Don't assume your reader is familiar with technical language unless that language is an integral part of the class. For instance, you don't have to explain chemical processes in detail if you're writing an essay for your chemistry teacher; if you're writing about the same process for a general audience, you should consider defining any technical terms you use. • Don't conflate two steps into one. When you revise, check to be sure each step represents a single action or occurrence. • Don't add extraneous commentary to your process description. • Don't make your essay more complicated than it needs to be. Describe the process in a simple and straightforward way.

Process Description in the Sciences

In science classes, a process description is considered different from a set of instructions. In the sciences, the term "process description" applies only to those processes that occur without the reader's intervention or participation. In that context, a "process" might be something like oxidation, evaporation, or photosynthesis—a phenomenon that occurs through a series of stages not influenced by the actions of the reader. Before you start your process description essay, be sure you understand what your instructor expects.

Useful Transitional Expressions

Process essays are usually organized chronologically and proceed step-by-step. To help readers follow the progress from one step to the next, use transitional words and phrases that express time relationships, like these.

After	First, second, third	Later
At the same time	Immediately following	Meanwhile
Before	In the meantime	Next
During	Initially	Simultaneously
Finally	Last	While

NOT LIKE THIS . . .

How to Make a Peanut Butter Sandwich

All very true, but this opening provides extraneous information rather than introducing the process description. Your introduction should set up the essay you're going to write, not make general commentary on a related topic.

The peanut butter sandwich is a staple of American childhood. Most of us grew up eating them, and many of us still rely on them for a quick snack or informal meal.

Making a peanut butter sandwich is simple. First take two slices of bread, of any variety. Spread the peanut butter on one slice and the jelly on the other. Put the two slices of bread together, and voilà! You have a peanut butter sandwich.

This student seems to have come to the end of the essay and felt he hasn't said enough. So he's added this last paragraph of filler about types of peanut butter and other ingredients. This information is tangentially related but doesn't pertain to the actual process of making a peanut butter sandwich.

There are many variations on this simple sandwich. First, there are different types of peanut butter you can choose from: crunchy or smooth. Then there is a variety of different jellies and jams that can change the flavor of the sandwich. Many people also use other "additives" to dress up the sandwich—from pickles to add tartness, to potato chips to add crunch, to marshmallows to add sweetness. Some people even deep-fry a peanut butter sandwich (which is not recommended). Which you choose depends on your personality and your tastes.

. . . LIKE THIS

How to Make a Peanut Butter Sandwich

This is a good opening that sets up the essay well.

Making a peanut butter sandwich is a three-step process: gathering tools and ingredients, spreading the peanut butter on the bread, and putting the sandwich together.

This student has taken the time to think about the question first. He thought through the process carefully before he started writing. The result is that his essay is clear and well organized, and all of it is relevant to the question asked.

The first step in making a peanut butter sandwich is assembling the tools and ingredients you will need. For tools, you need a knife and a plate or cutting board. The ingredients you need include a jar of peanut butter and two slices of bread.

In the second step, you will apply the peanut butter to the bread. Use the knife to extract peanut butter from the jar and spread it evenly on both pieces of bread.

The writer uses transitional expressions to lead the reader through the steps of the process.

Finally, put the two pieces of bread together; the peanut butter will make them stick to each other. If you wish, you can then use the knife to cut the sandwich in half for ease of eating.

COMPARE AND CONTRAST ESSAY

Compare and contrast essays may be required in many different classes—literature, history, social sciences, art, and others. Whatever the topic of your essay, the ability to compare and contrast is an essential skill involving critical and analytical thinking.

Introduction

The **purpose** of a comparison and contrast essay is to analyze the similarities (compare) and differences (contrast), usually between two things and sometimes among three or more things. Your **reader** will be looking for a clear and organized presentation of your facts, with strong transitions, to make the relationships easy to understand. You can begin **brainstorming** your essay by compiling two separate lists: one a list of the similarities between the two subjects and another a list of the differences. Making these lists can help you narrow the focus of your paper and identify the points of comparison you want to explore. For instance, if you are comparing two statues, you might look at the medium, the time periods in which they were produced, their size, the materials used, their subjects, and so on. Comparison and contrast essays are typically **organized** in one of two ways: the block method or the alternating method. For guidance, see the box "Organizational Structures for Comparison and Contrast Essays" (page 278). You may find that you develop new ideas as you write your **draft**. That's fine. Make a note of them and decide if you want to incorporate them in your next draft. It's wise to write a complete draft and leave it alone for a day or two. Go back and reread what you've written. Are the similarities and differences clear? Have you given more or less equal attention to the subjects you're comparing? Is there information missing? **Revise** to ensure your essay is clear, complete, and free of errors.

Organizational Structures for Comparison and Contrast Essays

There are two common organizational approaches for the comparison and contrast essay: the alternating method and the block method. Each has its own pattern.

Alternating Method

The alternating method can be most successful when you have closely related ideas and information about both A and B that lends itself to a point-by-point style of comparison.

- Introductory paragraph
- Discussion of A and B with reference to first point of comparison
- Discussion of A and B with reference to second point of comparison
- Discussion of A and B with reference to third point of comparison
- Conclusion

Block Method

The block method is most useful when your content does not lend itself to a point-by-point comparison between A and B. The block method is also useful when your ideas about B build on your ideas about A. It's a sensible structure to use when you want to compare and contrast three or more subjects. To help your reader follow your argument, present the different points of comparison in parallel.

- Introductory paragraph
- Discussion of A
  - Point 1
  - Point 2
  - Point 3
- Discussion of B
  - Point 1
  - Point 2
  - Point 3
- Conclusion

DO	DON'T
• Choose a basis for comparison. For most topics, you will need to limit the scope of your essay. For instance, in the example about cats and dogs below, the writer has chosen to focus on how these animals relate to people. An essay that attempts to explore all the similarities and differences between cats and dogs would be enormously long and complex.	• Don't choose subjects that cannot be easily compared. If you've been asked to come up with your own topic for your essay, take care in choosing a project you can accomplish easily and successfully. For instance, an essay that compares and contrasts two paintings will be easier and probably more successful than an essay that discusses a painting and a novel.
• Develop a thesis for your essay. It's not enough simply to list the similarities and differences between the items you're comparing. Your essay should have a focus that ties together all the information you intend to present. One way to begin to develop your thesis is to consider whether similarities outweigh differences or vice versa, and develop from there.	• Don't neglect your introduction. Your introduction and thesis establish not just the topic but also the basis of comparison. Your thesis presents an idea that you're going to try to prove. Without a proper introduction, your paper will likely read like a list of attributes, with very little point. (For guidance developing a thesis statement, see the box "How to Write a Thesis Statement" on page 264.)
• Use an outline. Not all writers like to outline before they write, but for this assignment, an outline is a must-have in order to help you organize your information. Your outline can be informal, and it's fine to use reverse outlining after you've started writing, but it's wise to outline at some point to ensure you're writing a balanced and complete essay. (See also the discussion on reverse outlining on page 16.)	• Don't try to combine the two organizational styles in a single essay. Your essay will be easier to follow if you choose either the alternating or the block format and stick with it throughout.
• Use transitional language to improve the unity of your essay and advance your argument. Useful words include "like," "similar to," "both," similarly," "in the same way," "share," "have in common," "also," "unlike," "differ," "however," "although," "in contrast," "while," and "on the other hand," among others.	• Don't write an unbalanced essay that devotes far more attention to one item than the other. Both items should receive equal or nearly equal treatment.
• Use topic sentences. Topic sentences at the beginning of each of your paragraphs help the reader	

> **DO** (CONTINUED)
>
> follow your argument as it develops. For more
> on topic sentences, see the box "Writing Strong
> Paragraphs" (page 271).
>
> - Devote more or less equal space and attention to
>   the items you're comparing.

EXAMPLES

EXAMPLE I

Title: A Cat or a Dog?

Thesis: Although cats and dogs are both very popular companion animals, prospective pet owners should understand the unique characteristics of each before deciding which animal to adopt.

ALTERNATING METHOD

Training
    Both—will accept a certain amount of training
    Cats—difficult to train, limited results
    Dogs—pliable and easy to train, accept and even welcome training
House-training
    Both—can be house-trained
    Cats—use litter box instinctually
    Dogs—require extensive house-training
Social behavior
    Both—can make good companions for humans
    Cats—primarily attached to territory rather than companions
    Dogs—pack animals, primarily attached to companions

BLOCK METHOD

Cats
    Training—will accept a certain amount of training, but difficult to train, limited results
    House-training—use litter box instinctually
    Social behavior—can make good companions for humans, but primarily attached to territory rather than companions

Dogs

> Training—pliable and easy to train, accept and even welcome training
> House-training—require extensive house-training
> Social behavior—can make good companions for humans, pack animals, primarily attached to companions

The eating disorders bulimia and anorexia are sometimes confused with one another. Both tend to affect women more than men, and both can have serious—even fatal—consequences. However, the two disorders are associated with different symptoms, behaviors, and medical risks, and parents of girls and young women should understand what to look for. **EXAMPLE II**

I. Symptoms **ALTERNATING**
> Anorexia—depression, fatigue, weight loss **METHOD**
> Bulimia—depression, fatigue, maintain stable weight

II. Behaviors
> Both—extreme concern with thinness, excessive exercise
> Anorexia—avoid eating/weigh food and count calories
> Bulimia—binge and purge

III. Medical risks
> Both—depression
> Anorexia—bone density loss, kidney damage, cessation of menstrual periods
> Bulimia—damage to digestive tract, stomach pains, tooth decay, organ damage
> Both—can result in death

I. Anorexia **BLOCK METHOD**
> Symptoms—depression, fatigue, weight loss
> Behaviors—extreme concern with thinness, excessive exercise, avoid eating/weigh food and count calories
> Medical risks—depression, bone density loss, kidney damage, cessation of menstrual periods, death

II. Bulimia

Symptoms—depression, fatigue, maintain stable weight

Behaviors—extreme concern with thinness, excessive exercise, binge and purge

Medical risks—damage to digestive tract, stomach pains, tooth decay, organ damage, death

ARGUMENTATIVE ESSAY

An argumentative essay requires you to take a position on a controversial issue and argue in favor of your position, defending it against opposing arguments. It also usually requires that you conduct research and present evidence from various external sources.

Introduction

The **purpose** of writing an argumentative essay is to develop your ability to reason and think critically about various issues. As you work on your paper, assume that your **reader** is a fair-minded person who does not have a strong opinion about the issue you are discussing. Your job is to provide background information and compelling arguments to persuade him to agree with you. **Brainstorm** widely, from both sides of the question, and conduct research. It's wise to **organize** your material by writing a formal outline. Winging it generally doesn't work, partly because you are likely have a lot of data to manage and partly because it's hard to organize when you feel strongly about something. Lay out your argument logically and dispassionately, and your essay will be more convincing. If you prefer not to outline before you start writing, be sure to create a reverse outline (see page 16) of your first draft, so that you're clear about the structure. Don't censor yourself as you write your **draft**. Instead, plan to go through several rounds of drafting and **revising**. Reread your first draft. Are your arguments strong? Do you offer enough support? You might find you need to go back and do more brainstorming and research. Revise to tighten your argument. Remember to proofread carefully, as errors can undermine your credibility.

MODEL OUTLINE

A common organizational structure for an argumentative essay is the five-paragraph format. It is not the only option, but it can be useful.
Paragraph 1: Present your topic and state your thesis.
Paragraphs 2–4: Provide several arguments supporting your thesis statement. Offer evidence in the form of facts, statistics, and corroboration from writers who agree with you. Present the opposing side's arguments and refute them.
Paragraph 5: Conclude your essay. Rather than just repeating your thesis statement, revisit it. State it another way, in light of the evidence offered in your essay.

DO	DON'T
• Choose your topic carefully. If you're free to choose any topic you wish, make sure you select one that has enough information available on both sides of the question. If you've been given a choice of topics, pick one that really interests you. You're going to be spending a fair amount of time on this assignment, so make sure it's something you're comfortable with and can engage with.	• Don't overuse "I think" or "I believe" in your essay. It's understood that you're expressing your opinion, and these phrases tend to weaken your argument.
• Do your research. Make sure you understand all sides of the question, not just the side you happen to agree with.	• Don't offer only moral or religious claims as evidence. Your essay should present facts that can be independently confirmed.
• Think before you write. Are you sure which side you're on? Don't be afraid to let the other side in. Your essay will ultimately be stronger if you truly understand the opposing point of view.	• Don't take for granted that the reader will agree with you about any facet of your argument. You must present evidence to support all your assertions.
• Come up with a clear and defensible thesis statement. You're going to organize your entire essay around this thesis statement, so make sure you're comfortable with it. Consider these two thesis statements, for example: "Marijuana should be legalized" and "Marijuana is no worse than alcohol." The ideas are similar, but the essays that follow them will be significantly different. Be sure you have a very precise idea what you're arguing for.	• Don't ignore opposing viewpoints. You have to acknowledge them and answer them. They won't go away.
	• Don't invent evidence to support your argument. You'll get caught.
• Think of several key reasons your thesis statement is correct. There may be many, but focus on the two or three you find most convincing. You won't be able to use all of them.	• Don't insult or denigrate those who disagree with you.
	• Don't introduce any new information or arguments in the concluding paragraph.
• Collect evidence that supports your thesis, and present it in the essay. Evidence may be expert opinions, statistics, facts, and research findings.	
• Present the opposing side's arguments fairly, and refute those claims. You gain nothing by trying to make others' arguments	

> He who knows only his own side of the case, knows little of that.
>
> —*John Stuart Mill,*
> *British philosopher*

DO (CONTINUED)

look weaker than they are. Take them on directly, and argue against them, presenting evidence to support your position.

- Limit your supporting paragraphs to one topic each.
- Use clear and logical transitions between paragraphs.
- Cite your sources. If you use other sources to support your argument, use the appropriate citation format to give credit where credit is due.
- Conclude strongly. Use your last paragraph to wrap up your argument, refer to important points in the essay, and revisit your thesis statement in light of the information you have just presented.

LIKE THIS

In 1984, Congress passed the National Minimum Age Drinking Act, effectively raising the legal drinking age to twenty-one in all fifty United States. The objective was to prevent alcohol-related deaths in young people ages eighteen to twenty-one. However, the act is inconsistent with the other responsibilities and expectations American society places on eighteen-year-olds. What's more, the act has not actually had the anticipated benefit of fewer drunk-driving deaths, in spite of what some of its supporters claim. Because it has unfairly infringed on the rights of young Americans, and because it has failed in its stated objective, the National Minimum Age Drinking Act should be repealed.

> The author presents a strong thesis statement.

The United States entrusts all citizens ages eighteen and up with the right to vote. This right is provided for in the US Constitution. Voting is a serious responsibility. The consequences of elections—especially national elections—can be very profound and far-reaching, not just in the United States but also around the world. If eighteen-year-olds were entrusted by the Founding Fathers with the right to vote in all elections, it makes no sense that this same group of people should be forbidden to have a glass of wine in a restaurant.

> The second paragraph develops one point in support of the thesis statement.

The right to vote is not the only responsibility given by the government to eighteen-year-old citizens. Young Americans are eligible to be drafted into military service starting at age eighteen. At various periods in history, eighteen-year-old males were routinely drafted into the US military and expected to fight in service of their country. Although the draft has not been in effect since 1973, young people are still required to register for the draft when they turn eighteen. In fact, failure to register is considered a felony.[1] If eighteen-year-olds are expected by society to go to war and risk their lives in the service of their country, why are they not permitted to order a beer with their pizza?

> The third paragraph develops a second point in support of the thesis statement.

Finally, supporters of the National Minimum Age Drinking Act claim that it has saved twenty thousand lives by preventing individuals under the age of twenty-one from drinking legally. This statement is not accurate. In fact, researchers Peter Asch and David Levy found that the "minimum legal drinking age is not a significant—or even a perceptible—factor in the fatality experience of all drivers or of young drivers."[2] Asch and Levy demonstrated that raising the drinking age simply transferred the deaths from the eighteen to twenty-one age bracket into the twenty-one to twenty-four age bracket. In other words, equal numbers of people are still dying as a result of drunk driving; they're just dying slightly later. Clearly the problem here is the misuse of alcohol rather than the age of the drivers. Drunk driving is the problem that needs to be addressed, and raising the drinking age has not addressed it. The act is therefore not justified by any increase in safety or decrease in fatalities among the group the act claims to protect.

> The fourth paragraph presents yet another point in support of the thesis. It fairly states the position of the opposition and refutes it using results from a research study. The study is cited appropriately, so that readers can consult it if they wish.

Young people in the United States are growing up faster and faster, and greater demands are being put on them. In general, they are proud to embrace the responsibilities they are entrusted with. Forbidding them to drink alcohol, while at the same time expecting they shoulder full adult responsibilities, is unfair and unjustifiable. The National Minimum Age Drinking Act has failed in its goal to reduce deaths from drunk driving and has only succeeded in limiting the rights of young Americans ages eighteen to twenty-one. The act has been in force since 1984, and it is long past time for it to go.

> The conclusion refers back to the arguments made earlier in the essay and presents the thesis again in light of those arguments.

[1] "Conscription in the United States," Wikipedia, last modified February 27, 2013, http://en.wikipedia.org/wiki/Conscription_in_the_United_States.

[2] Peter Asch and David Levy, "The Drinking Age and Traffic Safety," Cato Institute, accessed April 19, 2013, http://www.cato.org/pubs/regulation/regv11n2/v11n2-8.pdf.

"They Say/I Say": Some Strategies for Quoting and Responding to Sources

In most argumentative essays, regardless of the topic or the class, you'll be responding to the ideas of other scholars, critics, and researchers. *"They Say/I Say": The Moves That Matter in Academic Writing* is a useful book that offers strategies for framing your argument in the context of what others have written.

Here are a few sample templates excerpted from *"They Say/I Say"*:

Templates for Introducing What "They Say"

Americans today tend to believe that _____ .

In discussions of X, one controversial issue has been _____ . On the one hand, _____ argues _____ . On the other hand, _____ contends _____ . Others even maintain _____ . My own view is that _____ .

Templates for Introducing Quotations

X states, " _____ ."

In her book, _____ , X maintains that " _____ ."

Templates for Explaining Quotations

In other words, X believes _____ .

In making this comment, X argues that _____ .

Templates for Disagreeing, with Reasons

I think X is mistaken because she overlooks _____ .

I disagree with X's view that _____ because, as recent research has shown, _____ .

Templates for Agreeing

X is surely right about _____ because recent studies have shown that _____ .

I agree that _____ , a point that needs emphasizing because so many people believe _____ .

Template for Agreeing and Disagreeing Simultaneously

X is right that _____ , but she seems on more dubious ground when she claims that _____ .

For more templates and a comprehensive exploration of how to engage in the academic "conversation," see *"They Say/I Say": The Moves That Matter in Academic Writing* by Gerald Graff and Cathy Birkenstein, New York: W. W. Norton, second edition, 2010.

Plagiarism and How to Avoid It

Plagiarism is the practice of falsely representing as one's own any language, thoughts, ideas, designs, or expression in a paper, exam, or other work. Different schools, colleges, and universities may have slightly different definitions of the term, but they all amount to the same thing: plagiarism means taking someone else's words, ideas, or work and passing them off as yours.

Plagiarism is a serious violation of academic rules at every school, college, and university. The consequences of plagiarism can be very serious, ranging from failing the class to being placed on academic probation to—in some cases—being kicked out of the school entirely. It's critical that you understand what plagiarism is and how to avoid it.

Plagiarism isn't confined only to work done in an educational context. Plagiarism also occurs in the work world in the form of theft of original material for articles, books, journalistic reports, investigative reports, designs of all kinds, proposals, and many other work-related documents. If anything, the world of work is even less tolerant of plagiarism than the world of education, so you're well advised to understand the concept thoroughly to avoid running into serious trouble at work.

Common Forms of Plagiarism

Plagiarism may take many forms. Here are some of the more common forms that occur in an academic setting:

- Copying words or ideas from printed sources—books, journals, magazines, and so on—without citing the sources properly
- Copying words or ideas from web pages without citing the sources properly
- Copying all or part of another student's work and passing it off as yours
- Buying essays or papers from others, including off the Internet, and passing them off as your own

What Do I Have to Acknowledge?

The following guidelines apply to every academic discipline and every class you take:

- When you use someone else's **words**—phrases, sentences, and paragraphs—in your work, you must enclose them in quotation marks and give the writer credit by citing your source appropriately.
- When you use someone else's **ideas** in your work, you must cite the source.
- When you use someone else's **original research** in your work, you must cite that source.

Do I Have to Cite Everything?

No. You have to cite only that material that is the intellectual work of another person. If the piece of information you want to use is considered *common knowledge*, you do not have to cite it. If you have any questions about what is considered common knowledge in your field, ask your instructor. Here are some examples:

COMMON KNOWLEDGE

Drunk driving is a risk on the road.

NOT COMMON KNOWLEDGE

Over 1.41 million drivers were arrested in 2010 for driving under the influence of alcohol or narcotics. (Federal Bureau of Investigation, "Crime in the United States: 2010," accessed April 19, 2013, www.fbi.gov/about-us/cjis/ucr/crime-in-the-u.s/2010/crime-in-the-u.s.-2010/tables/10tbl29.xls)

COMMON KNOWLEDGE

Los Angeles has a large Central American population.

NOT COMMON KNOWLEDGE

In 2009, almost one in five Central American immigrants to the United States lived in the Los Angeles area. (Aaron Terrazas, "Central American Immigrants in the United States," Migration Policy Institute, January 2011, www.migrationinformation.org/usfocus/display.cfm?ID=821)

COMMON KNOWLEDGE

Edvard Munch's *Scream* is one of the most widely recognized paintings in the world.

NOT COMMON KNOWLEDGE

Edvard Munch's *Scream* was sold for $119.9 million. (Jori Finkel, "Edvard Munch's $119.9 million 'The Scream' to Go on View at MoMa," *Los Angeles Times*, September 18, 2012, http://articles.latimes.com/2012/sep/18/entertainment/lat-et-cm-edvard-munchs-recordsetting-scream-set-to-go-on-view-at-moma-20120918)

COMMON KNOWLEDGE

Teenagers tend to take more risks than young children.

NOT COMMON KNOWLEDGE

The rate of injury and death for adolescents is two hundred times greater than that for young children. (Rebecca Boyle, "Science Confirms the Obvious: Teenagers Take More Risks Than Adults," *PopSci*, October 15, 2012, www.popsci.com/science/article/2012-10/science-confirms-obvious-teenagers-do-more-risky-things-adults)

DO	DON'T
• Ensure you have read and understand your school's policy on plagiarism. If you don't know where to find it, ask. If you don't understand it, ask your instructor to clarify it for you.	• Don't assume you're safe from charges of plagiarism if you simply list all your sources in your bibliography. If you mention ideas or quote words from those sources in your paper, you must acknowledge them in the body of your paper, using the documentation format appropriate to your field.
• Keep careful notes as you do research. When you're reading a lot about a subject, it's easy to forget where you read an idea. It's also surprisingly easy to forget having read about that idea and to	• Don't assume you won't get caught, because it's extremely likely that you

DO (CONTINUED)

begin to think that it's really yours. Be aware of these risks and carefully notate the reading you do for your research.

- Use books and journal articles in your field as models for how to cite and quote sources. Published material will demonstrate the correct way to acknowledge the work of other scholars, critics, and researchers.

- Quote. If you really want to use someone else's words in your essay, you're allowed to do that. Sometimes the words of others can be an excellent source of support for your own arguments. But you must quote those words properly, that is, enclose the words, accurately transcribed, in quotation marks in your essay, along with a complete citation of the source where you found them.

- Paraphrase. Paraphrasing is another good way to borrow someone else's ideas while giving appropriate credit to the original thinker. When you paraphrase, you restate someone else's ideas in your own words. But although the words may be original to you, the ideas aren't, so you still need to cite them.

- Familiarize yourself with the appropriate citation documentation format for your field. Different fields of study have different preferred formats for citation and documentation of sources. Common formats include MLA, APA, *Chicago*, and

DON'T (CONTINUED)

will. The stylistic signs of plagiarism are typically very easy for your instructor to identify. In addition, your instructor is thoroughly familiar with the sources you're using and will almost certainly spot any swiped ideas and words. The advent of the Internet has made it a great deal easier to research and retrieve published work, which makes it easier for your instructor to pinpoint the exact source of stolen ideas or text.

- Don't think that you're the one super-smart, super-crafty student who's going to get away with it. I'm telling you, they've seen your type before, and other people have thought up the same trick you have. In addition, all the time you spend figuring out how to get away with plagiarism is time you could better have spent coming up with your own original ideas and avoiding the problem altogether.

- Don't think it's worth the risk. Plagiarism is never the solution to whatever problem you're facing with your paper or your studies. If you're starting your paper too late or having some other difficulties, you're far better off asking your instructor for an extension than turning in a plagiarized paper.

Turabian (see the box "Common Citation Style Guides for Papers" on page 238). Ask your instructor which format to use and get a copy of the appropriate style guide. If you have questions about formatting and cannot find the answer in the appropriate style guide, ask your instructor for help.

Why Is Plagiarism Such a Big Deal?

There are several reasons plagiarism is important. First, it's a legal issue: stealing is stealing. Authors have ownership and copyright on the content they've created. Plagiarism also violates simple fairness: consider how you might feel if you'd knocked yourself out to write a book or an article, possibly spending years on the work, and then someone came along and pretended your work was his. In addition, plagiarism speaks to your own sense of morality and personal integrity. Are you a cheat? Are you dishonest? No, and you don't want to be. Finally, plagiarism undermines the very educational process you're in school to experience. Ultimately, you're there to learn by doing the work yourself: coming up with your own ideas and expressing them in your own words. When you plagiarize, you not only violate the rights of others, you also cheat yourself.

INTERPRETIVE ESSAY

An interpretive essay is a paper in which you analyze a literary work or some other piece of writing. Interpretive essays are often assigned in English, literature, and writing classes. Although an interpretive essay depends on your understanding about the facts of the piece, it also requires that you develop and defend your own opinion about that piece. As its name suggests, it's an opportunity for you to interpret what you've read.

Introduction

The **purpose** of an interpretive essay is to explain the meaning—or one of the meanings—of a literary work or other piece of writing. Assume that your **reader** is someone who is interested in the topic but not an expert. You should be able to explain your interpretation and defend it in a way that's understandable to the average reader. Read the work carefully, more than once if you can, and see what ideas occur to you. Take notes as you read. Develop a thesis statement and **brainstorm** content that will support your thesis. Don't be rigid about your thesis until you feel you've found enough content to support it; reviewing the piece may cause you to refine or even change your thesis. Be open to this process and don't rush through it.

Once you have your thesis and supporting content, **organize** your essay. The Model Outline offers a useful organizational structure. Plan to go through more than one **draft** of your interpretive essay. Write a first draft and then take at least a short break from it. When you return to reread your draft, ask yourself if it flows well and if the evidence is convincing. You may find you need to go back to the text for more content or to do more brainstorming. You may also find that you have inadvertently included material that's not relevant. Take some time to **revise** your essay until it makes your case in a clear and compelling way.

MODEL OUTLINE

Opening: Lead with a topic sentence that identifies the work you're writing about and offers a strong thesis statement.
Middle: Present a series of paragraphs, each with a clear topic sentence, that expand on your thesis and present supporting evidence from the work.
Conclusion: Show how the arguments and evidence you have presented in the paper support your thesis statement.

What Is an Interpretation?

What does it mean when you're asked to "interpret" a piece of literature or other writing? What is an interpretation?

An interpretation is an analysis of the meaning of the work that goes beyond its surface meanings and finds deeper significance. Interpretation depends on "reading between the lines" to find what is suggested in the work, not just its literal meaning.

Many students fall into the trap of writing a plot summary rather than real interpretation. You may need to provide a brief plot summary to support your analysis, but you shouldn't substitute one for the other. Assume that your reader has read the text you're writing about, and offer a plot summary only to orient your reader and enlarge on your ideas.

Here are a few examples of how interpretation works:

Literal meaning: Shakespeare's *Richard II* is the story of a king who made bad choices, treated his supporters badly, and suffered the consequences of his behavior.

Interpretation: Shakespeare's *Richard II* examines ideas about kingship and the characteristics of a worthy ruler.

Literal meaning: Toni Morrison's *The Bluest Eye* tells the story of a little black girl who wants to be white.

Interpretation: Toni Morrison's *The Bluest Eye* explores the destructive consequences of the notion of ideal beauty to girls and women, in particular the destructive influence of the ideal of white beauty on girls and women of color.

Literal meaning: John Steinbeck's *The Grapes of Wrath* follows the lives of a family displaced by the Dust Bowl and looking for a better life.

Interpretation: John Steinbeck's *The Grapes of Wrath* condemns the inequitable economic system that forms the basis of modern capitalism.

How Do You Develop an Interpretation?

Developing an interpretation starts with a careful and alert reading of the text. There are many different questions you can ask to begin to reveal a text's deeper meaning. How does the setting of the story affect its meaning? Would a different setting change the meaning of the work? What about the time period? What physical details strike you—geography, weather, time of year? Who are the main characters? How do they speak? What do they want? How do they relate to one another? Are there conflicts among the characters? About what? Do the characters change? How? What is the main conflict in the work as a whole? How does it develop and resolve? Who narrates the work—is the narrator a character in the work or a voice outside the world of the work? Think about the kind of language used. Writers often use symbols and metaphors to help point readers to a deeper interpretation of their works. Titles often give an indication of deeper meaning of a work. What do you think the title means? Examining these questions will help you delve into the meaning of the work beyond the simple development of the plot.

Can an Interpretation Be Wrong?

A range of different interpretations of the same work may all be arguably correct. A rich piece of literature may have multiple meanings. For instance, you may interpret the novel *Moby Dick* in a variety of ways, focusing on issues of megalomania, social and class relations, or religion, to name just a few. However, not all interpretations are necessarily valid. Although an interpretation may be a personal reflection, it cannot be completely idiosyncratic. *Moby Dick*, which was written in 1851, cannot possibly be about the Internet or airplanes.

For an interpretation to be valid, you must be able to show evidence in the text that supports it. You may quote parts of the text that support the meanings you see, or provide a brief summary of the relevant incidents in the book. You may also quote from secondary sources (for instance, critical essays) to support your interpretation. See the box *"They Say/I Say"*: Some Strategies for Quoting and Responding to Sources" (page 286) for guidance in using secondary sources.

DO	DON'T
• Start early. The process of developing your ideas and writing your essay takes time, and it's difficult to rush it. Make sure you give yourself enough time to do a good job.	• Don't write a long summary and think you're done. You may want to summarize parts of the work to explain your analysis of it, but you need to go beyond summarizing and actually offer an interpretation.
• Choose an interesting thesis statement that you can support. Make sure you have enough evidence to support your thesis before you start writing. If you can't find enough, choose another topic for your paper. Trying to write an essay with an indefensible thesis statement is a miserable experience, and the end result won't be good. Take the time to develop a thesis statement that will work.	• Don't include a lot of random facts about the author and the literary work. Include only those facts that are relevant to your interpretations of the work.
• Use present tense, not past tense, to describe literary action. Write "Hamlet *sees* the ghost of his father," not "Hamlet *saw* the ghost of his father."	• Don't write about the author's life unless that information is directly relevant to your interpretation of the work.
• Make sure each paragraph has a topic sentence and covers only one main point.	• Don't quote any more from the work than is necessary to make your point. Learn to use quotations for the maximum effect rather than quoting very long passages.
• Use transitional sentences to link your points and advance your argument.	• Don't take passages from a book, article, or website without using the proper citation format. If you don't understand what you should cite or how you should cite it, ask your teacher or professor to explain it to you, or go to a school or campus tutorial center. Failing to cite other people's ideas can lead to charges of plagiarism, which can be very serious (see the box "Plagiarism and How to Avoid It" on page 287).
• Use quotations from the work to illustrate and support the points you're making.	
• Make sure the length of your quotations is appropriate for the overall length of the essay. If your essay is five paragraphs long, a quotation that itself takes up an entire paragraph is too long. Find a way to trim it so that you present only the most important and relevant part.	
• Sum up your essay with a strong conclusion. Make sure your conclusion refers back to your thesis and the evidence you've presented in the essay and doesn't go off in a different direction.	
• Consider quoting from other sources, such as literary critics, to support your position.	
• Choose a good title for your essay. Your title should reflect the content of your essay, not just repeat the title of the work you're writing about.	

NOT LIKE THIS . . .

The Great Gatsby

> This essay needs a better title, to give the reader a more specific idea of what it's about.

> This information is correct. However, it's very general and doesn't serve to introduce this writer's argument about the book. At this point, it feels as though the writer hasn't quite decided what he wants to write about and is just tap-dancing until an idea emerges. If you find your essay begins this way, go back and revise the opening once you have a clear idea of your thesis.

F. Scott Fitzgerald's novel *The Great Gatsby* was first published in 1925 and has been reprinted numerous times. A native of St. Paul, Minnesota, Fitzgerald is considered one of the greatest of American authors, and *The Great Gatsby* is rightly viewed as one of his masterpieces. *The Great Gatsby* was written in the years between the First World War and the great market crash of 1929, during a period of economic prosperity and social change known as the Jazz Age. *Gatsby* reflects many of the key issues of the Jazz Age.

> Yes, it does. But what are the key issues of the Jazz Age, and which ones in particular will this essay discuss? Any essay, particularly a short one like this, needs a tight focus and a clear thesis statement. There is no way this writer can cover all this ground here.

In the beginning of *The Great Gatsby*, we are introduced to the narrator, Nick, a young man who has come from the Midwest to work in the New York bond business. He rents a house on Long Island and finds that among his neighbors are his cousin Daisy and her husband, Tom. He visits Daisy and Tom in their mansion and finds Tom to be very wealthy but arrogant and bullying. There are also hints that Tom is having an affair and that Daisy is unhappy. Later in the novel Nick meets Tom's girlfriend, Myrtle, a shallow and pretentious woman who is not of Tom's social class.

> There's too much plot summary here and not enough analysis. The writer has identified some potentially interesting material—such as the disparity between Tom and Myrtle's social standing—but the essay doesn't get beyond plot summary into actual interpretation.

Nick's next-door neighbor is a mysterious wealthy man called Jay Gatsby. Nick hears wild rumors about Gatsby and the source of his wealth. People said that Gatsby made his money through criminal activities or that he came from a wealthy family, and there were rumors about Gatsby being a war hero in World War I. All Nick knows is that Gatsby throws wild and opulent parties. When Nick is invited to a party, he describes the scenes of excess.

> The writer has inadvertently slipped into past tense here. All literary action should be described in the present tense.

> This is quite a long quotation. The writer could have made his point with only a part of it.

On weekends his Rolls-Royce became an omnibus, bearing parties to and from the city between nine in the morning and long past midnight. . . . And on Mondays eight servants, including an extra gardener, toiled all day with mops and scrubbing-brushes and hammers and garden-shears, repairing the ravages of the night before. Every Friday five crates of oranges and lemons arrived from a fruiterer in New York—

every Monday these same oranges and lemons left his back door in a pyramid of pulpless halves. There was a machine in the kitchen which could extract the juice of two hundred oranges in half an hour if a little button was pressed two hundred times by a butler's thumb. (44).

Eventually Nick learns the truth about Jay Gatsby's personal background. It turns out that his real name was Gatz, and he was a runaway boy from a very ordinary family, not the aristocratic family he had pretended to be from. His money in fact comes from shady dealings with the Jewish gangster Meyer Wolfsheim, primarily from bootlegging liquor. Nick is shocked to discover the truth, but somehow still admires Gatsby and sympathizes with him.

> *The writer has drifted into past tense again here.*

> *In identifying Wolfsheim as a Jew, the writer has an opportunity to analyze the society in which The Great Gatsby takes place, but he doesn't take advantage of the opportunity to develop an argument.*

As the story develops, we learn that Gatsby and Daisy were previously involved in a relationship and that they are still in love with each other. In fact, Gatsby has been giving his lavish parties merely as a way to attract Daisy back to him. Gatsby and Daisy begin an affair, which eventually will become deadly for Gatsby. Through a series of events, Tom's girlfriend Myrtle is killed by Gatsby's car, and Gatsby is left to take the blame for the killing, even though it was Daisy behind the wheel. Myrtle's husband takes revenge by killing Gatsby, and Tom and Daisy leave town, refusing to accept responsibility for their parts in the deaths.

> *The essay lacks a thesis statement, and paragraphs lack topic sentences. As a result, the essay feels more like a wandering plot summary than an actual analysis.*

The Great Gatsby reflects the sense of discontent and corruption that lay beneath the glitz of the American Jazz Age. It is seen to be in fact a time of moral bankruptcy, perhaps foretelling the fiscal bankruptcy that is to come from the market crash and the Great Depression. At the end of the novel, Nick bids farewell to Gatsby's sadly abandoned mansion and leaves New York, back home to the Midwest and the solid values he remembers from there.

> *This is an interesting idea that could form the thesis for an entire paper. Unfortunately, it is not developed.*

> *Throughout the essay, the writer has depended more on plot summary than on actual analysis of the book. There are some good insights in this draft that could be developed much further into an engaging interpretation, but the writer has missed the mark.*

Work Cited

Fitzgerald, F. Scott. *The Great Gatsby*. 1925. New York: Scribner, 1995. Print.

...LIKE THIS

The Great Gatsby and the Dark Side of the Jazz Age

F. Scott Fitzgerald's novel *The Great Gatsby* is set in 1920s America, after World War I and before the stock market crash that brought about the Great Depression. Although Fitzgerald depicts scenes of great wealth, consumption, and glamorous parties, he also shows the "underside" of America at that time. Ultimately *The Great Gatsby* reveals how the corruption and decadence under the glitz of the Jazz Age undermined the American dream of the past and left the future uncertain.

| The first paragraph ends with a strong thesis statement. |

Although Jay Gatsby is initially presented as a charismatic character, ultimately his lifestyle and values are decadent and empty. Nick, the narrator, describes the casual excesses of Gatsby's famous parties: "There was a machine in the kitchen which could extract the juice of two hundred oranges in half an hour if a little button was pressed two hundred times by a butler's thumb" (44). There are rumors about Gatsby's past and the source of his wealth, but Gatsby tells Nick that he comes from a wealthy family and has an honorable past. By the end of the novel, however, we have learned that Gatsby comes from very humble beginnings and that he is not the American aristocrat he has pretended to be. Nor is he the honest self-made man that so many Americans aspire to become: his wealth actually comes from criminal activities. Gatsby has remade himself and compromised his integrity in the quest for wealth. His abandoned and dusty mansion near the end of the novel is a symbol of the emptiness and falseness of his adopted identity: "There was an inexplicable amount of dust everywhere, and the rooms were musty" (154).

| The writer uses quotations from the book economically to support his point. |

If Fitzgerald is critical of the sources and consequences of Gatsby's "new money," the world of "old money" in East Egg is shown to be equally morally bankrupt. Nick's cousin Daisy, whose rank and easy "natural" aristocratic manner Gatsby idolizes, is married to Tom Buchanan, the "hulking" and thoughtless heir of a large fortune. We learn early in the book that Tom is cheating on Daisy. In fact, he brings Nick along on a visit to his mistress. Tom's girlfriend Myrtle is shallow and pretentious. Near the end of the book, Tom and Daisy allow Gatsby to take the blame for Myrtle's death (which Daisy has caused), leading

| The third paragraph begins with a clear transition. The second paragraph has been about the emptiness of "new money," and this paragraph will be about "old money." |

to Gatsby's murder. Tom and Daisy leave the area immediately afterward. Later, Nick meets Tom on the street in New York, and Tom justifies his actions. Nick reflects that Tom and Daisy are "careless people" who "smashed up things and creatures and then retreated back into their money or their vast carelessness . . . and let other people clean up the mess they had made" (188).

> Rather than taking us through a plot summary, the writer carefully selects details from the book to support his argument about the book and to develop his interpretation.

Fitzgerald uses imagery throughout the book to illustrate the rot and destruction that underlies the glittering world of moneyed people. A remarkable passage early in the book sets the tone. Nick describes what he calls a "valley of ashes" that he sees every day from the train on the way into New York: "a fantastic farm where ashes grow like wheat . . . where ashes take the forms of houses and chimneys . . . and . . . of ashen grey men who move grimly and already crumbling through the powdery air." Nick explains that the train always waits at this industrial dumping site for at least a minute, "and it was because of this that I first met Tom Buchanan's mistress" (28). This shocking graphic scene hangs over the entire book, suggesting the consequences of material "prosperity" and its effect on human beings.

> A carefully chosen quotation closes the paragraph.

The Great Gatsby is a story of extremes—extreme ambition and wealth, and extreme decay and decrepitude. Fitzgerald shows the dark side of the glittering Jazz Age. Near the end of the book, Nick reminisces about his home in the Midwest and his memories. What is really important to Nick is the genuine warmth of human relationships. He describes scenes of young people returning from prep school for Christmas, meeting in a train station: "I remember the fur coats of the girls . . . and the chatter of frozen breath and the hands waving overhead as we caught sight of old acquaintances" (183–84). This warm scene seems far in the past, though. Nick will never get back to the innocence he had in those days, and for him the world will never be innocent again. The book ends with painful comment on our inability to reclaim our past and, by implication, the country's past, which is lost forever: "So we beat on, boats against the current, borne back ceaselessly into the past" (189).

> The beginning of the concluding paragraph ties together the content of the previous paragraphs.

> The closing paragraph returns to the idea of the thesis statement in light of the information provided in the essay.

Work Cited

Fitzgerald, F. Scott. *The Great Gatsby.* 1925. New York: Scribner, 1995. Print.

Writing in the Sciences and Social Sciences

SCIENCE PROJECT LOGBOOK OR JOURNAL

A science project journal or logbook provides a written record of a scientific experiment or project, compiled at specific, regular times over the life of the project. It provides a step-by-step record of your methodology, procedures, and findings so that other researchers can verify your findings. Keeping a laboratory notebook is a crucial skill for a scientist to learn. In professional research settings, a laboratory notebook is considered a legal document.

Your instructor may have special requirements for your journal or logbook. Be sure you understand what's expected of you.

Introduction

The **purpose** of a science journal or logbook is to provide a record of the entire process of your experiment or project. Keeping a journal faithfully can provide you with details you'll need if you write up a final report about the project. The process of keeping the journal also helps keep you organized over the life of the project. Ultimately, recording every stage of the experiment or project provides other scientists or investigators the information they need in order to replicate what you have done. Your **reader**, of course, will be your instructor. However, you should keep the journal or logbook as if you were a scientist recording your work for the benefit of other scientists. If you keep in mind that they will need your records in order to reproduce the procedure, your work will be more thorough and professional. Generating content for your journal is not so much a question of **brainstorming** as of keeping scrupulously accurate records. It is important to get into a routine of recording your data on a regular basis. Logbooks are **organized** chronologically, following the course of the project or experiment. Unlike with most other forms of writing, you should not plan on writing multiple **drafts** of your journal or logbook: the point of the document is that it is recorded in real time and not altered. You may **revise** your entries for spelling and clarity, but be careful not to change too much or the validity of your work may be challenged.

DO	DON'T
• Create a notebook dedicated only to your project. The best choice is a journal with sewn pages, so that pages cannot be removed. Your credibility is enhanced if it is clear that your notebook has not been tampered with. Number each page in the top right-hand corner.	• Don't skimp on details. It's better to err on the side of recording too much information than recording too little.
• Use permanent ink—not pencil or erasable ink—to record your entries. If you need to cross something out, do so with a single line through the deleted text. Don't black out anything or use correcting fluid: it may appear you are trying to hide something. Your records should be permanent and transparent.	• Don't remove any entry from your journal, even if it later seems irrelevant or seems to reveal an error on your part. It is more important to keep an accurate record than to perform every step perfectly.
• Begin the logbook with a short description of the experiment or project, including its objective.	• Don't feel you need to use formal language in your journal. Write your entries in informal, conversational language.
• Record your first entry on the first day of your project. Don't wait until the work is under way to start your journal.	• Don't "round" your measurements. Record each measurement to the maximum number of decimal points of the instruments you're using.
• Write legibly. The point of keeping a journal is so that others can read and understand what you did.	

DO (CONTINUED)

- Record every step of your process. If you are unsure about the level of detail you should use, ask your instructor.
- Write each entry immediately after each activity or observation. Don't count on remembering the details later. Record your activities and observations while they're fresh in your mind.
- Keep your journal faithfully. If you write irregularly or infrequently, you will certainly miss important information.
- Record all the calculations you used to process the data. Doing so will help you find and correct any mathematical errors that may occur.
- Note each measurement to the maximum decimal points of the equipment used.
- Write your entries clearly, in the active voice, in the first person. You should omit the pronoun "I": it's understood that you are doing the work. Many of your entries will be sentence fragments, for example, "Measured each seedling using metric ruler."
- Date and sign each entry.
- Title and date all graphs, charts, and figures.
- Staple, tape, or glue any computer printouts or photographs into your logbook in the appropriate place.
- Write a brief reflection on the results at the end of the experiment or project. Did you obtain the expected results? Did problems occur that might have affected the results?

LOGBOOK ENTRY EXAMPLES

Friday, March 9, 2013. Temp 16°C., humidity 70%. Hand-mixed compost. No changes perceivable.

Monday, March 19, 2013. Temp 19°C., humidity 72%. Decomposition has begun. Some food scraps still identifiable.

Friday, March 30, 2013. Temp 20°°C., humidity 61%. Decomposition continuing. No mixing. Added 125 g food scraps.

Friday, October 21, 2011. Plant A given a 6.0% saline solution. Leaves have begun to turn yellow.

Monday, October 24, 2011. Plant A drops a flower. Plant B given a 3.0% chlorine solution. Leaves have begun to turn yellow.

Tuesday, October 25, 2011. Plant C given only water. Appears limp.

MAKING CORRECTIONS IN ENTRIES

Mixture turned red after addition of ~~5 drops~~ 4 drops of catalyst. Weighed ~~0.76~~ 0.77 g calcium citrate (target was 0.80 g).

chloride
Weighed 0.33g of iron nitrate^ and added to a beaker of 7 ml ethanol with stirring.

and flanges
Affixed the pipettes^ to the frame apparatus. Forgot to use sealant. Repeated the procedure using sealant.

On March 9, 2013, reported that sample size of 33, but sample size was actually 31. Two units broke before beginning of experiment.

On September 10, noted that all specimens were male. In fact, 11 specimens are male and 2 are female.

LAB REPORT

A lab report is a common assignment in science and engineering classes. Each discipline has its own preferred format and style for a lab report—a lab report in biology differs from a lab report in chemistry, which in turn differs from a physics lab report. In addition, instructors may have personal preferences about how you write your lab report. What follows here is general guidance that applies to all lab reports. Be sure you understand exactly what your instructor expects from your own lab report.

Introduction

The **purpose** of a lab report is to document the findings of an experiment or procedure and to communicate the significance of those findings. Your report should also demonstrate that you understand the principles the experiment was built upon. Your **reader**, of course, will be your instructor. However, to get the most out of the assignment, you should write your lab report as though you were truly a research scientist documenting an experiment for an audience of scientists. To be scientifically valid, your results must be reproducible. Therefore, you must document your experiment thoroughly, such that another researcher could do what you did and obtain the same results. The process for gathering information for your lab report is not so much **brainstorming** as keeping accurate notes about your experiment as you go along. The Model Outline (page 305) gives an overview of an **organizational** structure for your lab report, but, as noted above, different disciplines have different requirements for lab reports, and you should check with your instructor to be sure you understand exactly what is expected of you. **Draft** your lab report as you would any other formal piece of writing, using grammatically correct English. Refer to your notes often to ensure your report is complete. It's a good idea to take a break after you finish the first draft of your report, so you can read the draft with a fresh eye later. Put yourself in your reader's shoes as you read over the draft. Is the report complete? Is it clear? Is there anything missing? **Revise** your draft as necessary to ensure completeness, clarity, and correctness.

Model Outline

———•———

The format and content of lab reports can differ significantly from one discipline to another and one instructor to another. This model outline contains the components typical of most lab reports. Check with your instructor to be sure you understand what is required of you.

Title Page. Your title page should include the name of the experiment, your name and the names of your lab partners, and the date.

Abstract. The abstract provides a summary of the purpose of the experiment, its key results, the significance, and your conclusions. The abstract may also mention the methodology you used or the theory that guided the experiment. The abstract is typically one paragraph long, with a maximum of two hundred words.

Introduction. In one or two sentences, the introduction of your lab report states the purpose of the experiment. It also describes the background and underlying theory that the reader needs to understand the experiment. The introduction may also mention specialized equipment used in the experiment and explain the importance of the experiment.

Methods and Materials. (Some lab reports substitute "equipment" for "materials." Some split this section into two separate sections.) Provide a brief description of what materials you used and how you used them. Offer enough detail in this section that another researcher could easily reproduce what you did. When you follow procedures laid out in a lab manual or other resource, it is enough to say so and cite that source. Some disciplines require that you note where and when your work was done.

Procedure. Some disciplines require a section that documents your procedures, step-by-step, in chronological order. Record your steps such that another researcher could duplicate your procedure.

Results. The results section should present the findings from the experiment without analyzing their implications. Equations, tables, and figures—

and sometimes photographs—are frequently used to present the data yielded by the experiment. All of your tables and figures should be self-explanatory.

Discussion. In this section you analyze and interpret the results of your experiment. Was your original hypothesis upheld or not? You may relate your results to existing knowledge and theory. If your results were different from what you expected, discuss the possible reasons. Discuss any experimental errors. Discuss the strengths and limitations of the research design. You may also suggest directions for future research.

Conclusion. Some disciplines require a conclusion to the lab report, which simply states what you know now as a result of this lab experiment. Suggestions for future research may also be placed in this section, depending on the discipline.

References or Literature Cited. List all the sources cited in your report, including your lab manual if you have cited it. Ensure you use the appropriate citation format for this section. Ask your instructor for help if you are unsure about what citation format you should use.

Appendices. If necessary, you may attach appendices to your lab report. These might include raw data or tables and figures that do not appear in the report itself. Be sure that you mention each of your appendices at least once in the body of the report. Give each of your appendices an appropriate, descriptive title.

DO	DON'T
• Give your report a descriptive and informative title. For example, instead of "Lab #2," use a title like "Lab #2: Transpiration" or "Lab Report 2: Melting Point Determination."	• Don't simply rehash the information in the lab manual as background to your lab report. Demonstrate your own understanding of the issues underlying your experiment.
• Write your report in grammatically correct English. Don't be tempted to use shorthand or sentence fragments.	• Don't write the Method section as a how-to. Describe what *you* did, not what is supposed to be done.
• Use the appropriate verb tense. Because the experiment is completed, you should use the past tense when discussing the experiment. When you refer to the report itself, the theory, or the equipment used, write in the present tense (e.g., "The findings of the report suggest that . . ." and "The centrifuge is designed to test . . .").	• Don't use inexact language like "relatively close," "very similar," or "much higher." Instead, report your exact findings.
• Describe the steps you took in the order you actually took them rather than copying from your lab manual. If your instructor tells you that you can simply state you followed the procedure in the manual, be sure you note any occasions when you deviated from that procedure.	
• Write numbers as numerals when they are 10 or greater or when they are associated with measurements. Spell out all numbers that begin sentences.	
• Be careful that your pronouns have clear antecedents.	
• Number all your equations and define every symbol used in the equations.	

Project Proposal Format

Research projects in the sciences and social sciences, including theses, often begin with a project proposal. This box provides a general overview of proposal format. Different disciplines use slightly different formats and terminology, and project supervisors may also have requirements that differ. Ask your instructor, adviser, or mentor if you have questions about what's expected of you.

Student Name

Name of Faculty Mentor or Adviser

Introduction/Thesis Statement. Provide a basic introduction to the project you are proposing. Describe the topic and/or your thesis statement. Explain why you consider the research important. You may also explain how this project relates to your major field or your future career.

Background Information/Problem Definition. Provide an overview of the history of the subject you intend to study. Does your project address a known problem in the field? If so, articulate the problem clearly and describe its background.

Research Modalities or Methodologies. Detail how you plan to carry out the research. Will you rely on publications, interviews, surveys, experiments, or other methods of gathering information? Explain how you will use each.

Required Resources. Do you require any special resources to carry out your research: data, special software, and so on? Describe the needed resources here.

Goals and Objectives/Outputs Desired. Explain why you are doing the project and what you hope to learn or accomplish through your research. Outline your specific goals and objectives. This section is typically the longest part of the proposal.

Final Presentation. Describe how you will present the findings of your research. Will you write a paper? Will you give a presentation? To whom, and what will the presentation include? Will you offer recommendations for future research?

LITERATURE REVIEW

A literature review may be a stand-alone assignment, part of a research paper in the sciences or social sciences, or a separate section or chapter in a senior thesis paper. It may take the form of an annotated bibliography. A literature review consists of a listing and critical discussion of previous work published on the topic you're writing about, including books, journal articles, and previous literature reviews. It may also include unpublished research as long as you have permission from the author to mention it. The format of a literature review may differ across disciplines, so be sure to ask your instructor what is expected of you.

Introduction

The **purpose** of a literature review is to provide a critical analysis of published work relevant to the field in which you are conducting research. Your review should classify the relevant research studies, describe the evolution of knowledge in that field, compare the works you're reviewing, and situate your own work within the context of the existing literature. Your **reader**, obviously, will be your instructor. However, to get the most from the assignment, you should write as though you are a professional researcher writing to an audience of your peers. **Brainstorming** your literature review consists of doing thorough research, understanding the different perspectives and approaches of the sources you are reviewing, and placing your own work within the appropriate context or contexts. You should pay particular attention to identifying and classifying trends in the sources you are reviewing. Depending on your field of study, you may group your sources according to theoretical approach, methodology, subject studied, sample data, or other characteristics. You may find it useful to create lists or even flow-charts to map out the relationships among ideas and research streams. Be willing to go back and revise your classifications if you come across additional information later in the writing process. You can use the Model Outline (page 310) to help you **organize** your literature review. Write your **draft** using an objective, scholarly tone. You are free to express your opinions about the work—indeed, you should do so—but remember that you are a professional writing to other professionals. It's a good idea to take a break before you finalize your draft. Then come back, reread your first draft, and **revise** for completeness and accuracy.

Model Outline

A literature review may range in length from several paragraphs to several pages. The length will be dictated by the number of different streams of literature reviewed, the number of studies within them, and their relationship to your own project. Your review should be as long as it needs to be to be comprehensive.

Introduction: Introduce your topic or area of study. Then provide a high-level overview of the previous studies in the same area, or those that will influence your own work. Identify trends in previous research, and briefly situate your work in that context. Present the criteria you will use to review the existing literature and explain the scope of your review (which studies will you review, which will you omit, and why).

Body: Group the various studies you are reviewing into categories, according to chronology, research questions explored, methodological approaches, objectives, findings and conclusions, and so on. Consider that some studies may fit in more than one category; it is acceptable to mention a study twice if it does belong in more than one place in your review. Allocate more space to those studies you consider more significant. Make sure the similarities and differences between studies are clear.

Conclusion: Summarize the major contributions of the studies you have reviewed, keeping in mind the criteria you laid out in the introduction. Offer an overall assessment of the current state of knowledge and research in the field, and point out any major gaps, theoretical methodological shortcomings, and inconsistencies. Identify directions for future research.

DO	DON'T
• Be precise about which field(s) you are reviewing.	• Don't rely on others' literature reviews to construct yours. It's appropriate for you to consider other reviews of the literature, but it's not a substitute for reading and evaluating the literature yourself.
• Ensure your categories and subcategories are logical and make sense.	
• Group like with like. Part of the purpose of a literature review is to trace the development of streams of literature. Ensure that you discuss studies along with those that are similar, and trace the lines of influence among them.	• Don't review a source you haven't read.
	• Don't just supply a list of references without providing analysis about them. Your literature review should not just be descriptive—it should be analytical.
• Be sure to characterize each work and its contribution to the field fairly and completely.	
• Make your literature review as comprehensive as possible. Be sure you find all the relevant studies within the stream(s) you are reviewing.	• Don't include sources that are not related to the topic you're writing about. In some fields there is a tremendous amount of published research. Focus only on those sources that have a bearing on your own work. If there is very little previous work in your area, say so in your review.
• Use strong topic sentences and transitional devices to help the reader follow your argument. (For guidance, refer to "Writing Strong Paragraphs" on page 271.) Your literature review should read well as a piece of prose.	
	• Don't be dismissive or insulting about another piece of work, even if you disagree with its conclusions or feel it was badly executed. State your criticisms, but maintain a professional approach throughout your literature review.
	• Don't omit research from your literature review just because it takes up a position contrary to yours.

HISTORY ESSAY

Writing about history involves more than just stating facts and regurgitating dates. A key part of the study of history is the ability to assemble facts, draw provisional conclusions from them, and support those conclusions. Writing a history essay gives you the opportunity to practice those skills as you explore a question that interests you.

Introduction

The **purpose** of a history essay is to explore a question about history and propose an answer to that question. Your **reader**, of course, will be your instructor, but you'll have more fun and produce a better essay if you imagine yourself to be a professional historian writing for an audience of other historians—people who are interested in your topic and expect a high level of professionalism in your work. Your essay thus becomes part of an ongoing discussion that attempts to understand the part of history you're exploring. **Brainstorming** your paper begins with selecting a good historical question (see the box "Asking Historical Questions" on page 315). Your choice of topic will naturally be limited by the scope of the class, but you should make an effort to find a question that genuinely interests you. You'll be spending a lot of time exploring this topic, so make sure it's one you really want to study. A history paper is generally an argumentative essay—that is, you're trying to prove a point—and, as such, is **organized** around a thesis statement. (For additional help, see "Argumentative Essay" on page 282 and the box "How to Write a Thesis Statement" on page 264.) Your thesis statement will likely be the result of repeated rounds of brainstorming and research. Be sure you allow yourself plenty to time to do research and develop your paper: you may find that you have asked an interesting question but cannot find enough evidence to support your ideas. You will need to be flexible until you hit on just the right topic and thesis. It's very helpful to use an outline as you write your **draft**. Historical topics can lead in many different directions, and it's easy to go astray unless you have an outline to guide you. Allow yourself enough time so that you can take a break between your first draft and your final **revision**. As you review your draft, ask yourself if your thesis is clear and if the content of the paper really supports it. Consider rephrasing your thesis if necessary. Is anything unclear? Are your facts and citations correct? Have you included anything irrelevant? Proofread carefully before you submit your essay.

DO	DON'T

DO

- Allow yourself plenty of time to write your history essay. This is not the sort of assignment you can expect to do the night before it's due or even a few days before it's due. You will need time to conduct research and do some serious thinking.

- Develop a plausible and specific thesis statement for your essay. Your thesis should be narrow enough that you can cover it thoroughly in your paper. (For help in creating and refining thesis statements, see the box "How to Write a Thesis Statement" on page 264.)

- Make sure you are arguing a specific point of view in your paper. It is not enough simply to assemble facts and recount events—your thesis must express a point of view.

- Connect your essay to research done by other historians. Unless you are working exclusively with primary sources, be sure you look carefully for work done on the topic by historical scholars, and situate your paper in the context of their research.

- Make your position in the debate clear. If you are writing about a topic on which others have taken opposing viewpoints, be sure to make it clear where you stand. Don't be shy about declaring your position.

- Think critically about your sources. Whether you are using primary or secondary sources, or both (see the box "Primary and Secondary Sources in Historical Research" on page 320), you should be careful to confirm the validity of those sources and compare them against other relevant source materials. Also consider the biases of your sources. Do they express a point of view? How does that point of view influence their usefulness as sources for your paper?

- Take the time to read the footnotes and endnotes in your sources carefully. It's tempting to skip

DON'T

- Don't slip into simply recounting events without connecting them to your argument.

- Don't include irrelevant details, no matter how interesting they are. Everything in your paper should be related to your thesis. If it's not, cut it out.

- Don't ignore evidence that runs counter to your position. Your paper will be stronger if you can refute opposing evidence. If you cannot, you must at least acknowledge it.

- Don't twist evidence to make it fit your essay better. It can be frustrating to find material that says almost—but not quite—what you'd like it to say, but you must represent the content of all your research fairly and accurately.

- Don't use the subjective "I" in your essay. It's understood that the position you're arguing for is the one you believe.

- Don't claim other people's original ideas as your own. Keep detailed notes as you do research, and cite your sources carefully. See the box "Plagiarism and How to Avoid It" (page 287) for help in understanding what you need to cite. If you are still unsure about what to cite, ask your instructor for help.

- Don't rely on emotional arguments to support your position. You may have strong feelings about what you're writing about, but your paper will be stronger if you argue dispassionately and present facts than if you make an emotional appeal. Emotion-driven arguments are easy to dismiss.

DO (CONTINUED)

footnotes, but they often contain a great deal of information that can help you in your research.

- Respect the culture and time period you are writing about. Values and norms change over time, and hindsight gives us the benefit of information that was not available in the past. Even if you disagree with the values of the people you are writing about, try to understand them on their own terms and avoid imposing your own values on them.

- Be aware of your biases. Opinions and mores change over time and are shaped by individuals' background and culture. Try to be aware of any biases or assumptions that might influence your perspective and the argument you're making in your paper.

- Maintain your argument throughout the paper. It's easy to slip into simply describing events in a history paper. If you choose to narrate the course of historical events, be sure there's a good reason to do so. All the details in your paper should support your thesis.

- Write in the past tense. If you're used to writing papers in English classes, you've been taught to recount literary action in the present tense. However, the past tense is appropriate for writing about history.

- Document your sources carefully and appropriately. Take notes carefully while you do your research, and note where you read facts and ideas. Use endnotes or footnotes in your paper to cite your sources. The preferred guide for citations in history papers is generally *The Chicago Manual of Style*, but you should confirm your instructor's preference about citations (see the box "Common Citation Style Guides for Papers" on page 238).

Asking Historical Questions
by the American Historical Association

———————————●———————————

Narrow the Topics

Topics are almost always too broad at their birth. Refining a research topic is necessary because the world of sources is wide and you have only so much time for any one project. Here are three quick ways to narrow:

- Limit the scope—Focus your topic geographically, by time period, or by groups of people. Restrict the topic by looking at only one country or region, one short span of time, one organization, or even one or two individuals.

- Choose an angle—Include a theoretical perspective to frame or guide your work. Emphasize one aspect of identity such as class, gender, race, or ethnicity, or a social process like secularization, nationalism, or capitalism. Consider approaching the problem from a particular kind of history: intellectual, environmental, cultural, social, labor, military, or political.

- Pick among possible sources—Restrict yourself from the start to a range of sources—a couple of books by two authors; readings in an anthology; a set of newspapers—while taking care to distinguish between primary and secondary sources.

Compose a Research Question

Restating a refined topic as a question can be harder than it seems. So spend some time on this.

- Types of historical questions—Some questions cannot be answered by historical research. So it may help to note that historical questions tend to focus on three types of problems. The comparison of similarities and differences between two moments in the past is a problem of *continuity or change over time*. An assessment of the array of significant factors and circumstances that influenced individuals and events in the past is a problem of *context*. The understanding of the ideas, states of mind, and experiences of people in the past is a problem of *meaning*.

- Writing the question—Research begins with the question. So write yours out as a single sentence ending with a question mark. Be prepared to rewrite the question as your research progresses.

- Working thesis statements—The point of research is to investigate difficult questions without obvious answers. But it is never too early to posit possible answers (or theses). A thesis is an argumentative answer to a question. Try writing out one or more working theses that can be modified as your research progresses.

The American Historical Association (AHA) is a nonprofit membership organization founded in 1884 and incorporated by Congress in 1889 for the promotion of historical studies. Its website is www .historians.org/.

LIKE THIS

Widows in Early Modern England and Spain

During the early modern period, England and Spain were the two most powerful nations in Europe. How were women treated in these countries? One interesting way to explore this question is to delve into the treatment of widows in these cultures. Widows are an important case, because they represent contemporary women at their most free: no longer under the control of either father or husband. Although some historians have pointed to the Reformation as a key point in the development of women's rights in Europe, other evidence suggests that Spanish widows may have had greater legal protections and social acceptance than their English counterparts.

In Spain, a highly unified, state-sponsored orthodoxy—the Catholic church—laid down strict guidelines for the behavior of widows. They were to spend their lives in quiet contemplation, and they were not to remarry. In Catholic countries, widows might enter convents, either as nuns or, more commonly, as residents.[1]

The teachings of the Christian church were frequently disseminated through popular "behavior manuals." According to P. Renée Baerstein, "The special role of the widow as a model of piety has been developed in Christian thought from early Christian times: Ambrose,

---

[1] For a discussion of the convent as a place of refuge for widows in late medieval Milan, see P. Renée Baerstein, "In Widow's Habit: Women between Convent and Family in Sixteenth-Century Milan," *Sixteenth Century Journal* 25, no. 4 (1994): 787–807.

Jerome, and Augustine all wrote on the subject. The genre exploded, however, in the late Middle Ages with behavior manuals on the three 'states of life' of laywomen."[2] The most prominent theorist on women's conduct at this time was the Spaniard Juan Luis Vives, the author of *De institutione feminae Christianae*.[3] The third section of *De institutione* is devoted to the conduct of widows. While Vives does not condemn remarriage in every case, his strong preference is that a second marriage not be necessary. He quotes Paul's advice that it is better to contain oneself than to remarry.[4] In addition to remaining single, widows were to stay at home as much as possible—except to go to church—to avoid contact with male servants, dress modestly, devote themselves to their children, and pray day and night.

However, despite the teachings of the church and domestic theorists like Vives, Spanish widows at this time had significant legal rights. According to David Vassberg, the early *fueros* (law codes) assumed that widows were "poor" and in need of protection and support. In a legal sense, widows were "much better off" than married women.[5] The law protected the property rights of widows. Widows were allowed, for example, to continue to hold an *encomienda* (a land grant conferred by the Crown) awarded to their husbands even after their husbands' death.[6] As Melveena McKendrick writes, "When her husband died, a woman became the legal head of her family, controlling its affairs and arranging the marriages of her sons and daughters." In fact, widows were the only women in Spain who could legally act as family heads. Mary Elizabeth Perry's study of early modern Seville has found that in spite of various attempts to restrict their behavior, widows were active members of the city's economic and social life: "Widows protected property, were legal guardians of minor children, provided dowries, signed rental agreements, bought and sold property, wrote their own wills."[7] Despite the strict teachings of the church and its agents, according to David Vassberg, "A widow in Spanish society was accorded considerable respect."[8]

In England, the Reformation made the widow's situation far more complicated. At this

---

[2] Ibid., 789.

[3] Juan Luis Vives, *A Very Fruitful and Pleasant Book Called the Instruction of a Christian Woman* (1523), trans. Richard Hyrde, London [1529?]. A facsimile reproduction of an early printing is available in Diane Bornstein, ed., *Distaves and Dames: Renaissance Treatises for and about Women* (Delmar, NY: Scholars' Facsimiles and Reprints, 1978).

[4] "Therefore I say vnto the vnmarried, and vnto the widowes, It is good for them if they abide euen as I doe. But if they cannot abstaine, let them marrie: for it is better to marrie then to burne" (1 Corinthians 7: 8-9). *The Geneva Bible: The Annotated New Testament, 1602 Edition*, ed. Gerald T. Sheppard (Cleveland: Pilgrim Press, 1989).

[5] David Vassberg, "The Status of Widows in Sixteenth-Century Rural Castile," in *Poor Women and Children in the European Past*, ed. John Henderson and Richard Wall (London: Routledge, 1994), 185.

[6] Melveena McKendrick, *Woman and Society in the Spanish Drama of the Golden Age: A Study of the* Mujer Varonil (Cambridge: Cambridge University Press, 1974), 42.

[7] Ibid., 17; Vassberg, "Status of Widows," 180; Mary Elizabeth Perry, *Gender and Disorder in Early Modern Seville* (Princeton, NJ: Princeton University Press, 1990), 15.

[8] Vassberg, "Status of Widows," 182.

time, England was in the middle of a very rough religious and social journey whose destination was unknown: "What had been for centuries a Catholic country was now moving irrevocably toward Protestantism and no one had any definite idea of just what social relationships—especially for women—might be like in this 'new' society. Attitudes toward women were changing in some quarters, but society as a whole could not accommodate itself to the change."[9]

The advent of Protestantism, in spite of its rhetoric of sexual equality, entailed real losses for many English women: "Henry VIII's destruction of the monasteries and convents, coupled with the growing Protestant focus on marriage as the only acceptable social condition, impacted heavily upon women. That women had no other occupation but to marry doomed those women who could not, or would not marry, to a life on the virtual fringes of society."[10] Curiously, in arguing a widow's right to make her own choice of second husband, the Puritans actually constricted the choices she could make comfortably within the orthodoxy of these teachings. Even married women found their roles transformed in ways they may not have appreciated. The Protestant insistence on the husband as head of the family relegated the woman to the status of "helpmeet" in an arena where she had historically held authority: "Married, she had lost many of the functions which would have been hers in a Catholic household; unmarried, she had lost the chance to become a nun."[11]

English widows lost not only the option of cloistering themselves in convents. They also lost the popular *model* of the secluded and single widow: "Unlike their Catholic counterparts, Protestant women had no religious justification for a lifestyle that excluded men and, therefore, they experienced widespread economic and social discrimination." Increasingly, the popular imagination lost the ability to accommodate the widow as a legitimate person; once widowed, she became either a woman "to be married" or an anomalous—and unnatural—figure making her way alone in the world: "widowhood transferred women to a status that made it difficult for them to mingle in society."[12]

Spanish and English cultures had very different ways of *conceiving* of the widow, not only in religious and quasi-religious writings but also in popular stereotypes. Spanish widows were popularly characterized as poor, whereas their English counterparts—regardless of their actual economic status—were routinely assumed to be rich. David Vassberg declares that "the phrase 'poor widow' was employed so frequently in Spanish documents of the time

---

[9] Theodora A. Jankowski, *Women in Power in the Early Modern Drama* (Urbana: University of Illinois Press, 1992), 37.

[10] Ibid.

[11] Patrick Collinson, *Birthpangs of Protestant England* (Basingstoke, UK: Macmillan, 1988), 74.

[12] Jankowski, *Women in Power*, 37; Retha M. Warnicke, "Eulogies for Women: Public Testimony of Their Godly Example and Leadership," in *Attending to Women in Early Modern England*, ed. Betty S. Travitsky and Adele F. Seeff (Cranbury, NJ: Associated University Presses, 1994), 174.

that it almost seems to be a single word." Vassberg's observation makes an interesting contrast to a different linguistic phenomenon in English. The notion of the rich widow became such a commonplace in England that rhetorician George Puttenham used it in an example: "When you will place your adjective after your substantive, thus: *Mayde faire, widow riche, priest holy* and such like."[13]

Of course both stereotypes were distortions. Although Vassberg concludes that his study "confirms the stereotype of the 'poor widow' in Golden Age Spain," he offers a number of questions to be addressed by future research; among his suspicions is the idea that some Spanish widows may have made themselves appear poorer than they actually were to avoid being placed on the tax rolls. And Merry Wiesner reports that in England widows often stressed their poverty in successful appeals to city and guild representatives; the term "poor widow" is certainly not unknown in English.[14] Still, the two opposing constructs of these stereotypes point to important differences in the way the two cultures understood the widow.

There is at the moment a far greater body of research into the lives of women in early modern England than the lives of their Spanish counterparts during the same period, and much more needs to be done. But early exploration suggests perhaps a surprising conclusion: that widows in Catholic Spain enjoyed more freedom and respect than those in Protestant England.

[13] Vassberg, "Status of Widows," 185. George Puttenham, *The Arte of English Poesie* (1589) (Menston, UK: Scolar Press, 1968), 212.

[14] Vassberg, "Status of Widows," 192; Merry E. Wiesner, *Women and Gender in Early Modern Europe* (Cambridge: Cambridge University Press, 1993), 104.

Primary and Secondary Sources in Historical Research

As you conduct research for your history paper, you will likely be working with one of two different types of information—primary sources and secondary sources. The difference between primary and secondary sources lies in the time they were created.

Primary Sources

Primary sources are materials that were created during the time period you are writing about. Common primary sources include newspapers and journals, maps, legal documents, business documents, speeches, letters, personal diaries, popular songs and ballads, oral histories, novels and poetry, and other types of books.

When you're writing an essay based mainly on primary sources, your objective is typically to present your own interpretation of events, based on your reading of sources from the time. Your essay should not just be a retelling of what happened but should rather take up a position that you can defend using information drawn from your sources. When you rely on primary sources, it's important to use multiple sources and check your facts carefully. Essays based on primary sources are often organized chronologically.

Secondary Sources

Secondary sources are materials that were created after the time period you are writing about. These include, of course, books and articles written by historians. They may also include things like novels, poetry, songs, or operas written about the historical period. Secondary sources also include scholarly introductions to collections of primary materials. Secondary sources typically express a retrospective point of view and interpretation of the historical events they cover.

When you are writing an essay based mainly on secondary sources, your task is to analyze the interpretations of other researchers and comment on their conclusions. You may agree or disagree with their positions, and you must provide evidence to support your position.

Finally, you should be aware that any given source might be both a primary and a secondary source, depending on your historical point of view. For instance, Walter Pater's collection of essays *The Renaissance* (1873) would be considered a secondary source if you were writing about the art and poetry of sixteenth-century Italy. However, if you were writing about the Victorian worldview, Pater's book would be considered a primary source.

Writing in the Arts

Art and art history classes often require students to attend a gallery or museum exhibition and submit a review of their experience. Writing a review gives you a chance to apply what you're learning in class to art that you encounter outside school.

Introduction

The **purpose** of an art review is to advise others whether the show is worth attending and to provide useful background information and interpretation for those who do attend. As you write your review, assume that your **reader** is someone with an interest in art and some knowledge of it, but not an expert or an art critic. **Brainstorm** from your reader's point of view. What would this reader find interesting and useful? What can you say to guide them and help them? Which pieces in the show will you focus on in your review? **Organize** your review from the general to the specific. Talk first about the artist or the overall show, and then discuss individual pieces. Expect to go through more than one **draft** of your review. Take a break from your draft, and then try to reread it from the point of view of someone who has not seen the show. Is there anything you should add to make the review more helpful to the reader? **Revise** accordingly.

DO	DON'T
• Be sure you understand the assignment before you visit the gallery or museum. Check to see if your instructor has asked you to pay attention to anything in particular in your review.	• Don't say anything rude or insulting. If you did not enjoy the show or the art, explain why without being rude.
• Do some background research on the artist(s) and the museum or gallery before you go. Doing so will enrich your experience and inform your review.	• Don't try to do too much. You won't have space to describe every piece in the show. Instead, focus on a few pieces to discuss in depth.
• Take your time at the show. Look at all the art carefully.	• Don't praise the work without offering analytical insight or supporting your opinion. Your review should offer more than just your likes and dislikes.
• Take notes as you observe.	• Don't say that you don't understand art or this particular art. If you're in an art class, you're expected to make your best effort to understand.
• Read all the information available at the gallery or museum, including wall texts and catalog copy.	
• Think about why the curator chose to show these works together, particularly if there are several different artists showing or just a small selection of a single artist's work.	
• Situate the work in a context. How is this artist similar to her contemporaries? Different from them? Which artists or artistic traditions may have inspired her? Does her work remind you of any other artist's work or "quote" other works of art?	
• Include information about the artist if it is relevant to the artwork.	
• Describe the work physically.	
• Include photos of the artwork, if possible. Some museums and galleries don't permit photography, so be sure to check before you take pictures.	
• Cite any sources you use in the review.	

Writing a Good Art Review

The three basic components common to most art criticism models are description, interpretation, and evaluation. A good art review will work through these components chronologically.

When you describe a work or exhibition, you want readers to picture it without seeing it. A good strategy is first to describe the general features and build toward crucial details. Be sure to mention the relative size and position of features, and be as detailed as possible. Ask a friend to read your description and then look at the work. Have your friend tell you what is confusing, misleading, inaccurate, or missing. Avoid the temptation to start interpreting the work too soon.

Your interpretation should build on the description. Resist the urge to be overly personal, funny, or brilliant. Before writing, consider different contexts of the show: What did the artist(s) intend? How do the works relate to each other and to the exhibition space? What could the works mean to naïve and knowledgeable viewers? Think about what the work reminds you of, how it makes you feel, and why. Would others share these associations? Think of how people of different cultural backgrounds, life experiences, and beliefs might respond. Sometimes it is appropriate to interpret art through a particular "lens," such as formalist, disability studies, feminist, and so on. This strategy can expose an artist or curator's unintentional bias, but you should be careful not to insert your own bias. Avoid interpretations that are too personal, and resist trying to be brilliant, humorous, or clever.

Evaluation is tricky, and it is usually unhelpful to grade or "rate" the work. If you're reviewing professional work, it's probably good. To evaluate the work, consider its effectiveness in terms of what you think the artist wanted, its context in the exhibition space or show, and the likely viewership. Instead of saying it's good or bad, describe what was most effective and why.

John Derby, PhD, is assistant professor of visual art education at the University of Kansas, Lawrence. He serves on the Editorial Review Board of the journal *Art Education*.

LIKE THIS

Mallory Paddock   Gallery Review

INTERESTING MEDIA

Fig. 1

"Metal sculpture, to me, is like a collection of bones taken from different places and reassembled into something that evokes a natural emotional response" (Johnson qtd. in Edrich). Eric Johnson is a metal sculptor from Birmingham, Alabama. He began to weld in his father's garage as a teenager and began his artistic career in 1991. Aside from his metals work, Johnson writes part-time and adds dynamism to his portfolio with wall art as well as furniture. He worked for a long time as a designer, but he explains that "it seemed like the job that was paying the bills was the one getting in the way" (qtd. in Edrich). So he left his career for a life of fine arts.

The majority of his sculptures are forms of abstracted figures or animals, reminiscent of some of the welded sculptures of Eila Hiltunen. Johnson has played with the human form and bends it to his will. In *Ready for Takeoff* (fig. 1) the figure is hunched over, and in the Art Center gallery a candle has been placed in front of him. His long and geometric features combined with the expression on his face give a sense of formulaic mischievousness.

What appears to be growing vertically out of his backpack is a long wire that ends at a propeller, hence the name of the piece. Like all of Johnson's works, an exoskeleton is used. The sculptures have nothing to hide and, in fact, viewers can see through the middle of some of them. Also common in his sculptures such as *Ready for Takeoff* is an emphasis through isolation. The figure stands alone, which works simultaneously with the viewer's personal reactions.

End of the Day (fig. 2), a depiction of a farmer at work, also stood out among the sculptures at the Art Center. Johnson shows a strong sense of line within the piece, using wire to align the fence. What is most impressive is Johnson's choice of wood for the plinth base. The natural curve of the wood imitates the effect of earth that the farmer figure is sowing. That natural movement creates a sense of legato rhythm that further illustrates the life of a farmer and the mood of a long day's work on the farm.

Fig. 2

Eric Johnson's sculptures are strange yet engaging and thought provoking. With process and materials being his expertise, Johnson's work is sure to inspire new approaches to art for the viewer.

Work Cited

Edrich, Alyice. "Interview with Eric Johnson, Metal Sculptor." *EmptyEasel.com*. Empty Easel, 14 April 2011. Web. 21 April 2012.

Mallory Paddock is a student at the Savannah College of Art and Design, class of 2015. Her website is www.mallorypaddock.com.

PERFORMANCE REVIEW

Drama, literature, music, and dance classes often require students to attend a performance and submit a review of their experience. Writing a review forces you to watch a performance alertly and allows you a chance to share your insights and opinions with others.

Introduction

The **purpose** of a performance review is to provide your readers with an impression of the show and help them decide if they want to attend, too. As you work on your review, assume your **reader** is someone who is interested in the topic but not an expert. Naturally, there is a lot you can say after a performance. **Brainstorm** your content from your readers' point of view. What kind of information will be most useful and interesting to them? **Organize** your review from broad topics down to smaller details: start with the work and the company, and work through to contributions of technical staff. Let your **draft** sit before revising it. Sometimes insights come to you a day or so after the performance, so allow yourself time to have some hindsight. As you **revise**, ask yourself if what you've written would be useful to people considering attending the performance: would your review help them make the decision and enrich their experience if they do decide to go?

To think of criticism as a conversation is to think of it as a social act, something that puts you in touch with other people who may think the way you do.

—*Arlene Croce, dance critic*

DO	DON'T
• Be sure you understand the assignment before you go to the performance. Check to see if your instructor has asked you to pay attention to anything in particular in your review.	• Don't say anything rude or insulting. If you did not enjoy the performance, explain why without being rude.
• Do some background research about the playwright, composer, or choreographer whose work you are about to see, as well as the performers you will be seeing. Do some research into the performance history of the piece. This information will enrich and inform your experience.	• Don't write exclusively about your experience or feelings about the performance and neglect to provide information about it.
• Take notes, discreetly, during the performance. It can be difficult to remember details afterward.	• Don't blame the performers or creative team if you didn't like the play, the music, or the dance. It's possible to distinguish between the piece being performed and the performers. You may see a good production of a play, dance piece, or musical composition that you don't really care for.

DO (CONTINUED)	**DON'T** (CONTINUED)

- Provide some information about the playwright, composer, or choreographer.
- Comment on any individual performances that stood out.
- Offer your interpretation of what the piece means, its general themes, or how it is relevant today.
- Offer at least a few comments on each piece, if the performance included multiple pieces.
- Suggest ways the production could have been improved, if you feel that it could have.
- Mention the set, costumes, and lighting. Mention the names of the designers.
- Offer readers information they will need if they decide they want to see the performance: place, date, times, and where to purchase tickets. If there are any special considerations for viewers— such as excessive violence or scenes unsuitable for children—let your readers know.

- Don't focus on one performer to the exclusion of others. Even if the piece features a star, be sure you give credit to other strong performers.

LIKE THIS

Red Bull Theater's revival of the little-known play *The Witch of Edmonton* illuminates a distant period in history that still resonates today. Written in 1623 by Thomas Dekker, John Ford, and William Rowley, the play shows what happens when an isolated community member becomes the scapegoat for all the community's problems.

The play was directed by Jesse Berger, artistic director of Red Bull Theater. His handling of the material brings to the fore the suffering and rage of the central character in the context of a suffocating and deeply prejudiced world.

It is difficult to single out any particular performers in this uniformly strong cast of classical actors. Charlayne Woodard as Mother Sawyer, the "witch," brings in a memorable and deeply moving performance. As the devil/dog who torments her, Derrick Smith is both seductive and terrifying, sometimes creeping along the ground and other times walking upright. Justin Blanchard is compelling as Frank, the hapless young man who ruins the lives of both of his loves, convincingly played by Christina Pumariega and Miriam Silverman. Sam Tsoutsovas does a very moving turn reminiscent of King Lear late in the play. Adam Green provides welcome comic relief as Cuddy Banks.

The ingenious set by Anika Lupes creates a claustrophobic hemmed-in world, while the monochrome costumes by Cait O'Connor suggest a community in which conformity is all. The stark lighting design by Peter West underscores the drama of the play. Daniel Levy's original music sets the tone. Rick Sordelet designed the extensive and sometimes spectacular violence.

The Witch of Edmonton, Red Bull Theater. Lucille Lortel Theater. Address 121 Christopher Street (at Bedford Street), New York City. Tuesday–Saturday at 7 p.m. Sunday at 2 p.m. Through March 14. Tickets at www.redbulltheater .com.

The Theater Review

———•———

Theater criticism requires double vision. On the one hand, you need to be able to experience a live performance in the present tense, as a work to which you react spontaneously—with laughter, tears, anxiety or flat-out boredom. But there also has to be another part of you that's analyzing your own responses and figuring out why what's being done on stage makes you feel the way you do. In other words, you've got to have your gut and your mind operating at the same time.

During a performance, I try to let my gut rule. Occasionally (and I mean this literally), I'll check my face to see if I'm smiling. If I am, the play is working for me. (That's true even if it's a tragedy.) It's when I sit down to write that the analytical side asserts itself. Then I step back to assess, more coolly, the intentions of the play's creators, and how successful they were in realizing those intentions.

Which brings you back to the gut, because that's your most reliable barometer of how good a performance was. Of course everybody's gut is different. But after you do the research and feel like you know what you're talking about, you have to go with your own subjective opinion. That's all you know, after all.

For me, the best criticism re-creates the visceral feeling of watching a performance, while placing it in the context of its time and place and artistic predecessors. It's a tricky balancing act. But both heart (or gut) and mind have to be present in any review. You can't have one without the other.

Ben Brantley is chief theater critic for the *New York Times*.

The Dance Review

───────●───────

Any viewer can appreciate the beauty or virtuosity of a dancer onstage. But dance is a wordless art expressed through ephemeral performances. Essentially there is no substitute for a live performance. A videotape of a performance is only a tool and flattens the choreography, never giving you a full picture.

So, if you are reviewing a high school or college dance concert and also, a major international dance company with a superstar, you are faced with the same specific problem: how to appraise this wordless art in words.

Introduce the reader to the kind of performance you are writing about. Dance is very popular and includes genres as diverse as ballet, modern dance, tap dance, folk dance, ethnic forms ranging from Indian classical dance to flamenco—not to speak of the ballroom dancing now seen in theaters and on television.

A lively image can be part of your first paragraph. But you must be a reporter too. The reader must know if you are writing about only two persons on stage, as in a duet, or a full company ballet with some 40 people in the cast. Provide information early on: the name of the group or the choreographer (especially if you will focus on new works) and the venues. Experimental dance is not always seen in a theater: performances can take place in a parking lot or a swimming pool.

You can sum up your opinion (even if it is mixed) near the beginning but keep in mind you will have to justify it in the review.

Define the dance piece visually, but steer clear of the floor-pattern school of criticism that describes movement after movement. You would not analyze an abstract painting by merely saying the red spot is to the left of a blue line, which is above a green circle.

Instead, you want to explain the concept behind the choreography. If you have not done the background research on a style or choreographer, know that dance communicates directly with the viewer. Your instinct and intelligence can guide you and tell you if what you are seeing is "good" or "bad."

But good or bad without ANALYSIS is not what a dance review is about. You can render an opinion in several ways. You can write in essay form and develop your argument. Or you can distill your analysis early and expand on it. If you have just discovered an exceptional dancer or seen a major premiere, say so boldly.

It is important to encourage new talent. A young choreographer may not succeed in his or her own goals but you can note that the ideas were interesting. If you dislike or do not understand a choreographer's esthetic, say so but do not question the choreographer's sincerity.

Technique in a dancer is important: discuss the quality of the dancing. This is distinct from discussing the choreography (its structure, relationship to music, novel partnering). Mention the lighting designers and conductors and composers.

The more you attend dance performances, the more you will know.

Anna Kisselgoff is former chief dance critic for the *New York Times*.

BOOK REVIEW

A book review offers you the opportunity to share your critical perception of a book's strengths and weaknesses, to share information that other readers might find useful, and finally to advise others whether they should read the book themselves.

Introduction

The **purpose** of a book review is to offer your critical assessment of a book—how successful and enjoyable you found it—and to recommend to your readers whether or not they should read it. Assume that your **readers** are interested in books but are not familiar with this book or the work of this author. **Brainstorm** from your readers' point of view. What information would be most useful to them? What would you have liked to know about this book before you read it? As you read, keep a running list of what you feel are the book's strengths and weaknesses, and select from these as you plan your review. The Model Outline provides a structure you can adapt to **organize** your book review. Allow yourself time to go through several **drafts**. You may find that your first draft is too long and not as tightly focused as you would like. Be aware that you probably won't have room to say absolutely everything you'd like to say about the book. Choose your content during the organizing process, further hone it as you draft, and finally **revise** to ensure that your review is as concise as possible. As you revise, ensure that you have all the details right and eliminate any typos and other errors.

MODEL OUTLINE

There is no single accepted structure for a book review. This outline provides a basic template you can adapt for your own purposes.

Introduction: Provide basic information about the book you're reviewing, including author, title, publication information (publisher and year of publication), and genre. In a few sentences, give the reader a general overview of what the book is about and your overall opinion of it.

Body: In the body of the review, devote several paragraphs to delving deeper into the book. Offer readers your insights about what you found most striking about the book, and provide specific examples. For a nonfiction book, you might discuss the author's purpose, thesis, arguments, and main points. What are the book's greatest strengths and weaknesses? Would you recommend this book to others? Why or why not?

Conclusion: Conclude by summing up your thoughts about the book. Remember that your readers are counting on you to help them decide whether to read the book. What is your overall message to the readers about this book?

DO	DON'T
• Start early on your book review. Allow yourself plenty of time to read the book carefully and to reread all or part of it. • Take notes as you read. Be sure to note the page numbers of important passages you want to discuss, so you don't have to waste time searching for them later.	• Don't be afraid to express your opinion. A book review is different from a book report, in which you are asked to be objective about the book. The whole point of a book review is to share your point of view. • Don't attempt to review a book you haven't read. It will be clear you don't know what you're talking about.

HOW TO REVIEW A WORK OF FICTION

There are many elements of a work of fiction to address in a book review. Here's a list of areas to consider as you plan your review:

Setting: Where is the book set? When does the action take place? How does the setting—both physical and temporal—influence the story?

Characters: Who are they, and how do they relate to one another? Do you find them believable? Engaging? Appealing? What is their dialogue like?

Point of view: Who is telling the story? Is it a third- or first-person narrator? Does the point of view shift? If so, what is the effect of that shifting? Which character or characters are the main focus?

Plot: Is it engaging? Easy or hard to follow? Surprising?

Writing: What is the author's writing style like? Are there distinctive features of the writing? How does the style influence your overall reading experience?

• Be selective. You will probably have a page limit for your review, and you should be aware that you may not have the space to say everything you want to say.

• Say *why* you liked or disliked the book—be specific.

• Support your points with direct quotations from the book. Keep these quotations brief: most of the review should consist of your insights about the book, not long quotations.

• Don't fall into the trap of summarizing the book. Provide just enough summary so that your points are clear to your readers. Your job is to share your insights about the book, not recount its contents.

• Don't include a lot of information about the author unless it's relevant to the book itself and to your perspective on the book. The author's birthplace, education, employment history, and family background may or may not yield interesting insights about the book you're reviewing. Use your best judgment, and resist the temptation to recite facts simply for the sake of reciting facts.

• Don't try to cover everything about the book in your review. You will have to be selective. Pick the things that interest you most, the most notable things, the things you think will be of most interest to your readers.

• Don't give too much away. If you're reviewing a work of fiction, don't spoil it for others by giving away key plot points or the ending of the story.

• Don't be nasty. If you didn't enjoy the book, don't be insulting or snide. Let your reader know—calmly and unemotionally—why you were disappointed in the book.

- Consider how the author's background may have influenced their writing of the book. Is this the author's first novel? Has the author written other books about the same kind of topic? Do you know of any experiences the author might have had that inspired or informed this book?
- Consider the projected audience for the book. Who do you think the author was writing for? Was it written for an academic audience? A specialist audience? History buffs? Romance fans? Self-improvement readers? A general reader?
- Take a stand. The ultimate point of a book review is to make a recommendation to your reader. Don't be afraid to share your opinion. Your verdict doesn't have to be an absolute yes or an absolute no. Perhaps you liked the book but have some reservations about it. Perhaps you basically disliked it but admired some part of it. Offering a nuanced opinion of a book often makes a more interesting review.
- Give your review a title that reflects the content of the review. Don't just use the book's title as the title of your review.

LIKE THIS

POLITICAL INTRIGUE AND
HIGH-SEA ADVENTURE

Master and Commander by Patrick O'Brian (W. W. Norton, 2009, first published in 1969) is a historical novel that tells the story of two very different men who become friends and end up serving on a Royal Navy vessel during the Napoleonic Wars. Jack Aubrey is a British naval captain, and Stephen Maturin is a physician and naturalist of mixed Irish and Catalan extraction. The two meet by chance in Mallorca. When Aubrey accepts command of the *Sophie*, he asks Maturin to join as ship's surgeon. *Master and Commander* creates an absorbing and entertaining world. Although fans of historical fiction and military history would particularly enjoy this book, *Master and Commander* provides an exciting and engaging story that any reader can enjoy.

Master and Commander provides a vivid depiction of the world of eighteenth- and nineteenth-century Europe. The book shows signs of careful research in its historical detail. The characters have distinctive speech patterns. Characters from different regions and classes speak with distinct accents. The descriptions of clothing are detailed without being tedious. The descriptions of life on board the ship—meals, sleeping arrangements, and the dangers of the service—are engrossing. Particularly interesting is a glimpse into the medicine of the time. Although Dr. Maturin is portrayed as an intelligent and skilled physician, the limits of medical science—before the development of anesthesia and antibiotics—are very striking, and some of the medical scenes are gory. To read *Master and Commander* is to take a trip back in time to a very different world.

O'Brian also does a good job of introducing the social and political complexities of the times. The story is presented from the point of view of the English in the Napoleonic Wars, but it's not a simplistic view of the political situation. Stephen Maturin is not English at all. He speaks Irish, Spanish, and Catalan fluently. He has been involved in some sort of Irish revolutionary activity prior to the opening of the book. The characterization of Jack Aubrey is also complex and serves to illustrate some of the splits in English society. His father is an army general who is a fierce Tory during a time when the opposing party, the Whigs, hold control. The blustering General Aubrey is not a political asset to his son, who is trying to rise through the ranks of the Royal Navy, which itself is highly politicized.

The book's greatest success is its vivid depiction of life and war at sea. O'Brian freely uses nautical terms, which is interesting but sometimes confusing for anyone who is not a specialist in this area. I found myself reaching for the dictionary frequently. The diagram of the sails of a square-rigged ship that appears in the front of the book is helpful, though the average reader would welcome a full glossary of sailing and nautical terms. The battle scenes are especially exciting. The book builds skillfully to several military encounters, and even if the terminology is not completely clear, it's virtually impossible to put the book down during these episodes.

The development of the friendship between Aubrey and Maturin is realistic and interesting. Both are likable, in different ways. Aubrey is an almost John-Bull type of Englishman, while Maturin is intellectual and eccentric. Their relationship is effective on a personal level and also helps portray the political complexity of a world that is shrinking owing to the technology of sail.

In conclusion, *Master and Commander* is enjoyable, interesting, and informative, and I highly recommend it. It is the first in O'Brian's seventeen-book Aubrey-Maturin series, and I am eagerly looking forward to reading the rest.

Other Forms of Academic Writing

COLLEGE OR SCHOLARSHIP APPLICATION ESSAY

Writing a college or scholarship application essay is one of the most important—and therefore most stressful—tasks a young person will do. The stress is compounded by the fact that, unlike grades or test scores, the student has immediate control over the quality of the essay. Although there are no guarantees in the college admissions or scholarship selection process, there's a lot riding on this essay, and students feel the pressure to perform well.

Introduction

Start as early as possible working on your essay—ideally, as soon as you know the required topic(s). Because it's such an important task, it's tempting to procrastinate. But you'll have a better experience and end up with a better end product if you start early and allow yourself plenty of time to revise your drafts.

The admissions committee already has your grades and test scores, the quantitative part of your application. The essay is part of the more subjective, qualitative part of your application. The **purpose** of the essay is to show the committee who you are as a person, what you value, and what you hope to do with your life. Equally important, the application essay serves as a writing sample that the committee can use to assess not just your grasp of grammar and vocabulary but also your ability to think critically and construct an argument.

Think hard about your **reader**'s expectations. Sometimes it helps to imagine your reader as a teacher in your school—one who doesn't know you or your work. That reader will expect a good essay, on topic, free from errors. Also bear in mind that your reader is probably reading a lot of other essays in addition to yours; do your very best to make his experience pleasant and rewarding.

Brainstorm extensively for these essays, both before you start your draft *and* during revision. Make sure your content is the best it can possibly be. Because this is a formal essay, you can be sure that your reader will be looking at how you've **organized** it. Is your structure logical? Take some time to outline your essay, and don't be afraid to reorganize it once you've drafted it; essays often evolve as you write them and may need to be reoutlined and adjusted during the revision phase.

Expect to go through several **drafts** before you finalize your essay. Give yourself plenty of time to write, **revise**, and rewrite. Don't feel you've failed if you don't write a perfect draft the first time through: editing and rewriting are part of the writing process. Proofreading is a critical part of the revision process. For obvious reasons, your spelling, punctuation, and grammar must be perfect. Good luck!

DO	DON'T
• Write it yourself. It's a good idea to have trusted friends, family, or advisers read your drafts and make suggestions. However, the essay must be completely your own work from start to finish. Admissions committees are very adept at detecting when someone else has written an essay for you.	• Don't let anyone else write any part of it for you. Your essay must be your work, and your work alone. The admissions committee will definitely know if your mom wrote even a little: nothing is more obvious to an experienced reader than changes in tone, vocabulary, and attitude. When you get feedback from friends or family, don't let them rewrite those sections for you. Absorb what they've said to you, and put it in your own words.
• Answer the question (or "prompt") exactly as it's posed. Some schools use the Common Application (often known as the Common App), which allows students to complete a single application packet	• Don't rehash quantitative information that appears elsewhere in your application. The admis-

for submission to multiple schools. However, not all schools use the Common App, and some might even require additional essays. If you're applying to multiple schools, it can be a hassle to customize your essays to meet their requirements, but doing so is absolutely critical to your success.

- Answer the whole question. Many questions have multiple parts. One typical question is to ask you to identify an important issue or person in your life and then to explain why. Don't neglect the "why" part of the question. That section is your opportunity to reflect, analyze, and show what's important to you as a potential member of the college community. Read the question carefully and be sure to answer it fully.

- Observe the conventions of a formal essay. Your essay should have a clear structure, with a consistent point of view, and it should be written with an eye to keeping the reader's interest. Your essay is not an e-mail to a friend, or a friendly conversation, or a list of accomplishments. It's a formal piece of writing with an introduction and conclusion—a clear beginning, middle, and end. Ideally, your essay should be interesting for anyone to read, not just the admissions committee.

TIP

No matter what you're writing, it's always a good idea to let your first draft "breathe" a bit before you revise it.

Try writing a draft of your essay, then leaving it alone for a *full week* before you look at it again. This trick will give you perspective on your essay and help you decide if the topic is one you really want to pursue.

- Be yourself. The committee wants to know who you are, so your essay should employ your natural voice, albeit in the context of a formal essay. Don't try to impress by using big words, convoluted

sions committee will look at your application as a whole including data such as test scores and grades. Don't waste the precious opportunity the essay affords by restating this information, no matter how impressive it may be.

- Don't use fancy words where ordinary ones will do. If you mean "praise," don't use "laud." If you mean "think," don't use "cogitate." If you mean "walk," don't use "perambulate." You don't get extra points for extra syllables. Write in your own, natural, intelligent voice.

- Don't indulge in excessive praise of the school you're applying to. Good schools already know how good they are. It's wise to show that you know something about the school you're applying to, but it's best to show this knowledge when you explain that you're an ideal fit for the culture and values of the school.

- Don't overemphasize what the university can do for you. You should show that you're aware of their offerings and emphasis, but you should put more emphasis on what you can do for the university community.

- Don't submit an essay with typos, misspellings, and punctuation errors. This essay is your writing sample, and it also demonstrates how much you care about your application. If you allow sloppy mistakes in your application essay, the admissions committee has every right to decide that you won't care about the work you do in college. Get several people you trust to proofread your essay before you submit it.

sentences, or pretentious ideas. Show the very best of who you really are.

- Use humor sparingly, if at all. Many students think that a jokey tone will convey their personality better or set them apart from other applicants. Be wary of self-deprecating humor, especially if it's used to provide reasons for a less-than-stellar academic record. This kind of approach almost always fails. If you have concerns about your test scores or grades, address them in a straightforward, serious way.
- Proofread, proofread, proofread. Do not rely on spell-check or grammar-check programs; they sometimes make mistakes. Proofread the essay carefully yourself; then give it to at least two other competent people (not your best friend who got a C in English) to proof it. It's even well worth the investment to pay a professional to proofread your final draft before you submit it.

NOT LIKE THIS . . .

Why have you decided to apply to the University of Central California?

My decision to apply to the University of Central California is influenced by two factors: my desire to remain close to my family and the excellence of the programs offered at UCC.

> The writer has an interesting premise for an essay here, but his treatment of it is vague and general. A more in-depth exploration of the topic might give insight into who he is and why he would fit well at UCC.

My family has lived in California for many years. In fact, my grandmother was born here in 1916, her mother came to California when she was 24. My grandfather was also born here. This makes us an "old" family by California standards. Because of this, I love California, and I plan to spend my life here. The opportunity to attend a fine California institutoin of higher learning and in the process to stay close to my family is very important to me.

I think I am an excellent candidate for admission to UCC. I have worked hard to prepare myself for the rigors of college life. My grade point average is 3.8, and my combined SAT scores are 1680, which I understand is considerabley above the average for the typical UCC student. I feel that I am well prepared to meet the expectations of a UCC student.

> The applicant's grades and test scores appear in other parts of his application, so it's not necessary to mention them here. Doing so interrupts the flow of the essay and doesn't contribute to answering the question.

The University of Central California offers several fine programs that interest me, in particular the program in business and agriculture program. My family has an agricultural background, and I hopes to follow suit in a business role, rather than in farming. I believe the program in Agricultural Business Management is ideally suited to my ambitions. I had the opportunity to meet with an Ag Bus major at UCC, who lauded the program highly, and I believe UCC's excellent reputation in Agricultural Business Management would provide many career opportunities for me after graduation.

> The poorly constructed paragraph is the result of only partially rewriting a prior draft, and failing to proofread carefully. This is the kind of mistake that's hard for a writer to catch but easy for another eye to find.

> This paragraph focuses too much on what the university offers the applicant and not enough on what he might bring to the community.

In addition to its academic excellence, UCC offers me many other benefits. As a relatively young institution, UCC does not suffer from the population density of the other UC campuses, and there are plenty of local apartments available where students can live comfortably in near proximity to the campus.

> The second sentence here was clearly written by someone other than the applicant. It sounds like it was lifted directly from promotional materials for the university.

As the denizen of an old California family and an aspiring expert in Agricultural Business Management, I feel that the University of Central California would meet my needs as a student and as a future California citizen. I hope very much to have the opportunity to join the UCC community as an undergraduate student.

> Using flowery language can get you into trouble, especially if you don't understand it. This writer doesn't mean "denizen"; he means "scion."

> The writer has missed a few punctuation errors and typos. A spell-checker could have caught two of them. The other, "I hopes," escaped the notice of the spell-checker. It's important to have someone else proofread your essay before you submit it.

. . . LIKE THIS

Why have you decided to apply to the University of Central California?

This writer tells a very interesting story about his family and does a good job of relating his family background to his interest in the university.

I have a deep commitment to the state of California and to California agriculture. California became a state in 1850. My family has been here for most of the state's history, with my great-grandmother's arrival in 1914. Most of that time, my family has been involved in agriculture. I am hoping to continue the family legacy of involvement in California agriculture, and the University of Central California seems like a perfect fit, both in its location in the Central Valley and with its excellent programs in agricultural education.

My grandparents on my mother's side came to California from Oklahoma when they lost their farm as a result of the Dust Bowl. As new Californians, they worked as agricultural laborers and eventually bought their own farm. My father is the son of citrus farmers and has worked for Sunkist for many years. My roots go very deep into the California soil, and I hope to sink them even deeper with a career in agricultural business.

Rather than concentrating on what the school can do for him, the applicant focuses on the good fit between the school's offerings and his interests. He also makes a good case that he would make an interesting contribution to the university community.

UCC's program in Agricultural Business Management seems like a perfect fit given my background and my career aspirations. I was fortunate to make a campus visit where I spoke with a current Agricultural Business major. I attended two of his classes with him and discussed the program in detail, and I am convinced that this program is an ideal fit for me. I am particularly interested in focusing on labor-management relations, which will be an increasingly important issue in the future. I feel that having both the labor and the management sides represented in my family, I have a unique perspective to contribute to the study of Agricultural Business Management at UCC. I am looking forward to joining the university community and making a contribution, and I hope very much that I will be afforded the chance to do so.

The essay is well edited, free from grammar, punctuation, and spelling problems that might distract the reader and create a poor impression.

The applicant writes in a natural voice that sounds like his own. He has obviously taken care with this essay, but he hasn't inflated it with fancy language. It is very pleasant to read, and it creates a good impression of the writer.

Please tell us what you find most appealing about Columbia and why.

Columbia College combines the best of both worlds: the excitement of its urban environment and the rich intellectual span of its curriculum. To be able to enjoy the influx of new ideas and opportunities that accompany a location in the country's busiest metropolis and also be introduced to the finest of the world's literary, philosophical, and artistic traditions is what I view as the ideal college experience.

Living in the heart of Manhattan has many attractions to the aspiring college student—and myself in particular. After all, only in New York could I pursue my interest in journalism in the home of the *New York Times*, or take a break from studying by catching a free concert in Central Park, or even catch a national controversy a mere subway ride away (the current Park51 initiative is a prime example).

But what separates Columbia from any other undergraduate experience in the city—Fordham, NYU, or even Barnard just across the street—is its academic centerpiece. The Core ensures that each and every Columbia student graduates fully versed in the great theories and ideas of thinkers as diverse as Homer, Locke, and Virginia Woolf. It is both a factor that unifies all students and one that diversifies one's perspective and interest: an engineer is introduced to literature, just as a writer is taught contemporary science. It is this that makes Columbia truly special: a classical education in the most modern of settings.

Alison Herman is a member of the Columbia College class of 2015.

Three Keys to a Successful College or Scholarship Application Essay

Your college or scholarship application essay is one of the most high-stakes documents you'll ever write. These tips can help you take advantage of the great opportunity your application offers you.

- Answer the question asked. It's fine to recycle content from other essays, but don't submit an essay that only sort of answers the question. Take the time to revise and customize your essay so that it responds explicitly to the question.

- Show your personality. An essay gives you the chance to show your true self. Instead of *just* trying to sound smart, be genuine and sincere and show the committee who you are as a person.

- Ensure your grammar, spelling, and punctuation are perfect. Submitting a sloppy essay suggests that you don't really care. Get help with proofreading so that your essay is as flawless as it can be.

The Best College Essay Is Really a Conversation

I'm surprised when students have trouble writing their college essays. I hear these same students in the hallways, talking about everything from the answer to a complicated math problem to the great college they visited last weekend to the girl in homeroom who has just noticed them for the first time in four years. Students have keen powers of energetic observation about themselves and the world around them, but ask them to share any of those ideas in a college essay, and the silence speaks volumes.

It's the title that scares them. To the average high school senior, "essay" either conjures up images of a high-stakes speech where they have to create noble images, or a tedious five-paragraph exercise that provides modest information with little passion. If they see it as a speech, they think they aren't up to the task; if they see it as one more English assignment, they're sure they don't want to do the task. Either way, they panic.

The best way to move forward is to see a college essay as a conversation. If they could, colleges would welcome you to campus and ask you questions for hours—but if they did that, no one would be admitted to college until they were 43. To accelerate the process, they want you to talk on paper; let them get to know you by giving them a guided tour of your heart, your brain, and your life. If you succeed, they will look up from reading your essay, and be surprised you aren't in the room; indeed, they will swear the chair next to them is warm from your having sat in it since Tuesday.

Patrick O'Connor is assistant dean of college counseling at Cranbrook Kingswood School in Bloomfield Hills, Michigan, and the author of *College is Yours 2.0*. His website is www.collegeisyours.com.

Teacher Recommendation for an Applicant to College

Many colleges in the United States admit students in a mechanical way (using a formula based on grades and test scores) or admit a very high percentage of those who apply. However, the most selective colleges require applicants to provide teacher recommendations, and those teacher letters can have a big effect on how that student looks to a college admissions office.

As you write a letter on behalf of one of your students think about who will read the letter and what that person is looking for.

What not to do

The college already has the student's high school transcript and test scores. You don't need to repeat what they see there. The college has already asked every applicant to list extracurricular activities, achievements and awards. You don't need to repeat what they already have from the student. In fact, if you fill sentences and paragraphs with what they know from other parts of the application, they may not read the rest of what you write.

What you should do

There are at least three things you should include in your letter. First, establish clearly how you know the applicant. For example, "Jane was my student in Algebra in the ninth grade and Pre-Calculus in the eleventh grade." "I taught John American History in the honors section in tenth grade and I have been his soccer coach throughout his high school years." "Weihui was not a student in my class but she is the editor of the school newspaper, which I serve as faculty adviser." Second, provide information about the student's achievements you observed first-hand and that goes beyond what appears on the transcript. It adds nothing to say "Sue got a 95 in my class." It adds a lot to say "Sue received the highest grade in my class during the year I taught her," or "Tomas wrote an outstanding paper on *Huckleberry Finn*. He submitted an early draft that showed some good ideas and then took my advice about how to turn those good ideas into original and outstanding ones," or "Mike came up with an imaginative explanation for the US immigration limitations implemented in the 1920's and was able to explain and defend his views in a very heated class discussion" or "Aliyah was able to grasp the concepts in my calculus class quicker than other students. Rather than keep them to herself to get a better grade than the others, I saw her many times help explain those concepts to her less talented classmates." Colleges want to hear what you know first-hand and they couldn't know unless you tell them. Third, provide a summary recommendation at the end. If you've done the first two things well, it will be persuasive when you finish a letter with "Ben is a wonderful applicant and has my strongest support." If you haven't established your credibility in steps one and two, your final sentence will be ignored even if you write "Lucy will be the next Einstein."

Ria M. Coyne and Roger Lehecka are partners at R&R Education Consultants.

REQUEST FOR RECOMMENDATION

A recommendation from a teacher or professor is often required when you're applying to college, graduate or professional school, for a fellowship or scholarship, or in some cases for a job.

E-mail is generally the most efficient way to request a recommendation, and most recommendations are submitted via the Internet.

Introduction

The **purpose** of a request for a recommendation is to enlist the help of a teacher or professor in providing a reference for you. You should assume that your **reader** is busy and that your request won't be at the top of her to-do list. One of your tasks, then, is to make it as easy as possible for the reader. **Brainstorm** information that will help the instructor understand your goal and write a compelling letter—let her know where you're applying, why you're interested, and why you think you're a good fit. Consider attaching your résumé and the statement you've written for the application. **Organize** your message so that it's easy to follow: the Model Outline provides a structure you can use for your request. Allow yourself time to go through a few **drafts**. (The more requests you write, the better you'll get at it.) Reread the draft from your reader's point of view. Have you identified yourself adequately? Have you explained the opportunity and your interest in it? Have you made a case that you're an appropriate candidate for the opportunity? **Revise** to be sure your message meets these criteria and is free from typos and other errors.

MODEL OUTLINE

A request for a recommendation should make it easy for your reader to understand and comply with your request.

Opening: Let your reader know right away why you're writing. Remind your reader who you are—which classes you took and when. Provide the deadline for the recommendation.

Second paragraph: Explain why you are interested in the program or other opportunity you are applying for. Demonstrate a good fit between the opportunity and your interests and qualifications.

Third paragraph: Give some hints about what you would like the reference letter to say. Provide information about yourself that the instructor may not have. Let her know what other references might be writing about and where she might have unique knowledge about you.

Conclusion: Finish your message by thanking your instructor, and offer to provide additional information about yourself.

DO	DON'T
• Choose your recommenders carefully. Select instructors who are likely to remember you. Did you do well in the class? Did you take more than one class with that instructor? Did you speak to that instructor outside class? An instructor who barely remembers you is not likely to be able to give you a very specific recommendation. It's also wise to request recommendations from the most senior instructors you know; their recommendations carry more clout than those from junior faculty.	• Don't assume the answer is yes. It's part of an instructor's job to write recommendations for deserving students, but that doesn't mean she is obliged to write a recommendation for every student who asks.
• Make your request well in advance of the deadline for the application. Give your reference plenty of time—at least six weeks—to write your recommendation.	• Don't use an informal tone in your request. Your message should be courteous and professional.
• Use an explicit subject line for your e-mail: "Request for Recommendation."	• Don't say anything in your request that suggests you're taking the answer for granted.
• Ask your instructor and wait for him to say yes before you enter a name on any website that handles your application. Once you enter the name of a reference, the system will be expecting a letter from that person. If you enter a name and the instructor says no or does not respond to you, the application site will mark your application incomplete.	• Don't dictate what you would like said in the recommendation. A polite request is fine, and instructors often appreciate that kind of guidance, but telling the instructor what to say is rude.
• Treat your request as a formal letter, even if it's an e-mail. Use a formal salutation and be polite. Unless you were on a first-name basis with the instructor, use the honorifics Mr., Ms., Dr., or Professor.	• Don't suck up. It's fine to say you enjoyed the class(es) you took with the instructor, but don't go overboard with the flattery.
• Identify yourself. Don't assume your instructor will remember who you are. He teaches a lot of people, and he's more memorable to you than you are to him. Give him your full name, tell him which class(es) you took from him, and remind him when you were his student.	• Don't ask to read the letter before it's submitted. Recommendations should be strictly shielded from the applicant, so the recommender can express his thoughts freely. If you have any doubts about whether this recommender will give you an enthusiastic endorsement, ask someone else.

- Provide a copy of your application statement, or offer to send it.
- Attach your résumé or curriculum vitae (CV), if relevant.
- Be sure to say "thank you."
- Proofread your message before you send it. Ask someone else to proofread it for you, if you're not confident about your skills. A message with typos and other errors sets the wrong tone for this communication.
- Send a follow-up thank-you note. After you learn that the recommendation has been received, send a note thanking the referee for providing a reference. Tell her that you will let her know the outcome of your application, and be sure you do so—and thank her again—when you get the news.

LIKE THIS

January 15, 2013

Dear Professor Cretcher,

I'm writing to ask if you would be willing to write a recommendation for me for graduate school. As you may recall, I took two classes from you during the 2011–2012 school year—The State and the Individual and Parliamentary Discourse—and earned A's in both of them. The deadline for my applications is March 1, 2013.

I'm applying to PhD programs in Political Science at Northwestern, Yale, the University of Chicago, and the University of Virginia. I've chosen these programs because they all have strong links to organizations that serve the developing world. My research interests include governance structures and sociocultural diversity, and I am hoping to pursue a career in policy with global applications.

I've attached a résumé, a draft of my personal statement, and the final papers I wrote in both your classes. I'm hoping that your letter might mention something about my analytical abilities. I learned a lot about analysis of evidence in your classes, and I know this is an important concern in graduate school admissions.

Thank you very much for your time and consideration. I enjoyed your classes a lot, and I would be grateful and honored to have your recommendation. Please let me know if I can give you any further information about myself or my goals.

Thank you again.

Sincerely,

Rosa Mendez

Dear Professor Wang,

I am writing to ask if you would be willing to write a letter of recommendation for me for the Meadows Fellowship. As you recall, I spoke to you in person last week and you suggested I follow up with an e-mail. The deadline for the fellowship application is January 27, 2014.

The Meadows Fellowship was endowed to provide support for students who wish to do research in areas related to literacy in the United States. I'm attaching a draft of the project proposal I'm submitting with my application, as well as my résumé. If I win the Fellowship, I plan to spend the semester studying English literacy among high-school-aged Chinese immigrants in Los Angeles. The outcome of the project will be a proposal that I will submit to the LA Unified School District.

I am applying because literacy has been a passion for me since I was young, and I am hoping to build my career as a literacy advocate after I graduate. As you know, I have volunteered in school and adult literacy programs for the past three years, and I have enjoyed discussing my activities with you. I am hoping your letter might give the committee some idea of the scope of my volunteer work and my dedication to it.

Thank you very much for your consideration. Please let me know if I can provide any additional information.

Sincerely,

Jenn Baxter

E-MAIL TO TEACHER OR PROFESSOR

Maybe you've missed class, and you aren't sure of the homework. Maybe you're stuck doing an assignment and need some help with it. Maybe you need an extension on a paper, or you're having trouble in the class. Or maybe you're interested in taking a teacher's class in the future and want to know if there's a syllabus or reading list you could look at. It's time to send an e-mail to the teacher or professor!

Don't hesitate to reach out. Teachers would much rather get an e-mail from you than have you come to class unprepared or simply not turn up at all. If you treat your teachers with respect for their position and their time, they're more than willing to help.

Sending an e-mail to a teacher or professor might be the first time you will have used e-writing to communicate with someone other than friends or family. It requires a somewhat more formal approach than what you might be used to. The guidelines below can help you navigate through this experience successfully.

Introduction

There are many reasons you might want to send an e-mail to your teacher or professor. You're usually looking for additional information or for some kind of help. As you write, be sure you're very clear about your **purpose** and that you state it explicitly. It will be much easier for your professor to respond if she knows what you're asking for!

Keep your **reader** in mind as you work on the message. Although your teachers and professors may be friendly, *they are not your friends.* They are authority figures who have power over you. They are generally very busy, teaching multiple classes, and may have many students. Make the message as easy as possible for your reader to process: it should be concise, clear, and courteous.

Messages to teachers and professors are generally brief, so you probably don't need extensive **brainstorming** or **organizing**. Do ensure, though, that your message contains all the necessary information you want to convey.

Be very alert to your tone as you **draft**. Your tone can be friendly, but it should also show the appropriate respect. Don't write to your teacher or professor in the same casual way you'd write to friends or family.

Double-check your tone as you **revise**, and be sure to check for completeness. Proofread carefully for spelling, punctuation, and grammar.

MODEL OUTLINE

An e-mail to a teacher or professor should ideally be brief.
Opening: Be sure you identify yourself. Let your instructor know which class you're in.
Middle: State your request politely, and if necessary, give the reason(s) for your request. Be as concise as you can while still remaining courteous.
Conclusion: Finish your message by thanking your teacher or professor.

DO	DON'T
• Contact your teacher or professor promptly if you need help or have a question. Waiting till the last minute suggests that you don't take the class seriously and that you expect your teacher to drop everything and help you. If you do end up writing late, acknowledge that fact and apologize for it rather than acting as though it's no big deal that you're asking for an extension two hours before that paper is due.	• Don't call your teacher or professor by his first name, unless you've been invited to do so. College instructors should be called "Professor." High school teachers should be called "Mr." "Ms.," or "Dr." as appropriate.
• Use a specific and courteous subject line. If you forgot what your homework assignment is, use a subject line like "Forgot the homework assignment" rather than "Need assignment." Never send an e-mail without a subject line.	• Don't make demands. Make requests instead, and ensure they are polite requests. Instead of "I need to know the reading assignment," try something like "Would you please let me know what the reading assignment is?"
• Use an appropriate salutation, like "Dear Mr. Blair" or "Hi Professor Rose." Don't write "Hey Professor" or simply launch into your message without a salutation.	• Don't whine. If you have a problem, explain it concisely and propose a solution. Teachers and professors have heard every crazy excuse in the book. They'll respect you more if you tell them the truth, without getting into too much detail, and make a conscientious effort to get back on track.
• Introduce yourself if you're writing for the first time. If it's early in the term, or the professor has many students, your professor might not recognize your name. Let her know what class you're in. If you're just shopping for a class or looking for a syllabus, let her know that.	• Don't say anything to indicate that their class is not an important priority for you. Your teachers and professors understand that you have a lot to do, but they expect you to do the work for their classes.
• Be specific about what you're requesting.	• Don't suck up. Just be courteous. Professors can spot insincerity a mile away.
• Be courteous and respectful. Teachers and professors have power over you.	• Don't use profanity, even in a joking or casual way. This is a formal communication, not a message to a friend.
• Keep your message brief and succinct.	
• Remember to say "thank you" if you're asking for a favor.	• Don't use texting abbreviations like "u r" or "2morrow" when you're writing to your teachers. Don't use emoticons. Write in real English.
• Sign your e-mail with your name. Don't just stop writing.	• Don't send unexpected attachments. If you have to miss class the day an assignment is due, ask your professor in advance if you may e-mail the assignment to her. Don't just assume she's going to print out your paper if you don't make it to class.
• Remember that e-mail is permanent. A thoughtless message can come back to haunt you, so be wise and sensible.	

- Don't be surprised if your professor asks you to come to office hours to discuss the issue you've raised in your e-mail. Face-to-face communication is often more effective, and you'll probably get a more complete and satisfying answer if you're able to talk to your professor in person

NOT LIKE THIS . . .

Who is this student? She never identifies herself or mentions which class she's in.

"Assignment" is misspelled. A spell-checker would have told the writer it was misspelled, but she seems to have been in too much of a rush to notice that red squiggly line. Notice also the sentence isn't properly punctuated; it's a question, so it should end with a question mark.

Topping off this festival of bad punctuation is this string of exclamation points. Though you may do it with your friends all the time, it's *never* all right to use multiple exclamation points in formal writing.

I missed class this week. Would you please send me the assigment. Also I'm not sure when it's due?

Thank you!!!!!!!!!!

This sentence is not a question, but it's punctuated as one.

. . . LIKE THIS

This student uses an appropriate salutation and signature.

Arielle is smart to remind Professor Post who she is.

Hi Professor Post,

I'm enrolled in your Thursday Shakespeare course, English 533. Unfortunately, I had to miss class yesterday because I had a migraine headache. Could you please let me know what the assignment is and when it's due? I'll get caught up by next week. Thanks for your help!

Arielle Booth

Arielle explains her absence and requests the assignment courteously.

She remembers to thank the professor and punctuates the sentence correctly.

NOT LIKE THIS . . .

David is making a request, but it sounds more like a demand. He's probably alienated Professor Saltzman already.

"Just couldn't get around to the paper"? Oops. Clearly David has a lot to juggle, but there's a more diplomatic way to make this point.

Perhaps sensing that he has made a mistake, David tries sucking up to Professor Saltzman. He also misspells "you're." If I were Professor Salzman, I wouldn't go out of my way to help this student.

Dear Professor Saltzman,

I would like to get an extension on my paper for your class. I had three midterms this week in other classes, including Chemistry and Bio, and I just couldn't get around to the paper. The chem one was 60 percent of our grade, if you can believe it. I slept a total of 6 hours over three nights before those exams. I am hoping to declare a pre-med major, so getting good grades in those classes is totally critical.

I really enjoy your class. Your a superlative teacher, and I really appreciate the opportunity to take the class with you.

Thank you very much for your consideration.

Sincerely,

David Cooper

This section combines whining with a description of why Professor Saltzman's class is not important to David.

The end of this e-mail sounds rather wooden and businesslike, not in keeping with the rest of the message. Worse, though, David has forgotten why he's writing and what he's asking for. He wants an extension on his paper? Till when? He needs to wrap up the message with some specifics.

. . . LIKE THIS

In this version, David makes a polite request for the extension and also reminds Professor Saltzman which class he's in.

David lets Professor Saltzman know that he values the class and links that to an appeal for the extension to get caught up.

Dear Professor Saltzman,

Could I possibly get an extension on my paper for your Asian History class? I'm taking a very heavy load of classes this term, and I had a lot of deadlines that turned out to be too much for me to manage. I understand your policy is not to accept late papers, but I am wondering if you would make an exception in this case. I really enjoy your class, and I'd appreciate the chance to get back on track. Would it be all right with you if I handed in the paper on Monday the 27th?

Thank you very much.

Sincerely,

David Cooper

David explains the problem of his heavy workload without whining and without making Professor Saltzman feel that the science classes are a more important priority. He takes responsibility for not being able to handle the competing priorities, and he proposes a way to fix the problem.

David proposes a specific date for the extension. He demonstrates that he is well organized, aware of the professor's policy on lateness, and working conscientiously to keep up with the class.

APPEALING A GRADE

Appealing a grade through e-mail is a tricky proposition. Before you write, you should weigh the consequences carefully: be aware that if you ask your instructor to recalculate your grade, the grade might actually go down rather than up. If you decide to move ahead, use these guidelines to help you write a courteous e-mail to your instructor:

DO	DON'T
• Understand why you feel the way you do. Do you think your instructor has made an error in calculating your grade? Can you point to specific reasons your grade should have been higher? Or are you simply feeling unappreciated and misunderstood? If it's the last, think hard about whether you should write, and be careful not to use an aggrieved tone in your message.	• Don't use the word "mistake." Rather than accusing your instructor of making an error, express puzzlement or confusion over the grade.
• Be extra polite in your message. An arrogant or brusque tone can be offensive.	• Don't talk about how hard you worked in the class. Instructors will sometimes give students a slightly higher grade for making a strong effort, but they are in no way obliged to do so. Also consider the possibility that your instructor might already have factored your effort into your final grade.
• Suppress your emotions. You may feel very angry or hurt, but don't share your personal feelings with your instructor. Keep your message business-like and professional.	
• Explain exactly why you're puzzled or confused. Be specific. Do you understand the basis for grading in the class and what percentage of your final grade each assignment accounts for?	
• Ask to see your final paper or final exam if you haven't seen it yet. If you haven't seen your grade on your final piece of work for the class, ask the instructor to return it to you. It might have had a large impact on your overall course grade.	
• Make an explicit request for the instructor to recalculate your grade. Vague and direct expressions like "I feel I should have done better" may sound like whining.	

LIKE THIS

Dear Professor Leighton,

I was a student in your Biology 5 class that met Tuesdays and Thursdays at 1:00 last term. I really enjoyed the class, and I learned a lot. I've just received my grades, and I'm confused about my final grade for this class.

Maybe my calculations are wrong, but I thought based on my labs and exams I had an A– going into the final. I'm just puzzled about how my final grade could have dropped so much. I'd be very grateful if you would recalculate my grade and help me understand it.

Thank you for your help. I really appreciate it.

Sincerely,

John Prusiner

ACADEMIC RÉSUMÉ

(See also *Résumé* on page 454.)

High school or college students sometimes find they need a résumé, for a job application, a scholarship application, or another use. Even if you have little or no experience in paying jobs, or if your work experience is not relevant to your current application, you can still create an impressive résumé by including information about academics, honors, and memberships as well as your work experience and volunteer experience.

Introduction

An academic résumé may be used for several **purposes**, including applications for scholarships, internships, and employment. Regardless of the reason for the résumé, you can safely assume that your **reader** is someone who is busy and is reading through many similar résumés. Make his job as easy as possible by making the résumé easy to scan and conforming to formatting conventions. Think about your reader's expectations in the context of your purpose. What might a college admissions officer or a potential employer be looking for in a résumé?

Brainstorm extensively about your activities and experiences. Give yourself plenty of time to make lists of your experiences and achievements. Talk with your parents and friends to get ideas; they might remember things you don't. You'll probably find that you have a lot more to say than you initially thought. Refer to the box "What to Include in Your Résumé" to get started brainstorming. Once you've chosen what to include, **organize** your résumé according to accepted formatting conventions: a résumé is no place to show creativity. The examples below provide models you can adapt for your own use. Expect to go through several **drafts** of the résumé before you finalize it. Your résumé should be no longer than one page, and your first draft will likely be too long. Allow yourself time to edit and trim the résumé. You may also find that working on the résumé jogs your memory, so you may come up with additional content. As you **revise**, focus not just on getting the résumé down to one page but also on including the most important information about yourself. You'll have to be selective. Proofread carefully for errors in grammar and punctuation and for typos. Give your draft to at least one other person and ask him to proofread it carefully. Errors on résumés create a very bad impression, so be sure yours is completely free from them.

What to Include in Your Résumé

High school and college students have slightly different needs when it comes to résumé content. See the two examples below for an illustration, and choose accordingly.

GPA

Major

Expected graduation date

Coursework relevant to the opportunity you're applying for

Independent study projects

Senior thesis

Academic awards

Dean's list, honor roll, and so on

Work experience

Extracurricular activities like clubs, societies, volunteer work, community service

Leadership positions

Sports

Foreign-language skills (indicate your level of competency)

Significant travel experience

Special computer skills

Musical instruments you play

Interests and hobbies

DO	DON'T
• Keep your purpose in mind. As you collect information and select which pieces to use, keep in mind what the résumé is for, and let that guide your choice of details.	• Don't go over one page in length. The people who will review your résumé are busy and are probably reviewing stacks of résumés. Make their lives easier by being concise. One that's too long looks sloppy and can cause resentment.
• Work with your parents and your counselor. They have experience with résumés and can help you jog your memory about experiences that you might have forgotten or might think are not important.	• Don't clutter your résumé with lots of different fonts and creative formatting. Use no more than two fonts, and keep your margins consistent at one inch on all sides. Your résumé should attract attention because of its content, not because of creative formatting.
• Use a professional format for your résumé. See the samples below for guidance.	• Don't embellish or fudge on your résumé. Tell the truth. Résumés can easily be fact-checked.
• Keep your formatting clean and consistent, and use one-inch margins all around.	• Don't ever send your résumé out without carefully checking for errors and typos. A sloppy résumé creates a bad impression.
• Be sure all your contact information is accurate and professional. If your e-mail address is something like iluvzombies@puffball.org, create a new account that includes your name to use for this purpose. Be sure the message on your voice mail is businesslike and serious.	
• Be willing to tailor your résumé according to the school or job you're applying for. For instance, if you know the school you're applying to has a strong core curriculum, be sure to note your reading of classical literature. If you're applying to work at an international aid agency, mention all your foreign-language skills.	
• Use strong action verbs to describe your activities. (See the box "Action Verbs for Résumés" on page 457 for suggestions.)	

LIKE THIS

Cameron Shapiro
2556 Ginger Tree Lane
Santa Lucia, CA 93454
555-111-9999
cameronshapiro@cihs.org

Personal Data

Date of Birth   January 15, 1995
Place of Birth   Santa Lucia, CA

Education

High School   Channel Islands High School
                           1673 Bay Street
                           Santa Lucia, CA 93454

GPA/Class Rank   3.85 / 37 out of 621 seniors
SAT Scores   620(W) 740(M) 620(CR)
AP Scores   Biology—5
                           United States History—4
                           English Language and Composition—4

Grade: 12

Honors and Awards

Zeigler Award for AP Biology (2012)
Honor Roll (2010–2012)
CIHS Student of the Month (2011)

School Activities

The Islander (student newspaper) (2011–2013)
      Features Editor (2012)
Science Club (2010–2013)
Finance Club (2011–2012)

Work Experience

The Gap (May–August 2012)
      Associate
Martin Fisheries (May–August 2011))
      Assistant

Community Service Activities

United Way Campaign (2011–2012)
Islander Outreach Volunteer (2010–2011)
Soup Kitchen Volunteer (2010)

Special Interests: Reading, swimming, marine biology

COLLEGE ACADEMIC RÉSUMÉ

Lisa Wattson
678 Dutton Hall
Ames, Rhode Island 02804
lmw2334@branston.edu
617-788-0985

OBJECTIVE
An entry-level position in book or magazine publishing.

EDUCATION
Branston College, Ames, RI
Bachelor of Arts in English expected June 2013, GPA 3.8/4.0
Dean's List (Fall 2009–present), Saltzman Prize (2010)
Senior Thesis: "The Book Publishing Industry in Nineteenth-Century New England"

RELEVANT EXPERIENCE
Gleason Publishing, Boston MA (Summers 2011 and 2012)
   Intern
   - Fact-checked and proofread nonfiction manuscripts
   - Conducted ad hoc research for selected authors
   - Participated in event planning for book launches and publicity events
   - Attended editorial meetings

Branston Bee, Ames RI (9/2011–present)
   News Editor
   - Edit copy and assist with layout and production for weekly college newspaper
   - Gather college-related news events through interviews with professors, students, and administrators
   - Recruit and supervise student reporters
   - Assist in selling advertising space to local merchants

ADDITIONAL EXPERIENCE
Branston College Learning Center, Ames, RI (9/2010–6/2011)
   Tutor
   - Assisted students with writing papers and conducting research
   - Designed and taught mini-sessions on grammar, punctuation, and presentation skills

ACTIVITIES
Ames Community Center, Ames, RI (6/2010–present)
   Volunteer
   - Teach reading skills to adults in an after-work literacy program
   - Tutor high school students in writing skills
   - Write catalog copy and copy for community e-mail blasts and advertisements

Chinatown Community Outreach, Boston, MA (Summers 2009 and 2010)
   Volunteer Assistant Teacher
   - Assisted in teaching weekly English-language classes to recent immigrants from Greater China

LANGUAGE SKILLS
Spanish (intermediate); French (basic); Mandarin (basic)

COMPUTER SKILLS
Proficient in Microsoft Office; some HTML and XML

References available on request

RECRUITING LETTER

If you're interested in being recruited as an athlete by a college or university, you can get a jump on the process by proactively sending the coach in your sport a recruiting letter to introduce yourself. The NCAA sets strict limits on coaches contacting potential recruits, but you're not bound by the same rules; you should feel free to write and introduce yourself.

Most recruiting letters are sent by e-mail.

Introduction

The **purpose** of a recruiting letter is to introduce yourself to a coach at a college or university you're interested in attending. It's the first step in what you hope will be an ongoing discussion with him, so consider your **reader**'s perspective. Coaches are busy people, and they receive a lot of e-mails from prospects like you. It's in your best interest to make their reading experience as pleasant and efficient as possible. Keep your message brief and to the point. **Brainstorm** your content from the coach's point of view. What can you tell the coach that will make him interested in you as a prospect? Focus not just on what you want but also on what you would bring to the team if you were recruited. The Model Outline (page 362) provides a format you can adapt to **organize** your own recruiting letter. Be sure you allow yourself enough time to write several **drafts** of your letter—this process is too important to hurry through. It's a good idea to ask your parents and your current coach to read your draft. Use their feedback to **revise** and refine your letter. Ensure that your message is complete but concise, and that you are sure you've eliminated all typos and other errors. You're making a first impression with this message—make sure it's a good one!

Model Outline

———•———

- Your letter should be addressed to the coach at the college, for instance, "Dear Coach Smith."

- The opening of your recruiting letter should address why you want to attend that school. "I really love your university, as I have visited several times with my parents for football games" or "I'm excited about the engineering program." Coaches want to know that you like their school, not just their sport.

- The next paragraph should demonstrate why you like this coach's athletic program. Do some research. Find something good about the team. Know what conference it plays in and how the current or most recent season went.

- Tell the coach about your academic situation. She wants to know that you are a serious student who can get into her school.

- Tell her about you as an athlete. Offer specifics about your accomplishments and how you can help her program.

- Offer two or three references with phone numbers and e-mail addresses.

- Finally, you should provide a link to your video if you have one. A YouTube video is fine and is preferred for most sports.

Wayne Mazzoni is an expert on the recruiting process and the author of *Get Recruited*. His website is www.waynemazzoni.com.

DO	DON'T
• Be sure you're directing your letter to the right person. Check on the college or university website to learn who the coach is in your sport. If you have any doubt, make a phone call to	• Don't use the generic salutation "Dear Coach." Take the time to find out the name of the coach in your sport, and direct your message to him. Check the website of the college or university you're

confirm the information on the website is correct.

- Personalize and customize your messages for each coach and school you write to. Sending something that's obviously a form letter sends the message that you don't really care which school you go to. Your letter must make the coach feel that his institution is one you're really excited about.
- Include your NCAA Clearinghouse ID number, if you have one.
- Let the coach know if you will be playing upcoming games or tournaments where the coach might come and see you.
- Include a link to your scouting report, if you have one.
- Include a link to your highlights video, if you have one.
- Show a genuine interest in the school you're applying to. Take the time to learn about the school, and show the coach why you're interested in attending the institution. Mention specifics— athletics, academics, traditions, religious affiliation, good experiences your friends might have had at the school—anything that will demonstrate you're sincerely interested in the school.
- Be brief, and format your letter so it's easy to scan. Coaches receive many e-mails and letters; make sure that yours is a pleasure to read. Keep your letter to a single page.
- Provide the coach with complete and accurate contact information for yourself and for your current coach.
- Follow up. If you don't hear back from the coach after your first message, send a follow-up note. Be polite and pleasantly persistent.

interested in. If you can't find the coach's name that way, make a phone call.

- Don't have your parents write to the coach. The coach wants to hear from you directly.
- Don't use slang or texting abbreviations. This letter is a formal communication, and you should write in correct English.
- Don't brag. There's a difference between recounting the facts of your career and boasting about them. If you're not sure your letter is getting it right, ask a parent or coach to read your draft before you send it.
- Don't focus exclusively on your stats and achievements. Let the coach know how you will contribute to the team and how you will fit in with the culture at the school you're applying to.

LIKE THIS

Dear Coach Schiffer,

I am writing to introduce myself. My name is Steven Randall. I am a senior (class of 2013), 5'11" 190 lbs. LH hitting first-baseman at Pioneer High School. I have been the starting first-baseman for the past 3 years. In my sophomore year, I was chosen by the PSAL to represent the United States to play baseball in Japan. My 2012 high school stats were .321 BA, .451 OB%, 3 2B, 4 3B, 3 HR, and 30 RBI. My NCAA Clearinghouse ID number is 1304768149.

I am interested in continuing my education and baseball career at Mason University. Mason offers me a great opportunity to pursue a degree in Education and play baseball at a high level. I take great pride in myself as a person, student, and athlete. I have a 3.50 GPA, and although that might not be as high as I would like, it does not reflect my desire to be a better student nor does it reflect a lack of effort. I am very active in my community. I participate in the annual Breast Cancer Walk and the Thanksgiving Food Drive for the Homeless and volunteer time for the Hanna Program for children with special needs.

I have a very extensive training plan that consists of:

- Parisi School—Strength, speed, and agility
- Hitting instructor—Frank DeLeon (10 years with St. Louis Cardinals organization)
- Fielding instructor—Ted Samuels (instructor at Patterson Sport Academy)

If you would like a professional talent evaluation I had one done by Ted Samuels, former Director of Midwest Baseball Academy and Director of Player Development at Sigma Training Facilities. His contact number is 888-400-7000. E-mail address: T.samuels@psacad.com.

I also have a college recruiter/advisor, Bill Kittredge (888-400-9999), guiding me in this important process. E-mail address: bkitt1991@lmvt.com.

I have attached a link to my video. I have also attached letters of recommendation and can provide references if you need them. If you have any upcoming camps or clinics please let me know, as I would like to attend. Thank you for your time, and I hope to hear from you soon.

Yours truly,

Steven Randall
9833 Appleton Road, Cordell, IA 86110
Class of 2013
888-111-0000
stevenrandall95.bb@phs.org
http://www.youtube.com/watch?v=dhvX_s9kKA&feature=youtu.be

Wayne Mazzoni is an expert on the recruiting process and the author of *Get Recruited*. His website is www.waynemazzoni.com.

ATHLETIC RÉSUMÉ/ATHLETIC PROFILE

An athletic résumé, sometimes called an athletic profile, provides recruiters and coaches with a summary of your athletic and academic background and achievements. It is not a comprehensive record of your entire career—more like a snapshot designed to pique the interest of the reader and motivate him to follow up and learn more. (See also Recruiting Letter on page 361.)

Introduction

The **purpose** of an athletic résumé or athletic profile is to provide an easily scannable summary of your athletic and academic achievements. Your **reader** is a coach at a college or university you're interested in attending. Bear in mind that coaches receive many such résumés, so make an effort to ensure yours is concise and easy to read. **Brainstorm** widely about all your achievements and activities—athletic, academic, and extracurricular. Making lists is a good way to jog your memory and collect information. You will probably come up with more information than you'll end up using in the final version. That's fine. It's better to start with too much than to forget something important. There is no single **organizational** pattern that's accepted for athletic résumés—just be sure your résumé is neat and easy to scan. Your initial **draft** will probably be too long. Keep **revising** and refining until you trim the résumé down to just one page. Get input from your parents, friends, and coaches as you streamline and polish the résumé.

What to Include in Your Athletic Résumé

————————————●————————————

There is no single accepted format for athletic résumés. Whatever format you use, be sure it's clear and easy to scan. It's typical to include the information below:

Contact Information
Who you are and how to get in touch with you

Academic Information
Class rank and GPA
PSAT, SAT, and ACT scores

Intended major
Academic achievements (honor roll, etc.)
Statement about NCAA core curriculum requirements

Athletic Information
Height and weight
Sport and position played
League
Stats
Awards
Other sports played

Extracurricular Activities
Volunteer work, school clubs, peer tutoring, student government. Other significant interests outside school

References
Names and e-mail addresses or phone numbers of references

DO	DON'T
• Allow yourself plenty of time to develop your athletic résumé. Starting at the last minute will almost certainly mean that you'll omit something important. Get started early, and budget enough time to go through several drafts.	• Don't ever lie on your résumé. Always be completely honest about your stats and your accomplishments. A coach who is interested in you will verify the information you provide.
• Make sure your contact information is businesslike. If your current e-mail address is silly or may be offensive, open a new e-mail account—ideally one that contains your name—to use for recruiting purposes. Make sure the message on your voice mail is businesslike and clear.	• Don't list people as references unless they have explicitly agreed to provide a reference for you. Let them know you are preparing an athletic résumé and would like to include them. Don't take for granted that people will serve as references for you—ask.
• Be completely honest about your abilities and your record. It's very easy to be caught if you embellish the truth. Save yourself and everyone else the embarrassment, and stick to the facts.	• Don't go overboard with references. Providing a large number of references won't help your chances.
• Keep your résumé to a single page.	• Don't send out your résumé until it has been carefully proofread by more than one person. Make sure it's as perfect as it can be.
• Format the résumé so it's attractive and easy to scan. Use plenty of white space, and don't pack the page with text. Remember, this is just a snapshot of your academic and athletic career.	
• Provide references. Don't include actual reference letters; simply give the coach the names and contact information of your referees. The coach will reach out to them if he is interested.	

LIKE THIS

Steven Randall
9833 Appleton Road, Cordell, IA 86110
888-111-0000
stevenrandall95.bb@phs.org

Personal

School: Pioneer H.S.

Class: 2013

Bats: Left

Throws: Left

Position: 1B, RF

DOB: 04/11/95

Ht. 5'11" **Wt.** 190

Parents: Duane and Lynn Randall

GPA: 3.50

SATs: Math 540 Reading 460 Writing 370

2012 HS Baseball Stats

BA: .321	Runs: 25	Hits: 40 for 115
HRs: 3	Doubles: 3	Triples: 4
RBIs: 30	BB's: 11	OB %: .451
Slugging %: .467	Fielding %: .941	Triples: 4

Academic Information

Graduation Year: 2013

GPA: 3.50 through 2012

SAT's: 1370

Other Sports

Varsity Basketball

High School Coaches

Tom Jepson /Pioneer H.S.   888-698-2000

Larry Spann/Prairie Stars   888-804-0000

Jose Reyes/Los Angeles Dodgers   888-400-5000

Frank DeLeon/Hitting   888-490-0000

Extracurricular Activities

Law & Politics Society

Participated in Holiday Chorus

Homework helper at Afterschool

Breast Cancer Walk & Blood Drive

Thanksgiving Food Drive for the Homeless

Volunteer Hannan Program for children with special needs

Summer Baseball/Camps

2009 Showcase Tournament Team

2010 Showcase Tournament Team

2011 Showcase Tournament Team

2011 Played on Iowa PSAL team that played in Japan

2012 Showcase Tournament Team

Academic Interests

Sports Management, Physical Therapy, Physical Education

Position/size/speed/strength

1B, RF, Ht. 5'11" Wt. 190, 60-yard dash: 7.6, Pop time: 1.97, Bench press: 220

Coach Wayne Mazzoni is an expert on the recruiting process and author of *Get Recruited*. His website is www.coach
.waynemazzoni.com.

Your Athletic Package

———•———

Your athletic résumé makes up part of your overall athletic package, which is intended to give the coach a clear idea of who you are. Your athletic package should contain items that answer the following questions:

—Can this student-athlete get into the school?
- This means you need to provide an official or unofficial transcript and board scores.

—Can this student-athlete play at my level?
- You need to have a video on DVD or as a link.
- Game schedule.
- Camps you plan on attending.

—What kind of person is this student-athlete?
- Coaches generally don't read reference letters, as the majority of them are all fluff and favorable. So it is best to list the names and contact info for a few athletic and academic people who know you—coaches, counselors, school administrators, etc.

Wayne Mazzoni is an expert on the athletic recruiting process and the author of *Get Recruited*. His website is www.coach.waynemazzoni.com.

INTERNSHIP LETTER

An internship letter accompanies a résumé you send to a company or other organization in applying for an internship. You should think of your cover letter as a kind of sales letter, intended to demonstrate what you can do for the organization and motivate the reader's interest in you.

This type of cover letter is also useful for recent college graduates applying for their first jobs.

Introduction

The **purpose** of an internship cover letter is to introduce yourself to the reader, express your interest in an internship, and convince the reader that you have something valuable to offer her. Most **readers** of internship letters receive a lot of them. You can make yours stand out by focusing not so much on what you want as on what you can bring to the internship experience. All your readers will understand that you want the experience. What do you bring to the table that will make you the right choice for the position? **Brainstorm** from your readers' point of view. What do you know about their needs, and how can you help meet those needs? Make lists of your skills and experiences. Think about what makes you especially qualified for the position. A cover letter generally follows a standard **organizational** format: use the Model Outline to help structure yours. Your first **draft** will probably be too long. At this stage, better too long than too short. Write it all out, and then try to take a break from the draft and return to it with a fresh eye. It's a good idea to show your draft to other people and ask for their feedback. As you **revise**, think about condensing and sharpening the letter so that it makes the best possible case for you. Ask others to help proofread your final draft carefully. Sending out a cover letter with typos or other errors can scuttle your internship application.

MODEL OUTLINE

Internship letters usually follow a straightforward format.
Salutation: Be sure you're directing the letter to the appropriate person, not just "To Whom It May Concern."
Opening: Let your reader know why you're writing and what you're interested in. If you were introduced or recommended by someone the reader might know, mention the connection by name.
Middle paragraphs: Making reference to your attached résumé, highlight the skills and experiences you have that make you a good match for the position.
Conclusion: Finish your message by thanking your reader for his consideration. Repeat your interest in making a contribution to the organization, and indicate how you will follow up.

DO	DON'T
• Give yourself plenty of time to draft and redraft your internship cover letter. A good cover letter is an important part of your application, so give it the attention it deserves.	• Don't hurry through this task. It may seem like just a formality, but your internship cover letter is important. Make sure you give it the attention it deserves.
• Personalize and customize each letter. You may be applying for many potential positions, but you must ensure that your letter is directed to the right individual and refers to the specific opportunity, company, department, or program you're interested in. Take the time to learn the name of the contact person and to familiarize yourself with the organization or program.	• Don't sound arrogant. Consider that you're presenting your credentials; do so completely and enthusiastically but not boastfully.
• Remember you are trying to persuade the reader. Don't write it like a sales pitch, but do keep your attention focused on benefits to the reader of choosing you as an intern.	• Don't propose a specific project for you to work on. You likely won't have any control over the project you're assigned to. Simply do your best to highlight your skills and enthusiasm.
• Focus on the fit. Take care to show how your experience and qualifications make you an outstanding candidate for the position.	
• Be courteous. Remember your reader is busy, and you're asking for her time. Be polite and respectful.	
• Proofread, proofread, proofread! You may have the best credentials in the world, but if your letter contains typos or other errors, it will be very easy for your reader to dismiss you.	
• Follow up appropriately. It's a smart idea to follow up to ensure your materials were received and to show your continuing interest. However, be respectful of the reader's wishes—if the listing says no calls, don't call.	

LIKE THIS

Larissa Walls
775 Landfair Ave. #8H
Haddon, NJ 02001
619-888-1111
lw2388@haddonuc.edu
March 15, 2013

Ms. Odette Wilson
McKinsey and Company
450 Madison Ave.
New York, NY 10022

Dear Ms. Wilson:

Your former intern George Kruper suggested I write to express my interest in the Marketing Internship position at McKinsey. George is familiar with my background in marketing and communications and felt that I would be an ideal candidate for a summer internship at McKinsey.

I am currently a junior at the University of Trenton. I am majoring in English, with a minor in Marketing. As my enclosed résumé shows, I have taken seven courses in marketing, communications, and public relations and earned an A in each of them. I have also worked for two summers as a marketing intern for Rational Networks, a small digital branding agency in Jersey City. My work at Rational Networks included participating on the branding strategy team, assisting with web design, and developing social media campaigns for clients. When I graduate next year, I intend to pursue a career in marketing.

Thank you for reviewing my application. I believe that my experience and my motivation will make me a strong asset to your marketing division, and I would welcome the opportunity to discuss the position. I can be reached at 619-888-1111 or at lw2388@haddonuc.edu. I will take the liberty of phoning you in two weeks to see if I can provide more information.

Sincerely,

Larissa Walls
Enclosure: Résumé

SCHOOL NEWSPAPER

Writing for your school or college newspaper is a great way to engage in the life of the school, hone your writing skills, find a social niche, and acquire experience that might be useful in the future. Many campus newspapers require no more than enthusiasm for the job and basic writing skills: they will teach you the rest. On the other hand, if you aspire to be a professional journalist, your campus paper is a great place to get experience and to start to collect clips you can show to prospective employers.

There are different genres of newspaper writing. This entry covers primarily feature writing—or newswriting. For information about writing editorials, see Editorial (page 183).

Introduction

The **purpose** of a school or campus newspaper, obviously, is to share information with the community. Your **readers** are typically your peers and classmates. Some of them will be intensely interested in your story; others will do little more than glance at it. Whoever your readers are, you must do your best to provide them with good information in clear and interesting prose. The most important **brainstorming** technique in newspaper writing is to consider the "Five Ws and One H" to ensure your story is complete. The box "The Five Ws (and One H)" (page 375) offers detailed guidance. Newspaper stories are usually **organized** with the information in descending order of importance. That is, the most important information should go in the first paragraph, and less critical information should appear in subsequent paragraphs. This structure is best for readers, who may not read the entire story. It also helps editors when they need to cut the length of a story; they know that cutting the last paragraphs won't deprive readers of essential information. Go through several **drafts** of a story, if possible, and give yourself time to revise. As you write, do your best to be objective and fair. Double-check all your facts, and proofread carefully for typos and other errors. Accuracy is important in journalistic writing, so **revise** until you're completely confident in your story.

DO	DON'T
• Educate yourself about journalism. Take a journalism class, if you can. Some high schools run the student newspaper as a class itself.	• Don't use extremely formal or flowery language. Newswriting should be crisp and to the point.
• Be willing to do other things besides writing when you're starting out at the paper, especially if you don't have prior journalism experience. Student journalists often start as copy editors or in other positions on the paper before they're assigned stories to write.	• Don't write anything unkind about anyone. • Don't put made-up content in your stories—ever. If you can't find the perfect quotation or the perfect statistic, do without it. It's never acceptable to use invented "facts" in a story.
• Choose topics that appeal to a broad audience. If you're allowed to choose what you're going to write about, make sure it's something your readers will want to read and not just something that interests you.	• Don't offer your opinion. Your job as a journalist is to collect complete information and present it fairly, without judgment or "slant."
• Take your work seriously. It may be "just" a school paper, and you may have classmates who don't take it seriously, but you must make every effort to treat your work as serious journalism. Your writing reflects on you and on your school as well.	
• Do your research. Get background information about the topic you're covering. If it's something controversial, be sure to get both sides of the story by interviewing a range of different people.	
• Be fair. If you are covering a controversial issue, be sure to tell both sides of the story and make an effort to get quotes from people on both sides of the question. Explain the opposing points of view accurately and without bias. Even if you have a strong opinion about the issue, your story must be scrupulously objective.	
• Report the facts accurately. Double-check the spelling of names and places, important dates, scores, dollar amounts, and every other fact in your story. Use a recording device, if possible, and take careful notes in a notebook.	
• Learn to use quotations well. Quoting people can add credibility and interest to your stories.	

Choose quotations that add a dimension to your story, not ones that simply repeat what you've just written. Always be sure your quotations are completely accurate.

- Cultivate an engaging style. Even if you're reporting straight news, you can write in a style that readers enjoy reading. The best way to develop your style is to read the work of professional journalists carefully and pay attention to things like word choice, sentence length, and transitions in your own writing. You should be aware when you write and know why you make the stylistic choices you make.
- Double-check your grammar and spelling. There's nothing more embarrassing than seeing a story in print, with your name on it, that's full of preventable errors.

The Five Ws (and One H)

The first paragraph of your story is its most important. Many people will read only the beginning of the story, so it's important that you include all the key information there. The mnemonic device of the "five Ws and one H" can help you be sure you've asked and answered all the key questions in your piece. Try to ensure your first paragraph answers these questions:

Who is the story about? Who was involved?

What happened?

When did it happen?

Where did it happen?

Why did it happen? (If there are competing explanations, be sure you report them accurately.)

How did it happen?

If your story provides good answers to all these questions about the event, you can feel confident you're reporting thoroughly.

LIKE THIS

Restoring Storm-Shaken School

Written by Bettina Edelstein

Standing on the corner of 246th Street as the storm was picking up, Director of Facilities Management and Security John Yeager watched and heard "crackling and lighting like the display of an electrical light show" after trees fell on electrical poles, he said.

With trees snapped over and blocking the streets surrounding school, power outages in all Upper and Middle Division buildings, and a roof ripped open in the Lower Division, maintenance and security staff immediately got to work clearing trees and repairing damage. Before the storm hit, the maintenance and security teams had secured anything that could be moved with wind and become a projectile.

Yeager, along with several maintenance and security staff, weathered the storm at school "ensuring that damage would be minimized," he said. "During the storm, our biggest concern was watching out for falling trees," he said. On Sunday night, while standing on the corner of 246th Street with 60 mph winds blowing, he heard "a loud cracking sound and then a tremendous, ground-shaking thud," as the 80ft oak tree next to the Business Office crashed to the ground, pulling down electrical cables and snapping the power pole in half. As he looked around through the night, he continued to see "bright flashes and hear loud humming sounds, as every time a tree fell the overhead lines also fell, creating havoc."

Yeager and the maintenance staff were ready to work early the next morning. Faced with clogged drains, trees fallen across streets, and downed power lines, the maintenance and security teams delved right into ensuring safety and restoring the school after Sandy hit. Broadway was closed because of a tree that had fallen from Van Cortlandt Park, but the full maintenance staff made it to school, as most of them live locally.

In evaluating the campus, "we really had to take a hard look at things. Some things may not be that obvious," Security Manager Mike McCaw said. For example, their greatest challenge was working with downed power lines because they did not know if the lines were still live, Yeager said.

This storm was different from past natural disasters, such as snowstorms, that the maintenance and security staff has faced. "Snow removal is snow removal, but this was a different challenge because of the strong winds," McCaw said. Typically, trees grow where power lines are, so if a tree falls, power lines fall, causing major problems.

Since Con Ed did not have the staffing to tackle the aftermath of the hurricane, power companies from Quebec, Buffalo, and Georgia were sent to the school to help the company, McCaw said. With all the contractors that Horace Mann deals with on standby, "the roof that was ripped open at the Lower Division was totally repaired, the Business Office parking lot that was damaged by an uprooted tree was repaved, and our arborist removed all dangerous and fallen trees from our vicinity within two days," Yeager said.

Generators brought light and heat back to Tillinghast and Rose Hall after the buildings lost power. "One of our top priorities was providing all employees living in HM houses with temporary power," Yeager said. The power was restored to the majority of HM buildings by last Thursday, but the Summer on the Hill house and Lisa Moreira's house did not regain power until Sunday, November 10th.

"I think we were right on point with our response to the storm. We were prepared, we managed it, and we were cleaning up and getting school prepared for students to return," McCaw said.

From Bettina Edelstein, "Restoring Storm-Shaken School," *Horace Mann Record*, November 16, 2012, http://horacemannrecord.com/articles/restoring-storm-shaken-school/.

UCLA receives $20 million grant for obesity prevention project

COLLEGE NEWSPAPER

The UCLA Fielding School of Public Health and the Jonsson Comprehensive Cancer Center received a new $20 million federal grant this week, which will fund a national project to combat obesity.

The grant came from the Centers for Disease Control and Prevention as part of the organization's Racial and Ethnic Approaches to Community Health initiative, according to a press release.

The Centers for Disease Control and Prevention gifted the money to UCLA to aid in a project promoting healthy lifestyles in public locations, such as schools and offices. The project, called "Healthy-by-Default," instructs community groups, such as Boys & Girls Clubs of America, how to provide healthy options in place of unhealthy ones, said Roshan Bastani, one of the two principal investigators for the project.

"We engage people where they spend a lot of (their) time, so we make the healthy option the default option," Bastani said.

Through the program currently, she said, researchers encourage local companies to have 10-minute exercise breaks once or twice per day to ensure that employees are active.

The grant came as a pleasant surprise to the entire team, Bastani said.

The new funding will allow the Healthy-by-Default program to expand its scope nationally and concentrate on metropolitan hubs where ethnic minorities make up a majority of the population, Bastani said.

Bastani and Antronette Yancey are both professors of health policy and management at the Fielding School and have spent 20 years researching various topics in health disparities, such as obesity prevention.

"We try to make a real difference in the communities we help," Bastani said.

Compiled by Stephen Stewart, Bruin reporter.

From "UCLA Receives $20 Million Grant for Obesity Prevention," *Daily Bruin*, October 5, 2012, www.dailybruin.com/article/2012/10/ucla-receives-20-million-grant-for-obesity-prevention-project.

WRITING AT WORK

Most of us do most of our writing at work. Whether it's simple internal communication via e-mail, planning and coordination of events, sales writing, or communication with customers and clients, writing skills are indispensable in business. E-mail has supplanted the phone call as the most popular form of business communication, and it brings with it the higher stakes of the paper trail it creates. Good writing skills at work can protect you and your company, improve your business, and help propel your career to greater heights.

The Basics

BUSINESS E-MAIL

E-mail is the most popular mode of business communication. Many of us spend much of the workday reading and writing e-mails. Although it's easy to go on automatic pilot when you open your inbox, you can significantly improve your productivity and success by paying more careful attention to how you write your e-mail messages.

You can have brilliant ideas, but if you can't get them across, your ideas won't get you anywhere.

—Lee Iacocca, American businessman, leader, and author

Introduction

The **purpose** of an e-mail is usually to make a request, provide information, or ask a question. To help make your message as concise and efficient as possible, it's important to keep your purpose clearly in mind as you write. Because e-mail is such a high-speed medium, it's all the more important to consider your **reader**'s needs, expectations, and likely attitude. If you can anticipate what your reader wants, you're more likely to get the job done with one e-mail rather than a long thread. If you're writing just a quick message, you won't need to do much **brainstorming**. If your topic is more complex, you'll need to give some thought to how to convey your message best. **Organize** your e-mail for maximum impact by letting your reader know at the very beginning of the message why you're writing. The Model Outline

MODEL OUTLINE

An e-mail should be as brief as possible to get the job done.
Opening: To orient your reader, say right up front why you're writing.
Middle: Fill in any details the reader needs. Keep this section brief. Use bulleted lists to organize complex information.
Conclusion: Finish your message by restating your main point (a request, next steps, etc.) and thanking your reader.

offers a structure you can adapt for your own purposes. Tone is a critical issue with e-mails, so be careful as you **draft**. Because we e-mail both our friends and our work associates, and because we're usually going so fast, it's easy to make a mistake with the tone. A very quick e-mail probably won't require **revision**, but a longer one might, especially to condense it for length. Proofread quickly for accuracy, to prevent misunderstandings that may require lengthy e-mail threads to sort out.

DO	DON'T
• Limit your e-mail to one topic only. When you try to cover multiple topics in a single message, you run the risk of burying important information.	• Don't send an e-mail when a phone call would be more appropriate. Don't engage in rounds of e-mail when a quick phone call could resolve the question. It wastes your time and your reader's.
• Use a concise and specific subject line. A good subject line can help readers prioritize messages and find them later. If your message is especially important, consider putting "important" or "response needed" in the subject line.	• Don't write anything confidential or private in an e-mail. Even if your e-mail is secure, be aware that this is not a private mode of communication. Protect yourself and your company by being discreet and following company policy.
• Begin your message with a salutation. Even if it's just the person's name with a dash after it, a salutation is courteous. It is acceptable to drop the salutation once you get into a thread of quick messages.	• Don't copy people on an e-mail unless there's a good reason for it. To some extent, the practices of your organization will guide you, but you should think carefully before you CC (courtesy copy) or BCC (blind courtesy copy) additional readers. Our inboxes are all full enough without e-mails we really don't need to see.
• Make your purpose clear at the beginning of the message. Don't count on recipients to read to the end to figure out what you want; many of them won't do it.	• Don't forward an e-mail without thinking about the consequences. When you forward an e-mail, be sure to look down through the entire thread to see if there is any content that should not be shared.
• Keep your message as brief as possible. It shows respect for your reader, and you have a better chance of being read and responded to.	
• Be courteous. We're all in a hurry, but it doesn't take long to type "please" and "thank you," and you'll get better results.	
• Make sure your tone is appropriate to your reader and your subject.	

- Remember to reply to all if the e-mail had multiple recipients. If you forget, it can be a hassle to get everyone caught up.
- Remember that e-mail isn't private. Your e-mails are the property of your company and can be subpoenaed. Even under less dramatic circumstances, your messages can easily be forwarded to others, so be sure you are discreet and sensible in everything you write. If you have a question about the appropriateness of what you're putting in your e-mail, err on the side of caution and pick up the phone instead.
- Sign your e-mail.

NOT LIKE THIS . . .

I've met with my staff, and we have some changes we'd like you to make in the Web site design. Overall we're very pleased with it. Can we change the color on the banner to a darker blue? Is there any way the font can be a little larger? It seems hard to read. A lot of our customers will be on laptops, so this is an important concern. Is this something we'll be able to change later?

I thought we had agreed to replace the inappropriate image on the home page.

Given these changes, let's push back the launch date by a couple of weeks. Would June 17 work for you?

Can we all get a tutorial at some point in the content management system?

In addition, Marco would like to speak with you about the security breach on the HR site. Is this under control yet? Please let me know ASAP.

Thanks.

What does "this" refer to?

Isabelle probably doesn't mean to sound quite so brusque here. She makes it sound as though there's a pornographic image on the home page. She'd be better off restating the agreement they had made earlier, in a more diplomatic way.

This is an important schedule change for the designer, and it should have been mentioned at the very beginning. It's a bit buried here.

This message reads like a quickly written and unrevised first draft. It's not well organized, and it's not easy for the reader to sort out all the information included here.

This is an afterthought about a different matter and doesn't belong in this e-mail. Given the apparently sensitive nature of the problem, it probably shouldn't be in an e-mail at all. The writer would be better off picking up the phone to get an update.

It would be more courteous for Isabelle to use a salutation at the beginning of the message and to use a proper closing.

. . . LIKE THIS

Hi Jon:

Thanks for the latest round of the website design. We really like it. We have a few changes to request, which will likely delay the launch. Is June 17 a good new launch date?

Here are the changes we'd like:

- Home page: As we discussed, we'd like to replace the stock photo of the guy with a group shot.
- Banner: Can we change it to a darker blue?
- Font: Can it be larger? The content needs to be easily legible on laptops.
- Content management system: Can we get a tutorial at some point?

Thanks again for all your effort. I think the site is going to look great. Please let me know if you have any questions, and please let me know if the June 17 launch date is good for you.

All the best,

Isabelle

> Isabelle alerts Jon to the new launch date at the beginning of the message.

> By organizing and formatting the changes in a way that makes them easy to scan, Isabelle helps Jon see at a glance the scope of the work he has to do.

> Isabelle's courteous salutation and closing make her message more pleasant to read and encourage cooperation.

> Isabelle reminds Jon of the change in the launch date and asks explicitly for a response.

For more sample e-mails, visit www.howtowriteanything.com.

Three Times You Should Never Send an E-mail

E-mail is literally at the tips of our fingers as we sit at our desks, but there are times when defaulting to this super-convenient mode of communication is not a good idea. Here are a few times you should *not* send an e-mail:

- When you know or suspect that anyone in your company has done something illegal or unethical. All written communication—including e-mail and instant messages—is discoverable in legal proceedings, and you could end up incriminating the parties involved. Such information is better discussed face-to-face.

- When you need to apologize and can do so in person. A face-to-face apology to a colleague means more than an e-mail mea culpa. If you have the chance to speak to the person you've offended, choose that route rather than an e-mail apology.

- When you're angry. Firing off an angry e-mail can feel good in the moment, but you're likely to say something you'll later regret. Take the time to calm down before you hit Send.

E-mail: Pet Peeves and Preferences

Everyone has a pet peeve when it comes to e-mail. For Len Elliott, financial aid director at a major Midwestern research university, it's thank-you e-mails. "The thank-you is implied. There is no question this is what I'm expected to do. I don't want a thank-you email. There's nothing endearing to me about the thank-you e-mail." Len processes financial aid payments to hundreds of students, including all internal and external awards for PhD students in fifteen research departments. He estimates he receives about seventy e-mails a day, thirty of which involve "serious problems" that each require as much as four hours of work. Sometimes during his busy season from July through September, Len misses checking his e-mails for several days: "I look at my inbox and it has four hundred e-mails in it. And I think, 'Is this something else I have to do?' I dread opening them. And then there's nothing worse than a stale thank-you."

But what about courtesy? Isn't it polite to say "thank you" when someone helps you? "I really don't need a thank-you," says Len. "But if it makes you feel better—if I really got you out of a bind or something—just put it in the subject line." Len goes on to talk about Katherine, a former colleague in the registrar's office. Once she had finished a task, she simply added the word "done" in front of the e-mail subject line, and her readers understood there was no need to open that message. " 'Done,' " says Len. "That's my favorite four-letter word."

Katherine's solution is one that organizations are adopting to cut down on the time spent on opening e-mails needlessly. Many people now write their entire message—if it's brief—in the subject line, followed by "(eom)" for "end of message." For instance, when a programmer writes, "Adam working from home today (eom)," his colleagues know they don't have to open that message; they can simply delete it from their inboxes.

As the technology of communication evolves, so do its protocols. Staying flexible and being sensitive to the needs of others is the cure for most e-mail pet peeves.

To share your own e-mail pet peeves, visit www.howtowriteanything.com.

REQUEST/INQUIRY

Requests and inquiries (requests for information) are some of the most common of business communications. Taking the time to plan and craft your request—rather than just winging it—can significantly increase your chances of getting what you want and can save you time and hassle over the long run.

MODEL OUTLINE

A request should be concise and clear.
Opening: Politely mention your request early in the message, so your reader knows why you have written.
Middle: Provide details about your request: the reasons behind it, reasons you are asking this reader, how important it is to you. Be concise and courteous.
Conclusion: Finish your message by restating your request and thanking your reader.

Introduction

The fundamental **purpose** of any request—be it for assistance, information, or any other goal—is to enlist the cooperation of the reader. Putting a request in writing also creates an official record of the request, even if you expect that it might be denied. Thinking from your **reader**'s point of view is key to writing a successful request. What is your **reader**'s potential attitude? What might make it difficult for her to say yes to your request? It's especially important to **brainstorm** around these issues, anticipate potential objections, and address those in your message. Think how to motivate your reader to respond positively. **Organizing** your request carefully can help: in general, it's best to state your request at the beginning of the message. The Model Outline suggests a good structure for your request. As you **draft**, use a courteous tone and avoid sounding demanding. You should plan to go through several drafts before you send out your request. **Revise** and rewrite until your request is clear, efficient, and persuasive.

DO	DON'T
• Address your request to the right person or at least to the right department. Misdirected requests can easily go astray.	• Don't take your reader, or his attitude, for granted. Don't assume he will say yes. Be respectful of his time. Be aware that the bigger and the more complicated the request, the harder you will need to work to motivate your reader to help you.
• Identify yourself in the opening of the message if the reader doesn't already know you. If he might remember you, give him information about where you have met.	• Don't use a demanding tone. There is a difference between a businesslike tone and an imperious one. Remember that you are trying to foster cooperation in your reader.
• State your request early in the message. Doing so helps orient the reader and allows him to decide whether to read your message now or wait until he can give it more time and attention.	• Don't make a vague request. An inquiry for "information" should be as specific as possible. Information about what?
• Be specific in your request. The more specific you are, the easier it will be for the reader to give you what you want, and the less potential there is for confusion.	• Don't go on too long. Give your reader the information he needs to make a favorable decision about your request, but not too much more.
• State the reason you're making the request.	• Don't bully or threaten your reader in any way. Taking a hostile or threatening tone can backfire. Unless friendly requests have failed repeatedly, be pleasant and cooperative.
• Give the reader all the information he needs in order to grant your request. Include any documentation related to your request. Let the reader know how you prefer to be contacted, if it's not apparent.	• Don't grovel. Don't apologize for taking up the reader's time or hassling him (unless your request really is onerous). If you are respectful and courteous, you needn't be self-effacing. People are actually *less* likely to help someone who grovels.
• Let the reader know how important the request is to you. How will you benefit if he grants your request? How might he benefit?	
• Give a deadline, if applicable and appropriate. A vague deadline like ASAP is easy to disregard. It's courteous to let the reader know the reason behind the deadline. People are usually motivated to meet a deadline if they understand it.	
• Remember to thank your reader.	

NOT LIKE THIS . . .

To: Mona Williams
From: Terry Hope
Re: Bob Donnelly

Dear Ms. Williams:

In reference to Bob Donnelly's visit next week, I am writing to confirm the following:

Car to and from JFK (itinerary attached)

Lunch provided (NO tree nuts). Private area for lunch.

The above in addition to the customary arrangements.

Please confirm ASAP. Thank you for your consideration.

Terry Hope

> Terry would be better off introducing herself and providing some context for this request.

> What are the "customary arrangements"? Will Mona know?

> What exactly does ASAP mean? Terry would do better to provide a specific confirmation date.

> Terry is a little high-handed and takes her reader for granted.

> This thank-you is a bit pro forma and doesn't sound sincere. Mona will probably help Terry, but she might not want to.

. . . LIKE THIS

To: Mona Williams
From: Terry Hope
Re: Bob Donnelly

Dear Ms. Williams:

I am writing on behalf of Bob Donnelly, who will be speaking at the Springs conference next week. Bob has asked that I work with you to iron out the details of his trip. I would appreciate it if you would make the following arrangements for Bob:

- Car to and from JFK. I am attaching Bob's itinerary.
- Lunch at the conference. Bob prefers to eat alone so he can review his materials. Please ensure his lunch has **no tree nuts**, as he is very allergic.
- Materials copied and distributed to participants. I am attaching a PDF of his handouts.

Let me know if you have any questions. Could you please confirm by March 28?

Thank you very much for your help.

Best wishes,

Terry Hope

> Terry introduces herself. She lets Mona know who Bob is and why the request is important.

> Terry provides a reason for this special request.

> Although these arrangements are customary, Terry spells them out anyway to make Mona's job easier.

> A specific confirmation date lets Mona know what the timeline is on the request.

> Terry is friendly and courteous throughout.

INSTANT MESSAGE

Sending instant messages at the office seems as quick and simple as having a conversation, but that very simplicity carries some risks. A little attention to etiquette and common sense will make your instant messaging with colleagues even faster and more effective.

Introduction

The **purpose** of an instant message is typically to send a quick message or ask a quick question of a colleague. Anticipate that your **reader** is just as rushed as you are, if not more so, and plan accordingly. While there's little **brainstorming** required for such a brief message, it's a good idea to spend a few seconds to be sure your IM is clear and specific. Sending a vague message that requires several rounds of messages to clarify defeats the purpose. **Organize** your message so its purpose is apparent right away. Instant messaging is no place for long preludes and explanations. Give your IM a quick proofread before you hit Send to be sure it's free of typos. A quick **revision** can save time.

DO	DON'T
• Respect your colleagues' availability status. If they're busy or unavailable, you may ask an urgent question if you let them know it's urgent. But don't expect a reply.	• Don't overuse instant messaging. Keep in mind that when you send someone an IM, you're interrupting him, even if he chooses not to answer you at that moment. Think before you ping. Do you need this answer right now? Is it worth interrupting your colleague? Would it be better to save up a few questions and ask them all at once?
• Ask if the person is busy before you launch into a long IM.	
• Make your "Are you there?" message more specific by letting the person know what you want to ping about.	• Don't use a very informal tone in work-related IMs. It's very easy to get very casual when you're communicating in this medium, especially if you're in the habit of using it with friends. Remember you're at work, and keep your vocabulary and tone appropriate for your setting.
• Wait for the other person to finish typing before you pile on more comments. If you see the other person is typing, wait until you see what she has to say. She may be in the process of answering the question you're still typing out.	
• Be sensitive to organizational culture in your use of emoticons. Emoticons can be useful in conveying tone when you're writing fast. However, not all	• Don't use humor unless you're sure your conversation partner will understand and appreciate it. Tone can be difficult to convey, and you're better off erring on the side of caution.

DO (CONTINUED)	DON'T (CONTINUED)
organizations view them as acceptable. Follow the lead of others in that regard. • Close the thread with a thank-you or some other courteous closing. • Be very careful what you're doing if you have more than one instant messaging conversation going at a time. Be especially careful if you have both personal and business chats open (not that you would ever do that at work). It's very easy to type in the wrong space when you have a lot of these windows open; be sure you aren't sending a message to your boss that you intended for your boyfriend.	• Don't use emoticons with your boss. Let your boss dictate the level of formality in your communication. If she sends emoticons, then you can, too. • Don't say anything in an IM that would embarrass you if it became broadly known. Instant messaging is not private! Although the instant messaging window disappears when you close it or shut down your computer, many instant messaging platforms have logging systems, and what you write may be recoverable. Like e-mail, instant messaging conversations are discoverable in legal proceedings, so proceed with caution.

NOT LIKE THIS . . .

Benjamin says: (10:21:31 AM)
r u there?

Steve says: (10:22:12 AM)
Yep

Benjamin says: (10:22:16 AM)
do you have a minute?

> Benjamin is considerate in asking Steve if he has time to chat, but he'd be wise to speed things up.

Steve says: (10:22:26 AM)
Just. Meeting at 10:30.

Benjamin says: (10:22:32 AM)
ok i have some questions about the documents for Ventana

> Steve has let Benjamin know he's in a rush, so Benjamin really should ask his question directly right now.

Steve says: (10:22:34 AM)
OK

Benjamin says: (10:22:40 AM)
i'm not sure what to do about the bios. should I be taking them off the website, or are there new ones for the pitch docs?

Steve says: (10:22:44 AM)
I'm not handling that. Ask Karen

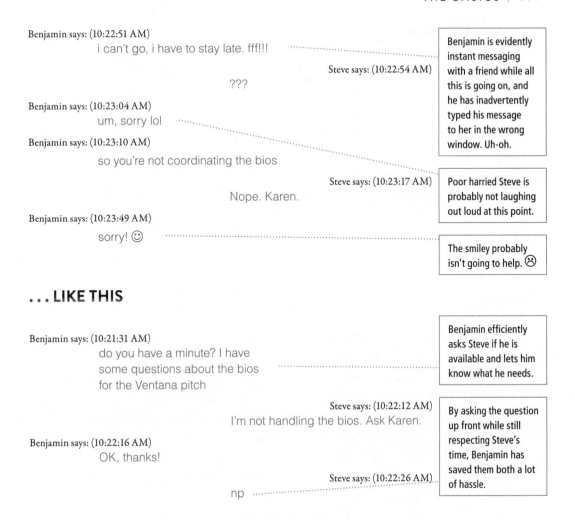

Benjamin says: (10:22:51 AM)
i can't go, i have to stay late. fff!!!

Steve says: (10:22:54 AM)
???

Benjamin says: (10:23:04 AM)
um, sorry lol

Benjamin says: (10:23:10 AM)
so you're not coordinating the bios

Steve says: (10:23:17 AM)
Nope. Karen.

Benjamin says: (10:23:49 AM)
sorry! ☺

> Benjamin is evidently instant messaging with a friend while all this is going on, and he has inadvertently typed his message to her in the wrong window. Uh-oh.

> Poor harried Steve is probably not laughing out loud at this point.

> The smiley probably isn't going to help. ☹

. . . LIKE THIS

Benjamin says: (10:21:31 AM)
do you have a minute? I have some questions about the bios for the Ventana pitch

Steve says: (10:22:12 AM)
I'm not handling the bios. Ask Karen.

Benjamin says: (10:22:16 AM)
OK, thanks!

Steve says: (10:22:26 AM)
np

> Benjamin efficiently asks Steve if he is available and lets him know what he needs.

> By asking the question up front while still respecting Steve's time, Benjamin has saved them both a lot of hassle.

BUSINESS LETTER

E-mail has replaced the business letter for most day-to-day business communications. However, there are some occasions that still call for a formal business letter, printed on paper and sent through the postal mail. Cover letters that accompany contracts, agreements, or other documents are often old-style formal business letters. Sending a business letter through the postal mail return receipt requested is still a popular way to confirm that the recipient received your communication. And although it may be hard to believe, there are still some businesses that do not carry out transactions electronically. Writing a formal business letter may be a dying art, but it's one that you're likely to need at some point.

MODEL OUTLINE

A business letter follows a traditional outline.

Your **address** appears at the top, either as a part of your letterhead or typed out.

Date. Spell out the month, and include the year.

Inside address. The address of your recipient.

Subject line. Some letters include a subject or reference line.

Salutation. Use "Dear" followed by a colon (:).

Body of the letter.

Closing. "Sincerely" is the typical closing for a business letter.

Signature. Your handwritten signature.

Name and title. Your name, typewritten. Your title on the line below.

Identification line. If the letter was dictated, the intials of the writer appear in capital letters, followed by a colon and the initials of the assistant in small letters.

Enclosures. If your letter includes enclosed items, type "Enc." or "Enclosures." If your letter includes more than one enclosure, note the number in parentheses.

Copies. If the letter is being copied to multiple parties, indicate so by typing "CC:" followed by the names of the recipients.

PS. If there is a PS, it is typed here.

DO	DON'T
• Print your business letter on company letterhead. If your company does not have letterhead, or if you are writing as an individual on a business-related matter, type your name and address, centered, at the top of the page.	• Don't use a very informal tone. A business letter is more formal than an e-mail.
• Format your letter completely, with the recipient's name and address and date.	• Don't use stilted or legalistic language. A business letter is a formal document, but you should feel free to sound like a human being. Avoid using stilted "business-ese" (like "per your request, enclosed please find") or "legal-ese" (like "the undersigned" in referring to yourself).
• Use a formal salutation. For a formal letter, it's conventional to use "Mr." or "Ms." in addressing the recipient, rather than the recipient's first name.	
• Use a formal tone in your letter. In general, business letters are more formal than e-mails (although there are exceptions), so make sure your tone isn't too casual.	
• Use block or indented paragraphs in the body of the letter.	
• Use a formal closing. "Sincerely" is the most common and most widely appropriate closing.	
• Sign your letter.	
• Type your name under your signature.	
• If you have enclosed anything with your letter, type the word "Enclosure" or "Enc." below your	

name, near the bottom of the page. Note the number of enclosures in parentheses.

- If you are sending copies of the letter to people other than the recipient, indicate so by typing CC (short for courtesy copy) below your name, near the bottom of the page.

. . . LIKE THIS

Arroyo Theater Company
1776 Colorado Blvd.
Pasadena, CA 91108
626.798.0001
info@arroyotheater.org

October 3, 2012

Mrs. Lois H. Brown
2397 Bonnie Brae Rd.
Altadena, CA 91001

Dear Mrs. Brown:

    It was a pleasure to meet you at the theater on Sunday. I always enjoy meeting our patrons, and I was delighted to hear that you had been attending our performances for so long. Thank you for being such a loyal supporter of Arroyo.

    I had a look in our files, and I was able to find the enclosed program for last year's production of *Volpone*. I hope you'll enjoy it. That one was particularly fun to direct, and I have very fond memories of the production. I will ask Wendy if she has contact information for Lawrence.

    If there is anything else I can do for you, please let me know. I look forward to seeing you again soon at the theater. Next up is *Bartholomew Fair*, which opens November 20. I hope to see you there!

    Thank you again for your support for Arroyo Theater Company.

                    Sincerely,

                    Jeffrey Bergen
                    Jeffrey Bergen
                    Artistic Director

Enclosure
CC: Wendy Anderson

MEMO

A memo—short for "memorandum"—is a form of internal business communication often used to share policy updates, schedule changes, information about new hires, and other company business.

Once upon a time, paper memos were the staple of interoffice communication. Today most memos are distributed via e-mail. Some organizations still use paper memos for certain purposes, such as cover memos attached to documents or other printed materials. Whatever medium it takes, the memo form is still useful for communication within the office.

Introduction

The **purpose** of a memo is typically to convey information to your colleagues or to ask them to do something. The success of your memo hinges on your **readers** actually reading it. People sometimes assume that anything coming from inside the organization is less important than communications from clients or customers. To improve your chances of getting your readers' attention, make your memo easy to scan and make the stakes clear. Take the time you need to **brainstorm** the content. Make sure your memo is complete. Think from your readers' point of view. What information do they need in order to do what you're asking them to do? Be sure to **organize** your memo to make the most of your readers' time. State your reason for writing, and get the important information in early. If there are action steps for the readers, make those very clear. If possible, allow yourself a couple of **drafts** before you send your memo out. Write in a collegial tone to get the maximum attention and cooperation. As you **revise** your draft, try to see the memo from your readers' point of view. Is the message clear? Will the readers know what's expected of them? Check to make sure you correct any embarrassing typos or misspellings. A very important memo—for instance, one that describes a policy change—should be reviewed by management or someone else before you circulate it.

DO	DON'T
• Be clear about the purpose of your memo. A memo should have a single purpose; it should not be a compendium of different information you want to share.	• Don't drone on too long. The longer your memo is, the less likely recipients are to read it.
• Send your memo to the right audience. Make sure everyone receiving the memo really needs to read it.	• Don't obscure your meaning by using "business-ese." Rather than "commence" or "initiate," try using "begin." Instead of "subsequent to," try "after."
• Use an effective subject line. Whether your memo is an e-mail or printed on paper, use a concise and specific subject line to let readers know what it's about, and—if it's an e-mail—to make it easy for readers to find in their inboxes later.	• Don't use salutations or closings, as in a letter. The memo format does not include these.
• Use the appropriate format for a paper memo. The sample on page 397 shows the correct formatting.	
• Get right to the point. Make it easy for the reader to understand the reason for the memo.	
• Keep it brief and concise. Your memo stands a better chance of being read—and being read carefully—if it is brief.	
• Use formatting to make your memo easy to skim. Short paragraphs, bulleted lists, and subheadings can break up long memos into easily digestible chunks.	
• Be very clear about any action that is required.	
• Note at the bottom of the memo if there are any attachments.	
• Be polite, especially if you're asking the reader to do something.	

NOT LIKE THIS . . .

To: Futura Team
From: Lisa Meyers
Subject: Office Move
Date: 1/22/13

> Lisa should be more specific with her subject line. The staff have probably received several communications about the office move at this point, and they might not read this one. This memo isn't just background information or an announcement; it's asking the staff to do something. Make sure they read it.

> This opening paragraph is a bit misleading, and it's a missed opportunity. Lisa is not just outlining the moving process; she's also asking her colleagues to do a few specific things to prepare for the movers. If you're writing a memo to ask for action, make that clear up front.

> This very important point—that the company cannot afford any downtime owing to a mismanaged move—feels buried here. It's a good way to motivate people to get themselves organized for the move; Lisa should find a way to highlight it to let people know the stakes of getting it right.

> This paragraph reads very much like a first draft. It meanders, and it doesn't emphasize important points. It's a little hard to follow. Lisa would have better results if she made this information as easy as possible to scan rather than requiring her colleagues to read it carefully.

As you are aware, our office move has been scheduled for mid-February for some time now. We have just received a firm date from the movers, and I would like to take this opportunity to outline the process so you will be aware of what is happening.

The actual move will take place over the weekend of February 15, and we expect to be up and running in the new space on Monday morning, February 18. To accomplish this, we are all going to have to work together. The more fully you cooperate, the more smoothly the move will go. As you know, the annual goal-setting meeting is happening on February 24, so it is critical that we get the move done right so there is minimal disruption to operations.

The movers will pack up the office on February 15 and will effectuate the move over the weekend. Consequently, it is not necessary for you to come into work on the 15th. However, it is critically important that your office be prepared for the movers by the time you leave on Thursday the 14th. This means NO piles of loose paper on your desks, no food, no knickknacks that will slow down the movers. Ideally, bring your work to a temporary stopping point by COB Thursday. You may leave items in your drawers. If you know there is something you'll need on Monday morning, be sure you know where it is. If you have any breakable items of a personal nature—vases, plants, and so on—it would be wise to take them home for the weekend: better safe than sorry.

Please let me know if you have any questions. Thank you for your cooperation.

... LIKE THIS

To: Futura Team
From: Lisa Meyers
Subject: Office Move February 15
Date: 1/22/13

> Lisa uses her subject line to let the readers know the date of the move.

We finally have a date for the office move! The movers will be here Friday, February 15, and we'll be up and running in our new space on Monday the 18th. To be ready for the **annual goal-setting meeting on February 24**, we'll need to work together to make this move fast and smooth.

> Lisa gets the critical information into the first sentence of the memo.

> Lisa conveys the high stakes of this move to her readers, and highlights the information by bolding the text.

- Please have your desk cleared and ready to be moved by COB Thursday the 14th. This means NOTHING on the surface of your desk. You may leave items in the drawers.
- Don't leave anything breakable in the office.
- The office will be closed Friday, February 15.
- Be ready to hit the ground running on Monday the 18th. We'll celebrate the move after the meeting on the 24th.

> Breaking out this information in bullet points helps readers see what's being asked of them.

Please let me know if you have any questions, and thank you for your cooperation.

BUSINESS APOLOGY

Sometimes regrettable things happen at work: flare-ups between co-workers, misunderstandings, failures to meet the expectations of colleagues or customers. An apology can help put things right.

Some people worry that an apology makes them look weak. On the contrary, a sincere apology shows that you value the relationship and that you take responsibility for your actions.

Give some thought to the best way to deliver your apology. Sometimes a face-to-face meeting is the best choice. You can also use a typed note or an e-mail. The degree of the transgression and the nature of the relationship will help you decide the best format for your apology.

A business apology should be brief and to the point.
Opening: Begin your message with acknowledging the infraction and apologizing for it.
Middle: Offer the reader an explanation of what happened. Assure him it will not happen again. If appropriate, let him know what controls have been put in place to prevent a recurrence.
Conclusion: Finish your message by reiterating your apology and letting the reader know you value the business relationship.

Introduction

The **purpose** of an apology is to let your reader know that you're aware you made a mistake and you're sorry for the pain or distress it caused him. A message of apology also gives you the opportunity to show how you're going to fix the problem, if that's possible.

Understanding your **reader** and his likely attitude can help you shape your message. What is your relationship? Is your reader your boss, your customer, someone who reports to you? How is he likely to respond to your apology? Most people are willing to forgive if you address them appropriately.

Take some time to **brainstorm** what you want to say. A perfunctory and thoughtless apology can be worse than none at all. Think from your reader's point of view, and address the issues most important to him.

Organize your apology so that the actual apology—the "I'm sorry" part—comes first. Any explanation or elaboration can come later. The Model Outline provides guidance you can adapt for your own message.

Your tone will depend on the seriousness of what you're apologizing for, and your relationship with your reader. Unless your apology is very simple and straightforward, plan to go through a couple of **drafts** before you send it. Getting the tone right can be a little tricky. Once you have a draft, take a break and do something else for a little while. Then go back and see if you can put yourself in your reader's shoes, and then **revise** from there. Be sure your apology is sincere and not defensive. Also be very careful to avoid leaving typos and other errors in your note, which can send the message that you don't really care that much after all.

DO	DON'T
• Write as soon as you can after the offense. Delaying can make a bad situation worse.	• Don't make excuses. If you made a mistake, admit it. You don't have to beat yourself up, but be sure you don't say anything to suggest that your behavior was really no big deal.
• Apologize. Be explicit in saying that you are sorry. If the reader feels you're fudging, your apology could backfire.	• Don't shift the blame to others. If others genuinely played a role, you may include that information in your explanation, but don't use it to evade taking responsibility for your own actions.
• Keep it brief. As a business communication, the apology should be concise and to the point.	
• Be sincere.	

- Explain. Let the reader know the cause of the breach. He's entitled to an explanation, and he wants to know that you didn't act from a lack of regard for him.
- If there is something you can do to rectify the problem, let the reader know what you're doing.
- If appropriate, assure the reader that it won't happen again.

- Don't blame the reader. An apology that says "I'm sorry, but you should have . . ." is not going to be received well. Sometimes people are so uncomfortable with admitting they've behaved badly that they unconsciously blame the reader. This can be subtle, so be alert to the risk.
- Don't grovel. Maintain your dignity.
- Don't say anything that could create legal liability. Particularly if you are apologizing to a client or customer on behalf of your company, take care that you do not open yourself up to liability you don't want. If you are unsure about liability issues, consult with your manager or legal counsel.

NOT LIKE THIS . . .

Dear Team:

My behavior in the staff meeting this morning was unacceptable.

Frankly, the habitual lateness to these meetings has stressed me out, and my "episode" was a response to that. As you all know, I am embroiled in working out the final budget for next year, reviewing the folders, and interviewing candidates for Jan's position. I was in meetings solidly from 8 a.m. to 6 p.m. yesterday.

I hope we can get back on track. I very much enjoy working with all of you and look forward to smoother sailing in the future.

Best,

Henry

> Henry would be better off starting his note by saying he's sorry. He's critical of his own behavior, but he stops short of apologizing here, and it weakens his message.

> By blaming his staff's "habitual lateness" for his "episode," Henry is more likely to alienate his readers than placate them. It may well be that he had a good reason to be upset, but he should deal with that problem separately from the apology for his bad behavior.

> Again, Henry is sidestepping the apology and shifting the responsibility to other people.

> Henry's going on too long, and he's begun whining.

. . . LIKE THIS

Henry provides an explanation for his outburst and lets his staff know that he is working to remedy the cause of his stress. Doubtless the next time Beth sends out a meeting invitation, she will ask that participants arrive promptly, thus addressing the problem with lateness. But Henry does not dilute his apology by shifting blame to the latecomers.

Henry closes by repeating his apology and looking forward optimistically to the future.

Henry opens his note with a sincere apology and takes responsibility for his own behavior.

Dear Team:

I'm sorry for blowing my stack in the staff meeting this morning. My behavior was unacceptable, and I apologize.

As most of you know, I have been juggling a lot of competing priorities and am under a lot of pressure. But that's no excuse for my outburst. I am working with Beth to set up a more realistic schedule for meetings, and I expect to be using my time more efficiently.

Again, I'm sorry. I very much enjoy working with all of you and look forward to smoother sailing in the future.

Best,

Henry

APOLOGY WHEN YOU ARE NOT AT FAULT

It can be good manners and build goodwill to send an apology when you haven't done anything blameworthy but you know a situation will have a negative impact on your associates or clients.

Dear Team,

Beginning Monday, September 13, through Friday, September 24, the kitchen area will be completely out of service for renovations. I am sorry for the inconvenience this will cause. I know a lot of you use the kitchen to prepare your lunch and take snack breaks during the day. As you know, the kitchen is in a dilapidated condition, and I hope that this two-week disruption will be outweighed by the clean, new, functional facility we'll be able to enjoy once the work is done.

Thanks for your understanding.

Rebecca

APOLOGY FOR POOR CUSTOMER SERVICE

When a glitch occurs in your otherwise stellar customer service, you should take responsibility and apologize right away. Consider offering the customer some compensation. Handling the apology well can undo the damage done and actually strengthen your relationship with your customer.

Be especially careful to avoid the passive voice in your apology. Don't say "The wrong item was shipped." Instead, take responsibility: "We shipped the wrong item."

Dear Ms. Rodriguez:

We understand that we shipped the wrong item to you, and we apologize for the error. We shipped out the correct item this morning. Would you please use the attached label to return the item shipped in error?

We would like to extend a 10% discount to you on your next order. Please use the attached discount code the next time you order online, or provide the code to the associate if you order by phone.

Again, we apologize for the error. We look forward to serving you in the future.

Sincerely,

Simon Polis
Customer Service

The Office Apology

———————•———————

Making apologies in the office can be a challenge, but choosing the right form for your apology can make it more effective. When should you write, and when should you apologize face-to-face?

In-person apologies are often best, because they allow you to connect with the other person and convey your genuineness. Face-to-face apologies take courage; they require you own up to your mistakes while remaining calm and confident. If you've lost your temper over an ongoing issue, apologizing immediately may not be the best course. Consider instead waiting a day or two and then offering your apology along with a suggestion about how to address the issue going forward.

There are other times when a written apology is called for. If you are part of a virtual team or always on the road and unable to connect in person, a prompt e-mail apology is in order. You may also want to communicate in writing if you want to apologize to a group rather than an individual. Finally, a written apology (either an e-mail or a personal note) may be in everyone's best interest if you feel you may react emotionally to the other person, if you're feeling defensive, or if you're likely to go on and on explaining, rationalizing, or making excuses.

The keys to any effective apology—whether in person or in writing—are its sincerity and its timeliness. Own up to what you said or did; own up to how it has affected the other person without making excuses; and finally, change your behavior going forward. Whether you decide to apologize in person or in writing, be sure you don't leave it too long—even in a difficult situation, waiting weeks and weeks is not the answer. An apology that comes late and without real change attached to it is meaningless. The good news is that, whatever form they take, timely and sincere apologies are disarming and can go a long way to improving relationships at work.

Diane A. Ross is a speaker, writer, and coach, and the author of *The Elephant in the Office: Super-Simple Strategies for Difficult Conversations at Work*. Her website is http://dianeaross.com.

BUSINESS BIO

You may be asked to supply a bio of yourself for many different reasons—for instance, for use on the company website, when you're making a presentation or speech, or for a company-sponsored charitable initiative. For entrepreneurs, a bio can be a crucial selling tool. Done right, a bio can provide a quick glimpse of who you are, what you value, and what you can do.

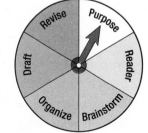

Introduction

The **purpose** of a business bio is to tell your professional story in an abbreviated form. A bio is different from a résumé in that it tells a story—it is not just a cold record of facts. The point of the story is always one of the following:

- "This person really knows what she's talking about; I think I'll listen to what she has to say."
- "This person's accomplishments are impressive. Acme must be a fine company to hire and retain talent like this."
- "This person has a lot of experience doing the kind of thing I need him to do for me. I feel comfortable that if I hire him he'll get the job done."

Your **reader** is looking for a quick digest of who you are. Many businesspeople keep several different versions of their bio available, tailored for different uses. **Brainstorm** about what your readers might be expecting to learn about you. If you're creating a bio for a particular occasion—perhaps a speech at an industry meeting—give some thought to who your readers might *imagine* you are and how your experience matches up to their expectations. Cast a wide net as you brainstorm: it's easy to overlook things in a long and varied career.

Business bios tend to follow a standard **organization**. Your readers will likely scan your bio rather than read it carefully, so be sure you make the information easy to access. The Model Outline can guide you.

Use a businesslike tone as you **draft**. Bios are usually written in the third person, as though someone else were describing you. Use an objective tone and stick to the facts.

MODEL OUTLINE

There's no hard-and-fast format for a business bio. However, most bios follow this general pattern:

Opening: State your current position and the major achievements you've been responsible for in this position.

Middle section: Provide information about past experience, including previous employment and achievements at past jobs. You may also want to include information about board memberships, community activities, and honors here.

Conclusion: Mention your educational background and any publications.

Optional: Some bios include personal information, such as place of birth and current residence, marital status, children, and hobbies. It's up to you—and sometimes your company—whether you include this information in your bio.

LET YOUR COMPANY HELP

If you've been asked to supply a bio for the company website or other publication, try to get a sample bio to model yours on—it can save you a lot of time and angst.

Find out if there are specific company policies about what can and cannot be included in a bio (e.g., personal information).

It can be difficult to fit all the content into your bio the first time through. Start early and make sure you have time to **revise** your draft. Show your draft to a few trusted colleagues or friends to get their objective opinion about the bio and to remind you if you've forgotten anything.

DO	DON'T
• Think in terms of your achievements, not just job titles. What have you accomplished in your job? What makes you an interesting speaker or a special asset to your company?	• Don't rely on impressive-sounding client lists to take the place of an in-depth bio. Remember, your bio is meant to tell your story, so use the opportunity not just to list facts and figures but also to show what makes you a particularly valuable person.
• Keep your bio brief—one page or less. This becomes more challenging the more senior you are. As you achieve more and more, you may have to make some difficult decisions about what stays in and what gets cut. Let the purpose for which you need the bio be your guide to what to include.	• Don't be offended if the person introducing you or publishing your bio makes significant cuts. Presenters often don't have time to absorb the bio fully, and publishers may need to adapt your bio to conform to everyone else's.
• Format your bio for ease of reading. Several short paragraphs are easier to read than one long solid block of text. Use paragraph breaks to indicate changes in topic.	• Don't reveal proprietary or sensitive information about a client or former employer, no matter how good it makes you look. You may have helped Acme Corporation cut its operating losses by 50 percent, but Acme may not be thrilled to have the whole world hear how badly they were screwing up before you came along. When in doubt, ask—or simply rephrase the information in a more positive light.
• Keep an updated version of your bio on hand at all times. Your "story" can change quickly, and you'll want to have the latest version on hand when someone requests it. Try to update your bio at least once a year.	
• Be ready to adapt your bio to different needs.	

NOT LIKE THIS . . .

Gloria Hanlon, Managing Partner
Ms. Hanlon oversees corporate finance, acquisition strategy, and investor relations for White Mountain Ventures. Ms. Hanlon brings over 20 years' experience in global operations, accounting and finance, investment banking, strategic planning, mergers and acquisitions, initial public offerings, and SEC due diligence and reporting. Ms. Hanlon's experience extends from executing turnaround strategies and providing financial management advice for large and small companies, which included Eluctant, Inc., fivewaves.com, Vellum Express Corporation, Maxxbank, Digital Technologies, Arthur Kane Corporation, Manitoba Beverage Corporation, Saunders & Colvin, LLP, and Erdelyi Financial Services. Ms. Hanlon is active on several advisory boards including the Brian Norton Institute, the High School of Economics and Finance and RePol, Inc. (an intelligence and securities company for which she is a Cofounder and Chief Financial Officer). In 1994, Ms. Hanlon was appointed by the Governor of Georgia, Frank Molton, to be a member of the Operation Legacy Project, responsible for attracting major corporations to the Revitalization Projects in preparation for the 1996 Centennial Olympics Games in Atlanta. In 1998, the Mayor of Newton, Massachusetts, Jeffrey Bonomo, assigned her to head the committee to replicate the High School of Economics and Finance in his district. Ms. Hanlon has been a frequent adjunct professor for Business and Finance at Boston University. Ms. Hanlon has BA in Accounting and MBA in Finance from the University of Pennsylvania. In 1981, Gloria Hanlon completed the Executive Management Program in Mergers & Acquisitions and Corporate Finance at Boston University and is a Licensed Certified Public Accountant in the state of Massachusetts. Ms. Hanlon speaks several languages, including French, Italian, and German.

> Yikes! Who wants to read this huge chunk of text?
> For your readers' sake, break a long bio like this into smaller, easy-to-read paragraphs.

> This bio doesn't really tell us much about Gloria Hanlon, does it? It's more like a laundry list than a person's story. It's great to include an impressive list of names and titles, but it's even better to use that information in a way that explains who you are professionally.

. . . LIKE THIS

> See how breaking the bio into paragraphs makes it much friendlier to the eye? It's easier for readers to process information when it's presented in smaller chunks.

Gloria Hanlon, Managing Partner

Gloria Hanlon oversees corporate finance, acquisition strategy, and investor relations for White Mountain Ventures. Ms. Hanlon brings over 20 years' experience in global operations, accounting and finance, investment banking, strategic planning, mergers and acquisitions, initial public offerings, and SEC due diligence and reporting. Before joining White Mountain, she was a Senior Consultant with the Senomar Group, where she executed turnaround strategies and provided financial management advice for large and small companies, including Eluctant, Inc., fivewaves.com, Vellum Express Corporation, Maxxbank, Digital Technologies, Arthur Kane Corporation, Manitoba Beverage Corporation, Bell & Colvin, LLP, and Erdelyi Financial Services.

> Adding this information about even one prior position provides a context for Gloria's experience with the companies she's worked with.

Ms. Hanlon is Cofounder and Chief Financial Officer of RePol, Inc., a Boston-based intelligence and securities company.

> This paragraph is about Gloria's "day job."

Ms. Hanlon is active on several advisory boards, including the Brian Norton Institute and Boston's High School of Economics and Finance. In 1994, she was appointed by the Governor of Georgia, Frank Molton, to be a member of the Operation Legacy Project responsible for attracting major corporations to the Revitalization Projects in preparation for the 1996 Centennial Olympics Games in Atlanta. In 1998, Mayor Jeffrey Bonomo of Newton, Massachusetts, appointed her to head the committee to replicate the High School of Economics and Finance in his district.

> And this paragraph is about her service.

Ms. Hanlon has been a frequent adjunct professor for Business and Finance at Boston University, where she completed the Executive Management Program in Mergers & Acquisitions and Corporate Finance in 1981. She holds a BA in Accounting and MBA in Finance from the University of Pennsylvania. Ms. Hanlon is a Licensed Certified Public Accountant in the state of Massachusetts. She speaks several languages, including French, Italian, and German.

> And this paragraph is about her education.

BIOS FOR THE SELF-EMPLOYED

Bios for consultants, entrepreneurs, and business owners tend to be more self-promoting than those for business employees. If you're counting on your bio to promote your own consulting practice or other business, it's important to begin your bio with a bang.

> Stephen Smith has been called "a turnaround artist," "a corporate miracle worker," and a "reengineering magician" for his ability to turn around companies teetering on the brink. His 42 years in corporate strategy, finance, marketing, and operations give him a uniquely broad perspective on the organization and its requirements. With clients ranging from small, family-run businesses to Fortune 500 corporations, Mr. Smith brings an unusually wide range of experience to his management consulting practice.

Bios for company websites tend to be one paragraph in length and highlight the achievements of the individual that support his or her current position.

> **Jeff Hyman**
> A senior project director at ART Technology, Jeff is responsible for overseeing all project management activity. Jeff's experience in managing projects is wide and diverse. Jeff has an extensive background in managing large-scale technology projects for clients such as Mutual Investments, MPR Global Communications, RobertsMason, Redolent Financial, JR Norman, CSUonline, and Level 4 Communications. Prior to joining ART Technology, Jeff was a project director at LearnOnline, where he oversaw client engagements and led a team of project managers. Jeff's experience also includes three years as director of software engineering at Wellesley Interactive and six years as a software engineer for PTE. Jeff received his MBA in finance and marketing from Holden University and a BS in computer science from the University of Minnesota.

A biography is considered complete if it merely accounts for six or seven selves, whereas a person may well have as many thousand.

—*Virginia Woolf*

SPEECH

Public speaking is said to inspire greater fear than any other challenge or phobia (even spiders). On the other hand, it can also offer great rewards. One way to help overcome your apprehension is to write a speech you're confident about. A good speech can inspire your listeners, enhance your reputation, and build your confidence. The more preparation you put in, the stronger the end product will be.

Introduction

The **purpose** of a speech might be to inspire, educate, persuade, entertain, or some combination thereof. If you've been asked to give a speech at an event, ask the organizers if they have something in mind so that you can tailor your speech to their purposes.

The primary audience for a speech is a **listener** rather than a **reader**, although you might be asked for a copy of your speech. (Make sure your speech is in good condition before you send it out. You may want to go back and make some edits to the text before you share it.)

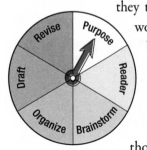

As you plan your speech, consider your audience carefully. What do they think and believe? What will they expect from you? What topic would most engage them? Your listeners will give you immediate feedback in the form of attention, applause, or yawns. Think hard about what it will be like to listen to your speech, and allow that information to shape what you write. An unsatisfactory speech can be painful for both listeners and speaker alike, so be sure you do your best.

Brainstorm widely. Your speech will be more interesting if you've thought carefully about your topic, examined it from different perspectives, and really sorted through what you think and what you want to say.

Organize your speech carefully. Your listeners depend on you to signal them the shape of your speech: the introduction of the main idea, transitions between points and the signal that the speech is drawing to a close, and the actual conclusion.

As you **draft**, keep in mind that the average speech goes about 120 words per minute. Use this to gauge length. Expect to go through several **drafts**. It's wise to ask a colleague or friend to read a draft of your speech or—even better—to listen to you practice and give you feedback. As you practice, you'll find areas that you want to **revise**, for instance language that looks fine on the page but doesn't sound right spoken aloud. You might also find missing content or that your speech is simply too long.

DO	DON'T
• Start your speech-writing or presentation project early, especially if you don't have a lot of experience giving speeches. You'll want plenty of time to find the right topic, go through a couple of drafts, and rehearse the speech before you deliver it. Don't leave it all for the last minute.	• Don't talk *at* your audience. Instead, talk *to* them. As you draft your speech, imagine you are talking to an individual.
• Make the topic of your speech relevant to your listeners. Select an issue that will engage their attention, and give it substantial treatment.	• Don't use fancy words where ordinary ones will do. Aim to impress your audience with the quality of your ideas, not your access to a thesaurus.
• Imagine a model listener. Who is that person you're talking to? What does he know about the topic? What does he care about? What can you share with him that will interest him? Imagining a single listener can be easier than writing a speech for a crowd.	• Don't feel you need to give a complete or comprehensive treatment of the topic. Rather than give an exhaustive account of something, choose a particularly interesting angle and explore it. Plan to talk about no more than three main points in your speech.
• Begin your speech with an attention grabber. You might use an anecdote, a joke, or a quotation. You might also pose a problem that you will solve over the course of the speech. Your objective is to hook your audience and motivate them to continue listening to you. A boring opening usually signals a boring speech.	• Don't exceed your time limit. Event organizers and listeners alike will appreciate it if you come in slightly under the time limit. Don't think that sneaking in just another minute or two will enhance your speech; it's likely just the opposite. Leave them wishing for more, not wishing you'd go away.
• Let your speech or presentation sound like spoken rather than written language. The language you use in your speech will likely be more formal than the language you use in the office day to day, but you should not sound like you're reading. Practice your speech; when you hit areas that are difficult to say, rewrite them in more conversational language.	
• Clearly mark transitions for your listeners. Readers have the luxury of going back and rereading if they lose the train of thought in a written piece. Listeners cannot do this. Offer brief summaries of your points as you go along, clearly state when you're shifting perspectives, refer back to earlier	

DO (CONTINUED)

parts of the speech, and let listeners know when you're about to conclude.

- Finish with a punch. Provide a conclusion that the audience will remember—sum up your points, end with a compelling story, or do something else to tie a nice bow on your speech. Leave the audience nodding in agreement or smiling.
- Print your speech so it's easy to read. Double-space it, and use a large font. You don't want to be squinting at the page or losing your place.

SPEECH EXCERPTS

Doug Bain, Boeing's senior vice president and general counsel, delivered a speech about company scandals at the Boeing Leadership Meeting on January 5, 2006.

OPENING

> Mr. Bain opens his speech with a joke that acknowledges the seriousness of the situation and engages his listeners.

> Mr. Bain uses plain, conversational English.

Good morning.

As I walked up here, I think I heard [Boeing Chairman and CEO] Jim McNerney mutter, "Here comes Dr. Death."

Jim asked me to give you kind of a candid assessment of our major scandals and how we got there.

My overall message is fairly simple: We as the leaders of the Boeing Company get to choose what kind of culture we are going to have. And we make these choices every day by what we do and frankly what we choose not to do. But the consequences of all those choices are our collective responsibility.

• • •

CONCLUSION

The cultural question we need to ask, of course, is are we going to model the leadership values? And are we going to hold accountable those of us in this room, our subordinates and even our superiors?

... I really feel that we've turned the corner and that there's a renewed emphasis and energy on doing the right thing. But the bottom line is, we just cannot stand another major scandal.

And all it takes for there to be a next time is one misstep by one employee, and it doesn't really matter whether that employee is a rank-and-file person or somebody in this room. Our jobs as the leaders of this enterprise is to establish a culture that ensures that there is no next time. And frankly the choice is ours.

Thank you.

Excerpted from "Transcript of Speech by Boeing's Doug Bain," *Seattle Times*, January 31, 2006, http://seattletimes.com/html/businesstechnology/2002772424_boeingtranscript31.html.

> Mr. Bain closes the speech, which has been about a difficult topic, on a serious but uplifting note.

Sheryl Sandberg, CEO of Facebook, addressed TEDWomen with the talk "Why We Have Too Few Women Leaders."

So for any of us in this room today, let's start out by admitting we're lucky. We don't live in the world our mothers lived in . . . where career choices for women were so limited. And if you're in this room today, most of us grew up in a world where we had basic civil rights. . . . But all that aside, we still have a problem, and it's a real problem. And the problem is this: women are not making it to the top of any profession anywhere in the world. The numbers tell the story quite clearly. 190 heads of state—nine are women. . . . In the corporate sector, women at the top, C-level jobs, board seats—tops out at 15, 16 percent. . . .

We also have another problem, which is that women face harder choices between professional success and personal fulfillment. A recent study in the U.S. showed that, of married senior managers, two-thirds of the married men had children and only one-third of the married women had children. . . .

My generation really, sadly, is not going to change the numbers at the top. . . . We are not going to get to where 50 percent of the population—in my generation, there will not be 50 percent of people at the top of any industry. But I'm hopeful that future generations can. I think a world that was run where half of our countries and half of our companies were run by women, would be a better world. . . . I have two children. I have a five year-old son and a three year-old daughter. I want my son to have a choice to contribute fully in the workforce or at home. And

OPENING

> Ms. Sandberg uses a casual, conversational style.

> Ms. Sandberg captures the attention of her audience by opening with a statement of a problem that interests them.

> This transition is clearly indicated, making it easier for listeners to follow the speech.

CONCLUSION

| The speech ends on an upbeat, inspiring note. | I want my daughter to have the choice to not just succeed, but to be liked for her accomplishments. |

> Thank you.

Excerpted from Sheryl Sandberg, "Transcript of Sheryl Sandberg's TED Women Video: Why We Have Too Few Women Leaders," August 9, 2011, reprinted at www.85broads.com/public/blogs/mareill-kiernan/articles/transcript-of-sheryl-sandbergs-tedwomen-video-why-we-have-too-few-women-leaders#PROVzU3uD1uebhKe.99.

POWERPOINT PRESENTATION

According to one estimate, thirty million PowerPoint presentations occur every day throughout the world. PowerPoint is ubiquitous in schools and workplaces, having supplanted more traditional visual aids like whiteboards, flip charts, and overhead projectors.

The term "death by PowerPoint" was first coined by Angela R. Garber and is widely used to describe the stultifying boredom that a bad PowerPoint presentation can cause. The web is awash in funny examples of terrible PowerPoint slides. But when it's your own presentation at stake, it's no laughing matter.

Introduction

Being clear about your **purpose** is absolutely crucial to creating a successful PowerPoint presentation. Is the presentation purely informational? Are you trying to sell something? If your purpose is vague, your presentation will be, too.

For PowerPoint presentations, it's probably more helpful to think of your **audience** than your **reader**. As you build your slides, think from the point of view of the people who have to look at what you create. What information do they need? What are they expecting from your presentation? How would you feel sitting through this presentation? How can you make the slides easy for the audience to read and ensure that they reinforce your main points? Putting yourself in the shoes—or the seat—of an audience member is an excellent way to guide your preparation of your slides.

Before you start, or as you develop your slides, **brainstorm** your content. Are you presenting complete information? Is anything missing? Think about the order in which you present your information. **Organize** your presentation for maximum effectiveness, and be willing to reorganize your slides, if necessary, as the presentation develops.

You can **draft** your slides in PowerPoint, in Word, by hand, or whatever way makes it easiest for you to generate content and see the full picture. Be aware that your first draft will probably be too long and too detailed, but don't worry—you can refine your presentation later.

As you **revise** your draft, take note that most of the problems people have in creating successful PowerPoint slides arise from trying to make the format do things it's not really suited to do. PowerPoint was developed as a visual aid to assist you when you're making a speech or presentation. Your slides should prompt you as you go through your talk, and they should serve as visual reinforcement for the audience of your most important ideas. PowerPoint was never intended as a way to communicate large amounts of data. Presenters run into trouble when they start using their slides as "data dumps." Think again about your purpose and the needs of your audience, and revise accordingly. Be sure your revision process includes careful proofreading.

DO	DON'T
• Choose the right template or design for your slides. Some organizations have templates available for your use, or at least a style guide to help you craft your slides. If no such template is available, consider asking colleagues if they have a template you can use. Templates are also available through the program itself or from Internet sites. There's no sense in reinventing the wheel when you create a PowerPoint presentation.	• Don't crowd your slides with a lot of text and graphics. Slides with plenty of white space are more inviting and easier to read.
	• Don't write out your entire presentation on your slides. Remember, the slides should contain just your main points. If the whole content is on the slides, why does the audience need you?
• Choose readable fonts, and limit the number of fonts you use. Some fonts are easier to read than others. Select fonts that look clean and clear on your slides. As a general rule, limit yourself to no more than two different fonts per slide. If you add more, your slide may look messy and distracting.	• Don't present graphics or text that are too small or too detailed for the audience to see easily. If you have a key chart or table that is complex, present a simplified version of it on your slide and give the audience the full version, printed on hard copy, to examine more closely.
	• Don't distract your audience with busy backgrounds. PowerPoint offers a lot of built-in

| **DO** (CONTINUED) | **DON'T** (CONTINUED) |

In addition, you should use fonts that are widely available. Very unusual fonts, even if they're attractive, may not read or align properly on other people's computers if you happen to e-mail your presentation. Stick to a few basic, simple fonts.

- Keep text to a minimum. You should present just your main points on your slides. An audience faced with a text-heavy slide will either lose interest immediately or start reading the slide. People can read faster than you can talk. If your audience reads every detail of your content before you present it, they'll stop listening to you. Putting too much content on your slides will inevitably cause your audience to disengage.

TIP

The old rubric "tell them what you're going to tell them, tell them, then tell them what you've told them" is very good advice for a PowerPoint presentation. Open the presentation with an overview slide to let the audience know what's coming. Coordinate subsequent slides with this overview. Then create a conclusion page that reinforces the key takeaway points of the presentation.

- Create a leave-behind with more detailed information. If you want to ensure your audience has every detail you mentioned in your talk, create and print a fuller version of your presentation and distribute it.
- Use animation and sound sparingly and strategically to support the message of your presentation. The golden rule is this: if it enhances the meaning and clarity of your presentation, use it. If it competes with your content, it will distract people.
- In bullet points, use parallel grammatical constructions to help people follow your ideas easily.
- Use formatting effects like bold and italic sparingly and consistently. Unless they clearly support

graphics and backgrounds, but that doesn't mean you should use them.

- Don't use meaningless animation. Again, the fact that fancy animation tools are available doesn't mean they're a good idea for your presentation. Use animation when it can help get your point across more successfully, not animation for its own sake. If people in the audience are sitting there thinking "cool animation," then they're not paying attention to your message.

your message, avoid using these potentially distracting formatting tools.

- Proofread your slides very carefully. Ideally, have someone else who is not familiar with the presentation proof it for you. A presentation that contains typos, misspellings, and punctuation errors can be very embarrassing and can undermine your credibility.

NOT LIKE THIS . . .

Best Practices During Phone Calls

Virtual teams typically meet by phone. Observing these guidelines can help participants work comfortably and productively on the phone.

- **Introduce yourself**
  - At the beginning of each phone call, be sure to introduce yourself if you are speaking with people you have not met before. Be sure to let others know your rold on the project.
- **Identify yourself when you begin to speak**
  - As the call continues, particularly if you are working with remote colleagues you do not know well, identify yourself when you begin to speak to avoid confusion about who is speaking.
- **State roles and responsibilities**
  - Ensure that every team member on the call understands what their role and responsbility is on the project.
- **Set expectations**
  - Set expectations at the beginning of each call, including how long you expect the call to last and what you expect to accomplish.
- **Review actin items and send out summary list**
  - At the conclusion of the call, review any action items. After the call ends, the project manager should sent around a list of agreed-upon action items, with deadlines, to the entire team.

This presenter has put the entire text of the presentation on the slide. The result is too much text, in a tiny, unreadable font.

This slide contains four different fonts, creating a busy and unattractive look.

There are several typos on this slide. The presenter likely didn't notice them because of the density of the slide, but someone in the audience is sure to spot them.

The presenter has tried to make the slide more interesting by selecting a background from PowerPoint's background library. But this graphic is too much on this already-busy slide.

. . . LIKE THIS

This much-improved slide contains just the main points, allowing the presenter to elaborate on the details. It's much easier for the audience to scan.

The background image is not distracting. It adds interest to the slide, and it's relevant to the topic of building global virtual teams.

Best Practices During Phone Calls

- Introduce yourself

- Identify yourself when you begin to speak

- State roles and responsibilities

- Set expectations

- Review action items

This version of the slide contains only two fonts, both easy to read, which creates a cleaner and more inviting look.

"What are those things in the background? Are those fish? Why fish? Maybe they're leaves. No, they really look like fish. I'd like some fish tacos. I wonder where I could I get fish tacos around here."
And your audience has just missed the conclusion of your presentation.
This "fossil fish" background comes with the PowerPoint software, but that doesn't mean it's appropriate for your presentation.
Be sure your backgrounds, graphics, and animations help get your message across rather than distracting the audience.

NOT LIKE THIS . . .

Conclusion: Keys to successful Virtual Teaming

- Strong **team-building**
- Choose the right **communication** method
- Best practices during **phone calls**
- Make a **connection** with your colleagues
- **Cultural** challenges
- Stay **open** to feedback

Some words on the slide have been bolded, but the pattern seems to be random. Elements that are formatted in this way should be parallel and consistent.

The bullet entries are grammatically inconsistent, which makes it harder for the audience to grasp the message.

. . . LIKE THIS

Conclusion

- Build a strong team

- Communicate appropriately

- Foster team connections

- Address cultural misunderstandings

- Encourage feedback

> The presenter has chosen a neutral background, which adds interest without distracting the audience.

> The bullet entries are grammatically parallel, each beginning with an imperative verb. As a result, the concluding message is clear and easy to remember.

Three Keys to Successful Presentations

As you develop the slides for your presentation, consider how the audience will experience them. Your slides should engage your audience rather than simply being a crutch for you.

- Don't put too much text on your slides. Effective slides are *scanned*, not read.

- Use your slides to pique the audience's interest. Put just your key ideas on the slide, not your entire talk. Make the audience curious about what you'll say next.

- Use your slides to reinforce your most important points. If information is both heard and read, your audience will retain it better.

QUESTIONNAIRE

A questionnaire is a kind of survey that's especially useful for collecting data from large numbers of people. Conducting a survey can be a significant investment of time and resources, and it's critical to take the time to design your questionnaire carefully.

Most business-related questionnaires are conducted online, where responses are easy to collect and tabulate, though some organizations still use paper surveys. Commercial websites like SurveyMonkey and Zoomerang allow you to create surveys free and will tabulate the results for you.

Introduction

The **purpose** of a questionnaire is to gather information from multiple people. Think carefully about what information you want to collect through your questionnaire. What problem are you trying to solve? How will you use the information you gather? The more specific you are about your purpose, the more helpful your questionnaire will be. Keep your **reader** foremost in your mind as you design your survey. Typically survey respondents are not required to cooperate with you, so you should make it as easy and pleasant as possible for them to assist you in completing the questionnaire. **Brainstorming** questions can help you pinpoint your exact purpose. It can be helpful to solicit questions from your colleagues. You will likely come up with more questions than you need. As you work, cull them down to only the essentials. **Organize** your questions in a logical order, progressing from the general to the specific or from factual to attitudinal, depending on the content of your questionnaire. Writing survey questions can be tricky, so you should plan to go through multiple **drafts** of your questionnaire. Share your draft with colleagues and **revise** according to their feedback. When you have a draft you're happy with, it's wise to pilot the survey to a small test group and interview them about how the survey went. **Revise** again before you send the questionnaire out to the respondents.

Types of Survey Questions

Consider carefully the types of questions you want to use in your survey. There are advantages and drawbacks to each.

Closed-ended questions give the respondent a limited set of possible responses. They may be yes/no questions, multiple-choice questions, or questions to be answered on a rated scale (e.g., from 1 to 5). Closed-ended questions provide results that are easy to tabulate and analyze.

Open-ended questions, on the other hand, provide respondents with blank space to write out their answer. They allow the respondent more scope in their answers and can provide interesting data. However, they cannot be tabulated and analyzed in the same way as closed-ended questions.

As you design your questionnaire, think ahead to how you want to tabulate, analyze, and report the results, and create your questions accordingly.

DO	DON'T
• Keep your questionnaire as brief as possible. In most cases, respondents are volunteering their time, and the longer the questionnaire, the less likely they are to complete it. Be sure you're asking only the essential questions.	• Don't write leading questions. Take care to phrase your questions in a neutral way without hinting at the answer you would like to receive. If you're unsure, ask someone to read your questions for you.
• Use simple language. Difficult vocabulary and complex sentence structure can make questions hard to understand.	• Don't use jargon or abbreviations that your readers might not understand. Keep your language as simple as possible. If you do have to use complex language or abbreviations, make sure you define them.
• Write short sentences. Questions become more difficult to understand and answer when they get too long.	• Don't write questions using double negatives. They can be difficult to understand.
• Begin the questionnaire with easy, interesting questions. Save the more difficult or intimidating questions for later.	• Don't write questions that are about more than one thing. For instance, the question "Do you

DO (CONTINUED)	**DON'T** (CONTINUED)
• Arrange your questions in a logical order, proceeding from the general to the specific. • Consider carefully the kind of questions to use. Closed-ended questions are easier to tabulate than open-ended questions. • Use a consistent rating scale. If you are using questions that have a rating scale for an answer, keep that scale consistent across the entire survey. • Test your questionnaire before you send it out. Try to get a test group of ten to fifteen people. Interview them after they've taken the questionnaire to find out if any of the questions were hard to understand or any of your questions were leading.	find weekly meetings and monthly debrief sessions useful?" should be split into two separate questions. • Don't ask questions about information that's difficult to recall. For instance, asking questions about the distant past is less likely to yield good data than asking questions about more recent events.

NOT LIKE THIS . . .

In order to improve our services in the future, Canyon Retreat Conference Center is requesting your assistance in completing this brief questionnaire about your stay with us.

Thank you for your participation!

> This question is awkward and a little difficult to understand.

(1) What is the frequency of your attending conferences on a yearly basis? (Please check one.)

☐ 1–2
☐ 3–5
☐ 6–10
☐ More than 10

(2) Of those conferences, how many take place at a commercial hotel vs. a purpose-built conference facility? (Please check one.)

> This answer should include 0.

☐ 1–2
☐ 3–5

☐ 6–10
☐ More than 10

(3) What do you perceive as the advantages of a purpose-built conference facility vs. a commercial hotel?
(Please check all that apply.)

☐ Staff more understanding of and more responsive to guest needs
☐ Conference rooms more comfortable
☐ Better acoustics
☐ Better climate control
☐ More comfortable guest rooms

> This is a leading question. Perhaps the respondent doesn't perceive any advantages at all, but there's no way for him to indicate that.

(4) Which disadvantages of a commercial hotel are least important to you?
(Please rank in order 1 to 4.)

_____ Staff not attuned to needs of conference guests
_____ Poor acoustics in conference rooms
_____ Too cold in conference rooms
_____ Lack of suitable areas for socializing

> This question contains a double-negative and is difficult to understand.

> A scale like this should specify what the numbers 1 and 4 mean. Most or least important?

(5) What is your favorite part of the Canyon Retreat experience, and why?

(6) If you would recommend Canyon Retreat to a friend, why?

(7) What part of the Canyon Retreat experience would you most like to be improved, and why?

> Questions 5–7 are open-ended questions. It's fine to have as many open-ended questions as you like, but you should be aware that it is more difficult and time-consuming to tabulate their answers.

... LIKE THIS

In order to improve our services in the future, Canyon Retreat Conference Center is requesting your assistance in completing this brief questionnaire about your stay with us.

Thank you for your participation!

> Phrased this way, the question is much easier to understand.

(1) How many conferences do you attend every year?
(Please check one.)

- ☐ 1–2
- ☐ 3–5
- ☐ 6–10
- ☐ More than 10

(2) Of those conferences, how many take place at a commercial hotel vs. a purpose-built conference facility?
(Please check one.)

> The scale now allows for an answer of 0.

- ☐ 0–2
- ☐ 3–5
- ☐ 6–10
- ☐ More than 10

> The question has been rewritten so that it does not "lead" the reader. The response "none of the above" has been added. Rewriting this question also allows the writer to eliminate the confusing question 4.

(3) Which features of a purpose-built conference facility appeal to you?
(Please check all that apply.)

- ☐ Staff more understanding of and more responsive to guest needs
- ☐ Conference rooms more comfortable
- ☐ Better acoustics
- ☐ Better climate control
- ☐ More comfortable guest rooms
- ☐ None of the above

> Question 6 above has been eliminated. It was close in meaning to question 5 and didn't justify the additional effort required to tabulate its answers.

(5) What is your favorite part of the Canyon Retreat experience, and why?

(6) What part of the Canyon Retreat experience would you most like to be improved, and why?

MESSAGE OF INTRODUCTION

Written introductions are a vital part of networking. When you have contacts or associates who you think might benefit from knowing one another, send an introduction to start the dialogue between the two.

In business, most introductions are made by e-mail. In some situations, you may still use a printed letter. If you do write a letter, bear in mind that it will likely be more formal than an e-mail introduction.

Introduction

The **purpose** of an introduction is to connect people who have common interests. An introduction is different from a letter of recommendation, which provides a detailed endorsement of the person; an introduction is usually shorter and less detailed than a letter of recommendation. Consider what your **readers'** attitudes are likely to be. Often you will have discussed the introduction with one or both parties prior to sending it, to assess the level of interest and to obtain permission. Even if you have discussed it before, though, remember that your readers don't know each other and will need to be reminded about the reason for the introduction. Unless it's a very brief and uncomplicated introduction, you're wise to spend at least a little time **brainstorming** the best way to frame the introduction. What information can you provide that will make the parties interested in one another? Most business introductions are brief, so don't require a lot of **organizing**. However, in some situations you should be sensitive to rank and seniority and ensure that you address the senior party first. The Model Outline provides guidance. It's not a bad idea to review your **draft**—even if it is very brief—before you send it out. Read over the introduction from the point of view of both parties. Is it clear why you're writing? Do you provide enough information about each party to make them interested in contacting each other? If not, **revise** until it works.

MODEL OUTLINE

An introductory message should be brief and to the point.

Salutation: Address both parties in the salutation. The senior party should be named first.

Opening: Use your first sentence to state that you're making an introduction.

Middle: State briefly why you think the parties might be interested in meeting.

Conclusion: If you are asking for a favor, explicitly or implicitly, thank the reader who might be granting the favor. End on a note of good wishes to both parties.

DO	DON'T
• Get consent from both parties before you make the introduction, if you feel there is any chance that either might be uncomfortable or unwilling. An unwanted introduction out of the blue can be very awkward, and it won't help your relationship with the reader.	• Don't make an introduction if you are at all uncomfortable about it. An introduction is an implied recommendation, so don't put your reputation on the line if you have any doubts about either party.
• Address both readers in your salutation. It's usually wise to place the name of the senior or more powerful person first in the salutation.	• Don't go overboard with your praise for one or both parties. Remember, this is just an introduction, not a full-blown recommendation.
• Remind the readers of the context of the introduction if you have mentioned it to them before.	• Don't go on too long. Keep the introduction brief and concise. If you wish to provide background information about either party, consider sending a bio or a link to that person's website either in this message or in a separate one.
• Offer a bit of information about both of the parties being introduced. In a quick e-mail, just a sentence can be enough.	
• If you are making the introduction specifically to serve the needs of one party, say so.	• Don't overstate the benefits of the introduction to both parties when it is clear a favor is being asked. If you are introducing a young graduate to an executive, for instance, it is clear that the introduction will likely have greater business benefit to the younger person.
• Mention how you met the parties, if that seems relevant.	
• Suggest how forging this connection could be beneficial for each of the readers. However, if it is clear that one party will benefit far more than the other, don't feel you need to invent benefits for the party who is granting the favor.	• Don't say anything to suggest that either of your readers is obliged to go forward with the meeting. Simply make the introduction and allow them to decide how to proceed.
• Close by thanking the party who is granting the favor. Wish both readers well.	• Don't offer to make arrangements for a meeting unless you are certain both parties are on board and comfortable with your playing this role.

NOT LIKE THIS . . .

Dear Smythe, dear Ron,

It's my pleasure to introduce you two. Smythe, Ron is a friend of mine from Hughes who has a background in commercial real estate and is hoping to get back into the field. I would very much appreciate it if you had the time to speak with him. Ron, Smythe is the sailing friend I mentioned who runs the tenant-rep agency in the city. His business is extremely successful; no one can give you better advice. I know you'll have a lot to talk about, and I hope the connection will be helpful for you both.

All the best,

Veronica

> Veronica should have cleared this with Smythe first. She's putting him on the spot with this introduction.

> Poor Smythe. Is Ron going to ask him for a job? Does he need this additional complication in his life? He was completely blindsided by this message.

> It's difficult to see how Smythe will be helped by this connection, since it's obvious that Ron is the one who needs help.

. . . LIKE THIS

Dear Smythe, dear Ron,

It's my pleasure to introduce you two. Smythe, thank you so much for agreeing to speak with Ron. I know how busy you are, and I appreciate it. I know you'll have a lot to talk about, and I hope you will enjoy meeting each other.

All the best,

Veronica

> Veronica has evidently communicated with Smythe prior to the introduction and received his okay. She will have briefed Smythe on Ron's background and his reasons for wanting to speak with Smythe.

> Veronica is straightforward that the introduction is really about Smythe helping Ron, and she thanks Smythe for his time.

> Veronica does not pretend that Ron, who is obviously junior, will help Smythe professionally. But this conclusion is pleasant and courteous and should put them both at ease.

MESSAGE OF COMMENDATION

A message of commendation conveys recognition of someone's achievement or deeds. You can send it to the individual you wish to commend, or to her supervisor, or to both. You might send a commendation to a person in your own organization or in a business you have worked with.

A letter of commendation is similar to a testimonial written for a business (see Testimonial on page 509). While the aim of a testimonial is typically to promote a business, the aim of a commendation is to promote an individual.

A message of commendation may be an e-mail or a printed letter. Generally a printed letter is more formal and carries more weight.

Introduction

A message of commendation may serve several **purposes**. It may be a simple acknowledgment of someone's achievement or good performance. It's also a kind of thank-you. As such, it can strengthen relationships and build goodwill. In addition, it can serve as a formal acknowledgment of someone's achievement: it may be placed into an employee's records. This kind of endorsement may come into play during future decisions about compensation or promotion. Your **reader** may be the person being commended or her supervisor. Even if you address the message to the commendee in question, you should think from the point of view of her supervisor. As you **brainstorm**, choose details that show most clearly the benefit of the person's actions. If a person was exceptionally courteous, that's nice, but if the courtesy helped the company secure a valuable account, that counts for more. The Model Outline provides an **organizational** strategy you can use. Your initial **draft** may be too long, particularly if you are recounting an incident. It's a good idea to write it all out and **revise** later, both for length and for impact.

MODEL OUTLINE

A message of commendation should be explicit and concise.
Opening: Let the reader know your purpose for writing at the very beginning of the message.
Middle: Provide details about what the commendee did, and the effect her action had on you.
Conclusion: As you close, repeat your message of commendation, thank the reader, and end on a note of goodwill.

DO	DON'T
• Send your commendation in a timely fashion. It will have more impact if it arrives soon after the event or incident you're writing about.	• Don't write a commendation in a slapdash way. If you're going to do it, take the time to make it as helpful to the commendee as possible.
• Try to send the message to the right person. Find the name of the commendee's supervisor if possible.	• Don't put anything confidential in the message. One of the primary purposes of a commendation is to be seen by people. You cannot control who will see your message in the future—a business might even put it on its website—so be sure there's nothing in it that might embarrass or incriminate anyone.
• State the purpose of your message explicitly in the first sentence or at the very least in the first paragraph.	
• Be specific about the achievement or accomplishment. Show that you have personal familiarity with it.	
• Be explicit about the value of the accomplishment	• Don't go on too long. Keep the message succinct.

> If it is possible to cut a word out, always cut it out.
> —*George Orwell, novelist and essayist*

to the organization. A commendation will be most useful to the recipient when you can show that her action ultimately benefited the organization.

- Don't recommend a course of action regarding the person. Don't recommend a promotion or a raise. Your reader knows her business.
- Don't trash other employees in the process of praising one.
- Don't say anything to suggest that the person has asked you to write on her behalf or has told you what to say. Your commendation is more valuable if it hasn't been choreographed by the commendee.

NOT LIKE THIS . . .

> The letter would be more effective directed to the appropriate individual.

To the Manager:

Last Saturday, May 5, I was shopping in Better Dresses on the 3rd floor. I was looking for a dress to wear to a friend's wedding. While I was shopping, your employee Patricia Bensman approached me and offered to help. This happens so rarely it got my attention. I didn't have great expectations, but Patricia surprised me. She knows her stock, she knows her designers, and she really helped me. She pointed me toward a couple of really nice dresses. When I couldn't find my size, she showed me I could wear the same thing in a petite and told me which size. I was very pleased with the selections she recommended.

I understand that Patricia is currently a temp and has applied for a full-time permanent position at Fulton's. I can't understand why you haven't grabbed her yet. She should be managing the department! She is head and shoulders better than the average Fulton's employees who stand around talking to each other and ignoring customers. Please hire her and promote her!

Sincerely,

Caroline Walls
Caroline Walls

> This implied criticism of the other staff isn't really helpful.

> This narrative would have more impact if Caroline took the time to condense it.

> This comment might make the reader suspect that Patricia asked for the commendation, which could undermine its effectiveness.

> Except that's what the reader is doing . . .

> This may be true, but Caroline shouldn't praise Patricia at the expense of the other store employees. She's better off just focusing on Patricia's performance.

> It's better not to make specific human resources–related requests in a commendation letter.

...LIKE THIS

Gina Quayle
Head of Retail Staffing
Fulton's Department Store
May 8, 2012

> By finding the appropriate person to write to, Caroline can be sure the letter gets into the hands of someone who can help Patricia.

Dear Ms. Quayle:

> Caroline is smart to put her commendation of Patricia in the first sentence of the letter.

Last Saturday, May 5, your employee Patricia Bensman was exceptionally helpful to me. I was shopping in Better Dresses on the 3rd floor, looking for a dress to wear to a wedding. Patricia really knows her stock and her designers, and she took the time to make some excellent suggestions. When I had trouble finding my size, Patricia showed me the right size of petite to try. I never would have thought of this, and I will be using this trick frequently in the future! Because Patricia was so knowledgeable and helpful, I ended up buying two silk dresses instead of the one I went for.

> Caroline makes the point that Patricia has shown her how to buy dresses more successfully, which should please the management of Fulton's.

> By showing that Patricia's helpfulness led to a larger purchase, Caroline demonstrates the value of this sales associate to the business.

It's rare to find a sales associate with the kind of knowledge and interest in customers that Patricia displays. She is truly an asset to Fulton's. I will certainly look for her the next time I'm in. Thank you for having such a fine associate on your staff.

Sincerely,

> Caroline makes the point that Patricia outperforms the other sales associates without insulting them or the store.

Caroline Walls
Caroline Walls

> Caroline suggests that Fulton's hire and promote Patricia without doing so explicitly, and she indicates that having Patricia on staff reflects well on the store.

(See also *Teacher Recommendation for an Applicant to College*, page 345.)

LETTER OF RECOMMENDATION

At some point you may be asked to provide a letter of recommendation for someone you know—perhaps an employee who is applying for another position or a young person applying for school or college. If so, you're in the happy position to do someone a great deal of good. Writing a letter of recommendation is a serious responsibility, and you should plan to invest some time and effort in making your letter of recommendation as convincing and powerful as possible.

Introduction

The **purpose** of a letter of recommendation is to offer your personal and professional insight into the fitness of a candidate. Your letter can testify for the candidate in a way that her résumé or class transcript cannot. The **reader** of a letter of recommendation is hoping to get a sense of who the applicant is; what she can do; and if she will be a good fit for the job, academic program, or other opportunity. As you plan your letter, **brainstorm** from your reader's point of view: what will he be expecting or hoping to hear from you? What special things can you tell him about the candidate that the rest of her record may not demonstrate? Think about what the new environment will demand of the candidate, and provide details that indicate she'll do well in that setting. The Model Outline contains a sample **organizational** approach for your letter of recommendation. Allow yourself plenty of time to write and revise several **drafts** of your letter of recommendation; don't let the deadline creep up on you and force you to write the letter at the last minute. It's very likely your first draft will be too long. Write it all out, and take a break from it. As you **revise**, consider your reader's likely response and revise to sharpen and condense the message. Proofread carefully to ensure you've left no typos or other errors that might undermine the credibility of your message.

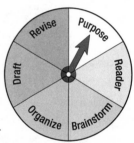

MODEL OUTLINE

A letter of recommendation should be one or two pages long. **Opening:** Announce at the very beginning of your letter who you're writing for and for what purpose. State explicitly that you recommend the candidate. Describe your relationship with the candidate and how long you have known her. **Middle:** Choose several points to discuss, and develop those. A laundry list of positive attributes will be less impressive than a thorough discussion of three or four. **Conclusion:** Close your letter by restating your endorsement of the candidate and hoping she will be successful in her application. Thank the reader for his consideration. Finally, let the reader know you are prepared to answer any questions he might have.

DO	DON'T
• Ensure you have all the information you need to write an effective letter. Understand the candidate's objective in asking for a letter of recommendation. It can be helpful to have a copy of the applicant's résumé on hand so that your comments are consistent with the candidate's work history.	• Don't agree to write a letter of recommendation for someone you feel is unqualified, someone you really can't support, or someone you don't really know. A lukewarm or vague letter of recommendation can cause damage, and it's better just to say no if you feel you can't offer good support.
• Announce in your first paragraph who you're writing for and why. Your first reference to the candidate should include both first and last name.	• Don't overstate the case. Unless the candidate really *is* the best employee you've ever had, avoid making such hyperbolic statements and stick to the plain truth.

DO (CONTINUED)	DON'T (CONTINUED)

- Use a businesslike tone. Even if you know the candidate personally, your letter will carry more weight if your point of view is professional.
- Make a clear statement early in the letter about how strong your support for the candidate is. Opening paragraphs make a powerful impression; don't wait until the end of the letter to let your reader know how you really feel.
- Let your reader know how long you've known the person you're writing for and in what capacity.
- Be specific and analytical about the person's qualities and accomplishments.
- Answer any questions you've been asked. For instance, if you've been given an application form that requests specific information about the candidate, be sure to supply it.
- Close your letter by repeating how strong your support is for the person, and make yourself available should the reader have any questions.
- Follow any instructions you have been given about how to submit the recommendation.

- Don't ignore weaknesses. If you are asked to write about the candidate's shortcomings, write about a weakness that can be overcome—or describe how the candidate is already overcoming it.
- Don't rely too much on vague descriptive terms like "great," "superior," and "outstanding." Instead, focus on the candidate's achievements, and the reader will get the point.
- Don't go on too long. Your letter should be no longer than two pages. Some applications will specify a length or provide a form to complete. If you go over the limit, you can actually hurt the candidate. Keeping the length under control will actually improve your letter by forcing you to select the most pertinent details and sharpen your argument.

NOT LIKE THIS . . .

> This statement is so vague it suggests Rob didn't really know Susan very well or what she did.

> This seems self-evident. It would be more compelling if Rob described Susan's responsibilities more specifically.

> Rob is clearly offering support for Susan, but overall his comments are rather vague and general.

> Rob mentions Susan's job title and the length of her employment, but he doesn't mention what their relationship was. This opening paragraph is not as compelling as it could be.

To the Hiring Manager:

I am writing to recommend Susan McCord for employment. Susan worked for Gibbons as Database Manager for seven years and did an extraordinary job for us.

Susan was an outstanding employee. As Database Manager, Susan was our go-to person for all of our database issues. Susan and her team worked extremely hard and always made deadlines, which were sometimes very tight. Throughout it all, Susan was always cheerful and helpful. We are all very sorry to see her go.

It is my pleasure to offer my support for Susan. If I can give you any further information, please do not hesitate to contact me at rstraker@gibbonintl.com.

Sincerely,

Rob Straker
Rob Straker

...LIKE THIS

To the Hiring Manager:

It is my great pleasure to recommend Susan McCord for employment. I supervised Susan in her job of Database Manager at Gibbons International for six years. We are all very sorry that Susan has decided to leave Chicago, but I am very pleased to offer my strongest possible recommendation for her in her new home.

> Rob notes how long he has known Susan, and in what capacity.

> Rob notes the strength of his support for Susan—his "strongest possible recommendation." The opening paragraph is very strong.

Susan headed a team that provided data for seven diverse groups of our organization, and she always carried out her work with diligence and aplomb. The Data Division received many requests for data, often sliced into unusual configurations. It's part of marketers' jobs to look for unusual and potentially fruitful patterns in data, and Susan's familiarity with our data and our software made these creative searches very successful. Many requests came in at the last minute, and Susan was ever unflappable, meeting one insane deadline after another.

> Rob supplies a description of Susan's job, the difficulties it entailed, and how Susan successfully coped with those difficulties.

In spite of her very high-stress and high-stakes position, Susan carried out her responsibilities with an almost superhuman goodwill. She was always a pleasure to be around and happy to do whatever it took to get the job done.

I should also mention that Susan was an exemplary role model and guide for the staff who reported to her. Many of her staff were recent graduates getting their first taste of a "real" job. Susan was brilliant at shepherding these entry-level employees, coaching them through stressful periods, and helping them grow into responsible and productive professionals. Susan's entire team was always ready to accept any challenge with diligence and good humor.

> This paragraph gives a vivid sense of what the job was like and that Susan made a very special contribution.

Rob repeats his endorsement of Susan in the closing of the letter.

In closing, it is my pleasure to offer Susan my very strongest recommendation. If I can give you any further information, please do not hesitate to contact me at rstraker@gibbonintl.com.

Sincerely,

Rob Straker
Rob Straker

LINKEDIN RECOMMENDATIONS

Recruiters and hiring managers do look at recommendations on LinkedIn. While those recommendations may not make or break an application, they can help. To make your recommendation as useful as possible, follow these guidelines:

- Provide a brief summary of how you know the candidate.
- Offer specifics about the candidate's performance, using measurable results wherever possible.
- Focus on transferable skills, since you don't know what positions the candidate might be applying for.
- Provide examples of the candidate's performance. Tell a story.
- For business owners, focus on how they stand out from the competition.
- Limit the recommendation to sixty to one hundred words.

AGENDA

An agenda helps participants prepare for a meeting by letting them know what topics will be discussed and what deliverables need to be prepared. An agenda also helps the meeting leader and participants keep the meeting on track. Afterward, an agenda can help provide structure and input for the preparation of the meeting notes or minutes.

Agendas are usually circulated by e-mail prior to meetings. It is helpful to have a way for participants to refer to the agenda during the meeting, so many people also provide printed copies of the agenda.

Introduction

The **purpose** of a meeting agenda is to let participants know what topics will be discussed in the meeting and what preparations they need to make. Ultimately, the purpose of an agenda is to ensure that meeting time is used productively and efficiently. The agenda is prepared primarily for the benefit of its **readers** so that everyone can be prepared and no one is blindsided by surprises during the meeting. As you prepare your agenda, think about what your readers need and expect. If the reason for the meeting is very straightforward, you may not need to do much **brainstorming**. That will depend entirely on the group and the organization. Some people circulate a draft to solicit input from others before finalizing the agenda. Most groups that meet regularly have a template they use over and over, swapping out the details. The Model Outline will help you **organize** your agenda. An agenda is often little more than a list of topics, so you don't have to worry about tone in your **draft**. Even if you don't circulate a draft widely, it's a good idea to have someone else check over your draft to ensure completeness. **Revise** according to their feedback.

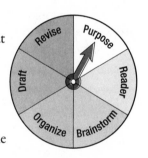

MODEL OUTLINE

An agenda provides a quick road map for a meeting. **Heading:** Include the title of the working group or meeting, if applicable, the date and place of the meeting, and the anticipated attendees. **Body:** List the topics to be covered, in order of discussion. Consider including the length of time budgeted for each item and the person responsible for that item. **Conclusion:** Note the date of the next meeting, if applicable.

DO	DON'T
• Note the time and place of the meeting as well as the names of the expected participants. If the meeting will take place over the phone, note the call-in details.	• Don't provide a lot of background information in the agenda itself. If participants need background information, attach that information to the agenda. The agenda itself should be an easily scannable road map of the meeting.
• List the topics to be covered in the meeting. Keep these lines brief and concise.	• Don't expect to run a meeting off an incomplete agenda. Allow yourself plenty of time to solicit input on topics from others. Coming into a meeting and realizing the agenda is incomplete defeats the purpose of having an agenda to organize your time.
• Note the approximate amount of time to be devoted to each topic on the agenda. Providing the timing can help participants stay on schedule and prevent the meeting from running late. Make sure your time segments add up correctly before you finalize the agenda.	
• Note the individual responsible for each topic on the agenda, if applicable.	• Don't forget to update the agenda. If you are using a template or an agenda from an earlier meeting, remember to update items like meeting date and participants.

- Use a template. If you expect to be responsible for creating the agendas for a series of meetings, develop an agenda template to help you save time in the future and create a standard that the group will expect.

LIKE THIS

Agenda

Lockstall Relocation Committee
June 7, 2013
11:00 a.m. EST
4th-Floor Conference Room

For Lockstall: Bryan Berman, Jill McDougal, Stephanie Page, Lin Yu.
By phone: Sherri Berndt, Ray Paredes
For Omega Properties: Lyn Wheeler

Call in: 888.999.0000 passcode 67540

Report on preliminary location visits—Bryan and Lyn (40 minutes)
Jpegs attached (sitevisits.zip)

Report on employee surveys and interviews—Lin (15 minutes)
Summary attached (staff.survey.draft.docx)

Report on proposed technology upgrades—Stephanie and Ray
(15 minutes)

Next meeting: July 6. Time TBA

Please contact Barb Jacobs at 212-800-0101 or
bjacobs@lockstall.net if you have any items you would like
placed on the agenda for the next meeting.

BUSINESS MEETING ANNOUNCEMENT

Many work groups rely exclusively on scheduling programs like Outlook to announce meetings and invite participants. If yours doesn't, you may need to compose your own meeting announcements. Writing a good announcement can be key to getting a good turnout and to ensuring that participants are prepared for their roles in the meeting.

Introduction

The **purpose** of a meeting announcement goes beyond simply letting people know there will be a meeting. The announcement should also let people know the stakes of the meeting and motivate them to attend. If your **readers** are required to attend, your task is pretty straightforward. If not, you need to consider what information might make them want to attend the meeting. As you **brainstorm**, make sure you're including complete information about the meeting—both its logistics and the purpose behind it. **Organize** the announcement so that its purpose is very clear; don't bury the lead. The tone you use as you **draft** will depend partly on your relationship with the readers. If you cannot compel them to attend the meeting, you'll need to put more energy into persuading them. Proofread your announcement very carefully before you send it out. If there are errors in the date, time, or place of the meeting, now is the time to catch them rather than after all your colleagues have seen them and confusion has spread. **Revise** accordingly.

DO	DON'T
• Develop the meeting agenda first. Include a copy of the agenda, or at least a summary of it, with the announcement. If you expect changes to the agenda before the meeting, let invitees know to expect an updated agenda.	• Don't wait till the last minute. People are busy, and meetings called on short notice may not be well attended.
• Note the purpose of the meeting on the announcement.	• Don't overwhelm readers with too much information. The meeting announcement should be concise. If you wish to include background information, supply that information as an attachment rather than in the body of the announcement.
• Let readers know what's at stake. Is this meeting a routine touch-base status conference, or is it critical to a project or an account?	• Don't take your readers for granted. If you're the boss, you can make people attend. If you don't

DO (CONTINUED)	**DON'T** (CONTINUED)

- Include all the logistical information about the meeting: date, time, place, and expected duration.
- Let readers know what—if anything—you expect them to do to prepare for the meeting. Do you want participants to provide a rundown of what they're doing? Do you want them to bring documents to share with each other? Let them know.
- Use formatting to highlight important information. Use spacing, bullet points, and bolding to make it easy to scan for critical information.
- Ask readers to RSVP, and let them know how.
- Send at least one reminder.

have the power to command, be sure you let your readers know why the meeting is important and that you appreciate their participation.

NOT LIKE THIS . . .

Last-minute meetings can be annoying, but they can also suggest a sense of urgency. Letting readers know why the meeting has been called late can engage their interest.

This invitation isn't particularly compelling and doesn't motivate readers to attend. The website is clearly going to happen anyway, so why make an effort to turn up?

Team:

Where?

Steve would like to meet about the website on Thursday at 11:00. Apologies for the short notice. He'd appreciate it if you could bring your ideas about how the new site could serve us best. It's very important that we get ideas from everyone, so please try to attend.

Thanks,

Amy

This is a good opportunity to appeal to the readers' interest. Why might the readers actually *want* to attend this meeting?

... LIKE THIS

Team:

Steve would like to meet about the website on Thursday at 11:00 in the 4th-floor conference room. I know it's short notice, but he just booked time with the designer on Friday and would like to get input from everyone so we can ensure the site serves everyone's needs. We need to get clarity on the following:

- Social media to appeal to younger market? Twitter feed on home page?
- Content management system to allow everyone to update their own pages. Do people want this?

Steve wants ideas from everyone, so please try to attend.

Please RSVP to me by COB on Wednesday.

Thanks,

Amy

> Maybe this is the same old meeting place, but it's helpful to be specific and it makes the meeting seem more important.

> Amy explains why the meeting is being called at short notice and indicates that the issue is fairly urgent.

> Amy lets readers know the stakes, which should motivate people to attend. These are important issues, and people will want to contribute their two cents.

> By setting an RSVP deadline, Amy reinforces the seriousness of the meeting.

MINUTES

The notes of a meeting, often known as minutes, provide a written record of the meeting. They include who attended, what was discussed, what decisions were made and who is responsible for carrying out these decisions, action steps to be taken for next time, and issues that were tabled for the next meeting.

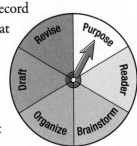

Minutes of meetings are often circulated by e-mail. Because minutes constitute an official record of a meeting, it is important that they be archived, either in print or electronic form.

Introduction

Meeting notes serve several **purposes**. They provide an official record of the meeting and may constitute a legal record of a company's actions. Good meeting notes can ensure that all team members are working with the same information. Minutes can also serve as a blueprint for future action. Meeting minutes may have several different kinds of **readers**: people who attended the meeting may use them to jog their memories about decisions made and responsibilities, and people who did not attend the meeting may rely on the minutes as an accurate record of what happened. Keep the needs of these various readers in mind. If you have kept accurate notes during the meeting itself, you won't need to do much **brainstorming**. If your memory is fuzzy or your notes incomplete, you may need to ask other meeting participants to fill in the details. Minutes are generally **organized** according to the order in which topics were discussed. Most groups that meet regularly have a template for meeting notes. The Model Outline will help you organize your minutes. As you write your **draft**, use an objective and businesslike tone. Once you have completed a draft of your minutes, check that draft against the notes you took in the meeting. It's wise to send the draft to another person who attended the meeting to check for accuracy and to proofread the document. **Revise** the minutes according to the feedback you get from your colleague.

MODEL OUTLINE

Meeting minutes provide a written record of what occurred in a meeting.
Heading: Record the name of the group and the purpose of the meeting. Note the date and time as well as the names of those in attendance.
Body: Record the topics discussed, in chronological order. Note any decisions made and the people responsible for carrying out those decisions. Note any agenda items tabled for the next meeting.
End: Note the time the meeting was adjourned and the date and time of the next meeting, if one was scheduled.

DO	DON'T
• Record the minutes from an objective point of view, using a neutral and businesslike tone. • Record all attendees at the meeting. If someone joins the meeting late, make a note of the time they arrived. • Record all topics discussed and all decisions made. Note who is responsible for carrying out any actions to implement those decisions. • Comply with your group's policy about how to report votes. Some groups record how each member voted on questions. Others keep this information confidential. • Format your meeting minutes for easy scanning. • Use the agenda. If there is an agenda for the meeting, it can be useful in organizing the meeting notes. • Ensure you are familiar with your organization's policies and preferences about meeting minutes. If possible, look at minutes from previous meetings as a model for yours. It is helpful for a working group to have continuity in the formatting and content of minutes over time. • Note the time and date of the next meeting, if it has been decided. • Note your own name as the person recording the minutes. • Develop a template. If your group does not already have a preferred format for meeting minutes, create a template that can be used consistently in the future. You may want to look at a variety of sample minutes to help you decide how to format yours.	• Don't editorialize. Meeting minutes are an objective record of what happened at a meeting. It's not appropriate to offer commentary or opinions. Be careful that you don't betray your opinions through selective choice of detail or use of a particular tone. • Don't provide a blow-by-blow account of discussions or arguments. There is no need to record the opinions of individuals. • Don't put anything confidential or sensitive in the minutes. Meeting minutes may have a wide readership beyond the attendees at the meeting and may be discoverable in the event of legal action. Many groups will go into "executive session" or the equivalent in order to discuss such issues off the record. If you have any question about what to include in the minutes, be sure to ask before you distribute them. **ROBERT'S RULES OF ORDER** Some organizations, including many nonprofit organizations with governing boards, follow Robert's Rules of Order for their meeting procedures, including the taking of minutes. Robert's Rules of Order was first published in 1876 and continues to be updated for modern use. Visit http://www.robertsrules.com/ for more information.

LIKE THIS

Meeting Notes

Lockstall Relocation Committee
June 7, 2013
11:00 a.m. EST
4th-Floor Conference Room

Attendance
For Lockstall: Bryan Berman, Jill McDougal, Stephanie Page, Lin Yu.
By phone: Sherri Berndt, Ray Paredes.
For Omega Properties: Lyn Wheeler.

Report on preliminary location visits—Bryan and Lyn
    Jpegs attached (sitevisits.zip)
Bryan and Lyn have made preliminary visits to four locations. Three were in Midtown, one was on the far Westside.
Lyn clarified that the sites visited are not under consideration to lease. The purpose of these visits is simply to give us an idea of what's out there. She encouraged others to come along with Bryan on future visits. Bryan agreed.
Bryan will have Sam let us know when his next round of visits will be.

Report on employee surveys and interviews—Lin
    Summary attached (staff.survey.draft.docx)
Lin reported on the results of a survey taken of all employees and a series of interviews done with division heads. (Printed report is attached.)
Key findings:
Office Location
78% of employees strongly prefer staying in Midtown.
96% of employees are concerned with added commuting time.
3% of employees say that added commuting time could cause them to resign.
Workspace Plan
67% of employees are opposed to an open floor plan.

89% of employees would feel better about an open floor plan if they could telecommute.

Lin reported that division heads are concerned that their work groups stay together. Accounting is currently in three locations, and that is extremely difficult. Communications is concerned about noise levels in an open floor plan.

HR has serious questions about confidentiality if we move to an open floor plan.

Bryan thanked Lin for the report.

After discussion, it was agreed to focus our search efforts on Midtown.

Report on proposed technology upgrades—Stephanie and Ray

Stephanie and Ray reported that the system upgrades in Chicago were overall successful. Similar upgrades could be accomplished in the New York office. It would be costly and impractical to implement these upgrades before a move. Recommendation to work with what we have and upgrade when we are in new space. It is easier to install needed wiring, etc., without furniture and people in the space.

Lyn agreed that conclusion was consistent with her experience.

Bryan asked Stephanie and Ray to begin pricing the upgrade, under two assumptions: an open floor plan and a traditional floor plan 10% larger than our current space.

Submitted by Lauren Itano

Next meeting: July 6. Time TBA

The Job Search and Human Resources

JOB DESCRIPTION

Writing an accurate and complete job description can save you—and others—a great deal of time and energy. Although the interview process may help you refine your requirements for the job, it's inefficient and unfair to go into this process without having done as much of your homework as possible. Taking the time to describe the job accurately can help ensure you interview the right people and ultimately hire someone who can do the work.

Introduction

The **purpose** of a job description is to describe the functions and requirements of the job as well as to situate it within an organizational context. A job description may also provide a framework for conducting a performance review. Job descriptions have a variety of **readers**, both external and internal to the organization. External readers are job seekers who will use the job description to decide whether or not to apply for the position. Internal **readers** include managers, supervisors, and perhaps colleagues of the potential hire. For both audiences, the job description must be accurate and complete. **Brainstorming** the content involves conducting a thoughtful analysis of the requirements of the job and its place in the organization. Many companies have a standard format for a job description. The Model Outline will provide an **organizational** framework that you can adapt for your own use. Especially if you are creating a new job or significantly revising an existing one, you should plan to go through several **drafts** of your job description. It's a good idea to ask others to review your draft—especially managers or supervisors who will work with the new hire, legal counsel, and human resources professionals in your organization. **Revise** according to their input. You will likely go through several rounds of drafting, reviewing, and revision before you finalize your job description.

MODEL OUTLINE

A job description typically contains the following sections. Your company may organize this information differently.
Basic Information: Job title, department, supervisor's title, salary range.
Job Functions: A list of the duties to be performed and any objectives connected to those duties. Duties are usually listed in order of importance. The relative importance of these duties is sometimes reflected as a percentage.
Requirements: Requirements are generally listed in order of importance. This section is sometimes divided into "minimum requirements" and "preferred requirements."
Special Requirements: Required testing, licenses, clearances, and so on.

DO	DON'T
• State the name of the position.	• Don't post an out-of-date or inaccurate job description. Take the time to make updates before you begin the search. To do otherwise is a waste of your time and the applicants' time as well.
• State who the position reports to, including "dotted line" relationships.	
• List the job responsibilities. It is conventional to list the job responsibilities in order of importance. That is, state first the task or tasks the person will be performing most, and then work your way down to the less important or less frequent tasks.	• Don't ramble. To help you focus, try to condense the job into a one-sentence summary. Then you can break out the job into its component responsibilities.
• State the requirements the candidate must meet to receive consideration. You may want to divide this section into "minimum requirements" and "preferred requirements" in order to establish a baseline but allow for a larger range of applicants to consider. Think about what your must-have requirements are.	• Don't define the job too narrowly. Some jobs have a single clear-cut function. Many, however, involve responsibilities that expand. If you expect the job to grow, or if you think the incumbent may be performing duties that you cannot anticipate, leave yourself an escape clause by saying "performs related duties as assigned."
• Consider using an "ideal candidate" section to describe the exact set of qualifications, background, and attitude you are seeking in a candidate. Developing an "ideal candidate" section can	• Don't include nonessential job functions that represent less than 5 percent of the job. Instead, use an umbrella statement as a catchall for these functions.

DO (CONTINUED)

help you refine your own understanding of the job and can help potential applicants decide whether or not to apply.

- Consider writing a bit about your organization's culture, values, and mission in the job description. This gives potential applicants a chance to decide for themselves if they might be a good fit, and it also can also create a talking point for any future interview.

- Decide how you want to deal with salary requirements. Some organizations have a policy to say simply "salary commensurate with experience." Be aware, however, that this kind of open-ended statement may elicit applications from unqualified or underqualified individuals. Many organizations specify a salary range for the position. Check to see if your company has a policy about this issue.

- Use straightforward and clear language in your job descriptions. Avoid abbreviations or jargon that is exclusive to your company.

- Develop a template. If you work for a company that employs more than just a couple of people, it's a good idea to develop a job description template so that job descriptions are consistent. Using a template forces a logical approach to organization, supervision, and division of labor, and having standardized job descriptions can help organize the performance review process. It can also help protect you against any future accusations of unfairness or wrongful termination.

LIKE THIS

Position Title: Administrative Assistant

Administrative assistant for fast-paced boutique PR firm, in an environment where office relationships are very important. Client-facing. Reporting to the president of the company, the incumbent provides support to the president and 5-member team of PR professionals.

Job Functions

- Provides high-level administrative support to company president and 5 PR professionals
- Screens a high volume of incoming calls and e-mails from clients, press reps, and other parties
- Assists in developing presentations
- Prepares a variety of printed matter
- Prepares for meetings and conference calls
- Manages calendar and scheduling
- Makes travel arrangements, including creating itineraries and managing point-to-point arrangements
- Maintains and assists in development of office website
- Performs other duties as assigned

Job Requirements

Minimum Requirements:

High school diploma or equivalent
Strong attention to detail
Excellent communication and interpersonal skills
Good phone skills
Ability to manage multiple priorities
Maintain poise in deadline-driven environment
Discretion and diplomacy with client information

Advanced proficiency with Microsoft Office software
Familiarity with content management systems for websites
Proficient with technology and fast learner
3 years experience in comparable environment

Preferred Requirements:

AA degree or higher
5 years experience in comparable environment

Reading knowledge of French and/or Spanish preferred

JOB ADVERTISEMENT

Writing a job advertisement can be a pain in the neck, because it requires you to think carefully about the job and prioritize the most important qualifications. The way you craft your job advertisement can have an enormous influence on the kind of applicants you get and the amount of time you'll need to spend weeding through applications, so it's well worth investing the energy to do it right.

Introduction

The **purpose** of a job advertisement is to let people know about a job opening and attract the best possible applicants. The trick is to provide the kind of information that will help your **readers** understand the nature of the opportunity and self-select. As you **brainstorm**, it's important to think from the point of view of the people who will see the ad. You know all about the job; they don't. There are many acceptable ways to **organize** a job ad. Your best bet is to look at other ads in the venue in which you want to advertise, and model yours accordingly. If you're advertising a newly created position or one that has been substantially revised, you should plan to go through a few **drafts** before you finalize the ad. It's likely that your first draft will be too long. Have a friend or colleague review the job advertisement. **Revise** according to her feedback.

Only God gets it right the first time.
—*Stephen King, novelist*

DO	DON'T
• Think carefully about the job before you write the ad. What are the key requirements? What kind of people would you like to interview? Make a list of the most important skills and qualities for the job and work from there.	• Don't overwhelm potential candidates with a very long job ad. A job advertisement is rarely long enough to include the entire job description. (See Job Description on page 442 to understand what should be omitted.)
• Consult the supervisor for his input. If you are seeking a candidate who will be reporting to someone other than you, be sure you work with the supervisor to develop the job ad.	• Don't stuff your ad with clichés. Terms like "self-starter," "team player," and "highly motivated" are so overused they've become practically meaningless.
• Be concise. The job ad should include the key requirements for the position, usually ranked in	• Don't hype the job without giving much real information about it. Some job advertisements spend

order of importance. Newspapers usually charge by the word, so you'll want to be brief. Online ads are typically longer.

- Use key words. If your ad is online, using key words can improve search results.
- Use bullet points to make your job listing easy to scan.
- Look at models. Check in newspapers and online for advertisements for similar jobs in similar industries.
- Consider whether you want to mention salary or not. Some companies give a salary range to accommodate applicants who have varying experience.
- Mention other benefits like heath and dental insurance, life insurance, vacation time, and so on.
- Mention other benefits and perks. Flexible hours? Telecommuting? Are there other things that might make this company attractive? Mentoring program? Tuition benefits? What makes your place special and attractive to the right person?
- Describe the work environment. Including some information about your company culture can help ensure that you get the right kind of applicants. Be honest, and don't just use buzzwords that you think will attract people.
- Stand firm. To discourage unqualified applicants, consider including a statement that only candidates who meet the stated qualifications will be considered.
- Include instructions about how to apply. If you don't want phone calls, say so.

so much energy praising the company they barely mention the job itself.

- Don't omit essential qualifications. If the successful candidate must have an MBA, a driver's license, or some other qualification, make sure the ad mentions that.
- Don't forget soft skills. Think about the character and work ethic of your ideal candidate, and mention the soft skills—such as communication skills, flexibility, or collaboration skills—that are important for the job.
- Don't try to deceive applicants. If you can't afford to pay a good salary, don't say your compensation package is "competitive." If your business is underperforming, don't describe it as "thriving."

LIKE THIS

Administrative Assistant for Boutique PR firm

Interested in joining a high-energy creative team? JCBpr is seeking a highly motivated and tech-savvy administrative assistant to provide support to the company president and her 5-person team. **Must be diplomatic and discreet**. Opportunity for advancement. Great benefits.

Duties:
- Provides general administrative support to team
- Creates presentations and other documents
- Frequent phone and e-mail contact with clients and press reps
- Makes travel arrangements
- Maintains and develops office website
- Performs other duties as assigned

Required qualifications:
High school diploma or equivalent; some college preferred. A minimum of 3 years in a comparable environment. Strong communication and people skills. Advanced skills in Microsoft Office software. Experience maintaining websites.
E-mail letter and résumé to contact@JCBpr.com. NO CALLS.

Administrative Assistant

Fast-paced boutique PR firm seeks motivated and professional AA to support president and 5-person team. Must be highly tech-savvy. 3 yrs exp required. Great benefits. E-mail letter and résumé to contact@JCBpr.com. NO CALLS.

COVER LETTER FOR RÉSUMÉ

The cover letter you submit along with your résumé is an extremely important part of your job application. Your cover letter provides you with a great opportunity to communicate with the hiring manager and to set yourself apart from your competition. Make the most of this opportunity and craft a careful cover letter with each application.

Most online job applications ask you to paste your cover letter into an online form. For companies that also request a hard copy of your cover letter and résumé, you should format your cover letter as a formal business letter and sign it (see Business Letter on page 391).

Introduction

There are several **purposes** for including a cover letter with your résumé when you apply for a job. Your cover letter specifies which position you're applying for, directs the reader's attention to relevant information on your résumé, and makes an argument that you are an especially good candidate for the job. People who screen résumés and cover letters typically go through them extremely quickly. You'll have only a few seconds to grab your **reader**'s attention. **Brainstorm** from your reader's point of view. What information will make her put your résumé into the "maybe" file rather than the much larger "no" file? How can you tailor your cover letter to highlight the fit between your experience and the job description? Keep the structure of your cover letter simple and straightforward. The Model Outline offers an **organizational** structure you can use. Although the letter is brief, you're wise to go through several **drafts** and **revisions** before you send it. Enlist the help of a friend or family member to review your letter. Typos, spelling mistakes, and other errors can throw you out of the running immediately, so ensure that your letter is *perfect* before you submit it.

MODEL OUTLINE

A cover letter for a résumé should be brief and easy to scan.
Opening: Let the reader know what position you're applying for. Say you believe you are an excellent fit for the position.
Middle: Direct your reader to information on your résumé that makes you a good match for the job. Explain if necessary.
Conclusion: Express your interest in interviewing for the job. Thank the reader for her time.

DO	DON'T

DO

- Tailor your cover letter to the particular job you're applying for. If you are applying for one hundred jobs, you should plan to write one hundred different cover letters. Develop a few different templates to use as the basis for your different letters, but be sure the cover letter you send is customized to the job you're applying for.

- Address a particular person in your salutation. Try to avoid "To Whom It May Concern," if possible. Even addressing your letter to "Hiring Manager" is preferable.

- State why you are writing and which job you are applying for. If you're writing at the suggestion of a mutual acquaintance, say so and mention how you know that person.

- Refer to your résumé. Draw your reader's attention to information on the résumé that is particularly relevant to your application for this particular job.

- Elaborate on your résumé. Instead of just repeating the information on the résumé, use the cover letter to explain how and why your experience is relevant to this application.

- Focus on what you have to offer the employer, not what the job can offer you.

- Write in your own voice. Your cover letter is a business letter, so it should be businesslike. However, you'll make a stronger impression if you allow your own voice to come through rather than writing in "business-ese."

- Keep it brief. Your objective is to pique your reader's interest. You can go into more detail during the interview.

DON'T

- Don't rehash the information on your résumé. Your cover letter should motivate the reader to look carefully at your résumé, not simply reiterate the information there.

- Don't explain the company to the reader. Your reader knows that her employer is the world's leader in aeronautical design or the country's fastest-growing insurance provider or the region's largest employer of technology graduates or whatever other superlative you might find. Your job in the cover letter is to explain why you're a great fit for that job at that company.

- Don't fudge about salary issues. Companies ask about salary history because they are trying to see if you fit within their budget. If you are uncomfortable providing information about your current salary, instead provide a salary range that you would be willing to accept. Ultimately it's your decision how much you need and how much you are able or willing to compromise.

NOT LIKE THIS . . .

To Whom It May Concern:

My name is Linda Wei, and I am writing to apply for the position of Administative Coordinator at the Center for Entrepreneurship. I believe I am an exceptionally good fit for the position.

> Never, ever open a letter with "My name is . . ." The reader is very well able to look at your signature and learn your name. The opening of any letter is too important to waste this way.

> Linda has left a typo in the very first sentence. Many readers will stop reading here, thinking she is careless.

As my enclosed résumé indicates, I have substantial experience in related jobs. I worked for six years as Program Coordinator for the Business Institute at Northhampton University. My responsibilities included extensive writing and editing of business-related copy. I worked for several years as a freelance editor and writer, and my clients included a number of professors at the Wharton School. I also worked as Assistant Director (promoted from Coordinator after one year) in the Alumni Affairs Office of the University of Pennsylvania, where my responsibilities included event planning, program building, fund-raising, and general administration.

> This paragraph is too long. Rather than offering a summary of the résumé, it simply restates much of the information there. You want to point your reader to the résumé, not just rehash it.

The Administrative Coordinator job would be an ideal fit for me. My family owns and operates several retail businesses in the area, including several high-end clothing shops, and I have been hoping to find a long-term, stable, part-time job that would allow me to devote some time to the family business. It would be an added bonus for me to work for a center devoted to the study of entrepreneurship, since that is what my family is engaged in.

> Linda is smart to explain why she's willing to take a part-time job. However, this paragraph focuses far too much on the details of Linda's life and her family business. The reader needs reassurance that Linda will stay in the job, not details about her life and circumstances.

Thank you for your time and consideration. I am available for an interview if you so desire.

Sincerely,

Linda Wei

. . . LIKE THIS

To the Director:

Thank you for considering my application for the position of Administrative Coordinator at the Center for Entrepreneurship. I believe I am an exceptionally good fit for the position.

> Linda directs the reader to the résumé, presenting just a recap of her experience. This paragraph says, in essence, "I'm right for the job, and my résumé proves it."

As you will see from the enclosed résumé, I have extensive experience as a business writer and editor, and I have worked with a number of professors at the Wharton School. I also have substantial administrative experience at the University of Pennsylvania, including event planning, program building, fund-raising, and general administration.

> Linda reassures the reader that she is really interested in a part-time job and not likely to abandon it after a short time. She concludes the paragraph by expressing her eagerness to make a contribution to the center.

The job also looks like an excellent fit for my interests and needs. I am seeking a long-term, stable, part-time job while I assist in building my family's retail businesses in the area. I would very much enjoy working at Wharton and helping the Center achieve its objectives.

Thank you for your time and consideration. I look forward to speaking to you about the Administrative Coordinator position.

Sincerely,

For more sample cover letters, visit www .howtowriteanything .com.

Linda Wei

Cover Letters for Special Situations

●

When There's No Job Description

Sometimes you send around your résumé even when there is no job advertised. You might be interested in working for a particular company, or you might be trying to break into a new field. If you are sending a résumé to try to schedule an informational interview, say so in your cover letter. Highlight a few skills or experiences that would make you an interesting candidate for the target company.

Career Changer with Transferable Skills

If you are applying for a position in an area in which you have no work history, use your cover letter to argue that the skills from your previous positions are transferable to the one you are currently interested in. Highlight any comparable experience, and be specific about the skills and experiences you believe prepare you for the job you've targeted. Explain why you're changing careers and what attracts you to your newly chosen field.

Gap in Employment History

Employment experts disagree about whether it's wise to address a gap in employment history in your cover letter. Many feel that mentioning the gap just gives a potential employer an excuse to discard your résumé without viewing it. Others believe you can use your cover letter to preempt questions that might be in the reader's mind. If you decide to mention it, simply acknowledge the gap and briefly explain what you were doing during that time. Don't dwell on the issue, don't overshare, and don't apologize. Keep the focus of your letter on what you have to offer and how you can contribute.

First-Time Job Applicants

(See also *Internship Letter* on page 370.)

Young people just entering the workforce often feel their résumés are too brief to be of much interest. If you have little formal work experience, use the cover letter to highlight what you *have* done and what you *can* do. Mention any internships you might have done. Mention volunteer experiences, even if they were not formally arranged. Focus on your skills. Highlight your interest in the company or industry you're applying to. Be especially careful that your cover letter is very well written; many companies will regard it as a writing sample.

RÉSUMÉ

A résumé is a targeted marketing tool that can be revised and refined to make the strongest possible case that you are the right person for the job. It's wise to customize your résumé for each job you apply for. Fine-tuning your résumé can be time consuming, but a well-crafted résumé can set you apart from the competition and get you on the inside track for an interview.

Introduction

The **purpose** of a résumé is to provide a record of your employment and professional achievements and to sell yourself as a job candidate. Although you may have no idea who your **reader** will be, it is imperative that you put yourself in her shoes as you write your résumé. Be aware that most people who review résumés spend about ten seconds each on them. You *must* craft your résumé to catch their attention. Look at the job description for the position you're applying for, and **brainstorm** about what experience you've had that would support your application for that position. Make sure that your most relevant experience appears on the résumé. Most résumés are **organized** according to the conventional reverse-chronological format. The Model Outline provides an overview of this format. However, some people use a skills-based or functional format. If you are writing a résumé for the first time, or updating it after a long period of neglect, you should expect to go through several **drafts**. It's an excellent idea to ask a friend or trusted colleague to review your résumé and offer feedback. It's also vitally important to proofread for spelling errors, typos, and inconsistencies. Be prepared to **revise** according to the feedback you receive.

MODEL OUTLINE

The most popular format for résumés is the reverse-chronological format.
Heading: Include your name, address, phone number(s), and e-mail address.
Summary or Objective (optional): Highlight your most important and relevant skills and experience. Career changers typically use an objective to let the reader know what direction they're headed professionally.
Work Experience: Provide details about your jobs, in reverse-chronological order (starting with your current or most recent position).
Education/Training: List your education and training, starting with the most recent first.
Other Information (optional): List memberships, awards, honors, or volunteer work. Follow the standard practices in your field.
References: End your résumé by saying "References available on request." It's also a way of signaling to the reader that she's reached the end of the résumé and hasn't lost the last page.

DO	DON'T
• Tailor your résumé to the position you're applying for, if possible. Ideally, you should revise your résumé for each position you apply for, to highlight you're a good fit for the job. The more closely you fit what they're looking for, the more likely it is they'll want to interview you.	• Don't lie. Ever. With the advent of social media and other Internet sources, it's easier than ever to get caught if you lie on your résumé. The risk is never worth it.
• Familiarize yourself with résumé conventions in your field.	• Don't use tiny fonts and narrow margins to cram more information onto the page. Résumés are scanned before they're read, and huge blocks of text are extremely uninviting to the eye.
• Consider including an objective. Particularly if you are changing careers or reentering the workforce after a period of absence, an objective can help your reader understand the type of position you're looking for.	• Don't use a lot of technical or specialized jargon. Make sure your reader will understand your job descriptions.
• Lead with your strongest suit. It is traditional to place the employment section first. However, if you are a recent college graduate with little work experience, or if you are a career changer who has recently completed an education or training program related to your new career of choice, it makes sense to lead with the education section.	• Don't use unusual formatting to make your résumé stand out. Most large companies use software to screen résumés, and unusual formatting can cause the software to reject yours. Even if you're applying to a small company, it can be risky to be too creative with your formatting.
• Make your résumé easy to scan. People don't read résumés; they look at them. Using bullet points and attractive formatting can make your content more accessible.	• Don't recap your job description in the work experience section of the résumé. The job descriptions should be strategic. Highlight what you accomplished, and highlight what's relevant for the job you're applying for.
• Select details that support your goal. Focus on duties and achievements that make you shine as a candidate for the job you're going after.	• Don't leave gaps in your résumé. A missing year will create questions in the minds of your readers. If you are unemployed, consider enrolling in some kind of education or training program so that you can account for your time on the résumé.
• Use strong verbs in your job descriptions. Try beginning each bullet point with an action verb (see the box "Action Verbs for Résumés" on page 457). Make sure that your bullets are grammatically parallel.	
• Focus on achievements and quantify them. For instance, how much revenue did you generate, how many new clients did you recruit, by how much did you increase circulation?	

DO (CONTINUED)

- Consider adding a volunteer section. Volunteer activities can say a lot about your leadership skills and commitment. Consider your achievements in your volunteer positions and note anything exceptional, such as funds raised or number of volunteers organized.

- Consider noting honors. If you have received honors or awards in your field, say so.

- Be careful about hobbies. Hobbies can reveal something about your character, and they can be a good icebreaker during an interview. Beware, though. If your hobbies are things like golfing or swimming, you're not really setting yourself apart from other applicants. On the other hand, if your hobbies include skydiving or extreme sports, you may be raising a red flag about your risk of getting injured and missing work. Music, dance, martial arts, photography, and art are just a few hobbies that suggest self-discipline and acquisition of skills over time—characteristics that can impress a prospective employer.

- Format consistently and cleanly. Once you choose your visual style for the résumé, be eagle-eyed in ensuring your formatting—including punctuation conventions—is adhered to scrupulously.

- Proofread, proofread, proofread!

> **TIP**
>
> Keep several different résumés ready if you are interested in more than one type of job. Don't expect a single version to do all the work if you are pursuing different kinds of jobs. Remember, a résumé is a targeted marketing tool, not just a list of your previous jobs.

Action Verbs for Résumés

Beginning each bullet point of your résumé with an action verb can communicate your accomplishments with greater punch. Here are a couple of examples:

Instead of . . .

Responsible for the supervision of 7 staff members

Try . . .

Supervised a staff of 7

Instead of . . .

Duties included cultivating donors and soliciting contributions

Try . . .

Cultivated donors and solicited contributions

Here is a list of verbs you might use in your résumé:

Administered	Enhanced	Led	Oversaw
Assembled	Enlarged	Maintained	Participated
Assumed	Established	Managed	Performed
Budgeted	Expedited	Marketed	Pinpointed
Built	Fabricated	Maximized	Pioneered
Carried out	Facilitated	Mediated	Planned
Collaborated	Forecast	Minimized	Predicted
Coordinated	Fostered	Mobilized	Prepared
Costed	Furnished	Modernized	Presented
Created	Generated	Modified	Presided
Cultivated	Grew	Motivated	Prevented
Customized	Guided	Negotiated	Prioritized
Defined	Headed	Netted	Procured
Delegated	Implemented	Obtained	Promoted
Delivered	Improved	Operated	Proposed
Developed	Increased	Optimized	Proved
Devised	Initiated	Orchestrated	Qualified
Effected	Innovated	Organized	Raised
Empowered	Instituted	Originated	Ran
Enacted	Launched	Overhauled	Rated

Reached	Restored	Solved	Traced
Realigned	Restructured	Spearheaded	Trained
Realized	Revamped	Specified	Transformed
Recommended	Reviewed	Staffed	Troubleshot
Reconciled	Revitalized	Streamlined	Undertook
Redesigned	Scheduled	Strengthened	Unified
Reduced	Screened	Studied	Used
Referred	Secured	Summarized	Validated
Regulated	Served	Supervised	Vitalized
Reorganized	Serviced	Surpassed	Worked
Represented	Set up	Synergized	Wrote
Researched	Showed	Targeted	
Resolved	Solidified	Tested	

NOT LIKE THIS . . .

As you browse through Sandy's various jobs, it's not clear what her profession is. She's had a variety of different jobs. In cases like this, it's wise to use an Objective section, to help the reader process all the data presented on the résumé.

Scan this résumé quickly. Sandy is using six different fonts plus bold and italic. There are a lot of little bullet points that are unattractive. It's a visual hodgepodge, and it's difficult to read.

Sandy Egan
19 East Jerome St. #4A
Brooklyn, NY 10022
718.800.9999
sandy.egan@bunonline.net

Work Experience

Placing the dates here gives them special prominence. Better to move them elsewhere.

2011–present. Administrative Assistant
Stern School of Business, New York University
New York, New York

Sandy has to use a tiny font to get in all this information, and the résumé still doesn't fit onto a single page. She should think hard about her objective and see if she can condense some of these job description sections.

- Coordinate logistics for internal and external meetings, including scheduling, booking rooms, preparing materials, and arranging conference calls
- Create PowerPoint presentations
- Responsible for handling and delivering of documents between and among divisions and departments
- Provide assistance in creating reports and other documents
- Handles reimbursements and travel arrangements for speakers, faculty recruits
- Responsible for processing expense reports
- Send thank-you letters to donors; notify faculty of incoming gifts
- Input gifts data into SPARS
- Process and follow-up on invoices in APCAR and FFE

All these acronyms aren't going to mean anything to anyone outside the organization. Sandy should describe what she does in terms anyone could understand.

- Oversees and transmits internal and external communications
- Supervise one work-study student assistant

> "Oversees" and "transmits" aren't parallel with the other verbs. This is a dead giveaway that Sandy is copying from the job description.

2010–2011. *Program Assistant*
The Willet School
Brooklyn, New York

> The bullet points in this section aren't grammatically parallel. Try beginning each line with a strong action verb.

- Assisted in archiving of research data from parent survey
- Assisted in archiving of research data from alumni survey
- Assisted alumni relations and development office
- Responsible for scheduling of classrooms each term
- Assisted teachers in ordering books
- Handled filing and scanned files
- Sorted and delivered mail and faxes, maintained and organized kitchen area

> Overall the job description sounds disjointed. It was probably a catchall job, but Sandy should try to make it sound more organized.

2008–2010. *Teaching Assistant*
PS 127
New York, NY

- Provided assistance to three elementary school teachers
- Maintained classroom supplies
- Assisted with book orders
- Worked on classroom setup at the beginning of each year
- Provided in-classroom support during special projects and events
- Helped plan events
- Maintained and organized supply storage areas

> Why are these duties on the same line? Sandy's trying to include every detail rather than choosing those that are most relevant to her job application.

2005–2008 *Assistant*
YMCA of Brooklyn
Brooklyn, New York

- Provided general assistance to director and staff
- Responsible for maintaining rosters for voluntary classes.
- Planned meetings and took meeting minutes
- Responsible for the setup of meeting rooms and AV equipment for presentations and meetings
- Handled phone calls and walk-in inquiries
- Light bookkeeping
- Maintained inventory of office supplies and interfaced with vendors
- Assisted in maintaining office equipment such as copiers and printers
- Worked with community volunteers

> Is it "NY" or "New York"? Sandy has both. It's a small detail, but if the employer is picky, they may use this as reason to reject Sandy's application.

Education
Brooklyn Community College, AA Communications, 2005
William Dunbar High School, 2003

REFERENCES AVAILABLE ON REQUEST

. . . LIKE THIS

The résumé uses fewer fonts and has been condensed. It's much easier to read, and it will fit easily on one page.

It's very clear now what Sandy is looking for, and the résumé makes more sense in light of her stated objective.

Sandy has tightened up these lines. She's removed some place-names, where they're obvious from the name of the organization, and tucked the dates into a less conspicuous place.

By condensing and consolidating job descriptions, Sandy has given herself room to use a larger, more readable font.

Sandy's dropped the acronyms in favor of a clear description of her task.

All the bullet points now begin with an action verb.

This new bullet point creates an umbrella statement for the diverse tasks described below.

Sandy Egan
19 East Jerome St. #4A
Brooklyn, NY 10022
718.800.9999
sandy.egan@bunonline.net

Objective
A position as an administrative or executive assistant where I can use my organizational skills

Work Experience

Administrative Assistant

Stern School of Business, New York University   *2011–present*

- Coordinate logistics for internal and external meetings, including scheduling, booking rooms, preparing materials, and arranging conference calls
- Oversee and transmit internal and external communications
- Send thank-you letters to donors; notify faculty of incoming gifts; log gifts in database
- Deliver documents between and among divisions and departments
- Assist in creating reports and other documents; create PowerPoint presentations
- Handle reimbursements and travel arrangements; process expense reports
- Process and follow up on invoices in university-wide accounting systems
- Supervise one work-study student assistant

Program Assistant

The Willet School, Brooklyn, NY   *2010–2011*

- Provided diverse support services for independent school staff and faculty
- Assisted alumni relations and development office
- Assisted in archiving of research data from parent and alumni surveys
- Assisted teachers in ordering books

- Scheduled classrooms each term
- Filed, scanned files, sorted and delivered mail and faxes

Teaching Assistant

PS 127, New York, NY   *2008–2010*

- Provided assistance to three elementary school teachers
- Maintained classroom supplies and organized storage areas; assisted with book orders
- Worked on classroom setup at the beginning of each year
- Provided in-classroom support during special projects and events; helped plan events

Assistant

YMCA of Brooklyn   *2005–2008*

- Provided general assistance to director and staff
- Maintained rosters for voluntary classes
- Planned meetings and took meeting minutes
- Set up meeting rooms and AV equipment for presentations and meetings
- Handled phone calls and walk-in inquiries; worked with community volunteers

Education

Brooklyn Community College, AA Communications, 2005
William Dunbar High School, 2003

REFERENCES AVAILABLE ON REQUEST

For more sample résumés, visit www.howtowriteanything.com.

> Sandy has consolidated similar tasks onto one line, saving space. She's dropped the kitchen duty, because it's not relevant to her job search.

> In addition to condensing and consolidating, Sandy's decided to drop a few bullet points. This job is far in the past, and she's handled greater responsibility since then. It's well worth the sacrifice in order to cut the résumé down to a more reasonable length.

CURRICULUM VITAE

A CV (short for curriculum vitae) is an expanded version of your résumé usually used for academic, research, and scientific positions. It is also used in applying for grants. It is common for employers in Europe, Asia, Africa, and the Middle East to request a CV rather than a résumé.

A CV is significantly longer than a résumé. A résumé is generally one page long; a CV, depending on how long your career has been and how much you have accomplished, may extend to over twenty pages. A CV typically includes a list of publications, awards, service activities, honors, affiliations, licenses, and other information relevant to the position you are seeking. Overseas CVs also include more personal information than résumés, including date of birth, nationality, and place of birth.

RÉSUMÉS FOR RECENT GRADUATES

Recent graduates obviously have less work experience than people who have been out in the workforce for several years. Don't worry. No one expects you to show twenty years of experience on the job. Instead, begin your résumé with an Objective section that states what kind of job you're looking for. Next, describe your most recent—and important—activity: your education. Consider creating a section called Relevant Coursework in which you briefly describe any classes you took that have particular relevance to the job you're applying for. Describe relevant independent study projects. Describe your senior project. List internships and volunteer work in separate sections. If your GPA is 3.0 or higher, list it. Include any academic honors you've received. You see—you've done more than you thought! (For a sample and for more information, see Academic Résumé on page 356.)

CAREER-CHANGER RÉSUMÉS

People who are changing careers or reentering the workforce after an absence face special challenges. Incorporate an objective into your résumé that states explicitly what kind of job you're looking for. Just glancing over your past experience will not give a reader a sense of where you want to go professionally.

Three Résumé Mistakes That Can Scuttle Your Job Application

———————●———————

Creating a good résumé takes time and effort. Avoiding these three common mistakes can help keep yours out of the reject pile.

- Failing to adapt your résumé to the specific job you're applying for. No matter how many résumés you send out, each one must be tailored to match the requirements of the job.

- Failing to include key words from the job description in your résumé. Many companies use an automated tool to scan incoming résumés. If your résumé doesn't contain the key words the machine is looking for, it may never be viewed by a human.

- Allowing typos, spelling errors, and grammar errors to remain on the résumé. Recruiters and hiring managers are often looking for any possible excuse to eliminate a résumé from consideration. You could be the best fit in the world for the job, but if your résumé is sloppy, it will likely be discarded.

Using Keywords to Write a Winning Résumé

———————●———————

Your résumé is your personal marketing brochure. Unfortunately unless you follow some basic guidelines, it may not even be read by a human.

When you are drafting your résumé in response to a specific job ad, consider who you are writing it for. As with any piece of marketing material, you need to imagine yourself walking in the shoes of the reader—your customer. When you submit your résumé, you may be one of scores if not hundreds of applicants, all hoping for a precious interview. The only thing that will differentiate you from the others is your ability to show, through your résumé, that you are uniquely qualified for the role. Therefore the words you choose for your résumé are critical.

Many recruitment agencies use software to scan job applications electronically, looking for keywords that are specific to the role advertised. If your résumé does not contain the correct keywords for that role, no human eyes will ever see it. Job ads use very few words, and all are important. To make sure your résumé is read by a human, you *must use the specific keywords in the job ad.*

In the case where the recruiter does not use software to prescreen applications, your résumé may be sitting in a stack of 50 to 60 others. Make it easy for a tired and bored recruiter to notice that you are best qualified for the role, again including the specific keywords from the job ad into your résumé.

Consider italicizing some of these keywords to draw the reader's eye to them and to make it even easier for your recruiter to choose you over all the others.

Good luck.

Liz Cassidy is a speaker, facilitator, and executive leadership coach and the author of *Job Interview Questions & Answers*. Her website is www.lizcassidy.com.

INTERVIEW FOLLOW-UP

You've just had a good interview for a job you really want. It's not only good manners to send a follow-up to the person who interviewed you, but it's also good strategy to help you get the job. A follow-up offers you a chance to thank the interviewer, reaffirm your interest in the position, and share any information about yourself and your experience that you didn't cover during the interview. It's just one more opportunity to show yourself in a good light to a prospective employer.

If you have the e-mail address of the person who interviewed you, it's fine to send this thank-you as an e-mail rather than a hard copy. If there were several people at the interview, be sure to copy all of them on your thank-you message.

Introduction

A follow-up letter or e-mail after an interview can serve several **purposes**: demonstrating that you understand how to behave professionally and courteously, reaffirming your interest in the job, and highlighting your experience and your background.

Consider your **reader** when you write a follow-up. Everyone is busy, especially people who are hiring to fill positions, so keep your message brief and focused. The recipient will be regarding you as a potential colleague; this is a chance to show her that you can write concisely, specifically, and courteously.

A good follow-up message can set you apart from other job applicants, so be sure to put thought and effort into this document. **Brainstorm** the content that will support your purpose and appeal to your reader. Use the Model Outline to **organize** your message in a way that's easy for your reader to follow and ends on a strong note.

As you write your **draft**, remember that a follow-up letter or e-mail is a formal business communication. No matter how comfortable you felt with the interviewer or how good a rapport you established, don't be tempted to assume a casual tone in this message. Stay polite and somewhat formal. Think of this letter as the final piece of your job application. It's part of your "permanent record"!

Avoid the temptation to fire off a follow-up message when you're still riding an emotional high after the interview. Your follow-up should be prompt—within forty-eight hours—but not hasty. Take some time to think quietly about what you want to say and what your reader might like to hear.

If possible, show your draft to someone you trust before you send it. Ask him to think from the point of view of the hiring manager and let you know what kind of impression your message creates. **Revise** your draft accordingly. You may have to go through a couple of drafts before you're really happy with your letter. Be sure to proofread your message very carefully before you send it off: spelling, punctuation, and grammatical errors can undermine the good impression you've already made.

MODEL OUTLINE

An interview follow-up should be no longer than three or four short paragraphs:

Paragraph 1: Thank the reader for taking the time to interview you for the position, and remember to state the job title. Let her know you enjoyed meeting her.

Paragraph 2: Mention a memorable part of the interview: a particular part of the job where you feel you could make the greatest contribution or that interests you the most. If you have additional qualifications that make you a good match for the job, mention them here.

Paragraph 3: Conclude by repeating your thanks and your strong interest in the job. Offer to provide the reader with additional information, and wish her luck on finding the best candidate.

DO	DON'T
• Thank the reader for the time she spent with you, and for the opportunity to meet her.	• Don't write a vague, pro forma thank-you note, with no reference to what actually happened in the interview.
• Mention the title of the job you interviewed for.	• Don't focus exclusively on what the job will do for you. When you restate your interest in the job, focus on what a good fit it is and how much you have to offer the company, not vice versa.
• Mention something specific from the interview that you found interesting. Use this as an opportunity to restate what you can offer the company if you're hired.	
• Reaffirm your interest in the position.	• Don't propose plans for changes you'd make if you were hired or tell your reader what's wrong with her organization. If you've discussed a particular problem during the interview, you may mention it, but don't start doing the job before you've been hired.
• If you have experience or qualifications that you did not have a chance to discuss during the interview, mention them here.	

TIP

Some human resources experts advise looking for an opportunity to send a "gift" as part of your follow-up: not wine or chocolates, of course, but information the interviewer might find professionally useful. If you have talked about a particular trend or idea during your interview and you know of a useful article, you might want to include a link to the article in your follow-up.

Be careful to offer this "gift" in the spirit of collegial information sharing, rather than as an attempt to influence the interviewer's thinking.

DO (continued)	DON'T (continued)
• Offer to supply any additional information about yourself she might require, and indicate you are available for another meeting if she wishes.	• Don't assume you're going to be hired, no matter how well the interview went. At this point in the process, you are still "selling" yourself. Don't take anything for granted.
• Wish the reader luck in finding the best candidate for the job. You may feel sure that you're the best, but it's still polite to make this gesture in your follow-up.	• Don't be pushy about anything at this point. Don't ask how soon the hiring decision will be made or try to schedule a second interview (though you may let your reader know that you're available for further discussion). The ball is in their court; be gracious about that.
• Send your follow-up message promptly. There are likely to be other candidates for the same job, and a timely and thoughtful follow-up can help set you apart from the competition.	

NOT LIKE THIS ...

Dear Dean Morton:

Thank you for interviewing me on Thursday. I appreciate your taking the time out of your busy schedule to meet with me.

I believe my skills and experience make me an ideal fit for this job. In addition to my enthusiasm, I can offer strong writing skills and an extensive background in higher education. My detail orientation and ability to manage multiple projects make me the ideal person to carry out the many changes you envision. In addition, I enjoy working in a team atmosphere, and I am certain I would work well with the other members of your staff.

I am very interested in working for you, and I look forward to hearing more from you about this position.

Sincerely,

John Cunha
John Cunha

> In your opening, remember to name the position you interviewed for; Dean Morton may be trying to fill more than one position.

> John's second paragraph is vague and generic. He misses an opportunity to show how his specific qualifications make him the perfect fit for the job.

> The closing lets us know that John still wants the job, but he misses a chance to show what he can bring to the position. Remember to focus less on your needs and more on what you have to offer to the potential employer.

... OR LIKE THIS ...

Dear Dean Morton:

Thank you for taking the time to interview me for the Associate Dean position on Thursday. I remain very interested in the position and hope to have the opportunity to meet with you again.

As we discussed, staffing the Teaching Center poses an interesting challenge. I believe that promoting graduate student involvement with the Center would be a productive strategy. It also seems to me that hiring a part-time Administrative Assistant could take some of the pressure off the Director.

I look forward to speaking with you again in the near future and to becoming a productive member of your staff. Please let me know if I can provide you with additional information about myself prior to our next meeting.

Sincerely,

John Cunha
John Cunha

> John seems to have some good ideas about how to solve the dean's problems, but he hasn't been hired yet. This paragraph is a little pushy, and it doesn't touch on John's actual experience.

> John is proactive in making himself available for a follow-up meeting, but he seems to be taking for granted that he's going to get the second interview and the job. It's fine to display self-confidence, but that second interview has to be earned. The trick is to convince the reader that he wants to talk to you again.

. . . LIKE THIS

John uses his first paragraph to reaffirm his strong interest in the job. His tone is friendly but still formal.

The second paragraph follows up on the interview and shows how his experience is relevant to the job he's applied for. This information might make the dean want to interview him again.

John is proactive in making himself available for a follow-up meeting, but he is also gracious enough to wish the dean good luck in finding the right candidate. This kind of courtesy and professionalism can create a lasting and favorable impression.

Dear Dean Morton:

It was a pleasure to meet you and discuss the Associate Dean position on Thursday. Thank you for taking the time to speak with me. I think I am an excellent fit for this job, and learning more about the school and the office has increased my interest.

I was especially interested in your comments about the Teaching Center. While I was at Emory, I launched an initiative to employ graduate assistants in our Learning Assistance Center. It proved a good way to build on their prior teaching experience and to give them additional financial support. Perhaps Simmons could explore a similar arrangement as a way to augment the offerings of the Teaching Center. I would welcome the chance to discuss these questions further.

Thank you again for interviewing me. Please let me know if I can provide you with any further information about myself or my experience. I would very much enjoy meeting with you again to discuss the position further. Best of luck to you in finding the perfect candidate for the job.

Sincerely,

John Cunha
John Cunha

JOB CANDIDATE REJECTION LETTER

You've interviewed a number of people for a job, and you've found the perfect candidate. In addition to the happy task of bringing your new employee on board, you also have to follow up with the other people you've interviewed and let them know you will not be extending them an offer of employment. Handled well, a candidate rejection letter can soften the blow of the bad news and leave the candidate feeling good about your company.

The way you deliver the news may depend on a number of factors, including how many interviews the candidate did and what relationship you have with anyone who might have recommended the candidate. It's usually best to convey the news via a phone call followed by an e-mail or a rejection letter as an e-mail attachment.

Introduction

The obvious **purpose** of a candidate rejection letter is to let a job applicant know that you will not be extending her an offer. The less obvious purpose is to build goodwill for your company. Although the letter may be bad news from the reader's perspective, it gives you an opportunity to show that you behave well and value her good opinion. Naturally, the **reader** may be disappointed. Be considerate of her feelings. Because these letters are brief and rather pro forma, there is little content to **brainstorm**. If a candidate has particularly impressed you during the interview or with her skills, you may want to mention that briefly. Candidate rejection letters typically follow a standard format. Use the Model Outline to help **organize** your letter. As you write your **draft**, use a businesslike but cordial tone. It's wise to take a break between drafts and **revise** carefully.

MODEL OUTLINE

A candidate rejection letter should be brief but cordial.

Opening: Thank the candidate for her interest in the position, and let her know she has not been selected.

Middle: Mention that you enjoyed meeting the candidate, and let her know you were impressed with her qualifications. Suggest she apply at your company again (if you really mean it). Use this section to soften the blow.

Conclusion: Thank the candidate once again, and wish her well in her job search.

DO	DON'T
• Send the message promptly. Some people prefer to let the candidate know their decision by phone immediately. In general, the further you've gone in the interviewing process, the more personal contact you should plan to have with the candidate.	• Don't go on too long. Your letter should be cordial but brief and to the point.
• Keep the message brief—just long enough to deliver the news graciously and soften the blow of the rejection.	• Don't gush about the candidate's qualifications. Overpraising the candidate may leave her wondering why she didn't get the job if you thought so highly of her. It can also leave you in a vulnerable position in the event of future legal action.
• Thank the candidate for her interest in the position and the time she spent with you.	• Don't say that you have hired someone "better qualified" for the position. In the event of a lawsuit, this statement can be challenged and the résumés of other applicants subpoenaed.
• Be direct. The bad news should appear in the first paragraph of your message.	• Don't reveal too much. You are under no obligation to justify your decision or explain your decision-making process.
• Be very cautious about supplying a reason that you chose not to hire the candidate. Some human resources experts advise not offering a reason at all, because of the risk that any statement	• Don't encourage the candidate to apply again if you don't mean it.

DO (CONTINUED)

might expose you to accusations of discrimination later on.

- Be tactful.
- Tell the candidate you were impressed with her qualifications or with her performance during the interview(s), if you can do so honestly.
- Encourage the candidate to apply to your company again but only if you really mean it.
- Conclude on a positive note. Thank the candidate for her interest in your company, and wish her well in her job search.

NOT LIKE THIS . . .

> Ouch. After that very warm first paragraph, Erikka might have expected an offer rather than this rejection.

Dear Erikka,

Thank you for coming in to interview for the Administrative Assistant position on Friday. Tom and I enjoyed meeting you, and we were very impressed with your qualifications and your professionalism. Your experience at Weldons was truly extraordinary.

> This is the second time "impressed with your qualifications" has appeared in this brief message. Sharon needs to slow down and take more time with the message.

I am sorry to have to inform you that we will not be extending you an offer for this position. Although we were very impressed with your qualifications, we have decided to make an offer to another applicant whose qualifications are more suitable for the job.

> Be careful. You've just praised Erikka rather lavishly, so it seems strange you've found a better candidate. There's no need to tell her you're making an offer to someone else.

You were an exceptional candidate, and we hope you will apply for other openings in the school for which you qualify. Your future applications will receive thorough review.

> Poor Erikka feels like a Ping-Pong ball at this point. If she was so exceptional, why didn't you hire her?

Again, thank you for taking the time to interview with us. We appreciate your interest, and we wish you all the best in your future endeavors. Your future employer will be fortunate to have you.

Sincerely,

Sharon Bullen

... LIKE THIS

Dear Erikka,

Thank you very much for coming in to interview for the Administrative Assistant position on Friday. Tom and I enjoyed meeting you. Although we were very impressed with your qualifications and your professionalism, we will not be extending a job offer at this time.

> It's bad news, but Sharon gets it over with right away. This is the kinder approach.

I encourage you to apply for other openings in the school for which you qualify. Your future applications will receive thorough review.

Again, thank you for taking the time to interview with us. We appreciate your interest, and we wish you all the best in your future endeavors.

> The letter is restrained but cordial. It's better to err on the side of formality than send mixed messages.

Sincerely,

Sharon Bullen

JOB OFFER LETTER

You've advertised the job, screened the résumés, conducted the interviews, and finally found the perfect candidate. A job offer letter can be legally binding, so it's important to get it right.

Typically, job offers are made over the phone and followed up by a job offer letter, which may be sent through the postal mail, in PDF form as an e-mail attachment, or both.

Introduction

The **purpose** of a job offer letter is to extend an offer of employment to a job candidate. It typically provides the basic information about the job and requests that the candidate respond by a given date. A job offer may be construed as a contract, so it's important to be cautious about the content you include. Your **reader**, of course, is your prospective employee. Presumably she will be very happy but will also be scanning the letter carefully for the offered terms of employment. Take care that the content you've included is accurate, to avoid

A job offer letter should be businesslike but pleasant and welcoming.
Opening: Begin your letter by offering the job and expressing your pleasure at offering the candidate the position. Specify any contingencies on the offer, such as passing a drug test.
Middle: Offer a brief overview of the position, including salary, benefits, and start date. You may want to include a copy of the job description rather than rehashing all the information here.
Conclusion: Let the reader know what actions she should take to accept the offer. Close on a note of goodwill.

any discrepancy between what the candidate may have been told during the interview or negotiations and what the written offer actually looks like. A job offer letter should require little **brainstorming** if you've created an accurate and complete job description, which can serve as a basis for your letter. Job offer letters typically follow a standard **organizational** format. The Model Outline provides a structure you can adapt for your company. The tone of your letter should be businesslike but warm, reflecting your pleasure in making the offer. **Draft** your letter; then check it against the job description. Ask a colleague to proofread it for accuracy and to catch any typos before it goes out. Make any necessary **revisions**. Don't shortchange this step: inaccuracies are potentially embarrassing and costly.

DO	DON'T
• Be careful what you say in this letter. A job offer letter may be construed as a contract, so don't offer anything you're not prepared to deliver.	• Don't say anything that could imply a commitment to employ the candidate indefinitely. Some companies prefer not to include an annual salary in the offer letter, as it might imply a guarantee of employment and compensation for a full year. Instead, they provide monthly or biweekly pay information.
• Include details about the position: job title, supervisor (if you so choose), salary, other benefits, start date.	
• Give a brief overview of the duties of the job. If there are any special requirements for the position—for instance, nighttime or weekend hours—be sure you specify those in the offer letter. Some companies prefer to send a relatively short letter and follow up with a longer letter that contains the full details and a full job description once the candidate has accepted the offer.	• Don't imply any guarantees that don't exist. If the compensation package offers bonuses or any other compensation contingent on performance, make the terms of that compensation clear.
	• Don't assume that anything "goes without saying." If there's any possibility of misunderstanding, make those issues absolutely explicit in the offer letter.
• Inform the candidate of any contingencies to the offer such as drug testing, background checks, or confidentiality agreements.	
• Be sure your offer complies with federal, state, and local employment laws.	

- Let the candidate know how to accept the offer. For instance, some employers ask the candidate to sign and date the letter as acknowledgment that she will accept the offer.
- Let the candidate know how soon you would like an answer—typically within five to seven days. It's a good idea to give her a weekend to mull over the offer.
- Use a template. If you are planning to hire a number of employees, create a job offer letter template to save work and ensure that your offers are consistently expressed. Have a lawyer look over your template—as well as any other business forms you create—to make sure it is compliant with the relevant laws.
- Be careful with your template. If you do decide to create a template for this kind of letter, be very sure you review your final draft before you send it off to the candidate. Unless you proofread carefully, it can be easy to leave content in a letter from a previous use of the template. Be sure all the details you're including are relevant to this job and this candidate.

NOT LIKE THIS . . .

Skyline Engineering
778 Palm Blvd.
Long Beach, CA 92001
222-888-0000

August 14, 2013

Lisa Dobbins-Marcus
9207 Rose Pl.
Pasadena, CA 91107

Dear Ms. Dobbins-Marcus:

> Careful. Avoid using any language that might be interpreted as an obligation to provide employment long term. The word "family" conveys a false sense of permanence.

Skyline Engineering, Inc., is pleased to offer you a job as a Senior Engineer. We are confident that your knowledge and expertise will be a valuable asset, and we look forward to welcoming you to the Skyline family.

> Offering an annual salary might be interpreted as a commitment to employ the candidate for at least one year.

> Arielle makes it sound as though Lisa should expect a bonus as a matter of course. Are there conditions around the bonus?

We are pleased to offer you an annual gross salary of $97,000, paid in biweekly installments, plus bonuses. The offer also includes the standard Skyline-provided benefits:

401(k) retirement account
Annual stock options
Child day care assistance
Education assistance
Health, dental, life, and disability insurance
Sick leave
Vacation and personal days

> Arielle should give Lisa a deadline for response and also give her instructions about how to indicate her acceptance.

> Arielle has forgotten a start date.

> Are there any contingencies with this offer? A noncompete agreement? A confidentiality agreement? These should all be spelled out in the offer letter.

We hope that you will accept this offer. We look forward to welcoming you aboard. Please feel free to call me if you have any questions.

Sincerely,

Arielle Dover
Arielle Dover

> Apparently there are two documents enclosed with this letter, but Arielle hasn't mentioned them.

Enclosures (2)

... LIKE THIS

Skyline Engineering
778 Palm Blvd.
Long Beach, CA 92001
222-888-0000

August 14, 2013

Lisa Dobbins-Marcus
9207 Rose Pl.
Pasadena, CA 91107

Dear Ms. Dobbins-Marcus:

Skyline Engineering, Inc., is pleased to offer you a job as a Senior Engineer. We are confident that your knowledge and expertise will be a valuable asset, and we look forward to welcoming you to the Skyline development team.

Should you accept this job offer, per company policy you'll be eligible to receive the following beginning on your hire date of September 1, 2013:

> Arielle proposes a start date.

- **Salary:** Salary of $3,730.76 paid in biweekly installments
- **Performance Bonus:** Up to 3 percent of your annual gross salary, paid quarterly
- **Benefits:** Standard, Skyline-provided benefits for salaried-exempt employees, including the following:
  401(k) retirement account
  Annual stock options
  Child day care assistance
  Education assistance
  Health, dental, life, and disability insurance
  Sick leave
  Vacation and personal days

> By breaking out the salary into biweekly segments, Arielle avoids committing the company to a longer period of employment if things don't work out.

> Arielle is specific about the nature of the bonus—it's contingent on performance—and about its amount.

> Arielle outlines a very clear procedure for Lisa to accept the offer. She includes a deadline.

To accept this job offer:
- Sign and date this job offer letter where indicated below.
- Sign and date the enclosed Non-Compete Agreement.
- Sign and date the enclosed Confidentiality Agreement where indicated.

> By making these agreements part of the acceptance process, Arielle ensures they get signed.

- Mail **all pages** of the signed and dated documents listed above back to us in the enclosed business-reply envelope, to arrive by August 30, 2013. A copy of each document is enclosed for your records.
- Attend new-hire orientation on September 2 at 9:00 a.m.

To decline this job offer:
- Sign and date this job offer letter where indicated below.
- Mail **all pages** of this job offer letter back to us in the enclosed business-reply envelope, to arrive by August 30, 2013.

We hope that you will accept this offer and look forward to welcoming you aboard. Please feel free to call me if you have any questions.

Sincerely,

Arielle Dover
Arielle Dover

Enclosures (2)

LETTER ACCEPTING A JOB OFFER

You've been through the application and the interviews, and you've finally received a job offer that you want to take. Many companies ask you to sign and date the offer letter and return it to them to affirm that you accept their offer. In other cases, you'll need to write a letter formally accepting the offer that's been made to you. In all likelihood, you have already agreed to the offer and the terms over the phone: your acceptance letter simply formalizes and finalizes the agreement.

Introduction

The **purpose** of this letter is to let a prospective employer know that you accept their offer of employment and its terms and that you will turn up to work on the appointed day. Because the content of your letter probably won't be any surprise to your **reader**, there's no **brainstorming** to do per se. Simply state that you accept the job offer and restate the terms of the offer. Use the Model Outline (page 477) to **organize** your letter. The tone of your **draft** should be pleasant and businesslike. Even with this brief letter, it's a good idea to take a break after you've written your first draft, and then review and **revise** to ensure your letter is accurate and free from typos and other errors. You want to start the new job by making a good impression!

MODEL OUTLINE

A letter accepting a job offer should be brief and professional. **Opening:** Begin your letter by thanking the reader for the job offer and explicitly stating that you accept it. Indicate that you appreciate the opportunity being offered you. **Middle:** If you have not countersigned the offer letter, spell out the terms of the job offer in your acceptance letter. Indicate that you will be there on your start date. **Conclusion:** Close your letter by repeating your thanks and looking forward to beginning work.

DO	DON'T
• Be sure you mean it. In sending a letter like this, you are in effect executing a contract, so be sure you intend to take the job you are accepting.	• Don't gush. It's fine to express your happiness about receiving the offer, but don't overdo it.
• If you haven't already accepted the offer over the phone, respond initially with a phone call, and then follow up quickly with a letter.	• Don't rush. You may be very excited about the offer, but slow down and make sure your acceptance is as perfect as you can make it. Sending a message that contains errors is a bad start to your employment.
• Address your letter to the person who offered you the position.	
• Say "thank you"! Let your reader know you appreciate the opportunity.	
• Restate the terms of the job offer in your acceptance letter, such as your title, supervisor, salary and benefits, and whatever else is relevant.	
• Indicate that you will be present on the starting date specified in the job offer.	
• Keep it brief.	
• Keep it businesslike. You may be bouncing off the walls with joy, but make sure the tone of your letter remains professional. It's great to say you are pleased, but keep your letter unemotional.	
• Make sure your letter is free from typos and grammatical errors. Look at this letter as your first piece of work for your new employer, and do it right!	

LIKE THIS

March 29, 2013

Dear Mr. Toder:

As we discussed on the phone earlier today, I am very pleased to accept the position of Marketing Manager for Maryland Organics. Thank you for the opportunity. I am eager to work with everyone on the team to help Maryland achieve its goals.

As we discussed, my starting salary will be $65,000. Medical, dental, and life insurance benefits will begin after 30 days of employment.

I look forward to starting employment on May 22, 2013. I will contact you in early May after relocating to the area. In the meantime, please let me know if there is any additional information or paperwork you need.

Thank you again for the opportunity. I look forward to working with you.

Sara Dominguez
Sara Dominguez

LETTER DECLINING A JOB OFFER

You've been offered a job, but for some reason it's just not right. You'll need to let the employer know that you appreciate the offer, but that the answer is no.

It's just good manners to notify an employer as soon as possible if you're not going to accept their offer, and that usually means a phone call before you send anything in writing. Your follow-up message declining the offer can be a printed letter or an e-mail.

Introduction

The **purpose** of this letter is simple: to let an employer know that you will not be accepting the job offer he extended to you. And despite the fact that you're saying no, a well-written and courteous letter can also help build goodwill with the company and the people you've met there. Direct your letter to the individual who made you the offer, but be aware that your let-

MODEL OUTLINE

A letter declining a job offer should be brief, businesslike, and courteous.

Opening: Thank the reader for the offer of employment and let him know you will not be accepting it.

Middle: Offer a reason for your decision. Keep it brief and diplomatic. This section can be a single sentence in the first paragraph or a brief stand-alone paragraph.

Conclusion: Finish your message by thanking your reader again for the opportunity and wishing him well.

ter may have more than one **reader**: it may be seen by people in human resources and various people in the area where you interviewed. Don't say anything in your letter that you don't want these people to see. Keep your tone businesslike and courteous. It's not necessary to **brainstorm** a lot of content for this letter; in fact, it's better to keep it brief. The Model Outline (page 478) will help you **organize** your thoughts. As you **draft**, focus on keeping a professional and courteous tone. Proofread your draft carefully, and **revise** to eliminate errors and to ensure your tone is appropriate. If you're feeling at all emotional about the decision—disappointed in the offer, for example—ask a friend to read your draft and give you feedback, to ensure you're not saying anything you really shouldn't say.

DO	DON'T
• Start with a phone call; then follow up that phone call as quickly as possible with a written message. If you've accepted another job, you're about to get very busy, so send this message now while you have time.	• Don't say anything negative about the employer in your letter. Even if you think you'll never want to work for that company, it's wise not to burn bridges. Stay neutral and professional.
• Be courteous and professional. You may end up working for or doing business with this employer in the future—or even just networking with the people you met there—so maintain the relationship.	• Don't criticize the offer you've been given. Even if you think the offer was poor, this isn't the place for commentary. Be alert for passive-aggressive snarkiness, and edit out anything that isn't businesslike and courteous.
• Be complimentary about the company, if you possibly can, without going overboard.	• Don't use the letter to continue the negotiations. If you want to use the offer you've received to leverage a better one from this employer, don't put it in the context of declining this offer. Pick up the phone and negotiate in a straightforward way.
• Be diplomatic. If you've chosen another position that pays more, don't point this out. It's enough to say you've accepted a position that better matches your interests and goals. It's not necessary to tell your reader whom you're going to be working for, but you can if you choose.	• Don't provide the details about the offer you have accepted, if you've accepted one. It's not professional to say anything more than it's a better fit.
• Keep your letter brief. This letter ties the bow on a professional interaction. Convey your decision courteously, and get out.	
• Thank the company for their offer, and extend your best wishes for the future.	

NOT LIKE THIS . . .

It would be better for Todd to decline the offer in the first paragraph rather than leaving Evan hanging.

There's no need to mention the compensation. Evan is probably aware of what other companies in the industry can offer.

This is a little personal.

There's *really* no need to mention the compensation a second time. Todd's impulse to praise the employer is a generous one, but his harping on the money undermines the gesture.

Dear Evan:

Thank you very much for offering me the position of Assistant Director of Marketing at Greenton. As we discussed, I am interested in the work Greenton is doing in the field of renewable energy, and I consider that work to be very important.

Unfortunately, I am unable to accept the offer. I have received another offer from Elson Energy, with a significantly larger compensation package. It was a very difficult decision for me. I would have loved to have worked for Greenton, but it is not economically feasible at this time.

Thank you again for the offer. I wish you all the best in the future and I very much hope one day we will be able to work together when the time comes that Greenton can pay industry-competitive salaries.

Sincerely,

Todd Meller

All right already. Todd's regard for Greenton seems to be sincere, but this passive-aggressive complaining about the offer isn't going to get him invited back.

. . . LIKE THIS

Todd conveys the news quickly and efficiently early in the message. He makes clear his regard for Greenton and implies an ongoing interest. His use of the word "needs" strongly hints that compensation was the reason for his choosing another offer, but he doesn't beat Evan over the head with it.

Todd's closing is warm and sincere, and it leaves the door open for future discussions.

Dear Evan:

Thank you very much for offering me the position of Assistant Director of Marketing at Greenton. Although I strongly believe in the important work Greenton is doing and appreciate the opportunity, I have decided to accept another offer that better meets my current needs.

I very much enjoyed meeting you and the team, and I appreciate all the time you spent with me. I hope we can stay in touch. Good luck in finding the right candidate, and very best wishes for your continued success.

Sincerely,

Todd Meller

LETTER WITHDRAWING FROM THE JOB SEARCH

You've been lucky enough to be in contention for several different jobs. You've made your final decision, and now it's time to let the other employers know that you're withdrawing from the job search. Sending a courteous message withdrawing from consideration is a way to build and maintain goodwill for the future. Don't pass up this opportunity to make a good impression.

If you have been interviewed for a position, you should make a phone call followed up by an e-mail. Even if you've just sent your résumé, it's a good idea to let the employer know your status. If you don't have contact information for an individual, send your message to the same place you submitted your application.

Introduction

The **purpose** of an application withdrawal message is very simple: to let an employer know that you are withdrawing from consideration for the job you have applied for. A secondary reason is to preserve the relationship with this employer and build goodwill. A courteous letter can leave your **reader** with a good opinion of you. This message requires very little **brainstorming**. It is not mandatory to provide a reason for withdrawing from consideration, but it is polite to do so. Simply state that you have accepted another offer, decided to stay in your current position, decided to relocate, or whatever your reason for withdrawing. Keep your explanation brief and straightforward. Be sure to proofread your **draft** for typos and misspellings, and **revise** accordingly.

DO	DON'T
• Direct your message to the person you have been dealing with on the matter. If you haven't reached the interview stage, direct your message to the same person you sent your cover letter and résumé to.	• Don't go on too long. Your letter should be brief and to the point.
• Let the reader know why you're writing in the first paragraph. Don't make him wade through a lot of prose to get to the point of your letter.	• Don't gush about the job you have accepted, if that is your reason for withdrawing. You may be very excited about your new job, but keep those feelings to yourself.
	• Don't disparage any offer that you've been made. Don't say anything to suggest that you've found

DO (CONTINUED)	**DON'T** (CONTINUED)
• Make sure you specify which position you applied for. The reader may be running more than one search and may not remember you.	something better than the position with this company. Remember that part of your purpose is to foster goodwill for the future.
• Provide a brief explanation, if you so choose. It's more important to do so if you have actually interviewed with the reader. In that case, let him know, briefly, if you have accepted another job or made some other decision leading to your withdrawal from consideration.	• Don't burn bridges. Consider that you might want to work for this company at some point in the future, or that you might be doing business with it. Take care to preserve the relationship.
• Keep it brief. There's no need to provide a long, elaborate explanation for your decision.	
• Thank the reader for considering your application. It is especially important to thank the reader for his time and consideration if you have interviewed with him. Showing your appreciation creates a good impression and builds goodwill that might pay off in the future.	

LIKE THIS

Dear Ms. Burbage:

Thank you very much for including me in the interview process for the Security Technician position. I would like to withdraw from consideration for the position. I have decided to accept another employment offer that I believe is a good match for my skills and goals.

Thank you again for your consideration. I enjoyed meeting you and your staff, and I wish you all the best in the future.

Sincerely,

Desiree Washington

PERFORMANCE REVIEW

Writing performance reviews for employees is an important part of many supervisory positions. In large companies that have human resources departments, supervisors usually have very specific guidance about how to write these reviews. Smaller organizations often develop their own guidelines and practices.

While writing a performance review often feels like just one more task heaped on top of your regular duties, it is important that you take the task seriously. Performance reviews can have important consequences, including level of compensation, for the employee as well as for the organization. Performance reviews can have a lasting impact: they may remain in the employee's record longer than the supervisor remains at the company.

Performance reviews are generally shared with employees in face-to-face meetings. Confidentiality is of the utmost importance.

Introduction

The **purpose** of a performance review is to give an employee a candid appraisal of his performance, usually against previously agreed-on goals. When handled well, the performance review process can help employees and their supervisors come to agreement about expectations, provide support for employees who are struggling in their jobs, improve job satisfaction through transparency, and improve the overall function of the business or organization. Annual raises and other compensation are often tied closely to performance reviews. These reviews are often written collaboratively with significant input from employees themselves. The **readership** of performance reviews is typically extremely limited. Generally only the employee, his supervisor(s), and select individuals in management and human resources have access to performance reviews. There are many ways to **organize** a performance review. Some companies have sections for general performance, specific job performance, and future goals. Others organize their performance reviews around functional areas in the employee's job description. They may also be organized around the organization's core values or objectives. Some companies devise a numerical scale to rate employees' performance. The structure of the performance review will guide your **brainstorming** about its content as you carefully examine each area to be evaluated. It is important to take adequate time to mull over the content for the review. Take time with your draft, and allow time for **revision**. Let a day or two pass between drafts to ensure that your language is appropriate and your evaluation is based on facts rather than feelings. Some supervisors show a draft of the performance review to the employee prior to finalizing it.

DO	DON'T
• Allow adequate time to carry out performance reviews, including time to solicit employee input, review your records, and refine your draft of the review. Doing performance reviews at the last minute can lead to inaccurate and incomplete reviews and may alienate employees unnecessarily. Be sure you start well in advance of the date the reviews are due.	• Don't make remarks of a personal nature. Performance reviews should make statements only about an employee's performance, not her personality or character. An employee's attitude is fair game, but be aware that remarks that seem personal could get you in trouble.
• Familiarize yourself with any guidelines your organization might have for writing performance reviews, and follow those guidelines to the letter. There can be serious legal implications for not doing so.	• Don't use language that betrays emotion of any kind. A performance review should sound as objective as possible rather than showing anger, frustration, or even elation in the case of a very positive review.
• Consider asking your employees to draft their own performance reviews, or write self-evaluations. Allow them to use the same forms or set of guidelines you use. Employees are far more likely than you are to remember the details of their work and their performance throughout the year, and they are more familiar than you are with the challenges they faced in doing their jobs. Asking employees to participate in drafting their own performance reviews lets them know that you value their input, and it can help engage them in a positive way in the review process rather than feeling defensive about what their boss is likely to write about them.	• Don't write a review that is wholly negative. Even if the employee's performance was extremely disappointing, find something in her work you can praise. This is not just for the employee's benefit. It can also protect you against charges of discrimination or unfairness.
	• Don't praise the employee lavishly. Using phrases like "best employee we've ever had in this position" can make it virtually impossible to terminate that employee should a problem arise in the future. If you focus on writing balanced reviews that describe areas for improvement and future goals, you not only create a more realistic picture of the employee, you also avoid painting yourself into a corner.
• Review your e-mails and other correspondence to help jog your memory about what your employees	• Don't put anything in a performance review you wouldn't say to the employee's face. Don't say anything insulting or unprofessional.

worked on during the previous year and what issues might have come up.

- Evaluate the entire year. Events in recent memory stand out the most, but be sure your review provides fair coverage for the entire review period.
- Consider the use of both quantitative and qualitative measures. Quantitative measures track employees' performance through numerical means—how much revenue they generated, how many new accounts they initiated, how many units they sold, calls they handled, pieces they built, and so on. Qualitative measures track more abstract contributions, such as creativity, teamwork, problem solving, and leadership. Depending on the job description, qualitative and quantitative measurement may be of variable importance.
- Write a balanced review. Your review should include positives and areas for improvement. Even a problematic employee has done something right, and including that on the performance review will help him feel he's being treated fairly and make it more likely that he'll pay attention to your comments about where he needs improvement. Even the best employee can improve, and identifying development areas can help motivate him to reach new and higher goals.
- Be specific. Cite specific instances of good and bad performance. By specifying particular projects or activities where the employee has performed well or not performed well, you highlight specific behaviors for him to consider in the future.
- Look forward as well as backward. A performance review is an opportunity not just to review the previous year, but also to set goals for the coming year.
- Use neutral language. Describe the employee's actions; don't discuss your feelings about those

DO (CONTINUED)

actions. Focus on using descriptive and objective
language.

- Give an honest assessment of the seriousness of
any problems. There's a big difference between
"could improve" and "will be fired if doesn't
improve."

- Let the employee know if she is in danger of being
terminated as a result of her poor performance.

- Document ongoing problems as they occur, and
refer to them specifically in the performance
review.

- Remember that employees have access to their
reviews and will certainly read them carefully,
particularly if there is anything negative in the
review.

- Design a consistent system. If your organization
has several employees, it's worth taking the time
to develop a format that is flexible enough to
be used for every job function. It is also prudent
to use the same guidelines to evaluate all your
employees, to avoid charges of discrimination.

- Remember that a performance review is just
that, a "review" of the employee's performance
throughout the year. This means that areas of
both praise and concern should be discussed
as they happen throughout the year, not just in
this meeting.

SAMPLE EXCERPTS

Lateness continues to be a chronic problem for Paul. Despite repeated cautions, he appears to be unable or unwilling to get to work on time. His constant lateness is having a negative impact on his co-workers and on the division, and this behavior must be remedied going forward.

NOT LIKE THIS...

Paul has an ongoing problem with coming to work late. I spoke with him about this habit on 1/13, 2/26, and 3/2. I have explained that the counselors cannot begin their jobs until he arrives. He has said that he understood the impact of his lateness on the office and made promises to correct it. Nevertheless, he was late to work again 4/14, 4/20, and 5/10. Paul must come to work punctually every day if he wishes to continue working here.

... LIKE THIS

Colette is hands down the best administrator I've ever worked with. She is conscientious, resourceful, and consistently exceeds my expectations. She has materially contributed to my productivity, and I don't know what I would do without her.

NOT LIKE THIS...

Colette's performance this year has been outstanding. She is conscientious and resourceful. Her dependable and consistent performance has freed me to focus on other aspects of my job.

... LIKE THIS

Eric seems to dislike his job intensely, and I wonder why he stays. He is unreliable, sullen, and sarcastic. He seems to think the world owes him a living, and the rest of the staff are fed up with his attitude. He refuses to show any initiative and will deliberately complete an assignment incorrectly in order to sabotage the program.

NOT LIKE THIS...

Eric seems unhappy in his work. He seems disheartened, shows little initiative, and is sometimes unfriendly. He carries out assigned tasks slowly. He does not ask questions when he doesn't understand an assignment, instead carrying it through to completion, often incorrectly.

... LIKE THIS

WRITING YOUR OWN PERFORMANCE REVIEW

In some organizations, supervisors request that employees draft their own performance reviews as part of the annual review process. Self-assessments have become very popular, partly because employees have far more information about their own jobs and daily activities than their managers possibly could.

Here are some tips as you prepare your own performance review:

- Be sure you understand the format for the review and what areas you are expected to cover. If you don't, ask.
- Don't be too modest. Research shows that most employees rate themselves lower than their managers would. Some people are embarrassed at the prospect of praising themselves, so they are too modest in describing their achievements. If you feel this way, imagine you are describing the work of someone who reports to you, and give that person the credit they deserve.
- Use this opportunity to discuss problem areas. If you know your manager is unhappy about something, you have an opportunity to shape the discussion by addressing it right up front and presenting your perspective on the problem.
- Be diplomatic. If you feel something is being mishandled, find a neutral way of describing the problem. Don't make your boss defensive.
- Consider asking for feedback from your colleagues. Ask them to give you an honest appraisal of your performance as a co-worker.
- Be specific. If there are particular achievements you're proud of, or areas where you put in a special effort, highlight those.

Writing an Effective Performance Review

Whether you run a small company or work in a large multi-national organization, writing an *effective* performance review can motivate a high-potential employee, manage the departure (voluntarily or involuntarily) of a low performer, and may help to protect your organization from an unwanted wrongful termination or discrimination claim.

Some specific examples:

Your company is struggling and you don't have enough in the budget to pay your star performers as much as you'd like. An appropriately positive review can have a tremendous impact on morale. This is an opportunity to discuss future goals as well as what motivates him/her, which you may discover is not just money.

Your employee is not performing up to expectations. Perhaps you've had individual informal conversations with this worker. Many employees don't put two and two together unless it's spelled out for them—meaning they may think that these individual conversations aren't indicative of overall poor performance. The performance review period is the time to provide your staff with the "big picture" and make it clear what needs to be improved and in what time frame. If the situation is made clear, the poor performer will do one of two things: attempt to improve or look for a new job. In either case, your company is benefiting.

One of the many hats that an HR professional wears is to consult with managers when the difficult decision is made to terminate the employee's employment. In some circumstances, managers have never given the employee a formal review or, worse, have given them a positive review. In these situations, the company may decide that terminating the employee's job at that time is too risky and as a manager, you are put in a position to build a case for termination. This may take months depending on the length of service of an employee.

The first question I ask a manager who wants to terminate someone's employment is "Will this employee be surprised?" If an employee has no idea that his performance is poor, how will he know what to improve? One suggestion is to keep a simple log of issues, both good and bad, throughout the year. Make sure that you keep track of your e-mails and conversations in this log. This will make it much easier to recall the important events that happened months ago.

The bottom line is that keeping an open dialogue with your team, giving consistent feedback and reviewing performance and accomplishments at least once a year (twice is even better!) will help you to reach *your* goals at your organization.

Michele Cohen is managing director, Human Resources, Fortress Investment Group.

RESIGNATION LETTER

It's time to move on. Whether you've found a better job, decided to move away, or chosen to go back to school, it's worthwhile putting some care into your resignation letter. A well-written resignation letter can help preserve goodwill and leave behind a good impression.

Resignation is best handled through a face-to-face conversation, followed by a formal resignation letter delivered by hand. If for some reason e-mail is your only choice, be sure your resignation e-mail is a formal and correct business communication.

MODEL OUTLINE

Keep your resignation letter brief and professional.
Opening: Begin your letter by stating that you are resigning and give your resignation date.
Middle: Courteously state the reason for your resignation. If you are leaving because you've had a bad experience, do not allude to the problem in this letter. Simply express your appreciation for the opportunity you have had.
Conclusion: Finish your letter with good wishes, and express your interest in staying in touch in the future.

Introduction

The obvious **purpose** of a resignation letter is simply to let your employer know that you are leaving and the date of your resignation. A secondary purpose can be to foster goodwill with your soon-to-be former employer. Even if you have been less than happy in your job, a resignation letter can be a good opportunity to rise above the current difficulties and go out on a positive note. Don't worry about what your **reader** is likely to think. If you treat your reader with professionalism and courtesy, you have done your job.

There is little content to **brainstorm** here; in fact, less is usually more in these cases. Resignation letters should be brief, and they generally follow a standard format. Use the Model Outline to help you **organize** yours. The tone of your **draft** should be businesslike and cordial. If you are leaving your job because you are unhappy, it may be helpful to write a draft—at home, not at work—saying all the things you really want to say. Once you've got all that anger out of your system, sit down and write an appropriate and businesslike resignation letter. Consider showing your draft to a trusted friend, and **revising** it based on her feedback.

DO	DON'T
• Wait until you're ready to go. In some jobs, you may be asked to clean out your desk as soon as you've submitted your resignation letter, especially if the job involves sensitive information or security clearance. To avoid being caught off guard, be sure you are prepared to leave when you hand in your resignation letter.	• Don't write a resignation letter when you're angry. Any letter you draft in a state of high emotion is likely to be something you regret later.
• Keep it brief. Whatever the circumstances of your resignation, your letter should be concise.	• Don't resign if you don't really mean to. Resigning or threatening to resign as a negotiating tactic or a way to get what you want often backfires and will not endear you to your boss or your colleagues.
• State the date of your resignation. (Be aware that you may be asked—or required—to leave sooner.)	• Don't complain about the company, the job, your boss, or any of your co-workers. You could lose a potentially useful reference by being unpleasant. A formal exit interview—if you will have one—is a better place to discuss any problems you may have encountered.
• Be businesslike. Your resignation letter will go into your employee records, so don't say anything you might regret later on.	
• Offer a reason for your resignation. It's courteous to let people know why you are leaving. If you are resigning because of bad circumstances, keep your letter very neutral.	• Don't blame anyone. Even if you feel pushed out, it's better to take full responsibility for your decision.
• Say something nice. Even if you had a bad experience in the job, you can express appreciation for the opportunity you had or at least let them know you learned a great deal while working there.	• Don't write a passive-aggressive letter. It's easy to let resentment creep in without being aware of it. Have someone look over your letter before you submit it.
• Offer to help with the transition, if you are willing to do so.	• Don't say anything that will make you look foolish. For instance, you may feel they'll be sorry when you're gone and wish they had treated you better. But don't say that. You'll just look silly.
• Thank your reader. Wrap up your letter with an expression of goodwill and a desire to stay in touch in the future.	• Don't go on too long. Keep the letter brief and businesslike.

NOT LIKE THIS...

Dear Jerry:

This is my formal notice that I will be resigning my position as Account Executive. My last day will be March 30th.

While I appreciate the opportunity I initially had at Dunham, recent organizational changes have made it impossible for me to do my job. Supervision clearly does not understand the work we do, and I'm sure the severe lack of morale has not escaped your attention.

I regret having to make this decision, but I have been left with no choice.

Sincerely,

Linda Callabra

> Linda needs to cool down and rewrite this letter. She does no one any good by grousing about the job and snidely blaming Jerry for his poor management.

> Linda looks angry and unprofessional. She may be perfectly justified in feeling as she does, but she should take the high ground in her resignation letter.

... LIKE THIS

Dear Jerry:

This is my formal notice that I will be resigning my position as Account Executive. My last day will be March 30th.

I appreciate the opportunities I have had at Dunham, and I have learned a great deal here. I wish you and the team success in the future.

Sincerely,

Linda Callabra

> Linda's resignation is professional and concise. She does not air her grievances, nor does she misrepresent the working conditions she's suffered through. She simply conveys her message professionally.

NOT LIKE THIS...

Dear Claire:

As we discussed this morning, I am sorry to notify you that I will be leaving my position as Practice Manager. My resignation is effective June 23.

I have been offered a position as Assistant Director of Patient Relations at the Equine Medical Center. I am very excited about the opportunity, particularly as I will have the opportunity to work in patient outreach and marketing. I have learned a great deal working for you, and I am looking forward to implementing those lessons in my new position. I am also looking forward to a limited schedule with no after-hours responsibilities and a full staff to support me.

> Brian is going on too long about his new job, and he's beginning to sound like he's gloating.

> Ouch. That was a passive-aggressive swipe at Claire, disguised as excitement about his new job.

I would be happy to work with my replacement to assist him or her in getting up to speed so that the transition is as smooth as possible. However, I expect my new position will be very demanding, so I will have limited time to spend on the transition.

> What exactly does this mean? Is Brian available to help or not? He is sending a mixed message here.

Thank you again for the opportunity to work with you, Claire. You are an exceptional veterinarian, and it has been a privilege to work with you. I hope we can stay in touch.

All the best,

Brian

. . . LIKE THIS

Dear Claire:

As we discussed this morning, I am sorry to notify you that I will be leaving my position as Practice Manager. My resignation is effective June 23.

I have been offered a position as Assistant Director of Patient Relations at the Equine Medical Center. I have learned a great deal working for you, and I am looking forward to implementing those lessons in my new position.

> This is all Brian needs to say. It's understood that he's moving on to a "bigger" job.

I would be happy to work with my replacement to assist him or her in getting up to speed so that the transition is as smooth as possible. I start work at EMC on July 7. As we get closer to June 23, let's talk about how I can best support the transition.

> It's always a little complicated offering to help your replacement, since you don't know when that person will be hired or exactly what kind of help will be needed. Brian deals with this well by stating the outer limit of his availability and opening a dialogue about how to address the problem.

Thank you again for the opportunity to work with you, Claire. You are an exceptional veterinarian, and it has been a privilege to work with you. I hope we can stay in touch.

All the best,

Brian

TERMINATION LETTER

Terminating someone's employment is always difficult. A well-written letter can soften the blow, make the process smoother for everyone, and help protect your rights as an employer.

Terminations are best handled in person and followed up by a formal letter, delivered either by hand or via certified mail. It is not appropriate to send a notice of termination by e-mail.

Introduction

The **purpose** of a termination letter is to give formal notice to an employee that his employment is coming to an end, to notify him of his last day of work, and to state the conditions of his termination. If you have discussed the matter with the employee prior to giving him the letter, he should not be surprised by the news. However, you can expect that your **reader** will not likely be very happy about the letter and its contents. You can cushion the blow and make the process smoother for everyone by putting yourself in your reader's shoes and crafting the letter with his feelings and his point of view in mind. As you **brainstorm**, ensure your letter is complete. Your letter should answer all the employee's questions about the termination: the effective date, the terms, any action required by him, any benefits or pay still coming to him. The structure of a termination letter is simple and straightforward. The Model Outline provides a template you can adapt to **organize** your own letter. As you **draft**, make sure your tone is professional and businesslike. Once you have a complete draft, show it to an associate to ensure it is appropriate and complete. It is also wise to have an attorney review the draft. **Revise** according to the feedback you receive.

MODEL OUTLINE

A termination letter should be business-like and complete.

Opening: Mention your meeting with the employee, let him know his employment is terminated, and let him know the effective date of the termination.

Middle: State the reasons for the termination and review all efforts made to correct the problems prior to the decision to terminate.

Review the conditions of the termination, any benefits owed the employee, and any actions the employee is required to take.

Conclusion: Provide the employee with a contact should he have questions.

DO	DON'T
• Familiarize yourself with any guidelines your organization might have for writing termination letters, and follow them precisely. Failing to do so	• Don't show any anger or hostility toward the employee. Your letter should be professional and dispassionate.

can have serious legal implications. If you work for a small company that has no such guidelines, or if you are self-employed, it's wise to let an attorney look at your termination letter before you present it to the employee.

- Consider providing a reason. It is not always necessary to state the reason for the termination, particularly where the employment has been "at will" or you are releasing temporary employees. However, when an employee is fired for cause, you may wish to state the reason for termination, as well as documenting the steps taken to resolve the problem prior to the decision to terminate. Consult legal counsel to ensure your letter is appropriate and provides your company the strongest possible legal protection.
- Be consistent with your reasons for terminating the employee, both in your conversations and in the letter. If your reasons seem to shift, you may look dishonest.
- State the final day of employment.
- State any other terms of the termination, such as severance pay.
- Explain the disposition of any employee benefits: retirement plans, health insurance, life insurance, and other benefits the employee may have been receiving.
- State the terms for verification of employment. Many employers agree to provide verification of dates of employment only. Check with an attorney.
- State any responsibilities the employee has in the termination process, and give him a deadline. For instance, employees may be asked to return keys, ID cards, credit cards, uniforms, and so on. If these items are to be returned prior to the final day of employment, specify that date.

- Don't go on too long. This letter should not be a record of every mistake or violation the employee has ever made. If you choose to offer a reason, do so concisely.
- Don't apologize. You may feel bad about having to lay off employees, but apologizing for the decision can backfire. This is a business letter that reflects a business decision. You can use a gentle tone, but don't apologize.
- Don't be melodramatic. In cases where an employee is downsized through no fault of her own, it's appropriate to use a compassionate tone, but don't overdo it. Help the employee maintain her self-respect and protect your firm against charges of unfair dismissal.

DO (CONTINUED)

- Provide the employee with contact information if he has any questions.
- Use a template. You can make this job easier by creating a template that you can adapt for future events. It's a good idea to show the template to legal counsel to be sure it's appropriate and to help ensure that your organization is as safe as possible from future legal action.

NOT LIKE THIS . . .

The termination date is missing. This is an important omission, with potential consequences for compensation, benefits, and other issues.

What warnings? When? Tony could dispute this unless Sheri has documentation of these conversations.

This is beginning to sound like a laundry list of Tony's shortcomings. It's better to make one case strongly than to go on like this. Sheri runs the risk of sounding like she bears a grudge against Tony.

What about other benefits? Health insurance?

Which is when?

Dear Tony:

This letter confirms our discussion today that your employment with Cummings & Hyman is terminated.

As we discussed in our meeting, the reasons for the termination of your employment are persistent tardiness and poor job performance. Despite repeated warnings, you have frequently been late to work. In addition, the quality of your work has been poor and has repeatedly caused delays in the processing of applications and has caused co-workers to redo jobs that you have supposedly already done. Your refusal to learn the processing software to an acceptable level of competence has harmed our overall productivity.

Payment for your accrued vacation days will be included in your final paycheck, which you will receive this Friday. You may pick up your check from the reception desk or we can mail it to your home.

Please return your security swipe card and your office key prior to your last day of employment.

Sincerely,

Sheri Bigalow
Sheri Bigalow

...LIKE THIS

Dear Tony:

This letter confirms our discussion today that your employment with Cummings & Hyman is terminated effective as of this date.

> Tony knows he's fired as of right now.

As we discussed in our meeting, the reason for the termination of your employment is chronic tardiness. You were given written warnings on January 13 and March 23 of this year. During your performance review on June 6, I warned you that continued tardiness would result in termination. Nevertheless, you have been late to work on several occasions since then, including June 12 and June 19, when you were late by over an hour.

> Sheri focuses on one cause for dismissal and documents it carefully.

Payment for your accrued vacation days will be included in your final paycheck, which you will receive this Friday. You may pick up your check from the reception desk or we can mail it to your home.

You will receive a separate benefits status letter that will outline the status of your benefits upon termination. The letter will include information about your eligibility for Consolidated Omnibus Budget Reconciliation Act (COBRA) continuation of group health coverage.

> It's smart to create a separate document with information about benefits rather than including it in the termination letter.

We have received from you your security swipe card and your office key at the termination meeting.

Sincerely,

Sheri Bigalow
Sheri Bigalow

Promotion and Public Relations

BROCHURE

Although most businesses have information about themselves on their websites, many still find a need for printed brochures describing their products and services. Website copy and images can often be repurposed for printed brochures, and vice versa.

Introduction

The **purpose** of a brochure is to persuade potential customers that your products or services can benefit them and to convince them to contact you. Your brochure should motivate people to want to know more. Your **readers** can range from people who are already your customers to those who have stumbled across your business by accident and may not be convinced they need you at all. The more clearly you can show benefits to your readers, the more successful the brochure will be. **Brainstorm** your content from your readers' point of view. What information do they need? What questions might they have? What might motivate them to pick up the phone or visit your store to get more information? **Organize** your brochure so that it's easy to scan. This is a writing task that will certainly require multiple **drafts** and **revisions**. Show your copy and your design to people you trust, and use their feedback to improve your draft.

DO	DON'T

- Build rapport with your customers. Understand who they are and what they need. Your brochure should be tailored for your customers.
- Meet the needs of your customers. Think from the point of view of your potential customers as you write your brochure copy. What do they need? What do they want to know about your business, product, or service?
- Focus on benefits to the readers. In what tangible ways will your product or service help solve a problem?
- Focus on persuading your readers rather than just providing information. What benefits will customers gain? Focus on information that will persuade them to take the next step and contact you.
- Demonstrate your credibility. In addition to showing the benefits of your product or service, let your readers know why they should trust you to provide it. Include a brief overview of your credentials and experience.
- Use formatting and design to make the brochure inviting. People usually scan brochures before they decide to read the text.
- Break up the text into short sections. Long blocks of text are unpleasant to read.
- Use short sentences. People usually read brochures quickly. Make it easy for them to follow.
- Consider including an order form.

- Don't provide an information dump about your business, product, or service. A brochure is a sales and marketing tool, and everything you include should be tailored to meeting the customers' needs and persuading them to contact you.
- Don't feel you have to explain everything. You can't possibly explain all the benefits of your service or product in a brochure. The key is to provide enough information to pique your readers' interest.
- Don't flood your readers with technical detail. If technical specifications are essential to your product, consider providing them in a table or chart rather than explaining them in the text. It will make your copy easier to read and also make the technical information easier to absorb.
- Don't use too many fonts, too much bold, or too many italics. A clean, simple brochure is easier to read than a busy, crowded one—and it creates a better impression of your business.
- Don't neglect the cover of your brochure. Space is at a premium in a brochure, and you should put all of it to maximum use. Consider using the brochure cover to convey an idea, a compelling quote or statistic, or an engaging tagline rather than just your company logo or an image of a product.

NOT LIKE THIS...

> This writer isn't thinking from the point of view of her potential clients; she's making an argument and offering a long explanation rather than offering benefits.

> This sentence is way too long. Remember, readers will scan a brochure rather than reading carefully.

> The focus here is still very negative rather than on positive outcomes for the reader.

> The writer is over-using bold text. It's distracting rather than informative.

> Good information. Should be condensed for easy scanning.

> At last something to look forward to! Unfortunately, it's deeply buried under a lot of text.

CLINICAL HYPNOSIS
What it isn't ... and what it is:

People are often worried that hypnosis might be like truth serum or involve mind control. They fear that they might be forced to do things against their will, to reveal proprietary information or secrets, or otherwise be taken advantage of.

In fact, **hypnosis is not mind control**. Rather, it is a tool that allows individuals to learn to **access and maximize inner resources**, release old patterns and conditioning that have outlived their usefulness and may be **interfering with achieving desired outcomes**, and harmonize the different mind levels so that they work together instead of against one another. Thus, working with hypnosis leads to **greater self-control, insight, and mastery in one's own life**.

HYPNOSIS AND YOU
What to expect at your session:

Far from being some foreign, altered state of consciousness, hypnotic trance feels **familiar** because **trancelike** states occur **spontaneously** throughout the day. Clinical hypnosis involves following a set of instructions designed to **promote physical relaxation, minimize peripheral distractions, and create an inner-directed, alert attention**.

The aim of clinical hypnosis is to **bypass the conscious mind**, with its analytical thinking and inherent resistance to suggestion, and speak directly to the subconscious mind—the level from which **real and lasting positive changes** can be created.

Usually, clients report feeling **refreshed, energized, and centered** after a session. They are able to **think more clearly, to see things from new perspectives**, and **to approach challenges with a more positive and proactive attitude**.

SERVICES

Areas of expertise include:

Phobias and performance anxiety (including common phobias such as flying and public speaking, as well as exam anxiety, preparation for medical and dental procedures)

Smoking cessation (also as adjunctive therapy with medical treatment)

Self-confidence, stress release

Regression and past-life therapy

Hypnofertility therapy (also labor and delivery preparation)

Supportive therapy for intractable illness (including cancer)

Release of old patterns, habits, and conditioning

Pain management (for both old injuries and chronic disease)

CONTACT

Siana N. Attwell, PhD
Clinical Hypnotherapist
~by appointment only

Phone: (204) 951-2701
1405-120 Donald Street
Winnipeg, MB R3C 4G2
Canada
Siana_Attwell_Phd@yahoo.ca
www.Siana-Attwell-PhD.webnode.com

> Remember you can't expect to get every bit of content you have into your brochure. You just want to pique your potential customers' interest. The writer needs to make some choices here.

... LIKE THIS

CLINICAL HYPNOSIS
What it is . . . and what it offers you:

Clinical hypnosis is a tool that allows you to:

- Access and use inner resources
- Release old patterns, limiting beliefs, and conditioning
- Gain greater self-control, insight, and mastery in life

Clinical hypnosis can be used to address and resolve:

- Insomnia
- Anxiety, fear, and phobias
- Unwanted habits
- Pain management
- Low self-esteem
- Self-confidence problems
- Psychological blocks or obstacles

It can also provide adjunctive therapy for physical problems and illnesses, such as autoimmune disorders.

HYPNOSIS AND YOU
What to expect at your session:

Clinical hypnosis involves following a set of instructions designed to promote physical relaxation, minimize peripheral distractions, and create an inner-directed, alert attention. The hypnotic trance you will experience at your session feels familiar, because trancelike states occur spontaneously throughout the day.

The aim of clinical hypnosis is to bypass the conscious mind and speak directly to the subconscious mind—the level from which real and lasting positive changes can be created.

Usually, clients report feeling refreshed, energized, and centered after a session. They are able to think more clearly, to see things from new perspectives, and to approach challenges with a more positive and proactive attitude.

SERVICES
What is available:

Areas of expertise include:

Phobias and performance anxiety (including exam anxiety and preparation for medical and dental procedures)

The writer gets off on the right foot here by focusing on benefits to readers.

Using bullet points to enumerate the potential benefits makes it easy for readers to scan the text. The writer has replaced the long block paragraphs with lists of potential benefits to customers.

This section really does give readers an idea of what to expect, and it's presented in a positive light.

Self-confidence, stress release

Regression and past-life therapy

Hypnofertility therapy (also labor and delivery preparation)

Supportive therapy for intractable illness (including cancer)

Release of old patterns, habits, and conditioning

CREDENTIALS

Know that you are in safe hands!

Dr. Siana Attwell holds a PhD in Clinical Hypnosis from American Pacific University.

She has earned Clinical Hypnotherapy and Advanced Clinical Hypno-therapy certifications from the American Institute of Hypnotherapy.

She has attended numerous CE credit trainings at Omega Institute (upstate New York), at which her teachers have included:

*   Dr. Brian Weiss (Regression and Past-Life Therapy)
*   Dr. Deepak Chopra (Quantum Consciousness)
*   Dr. William Tiller (Psycho-Energetic Science)
*   Marshall Rosenberg (Non-Violent Communication)

In private practice since 1998.

CONTACT

Siana N. Attwell, PhD

Clinical Hypnotherapist

~ by appointment only

Phone: (204) 951-2701

1405-120 Donald Street

Winnipeg, MB R3C 4G2

Canada

Siana_Attwell_Phd@yahoo.ca

www.Siana-Attwell-PhD.webnode.com

Siana Attwell is a clinical hypnotheraphist in Winnipeg, Manitoba.

This section is much easier to scan now that the writer has focused on the most important services for her customers.

Adding a credentials section enhances the writer's credibility tremendously and can help allay any worries the reader might have about the practice.

NEWSLETTER ARTICLE

Organizational newsletters are a form of outreach to customers, potential customers, and business associates. Newsletter articles give you the opportunity to demonstrate the depth of your expertise and knowledge in a field.

Newsletters are often sent as e-mails, though some organizations still offer a printed newsletter. Some use both, offering augmented content in the e-version of the newsletter.

Introduction

Organizational newsletters serve several **purposes**: to provide information to your customers and business associates, to stake out your place as the experts in your field, and to keep your organization in the minds of its customers, even when you are not actively working for them. Newsletters are most successful when they provide real value to their **readers**, keeping them abreast of industry trends and providing information that they can use. With the amount of informational "noise" that we all encounter every day, it is very easy to lose newsletter readership, so think hard from your reader's perspective when you **brainstorm** ideas for your newsletter article. What kind of article might catch their attention? What kind of information would be most useful to them in their day-to-day activities? It's perfectly fine to promote your firm, but make sure your article is more than just glorified advertising copy. **Organize** your newsletter article like a news story; that is, lead with the most important information first, in case people don't read the entire article. As you **draft**, the tone you use should be appropriate to the topic. For example, an article about advances in hospice care will have a markedly different tone than an article about the latest trends in family travel. Your tone should also be appropriate to the image of your company: a graphic design firm's newsletter will likely sound very different from a newsletter put out by an insurance agency.

Only God gets it right the first time.

—*Stephen King, novelist*

Your first draft will almost always be too long. In general, it's better to write out a long draft, take a break, and then **revise** it, trimming it down to just the most interesting and useful information. Be sure to proofread carefully for typos and misspellings. Your company's reputation is at stake, so don't leave careless errors in your copy.

DO	DON'T
• Write a catchy headline. Your headline should make your audience want to read the story.	• Don't use an inaccurate headline just to get attention. E-newsletter writers sometimes use misleading headlines to entice the reader to click from their e-mail onto your website. It's a dirty trick, and readers often end up feeling shortchanged and resentful.
• Grab the reader's attention right up front. Think of an intriguing hook for your story that will motivate your audience to keep reading.	
• Make the article an easy read. Use short sentences and easy vocabulary. Imagine your reader glancing at your newsletter over a sandwich. Don't make it hard to digest.	• Don't write an article that's just a thinly disguised ad for your company. If your company is offering new products or services that are genuinely of interest to customers, it's fine to report those in the newsletter. Remember that every article must provide value for readers.
• Offer your readers information they can use. In newsletters for nonbusiness organizations, people are often very happy to read personal profiles and human interest stories. In a business-related newsletter, it's better to provide information that can help your readers, plus relevant news about your company.	
	• Don't go on too long. Newsletter articles are typically brief. You'll likely find that the process of cutting your draft to a shorter length forces you to make the article better.
• Cite your sources. If you're passing along news you've read elsewhere, make sure you cite your sources.	
• Let readers know where they can find more information about the topic. Include a link to your organization's website. Invite them to set up a meeting with you to explore the issues in the article, if relevant.	

LIKE THIS

Why Are We Raising Robots?

As parents and as a society, we are concerned about making sure that our children are prepared to compete in the new global economy. I get that. We all want our children to find success and happiness. And nobody wants their 40-year-old offspring still living in the basement!

But here's what doesn't make sense to me. The way that we have responded to this challenge has been to push kids away from play and unstructured free time into academically focused pre-schools, supplemental tutoring programs like Kumon, and absurdly early organized sports teams. We are building our child's college application résumé from the time he can toddle across the floor. This push-down of academics and parent-directed sports and activities may contribute to a child's earlier understanding of basic reading and math fundamentals and an ability to follow directions. But there's no evidence that this early skill development provides any academic advantage over time. And we are sacrificing creativity and emotional resilience, two important traits learned best through play, traits that the research clearly shows are hugely important to a child's future success.

Let's think about what it means to be competitive in our modern economy. We are no longer a newly industrialized nation looking for competent factory workers who can read and follow instructions, stay focused, and perform the same task multiple times per day. We now have machines that can perform much of these functions. What is building our economy now is entrepreneurism and innovation. And for that we need people with the imagination to see the problems of the future and then solve them, people who are willing to take risks, people who are willing to fail and learn from these failures, and people who are able to function as part of a team.

Researchers are increasingly looking for insights into the science behind creativity while more and more businesses are, knowingly or unknowingly, incorporating that science into their work cultures. This is why at Google's office buildings, you'll be greeted with scooters, Ping-Pong and pool tables, and other adult toys. Google encourages its researchers to spend 15% of their day pursuing a speculative new idea. What may seem to be merely a recruiting tool or frivolous perk is actually highly productive. In fact, Google's Innovation Time Off program has led directly to the development of an estimated 50% or more of new Google products. Similar initiatives are in place at 3M and Pixar, to name only two.

It's clear that our country's most successful and innovative companies understand what the science suggests: that creativity is not the product of sustained and constant concentration, but more typically strikes us when our brains most resemble those of children at play. So why are we cutting out recess, turning pre-school into kindergarten, and signing our children up for specialized tutoring instead of letting them loose to play? Doesn't anyone else find it ironic that companies are working to instill creativity in their adult employees, while at the same time we are slowly stripping it from our kids?

If we want our children to succeed, we must make A Time to Play!

Meryl Neiman, "Why Are We Raising Robots?" A version of this article appeared on www.playdateplanet.com, July 20, 2012.

PRESS RELEASE

Press releases (sometimes known as news releases) are announcements of new developments supplied to the press. Press releases are issued for a wide range of issues, including new product announcements, significant hiring news, financial reporting, PR initiatives, and more.

Press releases may be mailed, faxed, or e-mailed.

When even one reporter latches on to something, it's like inviting the whole world for tea.

—Tamar Myers, novelist

Introduction

The **purpose** of a press release is to supply timely and newsworthy information to the press from your company or organization, with the hope of getting media coverage about the item. Your **readers** are professional journalists, so you'll need to think like a journalist to make your press release attractive and effective. The easier you make it for your readers, the better your chances that they will pick up your news and help disseminate it out into the world. **Brainstorm** freely, with a focus on content that will engage your readers. You'll probably come up with too much information the first time around, and that's fine. The trick is honing in on the most relevant and newsworthy content and presenting it in a streamlined and engaging way. **Organize** your content according to the accepted format. The Model Outline will guide you. Unless you are in an extreme hurry, you're wise to go through several **drafts** of a press release, especially if you are not experienced in writing them. Your first drafts will likely be too long and unfocused. Keep **revising** until your press release is tight and engaging.

MODEL OUTLINE

A press release follows a standard format:
FOR IMMEDIATE RELEASE (or specify the release date)
Contact person and full contact information
Headline
City, state (or country), date
First paragraph: Present the essence of the message and answer the journalist's "who, what, when, where, why, and how" questions
Middle paragraphs: Should be brief and easy to scan
Bottom of page 1 (if press release continues onto a second page): -more-
Top of next page: Abbreviated headline
Page 2: Remainder of text
Restate contact information after the last paragraph
End of press release: # # # (indicates the press release is finished)

DO	DON'T
• Use the standard press release format. Failing to do so will make you look unprofessional, and journalists won't take you seriously.	• Don't issue a press release just for the sake of issuing a press release. Be sure you have something newsworthy and interesting to share. Don't cry wolf.
• Make sure your news is really newsworthy.	
• Understand the difference between publicity and advertising. Although you are using the press release to garner attention, focus on writing the content as straight news rather than promotional copy.	• Don't go on too long or provide too much detail. Think like a journalist, and supply only the key information. Provide your contact information so that your readers can request more information.
• Write a strong opening, and ensure that the most important information appears in your opening paragraph. Make sure that your reader can get the essential message if they read only the first couple of lines of the press release.	• Don't use flowery, complex, or emotional language. The object of a press release is often promotion, but the style must be journalistic rather than promotional.
• Use an inverted pyramid structure: your broadest and most general information goes at the top of the press release, and the details become more specific as you go on.	• Don't use unnecessary technical jargon. If you must use technical terms that are not widely understood, be sure you provide definitions of those terms.
• Be sure your first paragraph answers the journalist's "who, what, when, where, why, and how" questions.	• Don't write more than two pages. Attention will diminish proportionally as the press release gets longer. It's important to keep it as concise and punchy as possible.
• Make it easy for news professionals to do their jobs by writing clean, clear copy they can use in their own publications. Use short sentences and simple vocabulary.	
• Focus primarily on the news rather than who's announcing it.	
• Use bullet points as appropriate to make your copy easy to scan.	
• Consider using quotations for color and authority. Ensure you have permission to use any quotations.	
• Direct the press release to specific individuals, if possible, rather than to departments or organizations.	

- Proofread, edit, and revise. Ensure that your press release is error-free, clear, and easy to understand.
- Develop a template. If you expect to be writing lots of press releases, develop a template to help you save time. Have your heading and contact information in place; this will make it easier to get information out in a timely fashion. Just remember to keep your template updated to reflect any organizational changes that might take place.

LIKE THIS

FOR IMMEDIATE RELEASE

CONTACT:

Meryl Neiman

Phone: (412) 606-0408

Meryl@playdateplanet.com

www.playdateplanet.com

Playdate Planet Simplifies Playdate Planning
New Web site makes planning playdates easier and less stressful for busy parents, resulting in more great play for kids!

Frustrated with the hassles of trying to plan a playdate in the modern world of over-scheduled children and super busy parents, two moms decided to do something about it. The result is Playdate Planet, a new, free Web site that makes creating or accepting playdates a snap.

"Based on our own experiences as moms, we felt there was a need to make scheduling playdates less time consuming and more efficient," says co-founder Lisa Baslow. "Using the Web site, making a playdate has never been easier."

As *Parenting* magazine's September 2012 issue describes, before Playdate Planet, a mom could experience "three days of missed calls to schedule one lousy playdate. NOW: A website that does all of that juggling for you."

But the Web site is more than just a way to make scheduling a playdate easier for parents. "In today's fast-paced world, kids simply are not playing enough, and experts are concerned. We wanted to make sure

more

Planet Simplifies

our kids, and others, had sufficient opportunities for unstructured play and socialization with friends," adds Meryl Neiman, Playdate Planet's other co-founder. "We've never forgotten how important free play time was to our own development, and we thought making playdate planning easier would result in more play for kids everywhere!"

There's no charge to join or use Playdate Planet. To get started, parents just register and set up secure profiles for parent and child. One of the great things about the site is how it streamlines the planning process. For example, information fields let a member quickly identify whether her house has a pool, a trampoline, pets, etc., as well as if her child has any special needs, allergies, or medical conditions. These details need to be entered only once, and they will be viewable for any future playdate.

Once an account has been created, parents invite friends to connect and can start planning playdates. To create an event, a member simply enters the pertinent information—such as the date, time, location, and number of open slots—and then selects the friends she'd like to invite. Attendees are confirmed on a first-come, first-served basis up to the number of available slots selected so parents can feel free to invite a large number of friends to ensure the likelihood of someone being available without the danger of their house being overrun with children!

Everything is designed to make moms' lives easier. You can invite your friends to join you on the site via Facebook Connect or by importing any popular e-mail address book. There's a GoogleMaps link to the playdate address, handy reminder e-mails about upcoming dates, easy calendar export capability, the ability to sort your child's friends into groups of your own design (neighborhood kids, pre-school classmates, etc.) and lots of other great features.

Playdate Planet Founders

Playdate Planet is a mom-owned, mom-managed business created by Lisa Baslow and Meryl Neiman, friends who met in the first grade at a time when kids were lined up by height and they were the two shortest girls. Lisa, who works as a business analyst at an investment bank, lives just outside New York City in Nyack, New York, with her journalist husband, Jim, and their son, Tyler. Meryl hosts a parenting talk show on webtalkradio.net and is writing a book about the country's play deficit and what moms can do to reverse the trend. She resides in Pittsburgh with her husband, Dave (a psychiatrist), and their son, Drew, and daughter, Jessie.

For more information, visit the site at www.playdateplanet.com, follow it on Twitter www.twitter.com/playdateplanet, or join the conversation on Facebook www.facebook.com/playdateplanet.

Media Inquiries: e-mail Meryl Neiman @playdateplanet.com or call her at: (412) 606-0408.

   # # #

Meryl Neiman is cofounder of the website Playdate Planet and hosts the Internet radio talk show *Parenting with Playdate Planet*. Her website is www.playdateplanet.com.

TESTIMONIAL

(See also *Message of Commendation* on page 425 and *Online Review* on page 213.)

When a business has provided you particularly good service or you're especially happy with their products, you may decide to write a testimonial for them. A testimonial is usually written with the explicit understanding that the business will use your comments for promotional purposes, probably posting them on its website.

Introduction

The **purpose** of a testimonial is to endorse and recommend a business, its products, or its services by sharing your experience. Your **readers**, prospective customers of the business, may read testimonials to help them decide whether to do business with the company. Putting yourself in your readers' shoes can help you write the most helpful possible testimonial. **Brainstorm** content from your readers' perspective. To be most effective, a testimonial must address the readers' implicit questions about the company. Can they provide what I need? Is it worth the price? Can I trust them? Your testimonial should answer some of those questions. **Organize** your testimonial so that it's clear from the start that you're endorsing the business. Your initial **draft** will likely be too long. Your story is more interesting to you than it will be to other people, so your first draft will probably contain too much detail. As you **revise**, distill the essence of your story and the key message: how this company solved a problem for you or otherwise helped you. Typos and other errors can undermine your credibility, so proofread carefully.

Only God gets it right the first time.
—*Stephen King, novelist*

DO	DON'T
• Make your testimonial specific. Explain how you have interacted with the company—which products or services you used and what benefits you gained. A true story with true details is much more compelling than a list of vague superlatives.	• Don't write a testimonial for a company you haven't actually done business with. Your reputation is at stake. If that doesn't persuade you, you should remember that people have become very attuned to shilling on the Internet and are likely to sniff out phony testimonials.
• Be sure you are comfortable with your name appearing next to the testimonial on the Internet or on printed promotional materials. If you prefer to remain anonymous, let the business know that.	• Don't write a testimonial for your own company. As above, there are people on the Internet who actually enjoy outing company owners who write

DO	DON'T
• Be concise. Readers don't need to know all the details about the squirrels in your attic, the challenges of hosting a party for middle-school kids, or whatever the business did for you. Keep your focus on how the company helped you.	fake testimonials. It's a great way to damage your business.
• Be specific in your praise. Don't just say "It was great"; explain what exactly was "great" about it.	• Don't exaggerate. It's fine to show enthusiasm, but don't go overboard.
• If you were pleasantly surprised, say so. The most valuable testimonials are often those that come from people who were initially skeptical about the product or service.	• Don't write a testimonial unless you absolutely want to. A businessperson may ask you for a testimonial, but don't do it unless you believe in it. It's better to think of a diplomatic excuse than to get roped into writing a testimonial when you really don't want to.
• State explicitly that you would recommend this company or individual to other consumers.	
• Ask the business for guidelines for writing a testimonial. How long should it be? What kind of content would be most helpful for them?	• Don't go on too long. Your testimonial will likely be one of many the company has on its website or in its files. If you want yours to be read, keep it succinct.
	• Don't praise the business by trashing others. If you have truly had trouble getting good service in this industry and found a refreshing exception in this company, by all means say so. But watch your tone so you don't sound like a crank.

> Don't use words too big for the subject. Don't say "infinitely" when you mean "very"; otherwise you'll have no word left when you want to talk about something *really* infinite.
>
> —*C. S. Lewis, novelist*

NOT LIKE THIS . . .

Near the end of last summer, we started having leaks in the upstairs bedroom. When my husband went up to the attic, he found a pool of water had accumulated. We assumed the worst and called a roofer.

The roofer came out and confirmed that we were right—there was a serious problem with the roof and it would have to be replaced. We have a big house, and that was NOT in our budget. We honestly didn't know what to do.

Thank goodness we decided to call Rick's Roofing. Rick came

> Linda's at the end of her second paragraph, and it's still not clear why she's writing. The actual endorsement should be right up front.

by and confirmed there was a leak. But he said it was completely ridiculous to replace the whole roof. He inspected the whole roof thoroughly and found three places that needed repair. He got the work done within a week. Rick's company did a great job, and we were very happy with them.

> Careful. It sounds as though Rick is trashing the other roofer, which is not professional behavior. Keep your review diplomatic.

The roof was perfect all winter. After the big rainstorm in May, my husband went up to the attic to check again. It was perfectly dry up there.

> What does "a great job" mean? More detail would be helpful.

Rick saved us over $10,000. It's rare to find an honest contractor these days, as we saw from our experience with the other roofer, who frankly tried to cheat us. Rick is really a gem.

> It's fine to say that Rick compares favorably with the competition, but be careful not to go overboard in your criticism of others.

When the roof does need to be replaced one day, Rick is the ONLY roofer I'll consult!

> Linda obviously feels strongly about her experience, but she'd do better to condense this story. Not everyone will be inclined to read the whole thing.

Linda Sanchez
Oceanside, California

. . . LIKE THIS

When our roof started leaking into our attic last summer, my husband and I feared the worst. Thank goodness Rick's Roofing was one of the contractors we consulted. Rick repaired our roof and saved us over $10,000!

> Linda puts the actual endorsement at the beginning of her testimonial.

One roofer we consulted said the roof needed to be completely replaced and wanted to charge us over $12,000. Then we called Rick. He inspected the roof thoroughly and found three places that needed repair. Rick's team was professional and courteous and cleaned up carefully at the end of every workday. They got the work done within a week, and the roof was perfect all winter. We checked the attic after the big rainstorm in May . . . and it was completely dry. Nearly a year after we had the work done, the roof is perfect.

> Instead of trashing the other roofer, Linda lets the story speak for itself.

> Linda provides specifics about the good service they received.

Rick's honesty and integrity saved us over $10,000 and earned him a customer for life. When the roof does need to be replaced one day, Rick is the ONLY roofer I'll consult!

> Linda gets to tell her story, but she's condensed it so that it's much easier to read. She offers Rick a more powerful endorsement in the process.

Linda Sanchez
Oceanside, California

How to Get Great Testimonials

Writing a testimonial is easy; *getting* one is a bit tricky. Entrepreneurs and small business people rely on testimonials to build trust and gain new customers. In my business as a clinical hypnotist, testimonials are key to sales because most people have never visited or even seen a hypnotist before. Testimonials are the only way I can show my clients that they are not alone and that they can achieve success.

Asking for the testimonial is the simple part. Almost everyone will promise to mail or e-mail it to you. Unfortunately, people often forget, so I realized I needed to change my strategy to start collecting testimonials from satisfied customers. Here's the method I developed:

- Meet your customers in person and bring them a testimonial form on a clipboard. If you must do this via e-mail, create a simple form for them to complete—but be aware that your return rate will not be as good.
- Ensure that your testimonial form has a "permission release" area so that you can publish their testimonial on the web, radio, TV or wherever you need it. Check with an attorney for the language you need for your permission release.
- At the bottom of the form, there must be a place for their signature, the date, their PRINTED name, occupation and their city and state. You may not get all of these filled in, but you do need the first three.
- Make two copies and store one copy off-site. Your testimonials are like gold, so treat them as such.

So how well has this worked for me? Well, I've been in business a little over ten years, and I have *over 750 written testimonials*, more than any other hypnotist I know. My potential clients sometimes just *look* at the five-inch-thick binder and smile knowing that they are in the right place. Nice.

Hint: The best time to ask for a testimonial is just after your customer has complimented you on your product or service.

Bryan D. Toder is a professional clinical hypnotist and owner of the Plymouth Hypnosis Center in Lafayette Hill, Pennsylvania. His website is www.plymouthhypnosis.com.

WEBSITE COPY

A company's website represents its public face and voice and is potentially its most powerful tool for sales, marketing, and public relations. The site text—or copy—is just one of many components that make up the site, but it's a key vehicle for your company's message. Visitors aren't always aware when they're reading good copy, but they recognize bad copy right away. Taking the time to write great copy can set your business apart from the competition.

Introduction

The **purpose** of website copy is to articulate a company's voice and identity to the public. Copy can describe the purpose of the company, its products and services, its people, its policies, and its brand personality. (Content on an internal website is directed toward employees, but the brand personality should be consistent across the websites, internal or external.) Your **readers** are your customers and your potential customers. To craft successful web copy, you have to understand what they need and what they expect. Make an effort to define your audience specifically, so you can understand their needs. **Brainstorm** from your readers' point of view. Remember that people tend to scan web copy rather than reading it, and **organize** your copy accordingly. Make sure the most important content appears at the beginning of each section and that benefits to the readers are clear. Plan to go through several **drafts** of your website copy. Your early drafts will almost certainly be too long and may lack focus. Ask others to review your drafts and provide feedback. Is the copy easily scanned? Is it appealing to the target reader? **Revise** and redraft as many times as you need to. Revisit your purpose as you revise. Is your message clear and concise? Does the copy provide readers with what they need? Your web copy must be completely free of typos and other errors, which can seriously undermine your message and your reputation.

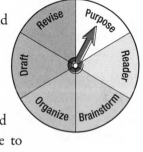

Writing a first draft is very much like watching a Polaroid develop. You can't—and, in fact, you're not supposed to—know exactly what the picture is going to look like until it has finished developing.

—*Anne Lamott,
novelist and essayist*

DO	DON'T
• Keep your readers in mind throughout the process. What are their needs and expectations? How does your company meet them? You should plan to return to these questions over and over again as you work on your website copy.	• Don't talk about yourself and your company too much. Instead, focus on what your readers can get from you. How you can help them? • Don't weigh down your pages with large blocks of text. People will not read them and will click away

DO (CONTINUED)	DON'T (CONTINUED)

- Focus on meeting your readers' needs rather than describing your company and its products and services. Every section of your website, including company history and bios of employees, should be organized around how your company and your people can help your customers.
- Think visually. Have you ever noticed that people say "Go *look at* my website," not "Go *read* my website"? The web communicates more visually than verbally. One implication is that you should limit the amount of text on your pages.
- Use short paragraphs and bullet points to break up your text. Writing for the web has been described as "chunking," that is, creating chunks of text that are easily scanned and digested.
- Use short sentences. Make the copy easy to scan and understand.
- Learn about search engine optimization (SEO). SEO can improve the visibility of your website on search engines through the use of key words and other techniques. Make sure your copy uses frequently searched key words and phrases that are relevant to your business.
- Use adequate spacing, white space, and other design elements to make your copy easy to scan. Work with your designer to make the text as accessible and palatable as possible.
- Review your copy in the website design. You will likely create the first drafts of your copy in a word processing program, but you cannot evaluate it effectively until you've seen what it's going to look like on the website itself. Ask your designer to flow your copy into the design and see how it looks.
- Ask others to review it for you. Ask them for their impression of how it looks (is it too long or too bulky?) and how it communicates your message.

from your site. Make the copy inviting and easy to scan.

- Don't focus on features rather than benefits to the reader. Don't just describe what you have or what you do—let readers know *what you can do for them*.
- Don't overuse jargon. You may need to use some industry-specific language, depending on your business, but don't overdo it.
- Don't use an extremely small font to fit more copy onto your pages. The effect is alienating, and site visitors will just click away rather than reading the tiny copy. Take the time to condense and refine your message.
- Don't treat all your pages the same. There are different requirements for landing pages, catalog pages, and so on. Think about the purpose of each page, and write the content accordingly.

- Include a call to action. Invite your readers to contact you, place an order, or take whatever action is appropriate.

NOT LIKE THIS . . .

HAHN REPLACEMENT WINDOWS

Installing replacement windows is a major improvement that can make your house feel more like home. Replacing your windows is a major investment. Beautiful design and increased energy efficiency make our windows not only a wise investment but also a great way to increase the comfort and beauty of your home. When done by the right contractor with the right materials, window replacement can be one of the most valuable home improvements you will ever make.

Hahn Replacement Windows has been Bangor's choice for quality replacement windows for over a generation. Our business has always been family owned and operated, and we do business based on traditional values. For more then 32 years we have served our community with pride and integrity. We are proud to put our family name on our business and on our work. We specialize in replacement windows, entry doors, sliding doors, and patio doors.

Hahn Windows utilizes the most advanced materials and techniques to provide you with the best possible product. Our low-E insulating glass, utilizing Argon gas fills, improves the performance of U- and R-values and makes Hahn Windows the most advanced replacement window products on the market today. Our test data meet standards set by the American Architectural Manufacturers Association (AAMA) and the National Fenestration Rating Council (NFRC) standards.

Glance quickly at this copy. Do you want to read it? Most site visitors wouldn't. The long block paragraphs are uninviting. When people visit a website, they scan first to decide if they want to read. Make your copy attractive to encourage visitors to stick around and read more.

This is a long paragraph that says very little of substance. The Hahns are sincere, but they're not doing a very good job of showing how their customers can benefit from their products and services.

A typo like this can undermine your credibility.

See how this sentence says almost the same thing as the first sentence of the paragraph? It's obviously an important point to the Hahns, but they need to make some hard decisions and cut this text down.

The Hahns are writing about what *they* think is important and assuming that their readers share their perspective. It's a good idea to establish the credibility of your business, but your copy should always be reader-centric rather than focused on yourself.

This important information—what the company offers its customers—is buried at the end of a long paragraph.

All this seems good, but what does it mean for the readers? What benefits will your customers get from doing business with you? What problems can your product or service solve for them? What are visitors supposed to do once they've read all of this? The page should include at least one call to action, asking visitors to contact the Hahns for an estimate.

This may all be true, but who the heck knows what it means? It's fine to provide technical details to back up your claims, but it's wise to do so in a way that the reader can understand readily.

. . . LIKE THIS

Glance over this page and imagine it on a website. The page is much less text-heavy and much more inviting to the eye.

This opening lets the visitor know what the Hahns do and establishes credibility very efficiently.

Aha! Here's a compelling benefit to the reader.

Here's an attractive call to action. This link clicks through to an e-mail sign-up page.

HAHN REPLACEMENT WINDOWS

Hahn Replacement Windows has been serving the Bangor community for 32 years with high-quality replacement windows, entry doors, sliding doors, and patio doors.

Replacement windows can not only beautify your home but also save you up to 50% on your heating bills.

Create a warm and snug environment for your family and save money while you're at it. Click here to get started.

Hahn manufactures its own windows, which meet or exceed the very highest industry standards for insulation and safety. For technical specifications and test data, please click here.

Hahn Replacement Windows is family owned and operated. Schedule a free no-obligation inspection and estimate now.

Potential customers need to know they're looking at a high-quality product. This brief section provides the key message about the quality of the windows and invites visitors to read more if they wish. By inviting them to click to another section, you keep visitors on the website longer. The technical page can also include a call to action, inviting potential customers to set up a consultation.

This will be an important selling point for many local customers, and it stands out clearly positioned here on its own.

A second call to action. This whole sentence will be hot and will allow visitors to enter their names and e-mail addresses for future contact. The copy as a whole is far more reader-centric, focusing on benefits to the potential customer rather than just reciting facts.

Social Media Tips for Business

Facebook and Twitter are good sites for reaching out to people in a social setting. When you're writing a post, it's important to sound like a human being—even if you're a business.

Facebook is a place where people spend time with friends, so they tend to "like" pages more when they already have a relationship with the company.

Red Lobster succeeds on Facebook by getting fans to do something that Facebook users already love to do: upload pictures of their food. Every week, the seafood restaurant invites its customers to send photos of their night out at any of Red Lobster's locations to compete for the coveted title of "Lobstar of the Week." By having a sense of humor about the brand, Red Lobster makes the corporate chain seem more personal and brings back good memories for the people who have been going there for years.

Local businesses can reward their regulars with a picture of their sidewalk chalkboard when they have a special or make pleasant conversation by saying that the patio is open on a beautiful, sunny day. If your message is casual and not too solicitous, people might even share the posts with their friends.

On Twitter, personal relationships are much less important, but personality helps. NASA charmed the Twittersphere by setting up an anthropomorphic Twitter account for the Curiosity Rover to chronicle its latest mission to Mars to more than 850,000 followers. The administrators sent pictures from space, made announcements, and answered questions with sparkling wit. When comedian Steve Martin wrote, "Just launched my own Mars lander to compete with NASA's. I sneezed on it before blast off. I hope that's okay," @MarsCuriosity replied, "Oh, Steve. That's snot okay. We have rules about that."

Devon Glenn is the editor of Mediabistro's SocialTimes, where she analyzes new social media sites and trends.

BUSINESS BLOG

Blogging is a valuable tool for businesses to maintain contact with their customers and attract new ones. Regular blogging can increase traffic to your website. By integrating your blog with Twitter, Facebook, and other social media, you can build an online community around your business and your area of expertise.

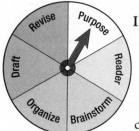

Introduction

The **purpose** of a business blog is to attract and retain customers by providing valuable content, promoting yourself as an authority in your field, and engaging with your customers in a rewarding and enjoyable way. Your **readers** will be existing or potential customers who are looking for information and who enjoy being part of an online community organized around a particular topic or field. **Brainstorming** is one of the most enjoyable parts of blogging. Think from your readers' point of view. What topics will interest them? What information do they need? What might amuse them? **Organize** each entry around an engaging hook that will grab readers' attention and motivate them to keep reading. As you draft, use a friendly, conversational tone; make your post easy and fun to read. Your first **draft** will likely be too long: it's smart to keep your blog entries relatively brief. Ask someone else in the organization to review your entries, and **revise** according to his feedback. It's tempting to click "publish" and be done with it, but remember that a blog is a public forum and careless errors can reflect badly on your company.

DO	DON'T
• Blog frequently. Regular readers will look forward to your newest offerings on your blog. On the other hand, readers get discouraged if they come back and see no new content, and they (rightly) question your commitment to the blog and to them. If you're going to do a blog for your business, plan on blogging a minimum of once a week.	• Don't use your blog only for brief, routine announcements such as sales. A blog should provide real substance to your readers. People will stop coming back if you don't offer anything of value.
• Offer something of value. Having a blog gives you the opportunity to show customers and potential customers that you know what you're talking about. Give your readers a sample of your expertise, and they'll be back for more.	• Don't attack competitors. Be nice. Your blog gives you a chance to demonstrate your excellence. Beat your competitors by providing superior information.
• Promote other businesses. Your blog doesn't always have to be about your business. Think about what your customers might enjoy. A garden center, for instance, might mention a nearby home store that's having a sale on outdoor furniture or a health food store that's stocking local honey.	• Don't abandon it. A company website that has a blog with only a few old posts looks bad—worse than no blog at all. You're better off not starting a blog if you can't make the commitment to post regularly. If you start a blog and can't keep up with it, hide the blog page or take it down entirely until you can make a commitment to posting regularly.
• Use formatting to make your blog posts easy to read and help your readers find important information. Long block paragraphs can be alienating. Use short paragraphs and bullet points to make your text easy to scan.	
• Use images, if appropriate. Images make your blog more attractive and engaging.	
• Learn to use tags effectively to improve search engine results.	
• Review the comments frequently. You may choose whether or not to allow visitors to comment on your blog. If you are able to monitor the comments regularly, it's a good way to foster discussion.	

LIKE THIS

**A KING AND NO KING NEXT UP
IN REVELATION READINGS SERIES**

An interesting hook that should make readers curious to read more about this "juicy" play.

Coming up on Monday, January 23, is Red Bull Theater's reading of Beaumont and Fletcher's juicy tragicomedy *A King and No King*, one of the best-known and most highly praised works in the Beaumont and Fletcher canon.

Short paragraphs make the post easy to read.

First performed in 1611, *A King and No King* remained popular during the 17th and 18th centuries because of its observations about the nature and limits of royal power . . . and what happens when the monarch falls short of the kingly ideal and transgresses against "natural law."

The play was frequently produced after the Restoration, and the phrase "a king and no king" entered the popular lexicon as a commentary on the problems associated with the kingship of Charles II. Prominent fans of *A King and No King* included Samuel Pepys and John Dryden, whose own play *Love Triumphant* (1694) bears a strong resemblance to Beaumont and Fletcher's play.

Michael Sexton, artistic director of the Shakespeare Society, will direct the reading. There will be a post-reading Bull Session with Professor Mario DiGangi.

A King and No King stars Matthew Rauch as Arbaces, the eponymous king (and yet no king . . . you'll have to come to the show to find out why). The wonderful cast for this reading also includes Michelle Beck, Guy Boyd, Jennifer Ikeda, Mark Nelson, Robert Stanton, and Sam Tsoutsouvas.

This cross-promotion helps both businesses.

**Acropolis Greek Restaurant offers a 10% discount
for all Red Bull Theater ticket holders! Reserve now at 212.555.1111.**

For tickets to *A King and No King*, please click <u>here</u>.
A King and No King
Monday, January 23, 7:30 p.m.
Lucille Lortel Theater
121 Christopher Street (at Bedford Street)
New York City

For more information about Red Bull Theater's Obie-winning Revelation Readings and this season's full schedule, please click here.

To make a tax-deductible contribution to Red Bull Theater, please click here.

Use Your Blog to Get Attention on the Web

Many businesspeople question the value of blogging in building their businesses. They're not sure they have any content to offer, and they think that paying marketing professionals for expensive search engine optimization (SEO) services is a better way to help ensure that prospective customers find their sites. For many businesspeople, though, regular blogging can have the same results as SEO services in promoting a business, at no cost at all.

Once you start blogging, you'll find that you have more content than you originally thought. After all, no one knows more about your business and how you can serve your customers than you do. Think about what kind of content your customers might be interested in. Tell stories, give tips, and help others learn about your niche. By sharing your expertise on your blog, you can become known on the Web as an expert in your field.

To help ensure your blog begins to appear in search engine results, be careful to use the keywords your customers frequently search. Research the most important keywords for your industry. You should use those keywords both within your blog posts and in the tags you attach to the posts. Make it easy for the search engines to find you.

Cooperating with other bloggers is another way to raise your profile on the Web. Invite guest bloggers to contribute posts, and write guest blogs for others. Sharing links in this way will help the search engines notice you. In addition, be sure to share your posts with other, relevant bloggers. Don't spam, and don't ask outright for links, but do send a courteous e-mail to let other bloggers know you've written something that might interest them.

Make sure your blog posts answer the questions people are asking online. Providing a little free information is the best way to establish yourself as an expert and to attract potential customers to your Web site. Engage the community in discussion on your blog, and respond to questions. The more you blog content that people search for, the more visible your blog will become in search engine results. More hits means more Web site traffic, which in turn means more sales.

Your blog can help the search engines find and love you. The fresher and more relevant your blog content to your market, the more the search engines will notice and rank it. By creating the right kind of content, cooperating with other bloggers, and encouraging community engagement, you can attract a huge amount of highly targeted and relevant traffic to your blog, thereby bypassing many of the expensive marketing channels your competitors rely on.

Cydney O'Sullivan is the author of *Social Marketing Superstars, Social Media Mystery to Mastery in 30 Days*. Her website is www.cydneyosullivan.com.

FACEBOOK STATUS UPDATE

Facebook offers businesses large and small an opportunity to connect with customers and potential customers in an entertaining and enriching way. Learning to write an effective Facebook status update gives you the chance to provide value to customers between transactions and can help you ensure that your customers don't forget you.

Introduction

The **purpose** of a status update to a Facebook business account is to promote your business and engage your customers. You can use Facebook to promote new products and services, announce special offers and events, provide valuable information to your customers, and build a community around your business. As you **brainstorm** about your updates, think from the point of view of your **readers**. How can you serve them? What will keep them informed, entertained, and engaged? Concentrate on providing value for them rather than just selling to them. Status updates should be kept short, so there's not much to **organize**. Consider starting with a catchy phrase, something to hook your readers' interest. Don't rush through the process of writing your status updates; the fact that they're short doesn't mean they're easy to write. Especially as you're learning, you shouldn't hesitate to go through a couple of **drafts** till you get it right. Type out your status update and read it out loud. Is it catchy? Is it interesting? If not, **revise** it until you hit just the right note.

DO	DON'T
• Post updates frequently. People will forget about your business if you don't update regularly. There's a lot of competition for attention on Facebook. If you don't show a commitment to your presence there, people will question your seriousness and lose interest.	• Don't use hard-sell tactics. If readers see nothing but sales pitches in your Facebook updates, they'll de-friend you fast. Focus on what you can offer your readers.
• Keep your updates brief. Facebook limits posts to 420 characters, and you shouldn't push that limit. Status updates of one or two sentences are best. People want to scan your update, not read a long screed.	• Don't post personal comments. Many small businesses rely on Facebook for promotion. Even if you are a small business or a one-person business, though, remember that your business updates should be appropriate for a business. Don't post about your personal feelings or opinions on this account.
• Use a conversational, friendly tone. Facebook is mainly a place where people connect with friends, so your updates should be warm and conversational.	• Don't post about politics. Using your company account to make political statements may alienate some customers, unless it's clearly related to your business. If, for instance, your business is tied to organic foods, it's not out of line to post information about government regulation of the food supply. Beware of asking your customers to advocate for you.
• Express your brand personality. Cultivate a consistent voice for status updates that is appropriate for your business.	
• Post questions for people to answer. Get them to interact. Don't post questions that require yes or no answers; really try to get a discussion going. Make sure that your questions are easy to answer and don't require a lot of thought or time.	• Don't post too much. Posting every hour is just going to annoy people. Focus on posting updates that provide real value to customers or build your customer community, not on making noise for its own sake.
• Consider using a poll to solicit engagement from readers.	
• Provide value. In addition to engaging readers in activities like discussions and polls, your Facebook	• Don't post the same content over and over. If you want to mention the sale again, don't just post it again. Some people may have missed it, but

DO (CONTINUED)	DON'T (CONTINUED)

page should offer useful content. For instance, if your business is seasonal, let customers know what they should or could be doing at each time of year. Your readers will come to think of your Facebook page as a useful source of information.

- Share photos. Not every update has to be wordy. Sharing relevant and interesting photos is a great way to engage people.

- Share updates from other businesses that provide goods or services that might be interesting to your customers. Your Facebook page will become known as a useful resource your customers can turn to.

- Change it up. Vary your posts among interesting facts, questions, photos, polls, and hints and tips, so that readers have some variety.

- Follow up on readers' comments on your update. Don't overdo it, but people like to know that you know they're there. Respond to questions that people ask and respond to interesting comments. You're the "host" of this community, so make your presence felt.

- Make sure all your posts are spelled correctly and grammatically sound. You don't want to look stupid in front of your customers.

- Learn about Facebook's metrics. Facebook, like all social media, is evolving. Educate yourself about the metrics Facebook uses to determine how much visibility status updates get, and keep up with any changes in these algorithms. A quick Google search can help you become better informed.

- Keep up-to-date on Facebook policy changes. Make sure you understand how it works so you can ensure people see your updates.

others have seen it and will be annoyed at repeated postings. If you want to call attention to something you've already posted, find a new way to deliver value to customers around the posting. Mention a special sale item, create a poll, or ask a question instead.

- Don't lose interest. It can take time to build a community on Facebook. Once you start, you should be prepared to go for the long haul, until people know about your business and you get the hang of using Facebook well.

LIKE THIS

Consider using these Facebook update styles to engage your customers.

Happy Mother's Day!
Save 10% on all parenting titles in the store, now through Sunday!

SPECIAL OCCASIONS

Reserve now for Thanksgiving!
A traditional meal with all the fixings. Reserve now—we sell out every year!

It's a rainy day in LA. We are open and warm and cozy and ready to cook you a lovely dinner!

TOPICAL UPDATES

Just a reminder we'll be closing early for the holiday on Friday. Happy Rosh Hashanah, everyone!

The peaches are here! Leslie's is celebrating peach season with homemade peach cobbler and peach ice cream. Mention this status update for a 10% discount on your whole meal.

SEASONAL UPDATES

It's September! Time to prune your roses for the winter season. Stop in for rose-care hints and tips.

Winter Solstice Sale! A special one-day event to observe the shortest day of the year. Buy one table lamp and get a second at 40% off. Let there be light!

Keep your family warm and dry this winter. Schedule a roof inspection by September 1 and receive a 10% discount.

Our three best-selling entrées are home-style meat loaf, lemon chicken, and mac and cheese. Which is your favorite, and why?

ASK A QUESTION

What was the name and species of your first pet? How old were you? Favorite memory?

CREATE A POLL   What's the most delicious gelato flavor?
**Mandarin orange
**Pineapple
**Kiwi

What's the BEST thing about moving to a new place?
**More space!
**Making a fresh start
**Exploring a new neighborhood

Three Keys to Promoting Your Business on Facebook

Businesses large and small are using Facebook to interact with customers, and you can, too.

- Being a regular and reliable presence on Facebook will keep your business at the forefront of your customers' minds.

- Offer real value. Your updates should do more than just promote your products and announce sales. Give your customers information they can use, and they'll begin to turn to you as an authority.

- Let Facebook's metrics show you what your customers like. Facebook sends periodic updates about how frequently people view and engage with your page. Use that information to provide more of what your customers want.

TWITTER

Twitter can help companies build relationships with customers and potential customers. Tweets are short—a maximum of 140 characters—but that doesn't make them easy to write. It takes time to learn how to make your tweets valuable and interesting to your public, but it can be well worth the effort.

Introduction

The **purpose** of using Twitter for your business is to create contact and interaction with your customers and provide them with valuable content. There is a *lot* of competition on Twitter. To build a successful community of Twitter followers, it's absolutely critical that you think from the point of view of your **readers**. Who are they? What will interest them? What will make your tweets more compelling than the dozens of other items vying for their attention? Don't skimp on time **brainstorming** about your readers' needs and interests. If you take your readers for granted or fail to understand them, you will lose them. Tweets are **organized** like headlines: the point is to attract the readers' interest and motivate them to click on a link. You should plan to work with **drafts** until you become adept at tweeting. Try reading your tweet out loud before you post it. Twitter is conversational, and your tweet should flow with the ease of conversation. Although tweets are brief, you shouldn't treat them carelessly. Be sure they're free from typos and misspellings. If it doesn't sound right, or if it contains errors, **revise** it. Practice makes perfect, and soon you'll find your own unique Twitter voice.

DO	DON'T
• Read a lot of tweets. If you're just beginning to tweet for your business, read extensively other companies' tweets to educate yourself about how those companies are using Twitter. Listen for their distinctive styles, and work to differentiate your voice and your offerings from those of your competitors.	• Don't use hard-sell tactics on Twitter. Twitter is really about marketing, not sales.
	• Don't tweet only about your company or your products and services. Retweet information from other companies or individuals your customers would find interesting. If your followers see you as a conduit to interesting content, they'll like you even better.
• Be extremely careful if you have multiple Twitter accounts. Be sure you're posting appropriately	• Don't use Twitter just to drive people to your

DO (CONTINUED)

on the right account. Inadvertently posting a personal tweet on your business page can cause big problems.

- Show some personality. A business account should have a brand identity and a unique voice. Make your tweets engaging and interesting to read.
- Tweet regularly. Your followers want to be able to rely on regular tweets. If you tweet only sporadically, followers will question your commitment and lose interest.
- Space out your tweets across the day. Don't dump a bunch of tweets in the morning and then ignore Twitter for the rest of the day.
- Provide real value for your customers. Share useful information. Ask questions that start interesting discussions.
- Share content from other businesses. Look for companies in other industries that share your customers, and retweet their content. A mortgage broker might retweet useful information from a financial adviser. A yoga studio might retweet information from a nutritionist. Think about what might interest your followers, and be creative.
- Shorten your links. Twitter provides a sidebar that makes this easy to do.
- Learn to use hashtags. A hashtag (the # symbol) is used to mark key words in a tweet in order to make your tweet more easily searchable. Check Twitter's support center (http://support.twitter .com/) for more information about using hashtags effectively.
- Respond to comments. Twitter is about conversation. If you want your customers to engage with you, you must engage with them.

DON'T (CONTINUED)

Facebook page, blog, or website. Tweets are short, but it's still possible to provide value to your customers.

- Don't post a tweet you think is dull or not your best. One of the keys to success on Twitter is consistently posting good content. If your latest effort seems below your regular standard, work a little harder on it till you have it right. If the quality of your tweets starts to slip, you will lose followers.
- Don't use celebrities as models. Some of the most popular people on Twitter are celebrities, but they typically don't make good models for businesses. Celebrities can get away with silly empty tweets full of typos; you can't.
- Don't tweet too frequently. Frequent, regular tweets are a good thing, but each one must really provide valuable content, not just make noise for the sake of making noise.
- Don't rely too much on retweets. It's great to share interesting stuff from others, but be sure you are offering enough original content to make your followers value you for yourself.
- Don't give up. It takes time to learn to write good tweets, and it takes time to build followers. If you want to use Twitter for your business, make a commitment to spending the time to do it and do it right.

- Write your tweets so there's room for them to be retweeted. Aim to use no more than 110 characters if you want to be retweeted.
- Check that your links work. This step is especially important with shortened links.
- Give credit when you retweet.
- Make sure your tweets are free from typos, poor grammar, incorrect punctuation, and misspellings. Careless errors really stand out in tweets, so avoid them.

LIKE THIS

INSTEAD OF THIS . . .	Spring sale! www.gardncntr.com
. . . TRY THIS	Renew your lawn at sale prices! www.gardncntr.com
	Learn to plant bright floral borders! http:/bit.ly/5w3pjM
	Free climbing rosebush if you mention this ad! www.gardncntr.com
INSTEAD OF THIS . . .	Great article on mutual funds in WSJ!
. . . TRY THIS	Great article in @WSJ discusses the future of mutual funds. http:/bit.ly/9u0lmN
INSTEAD OF THIS . . .	Check out our latest blog post on preparing your home for sale—http:/bit.ly/6z0ppK
. . . TRY THIS	"Five Ways to Make Your Home Irresistible to Buyers" —http:/bit.ly/6z0ppK

Twitter for Business

Twitter can be an amazing tool for business . . . but only if you use it right. If you do it wrong, your tweets can drown with all of the others that make up the River Twitter. There are therefore two ways to stand out and use Twitter effectively for business:

1. As a broadcast tool: Because of its sometimes-frustrating 140-character limit, Twitter is uniquely designed to impart short bursts of information quickly. The key is to use the 80–20 Rule: 80% of your tweets should benefit your customers/followers. Give them a link to an interesting article or a quirky video. Offer them something that makes their day or business better.

The real magic of Twitter in this regard is when your tweets get retweeted. That is the 21st-century form of word-of-mouth advertising. It is a follower telling his or her followers, "Hey, this is something valuable I found that I think would be of interest to you." That is how you grow your following and extend your brand. But you only get that if 80% of your tweets add real value to your network.

The other 20% of your tweets can then be more self-serving—mentioning a sale you are having, or a new product you are rolling out, that sort of thing.

2. As a networking tool: The other smart way to use Twitter is as a way to converse with and meet new people, people you would not otherwise have a chance to meet. There are conversations about your industry and business going on all the time at Twitter. Once you begin to inject yourself into these conversations in a meaningful way, you will meet new people and that will lead to new opportunities.

Happy tweeting!

Steve D. Strauss is a *USA Today* senior columnist on small business topics. He is president and CEO at The Self-Employed (www.theselfemployed.com).

Reports

BASIC REPORT FORMAT

Business reports can range in length from a single page to hundreds of pages. Short, informal reports may be formatted as simple memos. Longer, more formal reports follow a conventional format, partly for the ease and convenience of both writer and reader.

Organizations may have their own conventions for writing and formatting reports. You can adapt the structure below to suit your needs.

Letter of Transmittal

A letter of transmittal accompanies the report and is directed to the report's key audience, often its sponsors. It may highlight specific sections of the report, including conclusions and recommendations (see Transmittal on page 535.

Front Matter

Title page. This page includes the report's title, its author(s), sometimes its sponsor(s), and the date.

Abstract. An abstract is a summary usually 200–250 words in length.

Table of Contents. For ease of use, be sure to list all the sections and the subheadings in the report.

List of Figures. Create a list of figures if your report includes more than five charts, graphs, illustrations, drawings, or photos.

List of Tables. Create a list of tables if your report includes more than five tables.

Foreword. A foreword is an optional introductory statement written by someone other than the authors of the report who is in good position to place the report in context. Including a foreword is optional. The foreword generally offers background information and may address the purpose of the report.

Preface. Including a preface is optional. A preface may discuss the background, purpose, and scope of the report. It may also contain acknowledgments of people and organizations that provided assistance in compiling the report.

List of abbreviations and symbols. Create a list of abbreviations and symbols whenever there is a chance that your readers will not understand all those used in your report.

Body

Executive Summary. An executive summary is typically shorter than an abstract, no more than 10 percent of the length of the report (see Executive Summary on page 537).

Introduction. The introduction provides the reader basic knowledge and background they need in order to understand the report. Include the subject, the purpose, and the scope of the report as well as an explanation of the approach you took in researching and writing it.

Text. The text of the report should include descriptive headings to make it easier for readers to browse.

Conclusions. The conclusions section summarizes the main findings of the study.

Recommendations. Offer your suggestions about what should be done, based on the findings of the report.

References. List any studies, books, articles, and web resources mentioned in the report. Include any interviews and surveys cited in the report.

Back Matter

Bibliography. List any printed sources or web resources used in researching the report.

Glossary. A glossary is a list of special terms and their definitions. Create a glossary when you are not sure your audience will understand all the terminology used in the report.

Index. An index is a list of key terms of interest to readers, along with the page numbers where those terms appear. An index can make it significantly easier for readers to navigate long reports.

TRANSMITTAL

A transmittal is a cover letter or memo that accompanies another document—a report, contract, proposal, or a working draft of a document. It typically includes information not found within the other document, including background and due dates. It might also direct the reader's attention to sections of the main document that will be of particular interest or relevance. In some cases, transmittals may also contain sensitive information, such as a password for a protected electronic document.

A transmittal can be part of an electronic document, a cover e-mail, or attached to a paper document.

Introduction

The **purpose** of a transmittal letter or memo is to provide a context for the accompanying document and to discuss its content less formally than in the document itself. Your **reader** will typically be some stakeholder in the project, often the person who commissioned it. A transmittal is usually brief, so there is little content to **brainstorm**. However, you do have the reader's attention in a transmittal, albeit briefly, and it offers a good opportunity to highlight important findings, upcoming deadlines, and other critical information. Although a transmittal may be brief, it's still wise to let your first **draft** sit for

MODEL OUTLINE

A transmittal should be brief and easy to scan.
Opening: State your reason for writing and what you are sending. Provide the title of the document and restate the terms under which it was prepared.
Middle: Provide a brief overview of the purpose and the contents of the document you are sending. Note any outstanding issues, such as deadlines for further action. For the convenience of the reader, a transmittal may also highlight a key finding described in the attached document.
Conclusion: Thank your reader. Request approval or acknowledgment and provide a deadline, if relevant. Offer to answer any questions the reader might have.

a while and revisit it later. As you review, think from your reader's point of view. Have you overlooked anything she needs to know? **Revise** to eliminate typos and ensure completeness.

DO	DON'T
• Get to the point right away. State your reason for writing in the first sentence.	• Don't write a transmittal in a slapdash way. At the very least it's an opportunity to create goodwill.
• Use formatting to make the transmittal easy to scan. If the transmittal is long, use subheadings to break up the text. Consider using bold to highlight any critical findings or upcoming deadlines.	• Don't overlook any deadlines or critical information.
• Ensure your reader has your contact information, and encourage her to reach out to you if she has questions or comments.	

NOT LIKE THIS . . .

> This transmittal is fine as far as it goes, but John misses an opportunity to convey information that might be useful for Ms. Chen. She's more likely to read the document if she thinks there is something interesting inside.

Dear Ms. Chen:

Enclosed is the report tracking the effectiveness of our Employee Wellness Initiative over the period of 2011 to 2013, as requested by Arielle Dunham, Vice President, on October 3.

If you need any further information, please do not hesitate to contact me at 212.888.1111 or at jblock@tfbfhindustries.com.

Sincerely,

John Block

Enclosure

. . . LIKE THIS

Dear Ms. Chen:

Enclosed is the report tracking the effectiveness of our Employee Wellness Initiative over the period of 2011 to 2013, as requested by Arielle Dunham, Vice President, on October 3.

The report is the result of meetings and interviews with regional heads of HR for each of our divisions, as well as nationally administered surveys of line employees and supervisory personnel.

Findings suggest that the Employee Wellness Initiative has resulted in significant improvement in employee attendance and a drop in sick days. Details of these findings, including a statistical breakout of findings by region, can be found in the Results section of the report.

If you need any further information, please do not hesitate to contact me at 212.888.1111 or at jblock@tfbfhindustries.com.

Sincerely,

John Block

Enclosure

> Just a couple of lines can convey the methodology of the study and make its findings look more authoritative.

> John notes the most important findings of the report and makes them easy for Ms. Chen to scan by formatting them in bold. He also directs her to the section of the report where she can read more details.

EXECUTIVE SUMMARY

The executive summary of a report includes only the highlights of the report and is designed primarily for decision makers. Readers will typically glance over the executive summary and use it to help them decide whether to read the entire report and which sections to read carefully.

Introduction

The **purpose** of an executive summary in a report is to provide a quick overview of the content of the report, for readers who may or may not read the entire document. A well-written executive summary can also pique the interest of readers and encourage them to read the report more fully. Assume your **readers** are in a hurry and need a condensed version of the report and its findings. **Brainstorm** from your readers' point of view: what do they need to know in order to grasp the essence of the report? What might make them want to read more? To identify critical information to include in the executive summary, reread the report and highlight areas of interest as you do. The **organization** of an executive summary typically follows the outline of the report. **Draft** your executive summary, and then give it to someone who is not associated with the project to review. Ask him if the summary makes sense and if he has any questions after he reads it. **Revise** according to his feedback. Ensure that the summary is free of typos and other errors.

DO	DON'T
• Understand your organization's norms when it comes to the length of an executive summary. Some organizations limit a summary to one or two pages; others have a word limit. In any case, no executive summary should be longer than 10 percent of the entire report.	• Don't provide unnecessary technical detail in the executive summary. Use only as much technical content as is required to help your readers understand the report.
• Describe the report accurately and objectively. Don't "spin" any of the content.	• Don't introduce any information or recommendations that are not included in the report.
• Cover every main section of the report, and provide proportional coverage to each.	
• Describe the problem or opportunity that motivated the report.	
• Describe the method(s) that were used to conduct the investigation.	
• Summarize the report's findings.	
• State any recommendations offered in the report.	
• Use formatting like subheadings and bulleted lists to break up a long executive summary and make it easier to scan.	

LIKE THIS

Each year employee illness leads to significant costs in health care expense as well as lost productivity. This report was commissioned to track the effectiveness of DBFH's Employee Wellness Initiative over the period of 2011 to 2013.

The Employee Wellness Initiative was initially launched in mid-2008 with the aim of reducing sick time and health care expense. In the period of 2008 to 2010, it is estimated that the Initiative cut sick time by 4% and health care expenditure by 2% nationwide. In 2010, it was decided to revamp the Initiative to improve results and to evaluate its effectiveness after two years of operation.

Research for this report was carried out through surveys of line employees and supervisory personnel in each of DBFH's US divisions. Survey results were then shared with regional heads of HR for each division and follow-up interviews conducted. This report presents both quantitative data from the surveys and the qualitative findings from the interviews.

Findings suggest that the Employee Wellness Initiative has resulted in significant improvement in employee attendance and a drop in sick days nationwide. Absenteeism dropped by an aggregate 5% during the period studied. Costs for health care dropped by an aggregate 3%. DBFH's Western region saw the greatest improvement in both areas, with the Midwest, Eastern, and Southern following in that order. Overall the improvement in the Southern region was weakest, with some areas of the Southern division actually reporting increases in absenteeism and health care costs.

It is recommended that:

- The Employee Wellness Program be continued at the same level of funding (adjusted for inflation) for another two-year period.
- A follow-up study be conducted in 2015 to assess the effectiveness of the program.
- Follow-up studies be conducted to determine the causes of the anomalous findings in the Southern division and to develop recommendations to improve rates of illness and absenteeism in that division.

INCIDENT REPORT

An incident report—sometimes known as an accident report or trouble report—provides a timely record when something goes awry. Some companies have incident forms to fill in; in other cases, you'll need to write it out yourself. Incident reports may be used in legal proceedings, so it's wise to take the task seriously.

Introduction

The **purpose** of an incident report is to provide an official record of an unusual occurrence at a place of business. These reports may be reviewed in order to improve safety procedures, to determine if insurance claims should be paid, and in some cases to assess legal liability. The **readers** of an incident report are generally supervisors in charge, their supervisors, insurance adjustors, and potentially legal counsel. They will expect a complete, objective, and clear description of what happened. Your **brainstorming** in this case involves assembling as complete a view of what happened as possible. The sidebar "Incident Report Checklist" suggests a format that you can use to **organize** your report. As you write your **draft**, use an objective and neutral tone. Unless the incident was quite minor, you will want to go through a couple of drafts to ensure completeness. Review and **revise** to ensure your report is complete and the tone is appropriate.

INCIDENT REPORT CHECKLIST

An incident report provides as complete an accounting of an incident as possible. Your report should contain the following information:

- Exact time, date, and location of the incident
- Who was involved
- Exactly what happened
- Any injuries that occurred, and any treatment given
- Any emergency personnel who were summoned, and the time they arrived
- Any property damage
- Any work stoppage or delay
- Any witnesses, and their complete contact information

DO	DON'T
• Write your report as soon as possible following the incident, so your memory—as well as others' memories—is as fresh as possible.	• Don't express any emotions or opinions about the incident. Your report should be objective and matter-of-fact.
• Use neutral language. Focus on creating a complete report of what actually occurred.	• Don't assign blame for what happened, or use language that implicitly blames anyone. Your report may be used later to help determine responsibility for what happened, but it is not your job here to render a verdict of responsibility.
• Be as comprehensive and detailed as possible. A detailed and complete report can help investigators understand exactly what happened.	
• Note other contributors to the report, as necessary. If you did not witness everything yourself, you may need to ask others for information. Make a note of the information supplied by others.	• Don't include recommendations for preventing a similar incident in the future. Remember, you are just recording what happened.
• Supplement your report with photos, drawings, or diagrams.	

LIKE THIS

> The report makes it clear that Charlayne was the source of the information about how the accident happened.

> We know exactly what Donna did and that her action was appropriate and did not cause further harm.

At approximately 9:17 a.m. on February 11, Charlayne Peters incurred a severe burn on her left hand from the coffeemaker in the staff kitchen. According to Charlayne, the glass pot exploded, sending hot water flying. Charlayne was in a great deal of pain and crying, and her hand was blistered. Donna Bunini assisted by administering first aid to Charlayne by helping her hold her hand under cold running water. At approximately 9:31 a.m., Charlayne decided to go to the emergency room. Donna accompanied her. Donna returned to the office at approximately 12:10 p.m. She reported that Charlayne was treated at the ER and sent home with a second-degree burn. Donna reported that the ER doctor expects Charlyane to be out of the office for approximately two days. The kitchen area was cleaned up and all broken glass removed.

Personnel involved:
Charlayne Peters   x45756 cell 515.888.1111   cmpeters37@cpsdelivery.com
Donna Bunini   x45788 cell 515.973.1111   dlbunini45@cpsdelivery.com

> The source of the information about Charlayne's condition is clear.

> It's a good idea to include Charlayne's cell phone number if she's likely to be out of the office for a few days.

Sales and Billing

SALES LETTER

Asales letter is a form of direct-mail marketing especially tailored for a targeted audience. Improved data gathering and processing techniques can make sales letters even more effective than in the past. Despite the explosion in e-mail marketing, e-mail has not yet supplanted traditional sales letters sent through the postal mail. A letter can still provide benefits that an e-mail cannot. A sales letter that contains useful information or an enticing promise may be kept and referred to long after an e-mail solicitation has been deleted. The trick is in making a convincing appeal to your readers.

Introduction

The **purpose** of a sales letter is to grab the readers' attention and convince them that your offer—whatever it is—is the best way to solve a problem they have and motivate them to call you or make a purchase. Thinking from the **readers'** point of view is absolutely critical in writing an effective sales letter. Mention the product or service you're selling *only* in the context of serving the readers' needs, not to praise it in and of itself. A list of features and benefits—no matter how impressive—is not likely to motivate a reader to take the next step. **Brainstorm** from your readers' point of view. What do they need, and how will your offer meet that need? Use the Model Outline (page 544) to help **organize** your letter. Plan to go through several **drafts** before you finalize your letter. It's a good idea to test your sales letter to see how people respond to it. Ask your test readers if the letter keeps their attention and if they would be motivated to call you or take the steps to make a purchase. Ask them what's missing. **Revise** accordingly. Proof-read carefully. Typos and other errors can damage your credibility, so be scrupulous about correcting them before you send out your letter.

Three Keys to Effective Sales Letters

Writing an effective sales letter is a skill that's honed over time. These three critical insights will help you understand your potential customers and the sales process.

It's not about you. Effective sales is about serving the customer, not fulfilling your desires. Nothing is more irrelevant than what you think people *should* want. What matters is what people *do* want. To write an effective sales letter, then, you need to learn about your potential market. Brainstorm, talk to people, and conduct interviews with your potential customers. Stay flexible, and be willing to adjust your pitch to accommodate what you learn. We often find there's a big difference between what we know to be true and what we hope to be true. Hope is a fine thing, but it's a poor basis for a sales and marketing campaign.

People buy outcomes. When people make a purchase, they're not really buying a *thing*; they're buying a perceived *outcome*. What do your potential buyers need? If they bought from you, what benefits would they enjoy? What would their lives look like? How would they feel? What would it mean for them? Understanding the *outcome* potential buyers are looking for will help you craft a letter that can really move them.

Understand why people don't buy. Now that you have some idea about why people buy, think a little about why they don't. What objections might they have to making the purchase? Face those objections head-on, and deal with them directly. Pretending those objections don't exist or don't matter is not an effective strategy; anticipating them and answering them in advance is.

Finally, and perhaps most importantly, **offer real value, and believe in what you sell.** Let's face it, some people perceive sales professionals as unscrupulous. The best way to deal with this negative stereotype is to embody its opposite. When you offer value to your customers and truly believe in what you're selling, selling becomes about serving the needs of others. Your customers will benefit from such an attitude, and so will you.

Steve Harrison's company, Bradley Communications, provides a variety of publications, services, and training events for authors, experts, entrepreneurs, nonprofit organizations, public relations professionals, and others to help them refine, promote, and monetize their message. Steve is the cocreator (with Jack Canfield) of www.bestsellerblueprint.com.

Model Outline

Unlike many forms of writing, sales letters often benefit from being long, often several pages. A typical flow for a sales letter is the following:

Headline

Opening paragraph with a compelling hook

Discussion of the problem that your product or service solves

Introduction of your product or service as the solution to the problem

Description of how your product solves the problem

Overview of features and benefits of the produce or service

Offer of a discount or a special, or set a time limit

Offer of a guarantee, if relevant

Concluding paragraph with a call to action. Sum up the value of the offer and the time limitation. Urge the reader to call you, visit your website, and so on.

PS in which you repeat the sales message and the call to action

DO	DON'T
• Develop a very clear and specific idea of who your reader is. What do they need? What are they looking for? What kinds of things might catch and keep their attention?	• Don't write long block paragraphs. If the copy looks difficult to read, it won't be read.
• Begin your letter with a gripping opening line. It's your chance to hook the reader. You may want to write the opening later, or rewrite it.	• Don't use a lot of jargon or unnecessary technical language. Of course, if you are selling a technical product, you will need to use technical language.
• Describe the problem and its consequences.	• Don't exaggerate or use inflated language. Strings of superlatives like "revolutionary" or "amazing" begin to sound silly pretty quickly. Focus instead on exactly how the product will meet the readers' needs.
• Think from your readers' point of view. They'll be asking "What's in it for me?" Make sure you let them know.	
• Customize your letters. Consider segmenting your readership based on data you have about purchase patterns, for example. Create customized letters that appeal directly to those consumers rather than sending everyone the same form letter.	• Don't mention price too early in the letter. It's generally wiser to wait to mention price until you've piqued your customers' interest, unless low price is the strongest selling point of your product.
• Start with a powerful headline. Often the headline can make the difference between your letter being read and being recycled. Many copywriters write the headline last, after they have crafted the entire message. Take your time to develop the right headline.	• Don't use multiple exclamation points. And use single ones sparingly. Your letter will begin sounding like a car salesman shouting on the radio or TV.
• Keep your letter reader-centric throughout. Don't write about yourself. Focus on your readers and their needs.	• Don't take the prospective customer for granted. Use a conversational tone, but be respectful. Don't patronize or harry or threaten the customer.
• Use a friendly and conversational tone. Write directly to the reader, as though you were talking to a friend.	• Don't try to put too many points in your letter. Focus on your strongest sales point. More isn't better; attention diffuses and diminishes. If you have a lot of points, plan a series of letters rather than trying to fit everything into one.
• Build trust with the reader. Include testimonials or mention other clients and customers—any way to build trust.	• Don't trash your competitors openly. It's alienating and makes you look bad.
• Use short paragraphs of three to five lines.	
• Format your letter so it's easy to scan. Readers will scan a letter before they decide to read it. In	

DO (CONTINUED)

addition to short paragraphs, use subheadings
and bulleted lists to make the text inviting.

- Include a call to action. Ask your readers to call
  you, e-mail you, or visit your website.
- Make it easy for readers to reach you. Make your
  phone number, e-mail address, website address,
  whatever, very easy to see in the letter.
- Use a PS. Many readers will read a PS before they
  read the body of the letter, so make the message
  strong and repeat the call to action in your PS.

LIKE THIS

An attractive and intriguing headline makes the reader want to read more.	**Enjoy organic produce grown in your own backyard —and never lift a finger**

Dear [Pasadena resident],

We Pasadenans live in paradise. We have fertile soil, sun year-round, and spacious yards. We can grow anything here. So why don't we?

Jacob lays out the problem: we're eating bad food, and worse, we're feeding it to our kids.	The sad truth is that we're all too busy to take advantage of Pasadena's fabulous growing power. We dash from the office, dash to the market where we pick up a meal someone else has cooked, and then dash home and throw it in the microwave. We're eating lot of food additives and not getting enough fruit and vegetables in our diet. What's worse, our kids are growing up without the simple pleasure of fresh, luscious homegrown produce. With our climate, that's almost a sin!

Jacob has the solution to the problem.	I know you don't have the time to plant and care for an organic vegetable garden in your backyard, but I do, and I'll do it for you!

Jacob describes the service, always keeping his focus on benefits to the reader.	Pasadena Greenyard is a unique garden care company that will come to your home, inspect your yard with you, discuss the fruits and vegetables you want to grow, and then plant and maintain your

very own organic produce garden. We'll take care of the weeding, non-toxic pest control and fertilizing, general plant care . . . we'll even do the watering for you. All you need to do is step out the door and pick what you want to eat, whenever you want it, straight from your own organic garden.

We'll also plant and raise fruit trees for you—oranges and lemons, plums, pomegranates, avocados, whatever you want. Most fruit trees start bearing within a year of being planted.

When you hire Pasadena Greenyard, you'll have fresh, homegrown fruits and vegetables year-round. A variety of lettuces for salads, delicious watermelon in the summer, beautiful pumpkins and other squash in the fall, tomatoes and carrots and radishes and beans. Beautiful purple eggplants, bright heirloom tomatoes . . . the sky's the limit.

> The middle paragraphs expand on what the reader can gain from hiring this company.

Just think how much you and your family will enjoy having your very own vegetable garden. Instead of coming inside for an unhealthy sugary snack, your kids can pick and munch on sweet blueberries and strawberries from the garden. Instead of snacking on salty, greasy chips, you could be enjoying your own fresh, crisp carrots, celery, and zucchini.

Studies show that having plenty of fresh fruit and vegetables on hand is key to losing weight and keeping weight off. Imagine if all you have to do is step out the back door to have all the fresh produce you and your family could ever want.

> Plus you'll probably lose weight! Who could say no?

As a special introductory offer, Pasadena Greenyard is offering complete service for only $200 a month. Consider what you'd spend on organic produce—or even regular produce from conventional farms that use pesticides—and you'll see that's a small price to pay for unlimited organic produce from your own home garden.

Once we have our first 20 customers, that price is going to go up, so call us now at 626-800-1111.

> Jacob offers a discount, with a time limit, and issues a call to action.

Doesn't your family deserve this healthy, sustainable, and fun treat? An organic garden is a gift you and your family can enjoy year-round, and

> Jacob repeats the call to action.

we'll do the work for you! Call us now at 626.800.1111 to set up your consultation.

Sincerely,

Jacob Marsh

Pasadena Greenyard

The PS offers a special incentive and again repeats the call to action.

PS—If you are one of the first 10 people to call, we'll throw in five fruit trees of your choice—a value of up to $150—and plant them for you absolutely free! We expect a lot more than 10 callers, so call us right away at 626-800-1111 to set up your service and reserve your fruit trees.

SALES PROPOSALS

Businesses provide sales proposals (sometimes just called "estimates") to potential customers to let them know the projected cost of job or a project. The content of a sales proposal will vary widely, depending on the kind of business you're in.

Some businesses will not start work until the customer has reviewed and signed the estimate authorizing them to do so. Sometimes estimates are binding. In other cases, the proposal contains a clause stating that the final cost may vary depending on a variety of circumstances. It's in your best interest, as well as your customers', to create as complete and accurate an estimate as possible in your sales proposal.

Introduction

The **purpose** of a sales proposal is to give a potential buyer or customer an idea of what he'll be spending if he decides to do business with you and exactly what he can expect to receive. A proposal can be a kind of contract, and deviations from the estimate will be discussed. Your **reader** will use the proposal to decide whether or not to hire you, so there should be no surprises. Be sure you **brainstorm** comprehensively about all the costs you will incur and will have to pass along to your customer plus the profit you need to make on the job. The example below provides a model for **organizing** your sales proposal. It's a good idea to **draft** the proposal and then take a break from it before you submit it to your potential client or customer. Go back and check to see that you've included everything, and that your numbers add up accurately. Errors can be costly or, at best, awkward. **Revise** accordingly.

ESTIMATING CHECKLIST

Consider the following costs in calculating your estimate:
- Labor (wages, insurance, Social Security for yourself and any employees)
- Transportation
- Materials
- Equipment rental costs
- General overhead
- Your profit (as a percentage of the subtotal)

Your estimate should include the following information:
- Overall price
- Cost breakdown, listing the components of the price
- Work schedule and deadlines detailing when work will be done or products delivered
- Terms and conditions for payment
- Time period for which the estimate is valid

DO	DON'T
<ul><li>Write your proposal on company letterhead or an official estimate form that carries your company name and contact information.</li><li>Calculate your labor and materials costs. Don't guess.</li><li>Date your proposal, and include an expiration date for the price quoted. Your costs will likely increase over time, so don't bind yourself to a price forever.</li><li>Include a statement that the price is subject to change, if appropriate. Be sure to outline very clearly the factors that may cause cost overruns, including unanticipated circumstances on the job or changes in the customer's requirements.</li><li>Consider providing several different estimates, if the customer thinks he might want different products or services.</li><li>Develop a template. If you are starting a business where you're going to write a lot of proposals, create a template for future use.</li></ul>	<ul><li>Don't neglect to include all charges in your proposal. There should be no surprises for your client or customer.</li></ul>

LIKE THIS

Page 1 of 2

Joseph Robertson
Robertson Business Associates
100 E. 55th Street
New York, NY 10022

8.24.12

RESPONSE TO REQUEST FOR PROPOSAL

A. SCOPE OF THE PROJECT

Stefan Killen Design proposes to design 1) a brochure and
2) a series of three pamphlets for Robertson Business
Associates. The pieces will extend the look and feel of the
client's current branding.

1. **Brochure:** 12 pages plus cover, 8.5 x 11, 4 colors,
   approx 10 photos throughout.
2. **Three pamphlets:** 8.5 x 15, tri-fold 8.5 x 5, 4 colors,
   approx 5 photos throughout.

C. SCHEDULE

We estimate that production of the brochure and three pamphlets
can be completed within the following eight-week schedule:

9.3 – 9.17	Design development phase, with presentation of initial concepts to client on 9.17.12.
9.19	Feedback on initial concepts due to SKD.
9.20 – 9.27	Design refinement phase, with presentation of refined concepts to client on 9.27.12.
9.28	Feedback on design refinements due to SKD.
10.1 – 10.16	Layout preparation phase, with presentation of initial layouts to client on 10.11.12.
10.17	Delivery of print-ready files to printer.
10.31	Delivery of printed material to client.

B. PROJECT DEVELOPMENT

The following outlines the development of the brochure and
pamphlets:

1. **Project clarification and goals:** Stefan Killen Design and
   client will begin the initial phase of the project by discussing
   the client's design ideas and goals.
2. **Design Development:** We will develop two design concepts
   for each item, and will present them for client review.
3. **Design refinement:** Client will comment on the designs. Up
   to two rounds of design revisions will be made to each item.
4. **Layout preparation:** Once final designs have been
   approved, and final copy received, we will prepare layouts for
   each project. If necessary, up to three rounds of proofreading
   revisions will be made to layouts.
5. **Delivery of mechanicals:** Upon final approval of layouts,
   we will prepare and deliver digital print-ready mechanicals
   to printer.

68 Jay Street, Suite 305 • Brooklyn, NY 11201 • 718-222-2960 • info@stefankillendesign.com • www.stefankillendesign.com

D. PRICING

Design and production of the following items:

1. Brochure design and production

Brochure design	$2,000
Brochure production	$3,700
Photography management	$1,500
TOTAL	**$7,200**

2. Pamphlets design and production

Pamphlet design	$2,000
Pamphlet production (for three pamphlets)	$3,600
Photography management	$1,100
TOTAL	**$6,700**

3. Print Management (If requested)

Printer and paper management	$300
Half-day press check	$600
TOTAL	**$900**

E. TERMS

Design and production of the following items:

Professional fees: Project fee will be billed in two phases, with the first payment for 50% of the total due upon signing of proposal, and the second payment plus reimbursable production expenses due within 30 days of completion of each project.

Expenses: In addition to fees, Stefan Killen Design shall be reimbursed for all outside services or expenses related to the execution of this proposal, including, but not limited to stock photography, professional photography, professional illustration, and messenger/delivery services.

Changes: Changes beyond the scope of the proposal will be charged on an hourly basis at the rate of $150.00/hr.

Termination of agreement: Assuming just cause, either party reserves the right to terminate this agreement after giving ten days written notice to the other. Stefan Killen Design shall be paid for services and reimbursables incurred under this proposal up to the date of such termination.

Proofreading: Client will be responsible for proofreading final mechanical.

Sales Tax: Sales tax is charged to for-profit clients within NY State at 8.875%.

Stefan Killen   Date
Stefan Killen Design, Ltd

Joseph Robertson   Date
Robertson Business Associates

68 Jay Street, Suite 305 • Brooklyn, NY 11201 • 718-222-2960 • info@stefankillendesign.com • www.stefankillendesign.com

Stefan Killen is a graphic designer and photographer whose work is included in the book *Out of Focus*. His websites are www.stefankillendesign.com and www.pinholeny.com.

LONG SALES PROPOSALS

In some industries and for jobs of a significant size, businesses will submit long sales proposals. These proposals are often written in response to a request for proposal (RFP), which is prepared and circulated by an organization in search of a vendor to do a particular job.

A long sales proposal is formatted very much like a formal report and may include the following elements:

> Letter of transmittal
> Title page
> Executive summary
> Description of current problem
> Description of current method
> Description of proposed method
> Analytical comparison of current and proposed methods
> Equipment requirements
> Cost analysis
> Delivery schedule
> Summary of benefits
> Breakdown of responsibilities
> Description of vendor, including team bios
> Vendor's promotional literature
> Contract

INVOICE

An invoice is a statement delivered to a client or customer outlining the nature of the goods or services provided and requesting payment for them.

E-mail invoices are common these days. It's fine for an invoice to exist only as an electronic document, but it's critical for you to have access to it in the future. If you send an invoice in the body of an e-mail rather than as an attachment, be sure you have it backed up somewhere you can find it later.

Introduction

The **purpose** of an invoice is to create a record of goods or services provided and to bill your client or customer for such. An invoice might also include a record of payments received or serve as a receipt for payment in full. An invoice serves as a kind of contract between you and your **reader** so that both of you know the nature and extent of what's being paid for and the price being paid. Many companies and consultants have templates for invoices that can be customized with new customer and product information. Whether you're writing a one-off invoice or creating a new template for your business, be sure to **brainstorm** all the information you will need: your name, contact information, payment information (including tax ID if necessary), and anything else you need to facilitate getting paid. Most invoices conform to a standard **organizational** template; the Model Outline provides a good starting point for you. There's not much to be **drafted** per se, just information to be completed. Before you send off your invoice to your client or customer, read it over to ensure it's complete and accurate, and **revise** as necessary. In particular, be sure to double-check the total being billed. Because an invoice may have the force of a contract, if you enter the wrong amount you may be creating problems for yourself and your customer.

MODEL OUTLINE

An invoice should supply all the information a client or customer needs in order to pay you.

Header: Include your business name, full contact information, invoice number, taxpayer ID, and the date, as well as your client's name and contact information.

Body: Itemize the products or services provided. Specify price per unit and amount for individual items.

Footer: Provide a grand total, including any tax amount, your return policy for goods, and any policies on late payment. End with a thank-you.

DO	DON'T
• Provide your full contact information on your invoice, including your postal address, e-mail address, and phone number.	• Don't assume your customer will understand what the invoice is for. Provide complete information about the goods or services provided and the billing period covered.
• Check with your client or customer to see what information their accounting department needs in order to pay you. To pay an independent contractor, they will likely need a taxpayer identification number or Social Security number. Large businesses generally have rather complicated and inflexible accounting requirements, so be sure your invoice conforms to the requirements of	• Don't submit an invoice without proofreading carefully. Errors can delay payment.

DO (CONTINUED)

your own company and the client's. Failing to do so will delay your payment.

- Date the invoice, and enter a unique invoice number for your own record-keeping purposes.
- Provide a clear description of the product or service provided and a clear breakdown of the costs.
- State the due date of the payment. Such a statement doesn't guarantee prompt payment, of course, but it gives you a discussion point if there does happen to be a delay in payment.
- Format your invoice so it's easy to scan. Take advantage of templates in Microsoft Word and others available on the Internet, so you don't have to reinvent the wheel.
- Be sure to say "thank you" somewhere on the invoice. The invoice is generally a rather cold and functional document, but it's nice to add this human touch. A prominent thank-you creates a good impression of you and your company.

LIKE THIS

Vincenti Builders, Inc.

Bill To:	**Invoice #** 10127	113 West Homewood Street
Mr. Greg Gold	**Invoice Date** 12.08.12	Noyes, NV 10025
1012 East Tanoble Street		Phone: 215.777.7721
Noyes, NV		info@vincentibuilders.com
10022		

Taxpayer ID: 543-21-0000

Service	Rate	Hours	Description	Total
Demolition	$40/hr	5	Demolish and remove existing front sidewalk	$200.00
Concrete installation	$50/hr	3	Pour and finish front sidewalk	$150.00
Repair	$50/hr	2	Patch and repair concrete steps—back door	$100.00
				$450.00

Remittance

Date:

Amount Due: $450.00

Amount Enclosed:

   Thank you for your business

COLLECTION LETTERS

Nearly everyone in business has dealt with a nonpaying customer at one time or another. Large companies have collections procedures in place and dedicated staff to handle them. Small businesses or entrepreneurs often need to write their own collection letters.

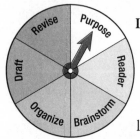

Introduction

The primary **purpose** of a collection letter is to convince a client or customer to pay an outstanding bill. Collection letters also have a secondary purpose: to maintain goodwill with the **reader**, your customer, in the future and to keep her business. As you write your letter, remember that there are many reasons people fail to pay their bills. It's usually a good idea to assume the best of your reader and treat the letter as a friendly reminder. You may need to send a series of letters, each more insistent than the one prior. As you **brainstorm** your content, bear in mind that you want to make it easy for your customer to pay. Don't guilt-trip them. Don't be emotional. State the facts dispassionately. The Model Outline provides a structure you can use to **organize** your collection letter. Pay close attention to your tone as you write your **draft**. It should be courteous and businesslike. If you are writing a series of letters, review the previous letters you have sent, and ensure that your demands are escalating in insistence. Review your letter carefully for typos and other errors, and **revise** accordingly.

MODEL OUTLINE

A collection letter should be brief and businesslike.

Opening: Notify the reader that her account is past due. State her balance, the date it was due, and the new deadline for payment.

Middle: If you are sending an escalated request, let the reader know the consequences of failing to pay by the stated deadline: late fees, additional interest charges, giving the account to a collection agency, or taking legal action, depending on the situation.

Conclusion: Finish your letter by restating the payment deadline and by encouraging the customer to contact you if she has questions or problems. Be sure to include your contact information.

DO	DON'T
• Be courteous, no matter how late the payment is.	• Don't use a menacing or bullying tone. Doing so will alienate the customer and actually make her less willing to pay.
• Assume the best: that the customer means to pay and that you will receive payment shortly.	
• Use a firm tone. Be polite, but let the reader know you take the situation seriously.	• Don't make threats that are inappropriate or illegal. If you end up taking legal action to collect the debt, you will be held accountable for anything you have written.
• State the amount due. If interest and late fees have accrued or are about to, let the reader know	

how much and provide a schedule of how additional charges accrue.

- State the deadline for payment. If a deadline has already passed, establish a new one.
- Keep your style simple and direct. Eliminate any risk of misunderstanding. Use short sentences and simple vocabulary.
- Keep your message brief, no longer than one page.
- Let the reader know if you are willing to arrange a payment plan or other arrangements to make her payment easier. Provide her with the details of the plan you propose.

- Don't make threats you are not willing to act on. If you tell a customer that you will turn her account over to a collection agency or that you will initiate legal action against her, be prepared to do so.
- Don't be patronizing or cute. Comments like "We've been wracking our brains trying to understand why we haven't heard from you" are just annoying.

Collection Letter Series

———•———

With any luck, you will need to write only one letter to remind your wayward customer to pay his account in full. If the nonpayment continues, however, you will probably need to send a series of collection letters, each more demanding than the last. Here is a useful overview of such a series:

Reminder letter. Use a friendly but firm tone to remind the customer of the overdue balance. Assume the customer has simply forgotten and intends to make the payment.

Second collection letter. Be more insistent. Note that you sent a reminder on the previous date and that payment has not been received. If late fees, interest, or other penalties have accrued, let him know. You may want to offer an olive branch and say you know it can be easy to overlook bills and that everyone is busy, but be firm. Let the reader know the new deadline for payment, and express your confidence that he will make payment immediately.

Later collection letters. Subsequent letters in the series may encourage the customer to contact you to discuss any circumstances that might be making it difficult for him to pay. Propose a payment schedule to pay down the debt over time. Appeal to the reader's sensibilities: that he has an obligation to do the right thing. Let him know that the consequences to his credit rating can be adverse.

Final appeal. Take a firm but dispassionate tone. State the facts: the amount due, how late it is, and the fact that you have made repeated efforts to contact the customer and collect the debt. State that you intend to turn the account over to a collection agency, report the customer to a credit bureau, take legal action, or any appropriate combination of the above actions if he does not make payment by the stated date.

Closing letter. If previous efforts have failed and you intend to take legal action or bring in a collection agency, you must notify the customer about the actions you intend to take and on what date those actions will be taken. Remember your collections practices are governed by relevant federal, state, and local laws, so be sure your actions are legal. Consult with your attorney if you are unsure.

LIKE THIS

January 11, 2013

Dear Mr. Gupta:

It has come to our attention that your account is past due $1,237.89. Please make payment to bring your account up-to-date.

Thank you for your prompt attention to this matter.

Sincerely,

Helen Sturtevant

February 15, 2013

Dear Mr. Gupta:

We wrote to you last month notifying you that your account is past due in the amount of $1,237.89. We have still not received payment. We value you as a long-term customer, and we assume this is simply an oversight. Please remit payment by February 28 to bring your account up-to-date.

We are confident you will remedy this situation promptly.

Sincerely,

Helen Sturtevant

March 11, 2013

Dear Mr. Gupta:

Your account is seriously past due. We have contacted you several times regarding your balance of $1,237.89, but we have not heard from you.

If there are circumstances preventing you from making a full payment at this time, please contact me at 818-555-1111 to discuss arrangements for a payment plan. We are willing to work with you, but you must contact us within the next 10 days.

Thank you for your prompt attention to this matter.

Sincerely,

Helen Sturtevant

March 29, 2013

Dear Mr. Gupta:

We have written several times about an ongoing past-due amount of $1,237.89 on your account, but we have received no reply.

We remain willing to work out a payment schedule with you. Please contact our office at 818-555-1111.

If we have not heard from you by April 7, 2013, we will refer your account to a collection agency, which may have a negative effect on your credit rating. Please contact us immediately to avoid this action.

Sincerely,

Helen Sturtevant

April 10, 2013

Dear Mr. Gupta:

Your account is seriously past due in the amount of $1,237.89. Despite repeated efforts to contact you about this matter, we have not heard from you.

Your account will be referred to a collection agency on April 24, 2013, if we have not heard from you. Please contact our office at 818-555-1111.

Sincerely,

Helen Sturtevant

For more information about writing and samples you can use for your own writing tasks, visit www.howtowriteanything.com.

Acknowledgments

Many people have helped me in the development and writing of this book. I am grateful for their knowledge, expertise, and support.

Many friends and colleagues generously read parts of the manuscript and made suggestions to improve it: Colette Sible Beauvais, Liz Cassidy, Michele Cohen, Bob Daugherty, Rachel Christmas Derrick, Erika Gaynor, Daniel Goldstein, Jennifer Gorman, Ronald Granite, Heidi J. Holder, Eugene D. Hill, June Cummins Lewis, Susan McCormick, Mary Olson, Alison Brown Paddock, Brandon Paddock, Mallory Paddock, Steve Paddock, David Rogers, Uptin Saiidi, Tom Tarduogno, Naja Touray, Martin Uniacke, Karen Vrotsos, and Alan Ziegler.

Jesse Berger and Wendy McClellan Anderson of New York's Red Bull Theater generously offered me quiet office space to complete the manuscript. Steve Harrison and Geoffrey Berwind of Quantum Leap provided invaluable guidance in developing the book.

Maria Boscaino helped me in many ways over the course of developing the book. She designed the original Writing Spinner graphic and kept tabs on "our book" as it grew. She calmed my nerves and provided expert help with a long and very unruly Word file. I am grateful for her friendship and moral support.

Very special thanks to Catherine M. Rose, my first English teacher and a lifelong inspiration; to Professor Howard L. Hertz, Professor A. R. Braunmuller, Professor Elizabeth M. Brennan, Professor James V. Mirollo, and Professor James S. Shapiro; and to Professor Ming-Jer Chen.

Leslie Adatto, Gail J. Anderson, Lisa Curry Austin, Jennie Cohen, Bob Fingerman, Catherine M. Gleason, Heidi J. Holder, Erin Langston, Jill Niemczyk, and Karen Vrotsos offered unflagging moral support over the long course of developing the manuscript. Thanks to Phyllis Mottola, Alison Brown Paddock, Patricia F. Brown, and David Walker Brown for their love and support.

My brilliant agent James Levine of Levine Greenberg believed in this project for many years before it finally got off the ground. Jim's creativity inspired me to create the Writing Spinner. And when the project was finally ready to go, he found just the right home for it. Thank you, Jim.

Finally, I am very grateful to Jill Bialosky, my wonderful editor at W. W. Norton. Jill's insights and suggestions improved the book tremendously. Thank you for the opportunity, Jill, and thank you for all your help.

ABOUT THE AUTHOR

Laura Brown, PhD, has taught writing to just about everyone—from corporate executives to high school students. Her expertise encompasses instructor-led training, individual coaching, classroom teaching, and e-learning development as well as audio, video, and webinar training for businesses, nonprofits, and educational institutions. She has more than twenty-five years' experience providing training and coaching in business writing and consulting on a variety of writing projects, with special expertise in designing customized writing training programs for organizations. She has partnered with Columbia University and General Electric to create a series of online business writing courses and has also worked with global companies helping executives from other countries transition to American business-communication conventions. She has also taught composition and literature at Columbia University and business and technical writing at Iona College. She lives in New York.

Information about Laura's consulting services and writing programs is available on her website, www.howtowriteanything.com.

Contributors

Many talented and accomplished people contributed sidebars and examples to this book. Their expertise on a wide variety of writing tasks has enriched the book tremendously, and I am grateful for their generous help.

Heather B. Armstrong is the creator and writer of the popular website *Dooce*. She is the author of the 2009 *New York Times* best-selling book, *It Sucked and Then I Cried: How I Had a Baby, a Breakdown, and a Much Needed Margarita*. Armstrong was recently named by *Forbes* magazine as one of the 30 most influential women in media. *Time* magazine has twice listed her website as one of the 25 best blogs in the world. She has appeared on many TV shows, including *The Oprah Winfrey Show* and *The Today Show*. Her website is www.dooce.com.

Siana Attwell is a clinical hypnotherapist based in Winnipeg, Manitoba. Since 1998, she has been helping clients to live more fulfilling lives by releasing problematic thinking patterns rooted in their subconscious minds. Her areas of specialty include regression and past-life therapy, fears and phobias (including preparation for medical and dental procedures), performance anxiety (including academic performance and exam anxiety), and adjunctive therapy for intractable illness. She also works with hypnofertility. Siana holds a PhD in clinical hypnotherapy from the

American Pacific University (now Kona University) in Hawaii. Her website is siana-attwell-phd.webnode.com.

Cathy Birkenstein is a lecturer in English at the University of Illinois at Chicago and codirector of the Writing in the Disciplines program. She has published essays on writing, most recently in *College English* and (with Gerald Graff) in the *Chronicle of Higher Education*, *Academe*, and *College Composition and Communication*. She has also given talks and workshops with Gerald Graff at numerous colleges and is currently working on a study of common misunderstandings surrounding academic discourse.

Ben Brantley became chief theater critic of the *New York Times* in 1996, after having served as its drama critic since joining the newspaper in 1993. Prior to joining the *Times*, Mr. Brantley was a staff writer at the *New Yorker* magazine and a writer at *Vanity Fair*. Mr. Brantley is the editor of the *New York Times Book of Broadway: On the Aisle for the Unforgettable Plays of the Last Century* (2001). He received the 1996–97 George Jean Nathan Award for Dramatic Criticism.

Jack Canfield is the originator of the Chicken Soup for the Soul series, which has sold over five hundred million copies worldwide. Known as "America's #1 Success Coach," Jack brings his critical insights to thousands of audiences internationally—sharing his success strategies in the media, with companies, universities, and professional associations. Jack is a Harvard graduate with an MA in psychological education, and he is one of the earliest champions of peak performance, developing specific methodologies and results-oriented activities to help people take on greater challenges and produce breakthrough results. Jack's latest book is the national best seller, *The Success Principles: How to Get from Where You Are to Where You Want to Be*. His website is www.jackcanfield.com.

Liz Cassidy is the founder of Leadership Mastery Institute and Third Sigma International, and is a speaker, facilitator, and executive leadership coach. Growing up during the Troubles in Northern Ireland, and with over twenty-five years of business experience in England and Australia, Liz brings an irreverent Irish perspective to life, the world, and business. As well as being a neuro-linguistic programming master practitioner, Liz is also a qualified practitioner in a range of tools including Myers Briggs Type Indicator and Apollo Profiling. She has a BS in chemical engineering. Liz's current books *Business Networking Success* (2012) and *Job Inter-*

view Questions and Answers (2012) are available on Amazon. Her website is www.lizcassidy.com.

Michele Cohen has over twenty years of human resources experience, including human resources information systems, benefits, employee relations, payroll, recruiting, and compensation. She started her career as an executive recruiter and moved into corporate human resources at Weiss, Peck & Greer, an institutional asset manager, in 1993. After eleven years at WPG, the last four as director of human resources, Michele joined Fortress Investment Group in 2004 to establish the HR function. Over the past eight years, Fortress has grown from two hundred to one thousand employees and manages $48 billion in institutional and private assets around the world.

Ria M. Coyne administers scholarship programs for foundations as a partner at R&R Education Consultants.

Crane & Co., Inc. has been dedicated to the art of classic correspondence for more than two centuries. Since 1801, the brand has been a leader in the social networking business, producing 100 percent cotton personalized notes, business stationery, wedding invitations, birth announcements, calling cards, and more. The seventh-generation family-owned business based in Dalton, Masschusetts, continues to celebrate treasured social connections and life's milestones through its exquisite quality, design, and craftsmanship. Its website is www.crane.com.

John Derby is assistant professor at the University of Kansas. He earned his PhD in art education with a graduate interdisciplinary specialization in disability studies from the Ohio State University; his MA from Brigham Young University; and his BS and BFA degrees from Bowling Green State University. His research intersects disability studies and art education as a transdisciplinary pedagogical project through contemporary art practices, the intermingling of art and writing, Foucauldian discourse analysis, and visual culture studies. He has published in the premier journals *Studies in Art Education* and *Disability Studies Quarterly*.

Devon Glenn is the editor of Mediabistro's SocialTimes, where she analyzes new social media sites and trends. Devon dabbled in music, educational publishing, and web development, and even cofounded a tutoring center before she decided to pursue writing full-time. Her work has appeared in the *Los Angeles Times*, the *Orange County Register*, and the now-defunct mobile magazine *U+Me*. She lives in Brooklyn.

Gerald Graff, a professor of English and education at the University of Illinois at Chicago and 2008 president of the Modern Language Association of America, has had a major impact on teachers through such books as *Professing Literature: An Institutional History, Beyond the Culture Wars: How Teaching the Conflicts Can Revitalize American Education*, and most recently, *Clueless in Academe: How Schooling Obscures the Life of the Mind*.

Steve Harrison's company, Bradley Communications, helps authors, experts, and entrepreneurs refine, promote, and monetize their message. Steve is the publisher of *Radio-TV Interview Report* and creator of the Quantum Leap program for authors and experts. He also presents the National Publicity Summit in New York. Steve's company has helped launch such best-selling books as *Chicken Soup for the Soul, Rich Dad Poor Dad*, and *Men Are from Mars Women Are from Venus*. He is the cocreator (with Jack Canfield) of www.bestsellerblueprint.com.

Alison Herman is a student at Columbia University (Columbia College class of 2015). She is a senior staff writer for the *Columbia Daily Spectator*, where she writes about food and the arts. She is also managing features editor for the *Eye* magazine.

Stefan Killen is a Brooklyn-based graphic designer and photographer. Stefan has been designing websites, brand solutions, annual reports, and book covers for over twenty-five years. His clients have included corporations, not-for profits, publishers, the US Navy, and small businesses. He has designed over seven hundred book covers for publishers around the United States. Stefan is also a fine arts photographer. His pinhole photographs are in private collections in the United States, Europe, and Japan and have been exhibited at the Alan Klotz Gallery in New York City. His work is included in *Out of Focus* (2012), which recently won a silver prize in the German Photo Book Awards. Stefan received a BA from the Evergreen State College, where he studied drawing and painting. He received a certificate in graphic design from the Basel School of Design in Basel, Switzerland. His websites are www.stefankillendesign.com and www.pinholeny.com.

Anna Kisselgoff was chief dance critic of the *New York Times* from 1977 to 2005, leaving the staff in 2006. She remains a contributor to the paper and to other publications. Ms. Kisselgoff graduated from Bryn Mawr College and has an MA in European history and an MS in journalism, both from Columbia University. Awards for her writing include the Order of the Dannebrog from Queen Margrethe II of Denmark, the Order of the Falcon from the Government of Iceland, and the Order of Arts and Letters from the French Government. She received the Distinguished Alumni Award from Columbia's Graduate School of Arts and Sciences and from Columbia's Graduate School of Journalism.

Abby Larson is the editor and founder of *Style Me Pretty* (www .stylemepretty.com), the style-savvy resource for the modern bride. Larson launched *Style Me Pretty* in 2007 as the ultimate insider's guide to all things wedding, changing the landscape for how brides plan their weddings through a unique approach of curating chic and stylish content online. Today *Style Me Pretty* is the leading and fastest-growing wedding blog, garnering over nineteen million page views per month and two million unique visitors monthly. Larson and *Style Me Pretty* have been featured on *The Rachael Ray Show* and *CBS Sunday Morning* and are regularly featured in top national publications, including the *New York Times*, *Brides*, and *InStyle*. Larson is a contributor to the Huffington Post, *Glamour*, and *Shape*. Larson recently debuted an entirely unique and photo-rich wedding book, *Style Me Pretty Weddings: Inspiration & Ideas for an Unforgettable Celebration* (2012).

Roger Lehecka served for nineteen years as the dean of students of Columbia College. He is a partner at R&R Education Consultants.

Wayne Mazzoni has been a college coach since 1992. He has coached at Fairfield University, Holy Cross, and Post University and is currently at Sacred Heart University (Connecticut). He is a 1991 graduate of Gettysburg College and also holds an MS in sports administration. He is the author of several books and videos, including *The Athletic Recruiting and Scholarship Guide* (2005) and *Get Recruited* (2009). Since 1998, Coach Mazzoni has spoken on this topic at over three hundred high schools. He has appeared on numerous local and national media outlets including Fox, ABC, News 12, *US News and World Report*, and five appearances on WFAN Sports Radio 660. His website is www.waynemazzoni.com.

Meryl Neiman graduated from Brown University and Duke University School of Law. After almost a decade working as a litigator for a large law firm, she leaped off the corporate ladder to devote more time to raising her kids and writing. She added entrepreneur to her résumé when she cofounded the website Playdate Planet, an online playdate scheduler for busy moms and dads. Meryl writes regularly about play-related topics, and she is working on a book about the importance of unstructured play for kids. She also searches for answers to parenting's most difficult questions on her Internet radio talk show *Parenting with Playdate Planet*. Her website is www.playdateplanet.com.

Patrick O'Connor is associate dean of college counseling at Cranbrook-Kingswood School in metropolitan Detroit. In addition to writing a weekly column for the website College Is Yours, he writes on education for the Huffington Post, and his writing has appeared in *High School Counselor Week*, the website myFootpath, the *Christian Science Monitor*, the *Washington Post*, the *Detroit Free Press*, and *Diverse: Issues in Higher Education*. Patrick has served as president of the Michigan Association for College Admission Counseling and the National Association for College Admission Counseling. He is on the board of directors of the Michigan College Access Network and on the credentialing commission for the American Institute of Certified Educational Planners. He is a recipient of the Outstanding Faculty Award from Oakland Community College, the Margaret Addis Service to NACAC Award, and the William Gramenz Award (for outstanding contributions to college counseling in Michigan). He holds five college degrees, including a PhD in education administration. His website is www.collegeisyours.com.

Cydney O'Sullivan is the author of *Social Marketing Superstars* (2012), *Social Media Mystery to Mastery* (2012), and *How to Be Wealthy NOW! 108 Fast Cash Solutions* (2012), founder of the websites Millionaires Academy and ExpertSocialMedia.com; and business turnaround consultant. After twenty successful years in a traditional retail business, she turned her attention to seeking out the strategies of the most successful social media marketers to assist other offline business owners and "work-from-home moms" like herself to understand the exciting opportunities in online marketing. She has since added international speaking to her services, and helps clients ready to move from making a living to thriving online. Her website is cydneyosullivan.com.

Mallory Paddock is a student at the Savannah College of Art and Design (class of 2015). She is studying production design and themed entertainment design. Her website is www.mallorypaddock.com.

Diane A. Ross is a speaker, executive coach, and author. She holds a B.Comm. in business and law from the University of British Columbia and spent fourteen years in litigation before moving on to become a certified executive coach and train in advanced negotiations at Harvard. She draws on these experiences to teach others simple strategies for having difficult conversations at work. Her forthcoming book *The Elephant in the Office: Super Simple Strategies for Difficult Conversations at Work* reveals how to deal with the "elephant" we create when we avoid a tough conversation. Her website is www.dianeaross.com.

Molly Stevens is an award-winning cookbook author and cooking teacher. Her cookbooks *All about Roasting: A New Look at a Classic Art* (W. W. Norton, 2011) and *All about Braising: The Art of Uncomplicated Cooking* (W. W. Norton, 2004) both earned James Beard and IACP (International Association of Culinary Professionals) Awards. Molly's articles and recipes appear regularly in *Fine Cooking* magazine where she is a contributing editor. Her recipes and tips have also appeared in the *Wall Street Journal, Every Day with Rachael Ray, Real Simple, Bon Appétit, Saveur, Eating Well*, and *Yankee* magazines. Molly is the coeditor of *The 150 Best American Recipes* (2006) as well as the annual Best American Recipes series. Previously, Molly coauthored *One Potato, Two Potato* (2001). She serves on the board of directors for the Intervale Center in Burlington, Vermont. Her website is mollystevenscooks.com.

Steven D. Strauss is often called "the country's leading small business expert." The senior *USA Today* small-business columnist and best-selling author, Steve's latest book is *Planet Entrepreneur: The Word Entrepreneurship Forum's Guide to Business Success Around the World* (2013). A lawyer, author, and public speaker, Steve regularly speaks around the world about small-business strategies and global trends in business, and he sits on the board of the World Entrepreneurship Forum. Steve has been seen on ABC, CNN, CNBC, MSNBC, and *The O'Reilly Factor*. His company, the Strauss Group, creates cutting-edge business content for everyone from Fortune 100 companies to small chambers of commerce. Steve's website for the self-employed is theselfemployed.com.

Bryan Toder is a certified clinical hypnotist and owner of Plymouth Hypnosis Center in Lafayette Hill, Pennsylvania. He's been in business at the same location since 2002, specializing in helping his clients lose weight, quit smoking, manage their stress, and even improve their golf game. Bryan was trained and certified in hypnosis and hypnotherapy by the National Guild of Hypnotists and the American Board of Hypnotherapists. Bryan's latest book is *Get Thin—Be Happy: The 6 Easy Steps to Weight Loss Success* (2011). His website is www.plymouthhypnosis.com.

Lawrence Wilson is public editor of the *Pasadena Star-News* and the San Gabriel Valley News Group. He has taught at the USC Annenberg School for Communication and Journalism and the New York Times Knowledge Network. His book *Twenty Surf Poems and a Song of Despair* is forthcoming.

Index